MUMMIES, DISEASE, AND ANCIENT CULTURES

Mummies, Disease, and Ancient Cultures

Edited by AIDAN *and* EVE COCKBURN

Abridged edition

CAMBRIDGE UNIVERSITY PRESS

CAMBRIDGE
LONDON NEW YORK NEW ROCHELLE
MELBOURNE SYDNEY

Published by the Press Syndicate of the University of Cambridge
The Pitt Building, Trumpington Street, Cambridge CB2 1RP
32 East 57th Street, New York, NY 10022, USA
296 Beaconsfield Parade, Middle Park, Melbourne 3206, Australia

© Cambridge University Press 1980

First published 1980
Abridged paperback edition 1983

Printed in the United States of America

Library of Congress Cataloging in Publication Data

Mummies, disease, and ancient cultures.

Includes index.

1. Mummies. 2. Paleopathology. I. Cockburn,
Aidan. II. Cockburn, Eve
GN293.M85 616'.00932 79–25682
ISBN 0 521 23020 9 hard covers
ISBN 0 521 27237 8 paperback

To everyone who made this book possible:

First, to our patient authors, who have responded nobly to our demands for four years, from every corner of the globe, giving unstintingly the fruits of their firsthand, original research and adapting with understanding to the format we required.

Second, to the many scientists who processed specimens, identified organisms, and generously gave of their knowledge.

Third, to the backstage workers who cannot be mentioned individually in the text – typists, technicians, and support staff of all kinds – without whose willing help a book of this complexity could never get off the drawing board.

Contents

Preface   page   ix

Introduction   1
AIDAN COCKBURN

Part I. Mummies of Egypt

1. Mummies of ancient Egypt   11
WILLIAM H. PECK

2. Diseases in ancient Egypt   29
A. T. SANDISON

3. Dental health in ancient Egypt   45
JAMES E. HARRIS and
PAUL V. PONITZ

4. A classic mummy: PUM II   52
AIDAN COCKBURN, ROBIN A.
BARRACO, WILLIAM H. PECK, and
THEODORE A. REYMAN

5. ROM I: mummification for the
common people   71
NICHOLAS B. MILLET, GERALD D.
HART, THEODORE A. REYMAN,
MICHAEL R. ZIMMERMAN, and
PETER K. LEWIN

6. Egyptian mummification with
evisceration per ano
THEODORE A. REYMAN and
WILLIAM H. PECK

Part II. Mummies of the Americas

7. Mummies and mummification
practices in the southwestern and
southern United States
MAHMOUD Y. EL-NAJJAR and
THOMAS M. J. MULINSKI

8. Aleutian and Alaskan mummies
MICHAEL R. ZIMMERMAN   118

9. Mummies of Peru   135
JAMES M. VREELAND, JR. and
AIDAN COCKBURN

Part III. Mummies of the world

10. Bog bodies of Denmark   177
CHRISTIAN FISCHER

11. Mummification in Australia and
Melanesia   194
GRAEME L. PRETTY and
ANGELA CALDER

12. Japanese mummies   211
KIYOHIKO SAKURAI and
TAMOTSU OGATA

13. Miscellaneous mummies   224
ANTONIO ASCENZI, AIDAN
COCKBURN, and
EKKEHARD KLEISS

Index   239

AIDAN COCKBURN

30 May 1912–19 September 1981

Scholar, scientist, physician, administrator, wit, raconteur; these words among many others, describe Aidan Cockburn. His contributions as an epidemiologist, specialist on the evolution and history of disease, and on paleopathology established him as an authority on these and other subjects long before his death in 1981. In a sense, however, words cannot capture the essence of the man. Aidan was a man of catholic interests and knowledge. He lived and worked in many countries of the world. (When I first met him his cat had traveled far more extensively than I – a fact that Aidan found most amusing.) The world view that arose from his global work and travel experience gave him a special perspective on many of the problems regarding the evolution of disease. He was the first to introduce me to the obvious but often overlooked concept that evolutionary processes would generally lead to the attenuation of virulence in bacterial disease organisms; the organism that kills its host usually dies as well, thus natural selection will favor the disease organism that does not kill its host. This concept is crucial to an understanding of the history of disease and to the interpretation of paleopathological specimens.

Aidan's influence on the development of paleopathology has been enormous. With Eve Cockburn, he founded the Paleopathology Association in 1973. This international and interdisciplinary organization today has a membership of more than 400. Although his great interest was in the general area of paleopathology, he became best known for his specific interest in the study of mummies. Despite this emphasis he gave enthusiastic support to all research on paleopathology. His interest in and support of the study of mummy tissues stimulated a whole new range of studies, many of which involve the latest technology and methodology in science and medicine.

Mankind may never completely eradicate infectious disease but certainly the perspectives provided or stimulated by Aidan will do much to illuminate those factors that affect human health and provide the time perspective needed to continue the quest to minimize the effects of disease on human life.

Donald Ortner

Preface

Why mummies? That is the question we are often asked. How did an otherwise respectable physician and a senior member of the University of Oxford, whose field is modern language and literature, find themselves regarded as "the mummy experts"?

The story begins in Aidan's early medical years. He is cursed with the 'satiable curiosity of the elephant's child and always wants to know "why?" Why are diseases the way they are? Were they always like this? Where did they come from? Under the influence of the nineteenth-century ideas of Darwin and Huxley, he worked out a series of theories that would explain how disease organisms evolved, how they changed during the different epochs of the development of human society, and how the interaction of these two streams of evolution resulted in our current infectious disease patterns. Eve, with her nonscientific background, found herself looking at these ideas with the cold and critical eye of an outsider, then helping with the sorting and organizing of theories – and so a partnership was born.

After Aidan's first two books on the evolution of infectious diseases (1963 and 1967), there was a hiatus of several years. Then came two casual conversations, which led to the present line of research and the present book. At a meeting of the American Association of Physical Anthropologists in Boston in 1971, Lucile St. Hoyme of the Smithsonian Institution remarked: "Aidan, why don't you apply for a grant from the Smithsonian to study in some area where you could find facts to back up your theories? We have local currency funds available in at least seventeen countries." She listed them, and the obvious one that would provide a fertile field for research was Egypt. Aidan applied for and received a grant to go to Egypt on a reconnaissance trip to investigate the possibility of organizing a project for the autopsy of large numbers of mummies, thus obtaining facts to back up his, until then, largely speculative ideas.

Then came casual conversation number two. Eve was talking to William H. Peck, Curator of Ancient Art at the Detroit Institute of Arts, about the projected trip. Bill asked whether Aidan had ever autopsied or in any way examined a mummy before, and when the answer was no, he suggested that Aidan might like to practice on one of those in storage in the institute's basement. The story of this first, primitive autopsy has already been fully described (*Smithsonian*, November 1973); its importance lies in the idea of examining mummies in American museums rather than those in Egypt.

While in Egypt, Aidan met David O'Connor, who became a major contributor to the final program. At the Pennsylvania University Museum, where he was Egyptian curator, there were several mummies, and David invited Aidan to examine these if he needed to. The first autopsy (PUM I), conducted in Philadelphia at the university, was an unmitigated disaster. No one really knew what to do, and readers of this book will find only passing reference to the project – but it *was* a valuable learning experience. The media had been invited and turned up in full force, so the examination became a three-ring circus, with photographers and cameramen taking over the autopsy room; at one stage there was even a class of visiting third-graders, complete with teachers, wandering through and getting underfoot. Not an atmosphere conducive to serious scientific work!

However, three more mummies were provided by David and successfully autopsied in Detroit, with conditions strictly controlled. The Smithsonian Institution, the Detroit Institute of Arts, and Wayne State University School of Medicine collaborated in the sponsorship of these studies. The first study, of PUM II, became the basis of the Paleopathology Association. Papers presented at the symposium held in conjunction with the autopsy, which had been given the somewhat fanciful name of "Death and Disease in Ancient Egypt," were printed with a covering letter of information under the grandiose title, *Paleopathology Newsletter*, Number 1. At

that time, it really was debatable whether there would ever be an issue number two! However, the publication found an immediate audience, and so the Paleopathology Association was born. There are no association dues, no formal organization, no by-laws. The *Newsletter* is now a viable entity, with more than 300 subscribers in 25 countries, and it is from these that contributors to the present book are drawn. During the past 5 years, a great deal of major scientific work has been performed, all on a strictly voluntary basis. People work because they are interested, consumed by that same 'satiable curiosity that started Aidan off in the first place. We are grateful for what their enthusiasm and energy has produced–and we hope readers of this book will feel the same.

E. G. C.

Introduction

AIDAN COCKBURN
President, Paleopathology Association
Detroit, Michigan, U.S.A.

What is a mummy? For most people, the word immediately brings to mind visions of Egypt and, in particular, pictures of a body wrapped in swaddling bands of cloth. This was the original idea of the term, and indeed from the earliest days of antiquity, the preserved bodies of ancient Egypt have gripped the imagination of all who knew about them, whether rich or poor, educated or not. This was so much the case that when the Romans took over Egypt and found the art of preservation to be badly degenerated, they tried to revive the old ways. But it was too late. The ability to read hieroglyphics and ancient writings had been lost when the Greeks under the Ptolemies conquered the country and introduced their much superior Greek script. However, some form of body preservation was continued up to the eighth century A.D. At that time, the invading Arabs swept all before them in Egypt. To them, the practice of embalming the dead was abhorrent, and they put a stop to it.

Today, the term *mummy* has been extended to cover all well-preserved dead bodies. The majority of these are found in dry places such as the sands of deserts or dry caves, where desiccation has taken place rapidly, doing naturally what Egyptians did by artifice. The basic procedure in either process is the same: Water is extracted rapidly from the tissues. There is no mystery in this, for people since antiquity have been preserving fish and meat in the same basic ways, either by drying in the sun or by packing in salt. The Egyptian embalmers used a naturally occurring salt called *natron* instead of common table salt and supplemented this with oils, resins, and bitumen. The word *mummy* is derived from the Persian *mumeia* or *mum*, meaning "pitch" or "asphalt." This substance had been used in classical times in medical prescriptions, but medieval physicians introduced a refinement with preparations of pitch from Egyptian mummies. These "exudations" of mummies became very popular and remained so up to the nineteenth century. The first use of the word referring to medicine dates back to the early fifteenth century (*Encyclopaedia Britannica* 1911). As applied to a preserved body, however, the earliest record is 1615 (*Oxford English Dictionary*).

Occasionally, bodies are found preserved in other ways. Most of these are frozen, like an Inca boy who had been sacrificed on a high mountain in Chile. Apparently, he had been drugged and left to freeze. In Siberia, mammoths and extinct horses have been found in the permafrost. In the Altai mountains of Russia, Scythian bodies from about 400 B.C. have been recovered, encased in ice, from their tombs. The first use of *mummy* applied to a body frozen in ice was in 1727 (*Oxford English Dictionary*).

More baffling is the wonderfully preserved corpse of a Chinese princess of 2,000 years ago. The coffin in the tomb was hermetically sealed and still contained the preserving fluid, a weak mercurial solution. The tissues were still elastic and the joints could be bent. Whether this survival was attributable to the exclusion of oxygen, as suggested by the Chinese scientists, or to the mercurial solution, or to a combination of both is uncertain.

Serious scientific studies of mummies on

an organized basis began in Egypt shortly after the turn of the century (Dawson 1938). This coincided with the period when Egypt was dominated by the British and with the foundation of a school of medicine and the creation of the first Aswan Dam. The two events were interrelated. The first great dam at Aswan was completed in 1902, and the reservoir behind it was filled in the spring of 1903. By this action, the First Cataract on the Nile was obliterated, Philae was inundated, and much of the valley of the Nile was flooded. Many antiquities were ruined and many ancient burials destroyed by the inundation and the seepage.

Much public resentment had been expressed at this destruction of historical records, and the pathetic sight of the Temple of Philae, standing half drowned in the muddy water, had appealed to innumerable tourists as a sacrifice of the beautiful and historic on the altar of modern utilitarianism. In 1907, the Egyptian Government proposed to increase the height of the dam by another seven meters. Such a project entailed the flooding of a very large area. The Government wisely decided that before the inundation took place, the area should be thoroughly surveyed and examined. All antiquities were to be recorded; all burials were to be examined, described, photographed, and rescued before the raised Nile could reach them. [Wood Jones in Dawson 1938]

Coincidental with this event was the founding of the English-language Government School of Medicine in Cairo on the ruins of the former French school, which had become defunct 10 years earlier. The professors at the school were excellent, and three of them shaped the future of the study of mummies for decades. They were Grafton Elliot Smith (anatomy), Armand Ruffer (bacteriology), and Alfred Lucas (chemistry). Elliot Smith left Egypt after 7 years to return to England, but for the rest of his life he continued to develop the ideas he had conceived in Egypt. Ruffer explored means of examining soft tissues, and his techniques are still used today. The world lost a distinguished scientist when he was killed during World War I,

while serving in a hospital ship that was sunk. Lucas continued in Egypt; when Tutankhamun's tomb was found, he was called in as a consultant. Elliot Smith made the greatest impact at the time, but today it is Armand Ruffer who reigns supreme in the field of paleopathology.

Elliot Smith began his studies of Egyptian bodies in the Thebaid in 1901, and in 1905 he made the first of his detailed examinations of the technique of mummification. In early 1903, the tomb of Pharaoh Tuthmosis IV was found, and Maspero, the director of the Service des Antiquités, ordered that the mummy of the king be unwrapped and examined. The result was a public spectacle for the elite of Cairo, but the examination had no scientific value. However, Elliot Smith was able to make a later, private examination that included roentgenography. At that time, there was only one X-ray machine in Cairo, so Elliot Smith and Howard Carter took the rigid pharaoh in a cab to the nursing home to have it X-rayed. This was a historic first. Following this, Elliot Smith made a study of all the royal mummies found in the two great caches of Deir el-Bahri (1881) and the tomb of Amenophis (1898). Later he investigated a series of mummies from different periods in order to determine how the embalming process had changed over the centuries. On a visit to his native Australia, he found two mummies of Papuans from the Torres Strait in a museum in Adelaide. These had so many features in common with the mummies of Egypt that he developed his concept of cultural diffusion, claiming that the idea of mummification had spread from Egypt to the Torres Strait. Pretty and Calder discuss this theory in Chapter 11.

The investigations that resulted from the raising of the Aswan Dam proved beyond the capacity of the staff of the Government Medical School, so additional assistance, notably that of W. R. Dawson and Frederic Wood Jones, was obtained from England. The task was so great that in one month in one small area, the archeologists uncovered the tombs of 2,000 persons. The workers did their best, but by modern standards the whole operation was a very crude and rushed affair. Under similar circumstances, it is doubtful whether we could have done any better today. Regardless of this, the pathologies of ancient Egypt were revealed for the first time. In all, autopsies were performed on about 8,000 mummies.

After that initial period of excitement, work on ancient bodies dwindled to almost nothing until recent times, when an even bigger Aswan Dam was built and the whole business of saving ancient relics began anew.

Sir Armand Ruffer's work was not in the blistering heat of the exposed desert, but within the four walls of his laboratory. Whereas Elliot Smith measured bones and studied mummification, Ruffer explored the possibility of restoring ancient tissues to something approximating their condition before death. He was so successful that Ruffer's fluid is still in use today. He was the first to show *Schistosoma* ova in kidneys, bacteria in tissues, and organized structures in organs dead for two or three millennia. We must all salute his memory.

Lucas, a painstaking chemist, analyzed the materials used by ancient Egyptians. By modern standards, his techniques seem old-fashioned, but his results have never been surpassed. His work (1962) is a classic that even today is indispensable. He also experimented with mummification. According to Herodotus, the body was immersed in a large vat that contained a solution of natron, although apparently this interpretation depends on the translation of a single word. If the word is taken in its other meaning, the interpretation is different. Lucas doubted that immersion in a solution of natron would produce mummies as we know them today, so he took pigeons, soaked them as described, and found that the flesh became soft and separated from the bones. Typical mummies could be produced by packing dry natron inside the birds and covering them with the salt externally. Treated this way, they dried out

quickly. The process was so successful that decades later his mummified pigeons still sit in the Department of Antiquities just as he left them, though kept at room temperature without any special care for so many years.

How many mummies are there in the world? This question is often asked, especially in criticism of the sometimes destructive methods used in an autopsy. The implication is that something irreplaceable is being destroyed, but this is not always correct, for two of the six mummies studied by our group have been enhanced in value and are now on exhibition in major museums instead of being hidden in basements.

A head count of mummies is not possible, but some idea of the total number can be gained by a review of their history. In desert areas of North Africa that have been dry for thousands of years, large numbers of bodies must still remain preserved in the sand. In Peru the same applies, with the additional factors of careful burial and wrapping in cotton. So over a period of 2,000 or 3,000 years, many millions of bodies must have been interred. To start with, artificial mummification in Egypt was probably reserved for the pharaoh, his family, and the nobles; but eventually, as everyone wanted to live for eternity, the practice spread. Even if the population had been no more than 1 million people (and surely it was much more), with an average life expectancy of 40 years, about 1 million mummies would have been laid in the ground every 40 years. In the course of 2,000 years this would amount to more than the present population of Egypt.

The question of numbers was discussed in Egypt in 1972 with officials from the Department of Antiquities. They say that tombs containing mummies are discovered almost every time a new road or airfield is constructed. There are so many mummies that those that appear to be of no special interest are reburied in the sand.

On the other hand, Egypt has been exporting or using mummies for centuries, so vast numbers must have been destroyed or dispersed. The process started in the fifteenth century, when it was claimed that ground-up mummy had medicinal properties, and this became an expensive and valued remedy for many diseases. How many hundreds of tons of mummy tissues were swallowed by credulous sufferers, before the practice died out early in the nineteenth century, is anyone's guess.

Another drain on the mummy population in Egypt was caused by lively interest in the Western world, possibly sparked by reports from the savants who accompanied Napoleon to that country. By the end of the nineteenth century, it was de rigueur for every museum to have at least one mummy on exhibition. Even today many small towns have a specimen dating from this period, although the larger museums frequently relegate the bodies to the basement.

In Canada during the nineteenth century, mummy cloth was used in the manufacture of paper. Because the supply of rags for paper making proved inadequate, Canadian paper manufacturers imported thousands of mummies just for their wrappings. What happened to the bodies is not known.

In *Innocents Abroad*, Mark Twain tells of another way in which mummies were destroyed. They were used instead of coal in the engines of the newly constructed railway! Some mummies were destroyed in areas where irrigation was extended and the level of the subsoil water rose. This was especially true in the delta region, where silt from the Nile pushed the land increasingly into the Mediterranean and the land sank slightly as a result of the extra weight.

The biggest destruction of mummies came in the period of dam building that began about 1900 and continues to the present. More and more land was covered by water, and any bodies interred there were damaged. Rescue operations touched only the fringe of the problem, and in any event, most of the bodies found were simply reinterred after a preliminary examination, then left to the mercy of the

rising waters. However, Nubia and the areas above the Aswan dams were not noted for the practice of artificial mummification, and so far the prime areas have been left undisturbed by this particular form of cultural development.

When all these factors are taken into account, it seems probable that many hundreds of thousands of mummies have been lost; even so, millions still remain in the sands and tombs of Egypt. Add to this figure the millions in Peru and other dry areas of South America, and it becomes clear that a huge store remains for future generations to study.

Of course, mummification was not confined to humans: Animals were treated the same way. The Egyptians embalmed specimens of almost every animal in their ecosystem – ranging from bulls through birds, cats, fish, and bats down to shrews – and the numbers were enormous. Their sacred bird, the ibis, may have become extinct simply because every one found was killed and stuffed.

It is in the cold regions, however, that future studies on animals look most promising, especially for the field of biochemistry. The frozen mammoths of Siberia are well known, and a baby mammoth in good condition was recently exposed by a bulldozer in Siberia (Figure 1). Rhinoceroses, horses, and small mammals have also been identified. The permafrost of the Arctic must be a well-stocked refrigerator whose contents are virtually unexplored. At the other pole, conditions are different, but the potential is also great. There, the extreme cold and dryness of the air freeze-dry any animals that die on ice or on land. Thousands of dead seals have been found, some thousands of years old, and there are even reports of bacteria remaining alive in the soil after 10,000 years. Possibilities like this make the future of mummy research most exciting.

Among the most satisfying discoveries associated with mummies are objects that have been included by chance. Quite apart from the religious ritual and ceremony that apper-

Figure 1. Baby mammoth found frozen in Siberia, 1977. (Courtesy of Professor N. K. Vereshchagin, Academy of Science, USSR)

tain to the processing of a body for preservation, objects were occasionally included that were insignificant to the embalmers but shed bright beams of light in corners that would otherwise remain dark for us.

Our own group experienced one such example of serendipity with the finding of a ball of cotton in the wrappings of PUM II. This is the earliest cotton recorded in Western civilization, although the textile was used in both India and America perhaps 2,000 years earlier. How it reached Egypt and what it was doing in a mummy's wrappings are matters for conjecture. Meryl Johnson, who was the first to notice it, is inclined to believe that perhaps the ball of cotton was regarded as a valuable object and was included for that reason (Chapter 4).

Another adventitious find was the only example of an Etruscan text that has come down to us (Wellard 1973). It was half a century before anyone realized the writing on the shroud was Etruscan, and in that time some 80 percent of the wrappings disappeared. The mummy was bought in 1848 by a Croatian, Michael Barie, who was employed by the Hungarian Chancellery in Alexandria. He took it home with him, and on his death his brother gave it to the museum of Agram (now Zagreb). The museum noted that the wrappings were "covered with writing in an unknown and hitherto undeciphered language."

Dr. Heinrich Brugsch, an Egyptologist, viewed the writing and could make nothing of it; he mentioned it to Richard Burton, the famous explorer and linguist, who was at that time British Consul at Trieste. The vice-consul copied part of the text for him, and this was published in the *Transactions of the Royal Society of Literature* in 1882. The previous year Burton had published a book, *Etruscan Bologna*, but in spite of these studies he did not suspect the nature of the writing. In the end, the bandages were sent to the University of Vienna, and there Professor Jakob Krall made the proper identification. How this inscribed linen came to be wrapped around a dead Egyptian girl is not known. It has been suggested that the linen had nothing to do with the girl, but that the embalmers simply bought a sheet of second-hand linen and tore it roughly into strips for their purposes. As will be seen in Chapter 6, a similar method was used on PUM III. We still do not know what the writing says, though it appears to deal with the religious code of the Etruscan people. Perhaps some day an interpretation will be made that will help us to understand more about these mysterious people.

Why were bodies preserved in this way, to last long periods of time? Naturally preserved bodies have come down to us simply because of accidents or environmental conditions, without deliberate human thought. The general climate or microclimate at the time of death produced a situation in which the tissues were dehydrated or frozen, so that the usual biochemical changes of degradation in dead bodies were inhibited. This occurred in hot dry areas, at high altitudes, or in arctic surroundings.

When, however, deliberate efforts were made to ensure that the body would continue to exist in a form somewhat resembling that of the living person, the questions of why this was done and how it was done become matters of considerable interest, going as they do to the very basis of man's attitude to death.

Death is a fearsome thing. Within a brief period – 24 hours in the tropics and a few days elsewhere – a close friend, a relative, or a colleague becomes a bloated, horrifying caricature of the living human being; the body melts and eventually turns into a heap of bones. This has happened since the origin of life and is a basic fact: Everything that lives must die.

The human race has constantly rebelled against this idea, producing various concepts to show that death is not the end and that life in one form or another continues after the physical disintegration of the body. This is the essence of most religions. There are many variations on the theme – the Valhalla of the Vikings, Paradise for Muslims, Resurrection among Christians, the reincarnation beliefs of the Hindus – but the central premise is that death is not final: Something better comes afterward.

In most cases where mummies have been preserved deliberately, the objective seems to have been to keep the body intact and recognizable for this afterlife, even to the point of burying with it clothing, food, and utensils for the future. The Egyptians believed that the spirit of a person could not continue to exist if the physical body disappeared; therefore, to attain immortality, the body had to be mummified. Eventually, almost all Egyptian bodies were so treated, to universal satisfaction: The people believed they had conquered death.

Not all peoples are afraid of death. One has only to think of Spartans at Thermopylae, Scythian youths going willingly to their deaths at the funeral ceremonies of their kings, sacrificial maidens of the Incas treated with the greatest respect during their lives and dying in full expectation of a magnificent thereafter, Christian martyrs in Roman times welcoming death in a state of ecstasy, or even, in modern times, the kamikaze pilots of Japan. To people like these, death is not a disaster, but the gateway to a better existence in another world.

Looking at the matter on a global scale, we can say that most people believe in some form of life after death and often come to the conclusion that the body of the deceased should be prepared for this continuing existence. This can be achieved either by burying the person along with objects for use in the next life or, better still, by preserving the body itself. It can be noted in passing that almost all dead bodies in the United States today are embalmed. This can have no other purpose but to give survivors reassurance that life continues in some way: From the purely public health point of view, it is meaningless.

Throughout the world, nations and tribes have striven to preserve the bodies of their leaders and great men. One unsuccessful effort was that of the Chinese ruler who had a marvellous suit made of small pieces of jade stitched together with gold wires and shaped to enclose his whole body. Jade was believed to preserve bodies, but in this case it was ineffective, and the body inside the suit changed into dust. In Vienna, according to Ekkehard Kleiss (personal communication 1977), there are mummies of the kings and princes of Austria. A peculiar feature here is that in some instances the bodies are kept in one cathedral and the internal organs in another. To this day, the bodies of the Jewish patriarchs and their families are kept in tombs in Israel. It is probable that all of them were mummified as described in the Bible.

Among mummies that have been lost are those of the Ptolemies in Egypt. These Greek pharaohs adopted the customs of their conquered country, and that must have included preserving the body after death. The greatest of all the Greek leaders was Alexander, and the site of his tomb in Alexandria has also been forgotten. An active search is even now in progress for the tomb of the world's first known genius, Imhotep, near the pyramid he built for his pharaoh. This step pyramid at Saqqara was the first one, and archeologists feel certain that Imhotep was buried near his master.

Preservation of the body was undertaken not only for the future good of the dead, but often out of fear by the living of the spirits of the dead. If there is life after death, as so many

people have believed, then it follows that the ghosts may return to haunt and hurt the living. Therefore, the dead must be placated by adequate care during burial and kept in a friendly state by presents of food and other gifts long after death. The ancestor worship of the Chinese is probably based on such beliefs. The mummies of the Inca rulers were displayed at intervals in the square in Cuzco, as though they were still living, and were offered food and drink.

In many parts of the world, bodies resting in churches, cathedrals, and temples were preserved by accidents of climate or circumstance. I saw one example in the making in 1959 in East Pakistan (now Bangladesh) while fighting a smallpox epidemic. One night in Cox's Bazaar, the district commissioner came to see me and asked me if I would visit a monastery 60 km away on a river that formed the boundary with Burma. Some 2,000 years ago, there had been 1,500 monks there, but now only one was left and he was very ill. On arrival, I was escorted to the temple, but had to enter alone.

The last surviving monk was lying before the statue of Buddha, almost unconscious, scarcely breathing, and with a very feeble heartbeat. His legs were gangrenous, and because this was the hot and dry season, they had dried up and were in fact mummified. He could not drink the water I gave him, and it was obvious that he was near death: In fact, he died the next day. In time, he would have dried up completely. But in that climate the body could not have stayed mummified for long; with the arrival of the monsoon rains, humidity, insects, rats, and fungi would soon have reduced the soft tissues to dust so that only a skeleton remained.

In many countries, however, bodies like his have survived. A spectacular example is in the Capuchin Catacombs of Palermo, Sicily, where 8,000 mummies of men, women, and children, dressed in their best clothes, line the walls, their flesh preserved by the dryness of the air. These mummies represent a cross section of the populace of the nineteenth century, coming from all sections of society. The practice was abandoned in the early twentieth century, but the mummies remain as dressed a hundred or more years ago.

In Venzone, Italy, there are mummies displayed in white sheets in erect positions (one wonders if they survived the recent earthquake that destroyed the town). In Vienna, kings and princes were preserved and their organs distributed among the cathedrals and churches of that city. In Corfu, Greece, the mummy of Saint Spiridion, patron saint of the island, is paraded with full ceremony around town during his festival. The list is endless.

An advance in embalming technology in which the tissues are infiltrated with paraffin wax first appeared in the Argentine at the beginning of this century. The most superb example of this method is said to be the body of Eva Perón, who appears to be merely asleep in spite of the peregrinations of her remains to Italy and back home again. Many observers have commented on the waxy face of Lenin, and some on that of Stalin, so perhaps they also had the paraffin treatment.

This longing for everlasting life has taken a new twist in recent years as a result of advancements in technology. It has long been known that freezing can, to some extent, suspend animation; for example, fish frozen in lake ice sometimes swim away when they thaw out. For decades microbiologists have preserved living viruses, bacteria, and simple organisms by keeping them at very low temperatures. Recently, it was reported from the Antarctic that living bacteria, up to 10,000 years old, have been found deep down in the frozen soil.

It is, therefore, not surprising that a new "science" of cryogenics has arisen in which the bodies of the dying or recently dead – the time at which the change from life to death takes place is a debatable legal point of considerable importance – are placed in deep freezes for revival in the future.

The reason this procedure is deemed worthwhile is the belief that a disease that kills today is likely to be curable tomorrow. It is hoped that, at some future time, life can be restored and the disease treated. In this way life can be continued, with occasional pauses for renewal, through eternity. Already, numerous bodies have been prepared in this way and stored in lockers at low temperatures. This technique may or may not work, but it will surely supply excellent specimens for research by paleopathologists in the future!

REFERENCES

Dawson, W. R. 1938. *Sir Grafton Elliot Smith*. London: Cape.

Lucas, A. 1962. *Ancient Egyptian materials and industries*, 4th ed., revised and enlarged by J. R. Harris. London: Edward Arnold.

Wellard, J. 1973. *The search for the Etruscans*. New York: Saturday Review Press.

PART I
Mummies of Egypt

1

Mummies of ancient Egypt

WILLIAM H. PECK
Curator of Ancient Art
Detroit Institute of Arts
Detroit, Michigan, U.S.A.

In the modern mind no single type of artifact from the ancient world excites more interest than the Egyptian mummy, and no other kind of object is considered more typically Egyptian. The very word *mummy* brings to mind a host of associated ideas – the Egyptian belief in life after death, the seemingly pervasive concern with the notion of death, and the elaborate preparations that were made for it. It is well to state at the outset that religious beliefs made it necessary to preserve the dead, and what seems a preoccupation with death was actually the outgrowth of a love of life and an attempt to prepare for a continuation in the next world of life as it is known in this.

A considerable literature, much of it of a speculative nature, has grown up around the modern interest in the process of mummification. In recent decades the progress of science has done much to dispel earlier misconceptions, but many of these have become firmly fixed and die hard. The process of mummification is still considered to be a "lost art" by many who would rather remain content with an intriguing mystery than be disappointed with a simple explanation. The process was the result of a continuous development based on trial and error and observable results. The details of technique can now be discussed with some confidence and accuracy.

Modern literature on the subject of mummification is extensive; the historic cornerstone of the study in English is Thomas Pettigrew's *History of Egyptian Mummies*, published in 1834. For the time at which it appeared, the work was a monumental undertaking. Based on scholarly research and practical experience, Pettigrew's work was a summation of almost all that was known concerning Egyptian funerary practices. He compiled all the ancient sources and commented on them, as well as discussing many examples of mummified remains investigated by or known to him (Figure 1.1). This work is illustrated by engraved plates by George Cruikshank (better known for his satirical drawings) that are the product of careful observation.

It was not until 1924 that another work of comparable stature appeared. *Egyptian Mummies* by G. Elliot Smith and Warren R. Dawson is still a standard text to which the interested reader can turn with confidence. Alfred Lucas was another twentieth-century pioneer in the scientific study of the process of mummification. In addition to many articles on various aspects of the subject, he devoted a chapter to his findings in *Ancient Egyptian Materials and Industries* (Lucas 1962). His work has been carried on by the Egyptian, Zaki Iskander (Mokhtar, et al. 1973). Recently, James Harris and Kent Weeks (1973) have published a popular report of the work done on the royal mummies in the Cairo Museum in *X-Raying the Pharaohs.*

The purpose of mummification in ancient Egypt was twofold. The body of the deceased, it was believed, had to be treated to render it incorruptible. At the same time the physical appearance had to be maintained as nearly as possible to what it had been in life. The Egyptian conception of life after death developed early, as is evidenced by the burials of the predynastic (prehistoric) age. It would seem that the notion of preserving human and ani-

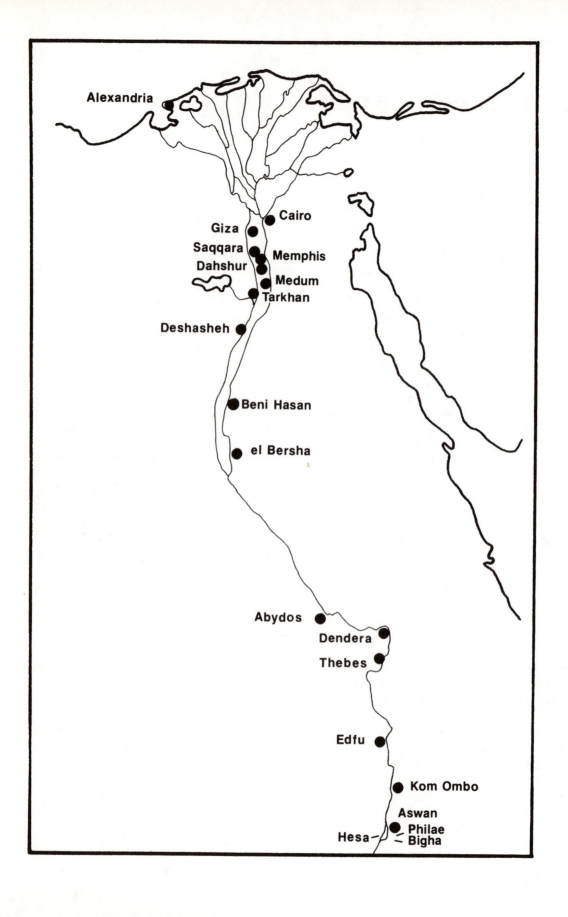

Alexandria

Cairo
Giza
Saqqara   Memphis
Dahshur
                 Medum
                 Tarkhan
Deshasheh

Beni Hasan

el Bersha

Abydos
Dendera
Thebes

Edfu

Kom Ombo

Aswan
Hesa   Philae
        Bigha

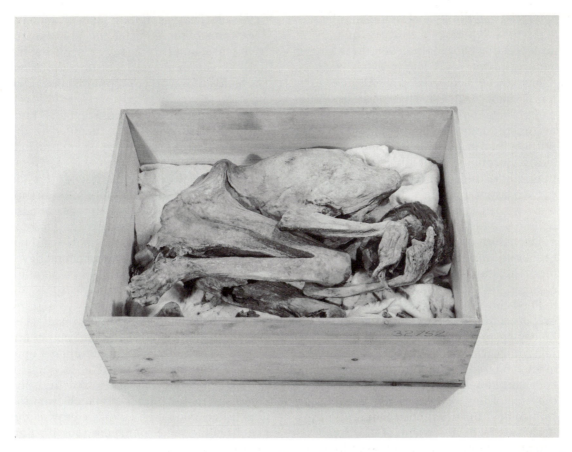

Figure 1.2. Predynastic burial, before 3000 B.C. British Museum 32752. The typical flexed position of most predynastic burials is illustrated here, as is the high state of preservation resulting from the dry sand rather than a complicated embalming process. The subject is an adult female.

mal dead came about naturally in the dry climate of Egypt. Predynastic burials were simple and practical (Figure 1.2). The corpse was placed in a hole in the sand, usually in a contracted position, accompanied by such grave goods as pottery and other useful objects. No embalming process was carried out; in no way was the body prepared (mummified) for the burial, but it was often wrapped in linen, reed matting, or hide. The pit was sometimes lined with matting, boards, or bricks, but the cavity that received the body was more grave than tomb. A small tumulus was erected over the grave, never large enough to interfere

with the warming effect of the sun. It was the hot, dry sand that served to desiccate the tissue. The result, to be observed in countless examples, is a well-preserved corpse. From the simple fact that objects were included with the burial, we can deduce that they were meant to serve the spirit of the dead in some fashion in the next life.

At the beginning of the dynastic age (around 3000 B.C.), the religious beliefs and accompanying funerary ritual appear to have been already well developed. The tomb structures of early dynastic kings were designed as imitation palaces and fortresses that must

Figure 1.1. Major sites in ancient Egypt. (Map by Timothy Motz, Detroit Institute of Arts)

have reflected the style of living architecture of the time. The great quantity of funerary offerings in these burials indicates that a king or member of the royal family expected to be able to use such material in a continued existence in the next life. The subsidiary interment of retainers nearby suggests the ability to confer immortality on them, if for no other purpose than to serve their master in the spirit world. As tomb structures became more complex, the position of the body in relation to the surface layers of warm sand was altered; the body was placed lower in the earth, at the bottom of a tomb shaft.

The notion of a "home" for the spirit continued throughout pharaonic history; the form of the structure underwent many changes, but the fundamental purpose remained the same. In the Old Kingdom the private tomb superstructure became more houselike, providing a protection for the burial, which was placed deep in the earth beneath it. The superstructure also provided the necessary rooms for the conduct of ritual at the time of the burial and after, as well as a storage area for ritual objects and offerings. Because the development of the tomb resulted in the removal of the body from the surface area of warm sand, it became necessary to invent a technology that would accomplish the preservation of the physical remains, a process that had occurred naturally in more simple times. In all cases where the body of the deceased had received "proper" burial, we can assume that some effort was made to treat the corpse and render it resistant to decay. The key factor in the preservation of the human body, as it was practiced by the Egyptians, is the removal of all body fluids. It is difficult to imagine the impetus for the initial steps in the development of the craft of mummification, but it has been suggested that some accidental knowledge of predynastic burials must have become available to the people of the early dynasties. By simple reasoning, it could have been determined that the removal of body fluid was the most important factor in the preparation of

the dead. The inspiration may even have come from observation of the processes of drying meat and fish. In any case, during the first 400 years of pharaonic history, the essential details of Egyptian mummification were evolved.

According to the *Oxford English Dictionary,* the word *mummy* is recorded in the English language as early as the fourteenth century. It existed in medieval Latin as *mumia* and was ultimately derived from the Arabic and Persian designations for an embalmed body by way of those for wax or bitumen. In modern usage, the word *mummy* is taken to mean the body of a human or animal that has been embalmed by the ancient Egyptian or some similar method as a preparation for burial. By analogy, many corpses are called "mummies" even if they have nothing to do with ancient Egypt. As a result, it is common to speak of Peruvian mummies, Aleutian mummies, the mummified Capuchins of Palermo, and the like. In English, the word *mummy* has been used to designate medicinal materials prepared from the mummified bodies of Egypt, a brown pigment from the same source used in oil painting, and, in a somewhat more specialized use, as a slang term for Egyptian issues on the English stock exchange. Current in the sixteenth century was the use of the word *mummy* for any dead flesh: "The water swells a man; and what a thing should I have been, when I had been swel'd? I should have been a mountain of Mummie" (William Shakespeare, *The Merry Wives of Windsor*).

It has been traditional in the past to base any study of mummification on the accounts given by a few classical authors. The few Egyptian texts that can be used to supplement these are tantalizing in the extreme. It is to be hoped that a complete account of the embalming process may be found for some period in Egyptian history, but until now, this has not happened. By accident of preservation, a composition entitled *The Ritual of Embalming* exists in a fragmentary state in two versions (Goyon 1972). The information it contains is more of a ritual nature than a step-by-step handbook on the technique of mummification. Its material consists of three parts: ceremonial acts to be performed on the mummy, prayers and incantations to be said during the process, and the methods of applying ointments and bandages to some parts of the body (arms, hands, legs, feet, back, and head). If either of the two late Papyri that contain this partial text were more complete, at least a sequence of wrapping the body might be explained. The most important lack is the absence of any information on the earlier stages of the mummification process, including evisceration and desiccation. From a number of minor Egyptian sources on stelae, ostraca, and papyri, the total length of time necessary for the total mummification process is established as 70 days. This includes the long period in which the body was allowed to dry.

The two classical authors who have given the best and most complete account of the process of mummification as they understood it are Herodotus and Diodorus Siculus. The account of Herodotus is by far the better known of the two, probably because the *Persian Wars,* of which it is a part, makes such interesting reading and because his account of Egypt has received such widespread publication. It must always be remembered that he was a Greek from Halicarnassus writing in the fifth century B.C. and that he is often accused by modern historians of reporting a considerable amount of what may be termed hearsay evidence. The reliability of Herodotus in regard to his descriptions of Egyptian customs and daily life has been the subject of much contemporary criticism; what he had to say about mummification must be weighed against the physical evidence of the mummies themselves.

Herodotus' account in the Rawlinson translation is as follows:

There are a set of men in Egypt who practice the art of embalming, and make it their proper business. When a body is brought to them these persons show the bearers various models of corpses, made in wood, and painted so as to resemble nature. The most perfect is said to be after the manner of him whom I do not think it religious to name in connection with such a matter; the second sort is inferior to the first, and less costly; the third is the cheapest of all. All this the embalmers explain, and then ask in which way it is wished that the corpse should be prepared. The bearers tell them, and having concluded their bargain, take their departure, while the embalmers, left to themselves, proceed to their task. The mode of embalming, according to the most perfect process, is the following: they take first a crooked piece of iron, and with it draw out the brain through the nostrils, thus getting rid of a portion, while the skull is cleared of the rest by rinsing with drugs; next they make a cut along the flank with a sharp Ethiopian stone, and take out the whole contents of the abdomen, which they then cleanse, washing it thoroughly with palm-wine, and again frequently with an infusion of pounded aromatics. After this, they fill the cavity with the purest bruised myrrh, with cassia, and every other sort of spicery except frankincense, and sew up the opening. Then, the body is placed in natrum for seventy days, and covered entirely over. After the expiration of that space of time, which must not be exceeded, the body is washed, and wrapped round, from head to foot, with bandages of fine linen cloth, smeared over with gum, which is used generally by the Egyptians in the place of glue, and in this state it is given back to the relations, who enclose it in a wooden case which they have had made for the purpose, shaped into the figure of a man. Then fastening the case, they place it in a sepulchral chamber, upright against the wall. Such is the most costly way of embalming the dead. [Herodotus, *History,* Book II:86]

If persons wish to avoid expense, and choose the second process, the following is the method pursued: Syringes are filled with oil made from the cedar-tree, which is then, without any incision or disembowelling injected into the bowel. The passage is stopped, and the body laid in natrum the prescribed number of days. At the end of the time the cedar-oil is allowed to make its escape; and such is its power that it brings with it the whole stomach and intestines in a liquid state. The natrum meanwhile has dissolved the flesh, and so nothing is left of the dead body but the skin and the bones. It is returned in this condition to the relatives without any further trouble being bestowed upon it. [Herodotus, *History,* Book II:87]

The third method of embalming, which is practiced in the case of the poorer classes, is to clear out the intestines with a purge, and let the body lie in natrum the seventy days, after which it is at once given to those who come to fetch it away. [Herodotus, *History*, Book II:88]

Herodotus' account may well give a description of the mummification process as it existed in the fifth century and as it may have been related to him, but it must be remembered that over 2,000 years of development cannot always be measured by a description of so late a stage. It will be helpful to suggest what can be learned from his account. That the embalmers were a special class of workers we are reasonably certain. The presentation of models of the various classes of mummification to the family cannot be verified, but contained in the description is a reference to "him whom I do not think it religious to name" (the god Osiris), which may be a reference to small mummiform statues, and an attempted explanation of their purpose. The brain was often removed through the nose, but evidence exists for its removal through the base of the skull and other openings. The incision in the abdomen usually was made on the left side and is seldom found to have been stitched up. Herodotus states emphatically that the body was covered with natron. This part of his description holds the most important key to the process. In earlier translations this was misinterpreted as natron in solution involving a prolonged soaking. It has been proved very satisfactorily that dry natron was used for the important step of desiccating the body and that the 70 days assigned to this stage actually refer to the entire mummification process. If the mummy was given back to the relatives for placement in a coffin, it was probably for an inspection of the embalmer's work. There is little evidence that the mummy was placed standing in the tomb, but mummy cases from the Ptolemaic period do have a baselike section at the foot. Good evidence of the second method exists, for mummies have been found with no abdominal incision, yet with internal organs missing and the anus plugged with linen packing.

Herodotus' account of mummification continues with some details that need not be quoted in full. He says that the bodies of women of high rank or great beauty are not delivered to the embalmers immediately, but after 3 or 4 days, to prevent the possibility of intercourse with the dead body. He also adds that the bodies of those who have fallen in the Nile, or who have been attacked by crocodiles, must be embalmed by the inhabitants of the nearest city and buried by them. Of the delay in embalming important women there is some evidence, but the second assertion is difficult to prove.

The second important classical source for the process of mummification is the account of Diodorus Siculus. A native of Sicily, as his name implies, he drew heavily on Herodotus, added a few details, and has left us some additional information. Because he was writing in the first century A.D., and because he agrees so much with Herodotus, it is hard to believe that his account contains an accurate description of mummification in his own time. To Herodotus' statement that embalmers were of a special class, he adds that the occupation was hereditary. This is likely, considering the number of other trades of ancient Egypt that were passed on in families. Diodorus adds designatory titles for the specialists who performed the different stages of the process. He identifies the heart and kidneys as having been left in place in the body when the other organs were removed, which seems to be accurate considering the number of times the heart has been found in mummified remains. He says that the cleansed corpse was treated with cedar oil and other substances, but he omits mention of the removal of the brain.

After listing the three grades of mummification, Diodorus describes only the most expensive, but gives prices for all three. Two interesting details are added in his account. According to him, the embalmer who made the incision in the side, even though it was necessary to the embalming process, had to flee to escape the wrath of his fellow workmen. The explanation given is that any injury to the body of the deceased had to be punished, and this suggests that the ritual of protecting the corpse was taken seriously by the practitioners of the embalming craft. The second addition supplied by Diodorus is a description of the embalmed body, which, according to him, was preserved in every detail. So lifelike was the state of preservation that the body could be kept as a sort of display piece for the edification of the living. This agrees with Petrie's theory that some mummies of the Roman period must have been on view in the home for a considerable time before they were interred. Petrie was referring to mummies that had painted face coverings; the implication in Diodorus is that the face was still visible. The latter would be particularly curious and is not supported by the evidence of existing mummies.

In addition to Herodotus and Diodorus, Elliot Smith and Dawson refer to several papyri that give additional information, such as the prices of the various materials used in the mummification process. They also cite several late references to Egyptian embalming from Plutarch, Porphyry, Augustine, and others. For a somewhat distant source that contains mention of mummification, the Book of Genesis in the Old Testament should be quoted: "And Joseph commanded his servants, the physicians, to embalm his father; and the physicians embalmed Israel (Jacob)" (Gen. 50:2); "And forty days were fulfilled for him; and so are fulfilled the days of those which are embalmed; and the Egyptians mourned for him, three score and ten days" (Gen. 50:3); "So Joseph died, being an hundred and ten years old; and they embalmed him, and he was put into a coffin in Egypt" (Gen. 50:22). These short statements from the Old Testament add little to the Egyptian or classical sources beyond suggesting that the author had some familiarity with, or

access to, a tradition concerning Egyptian mummification.

No ancient Egyptian illustrations of the mummification process exist as such. The tomb paintings that have been preserved depict stages in the ritual and the offerings of prayers, but none of the physical treatment of the body itself. There are numerous instances in which the mummy is shown on the funerary bier, while it is being transported to the tomb, and before the tomb entrance at the time of the Opening of the Mouth ceremony, but the physical mummification seems not to have been an appropriate subject for tomb decoration. Any modern study of the process of mummification is dependent, then, on the physical remains of mummified bodies supplemented by the Egyptian, classical, and other references that deal with mummification and that have to be tested against the examples of mummification preserved.

The preservation of buried bodies in the predynastic age has already been commented on. The state of the development of the art of mummification in the early dynastic period is difficult to determine and must be inferred from the evidence of examples of later times. From Petrie's excavation of the Royal Tombs at Abydos came the bones of an arm that was wrapped in linen and still decorated with jewelry, but this indicates only the use of wrapping and gives no indication concerning the other preparations of the body. Quibell found at Saqqara the remains of a female of the Second Dynasty (2780–2635 B.C.). A contracted burial contained in a wooden coffin, the corpse was wrapped in over 16 layers of linen, but again, the condition of preservation made it impossible to determine exactly how the body had been treated. One important burial from the beginning of the Fourth Dynasty does a great deal more to suggest the state to which the science had progressed. In the early years of this century, the Boston–Harvard expedition, working at Giza under the direction of G. A. Reisner, discovered a tomb of Queen Hetepheres, the wife of Sneferu and the mother of Cheops (Ca. 2500 B.C.). Apparently, the remains of the queen had been entombed first at some other location, perhaps Dahshur, for the simple shaft tomb at Giza gave every appearance of a reburial. When the stone sarcophagus was opened, the body was missing, but the compartmented chest that contained the queen's viscera was found undisturbed. The packages of internal organs were still preserved in a solution of natron. The fact that the solution was still liquid after 4,500 years was incredible, but the real value of the discovery is the evidence it gives for the developed practice at this early time of the removal of the viscera and their inclusion in the burial in a special container of their own. The course of events to be inferred is obvious. At some point between the end of the predynastic period and the time of Hetepheres' burial, the technique developed of removing from the body those organs that were most likely to decay. It is not surprising that, in the 500 years this historical period covers, methods of embalming should have developed to such an advanced state.

The outward form of vessels used in the preservation of the viscera varied during the dynastic period. In the case of Hetepheres, the container used was a compartmented chest of alabaster. Individual canopic jars of the Fourth Dynasty exist. The idea of sets of four containers (or one divided into four parts) continues throughout much of dynastic history. The form changes – a miniature coffin occasionally replaced the jars – but the central idea was that the parts removed from the body were still a part of it and had to be treated as the body was, as well as being buried with it. The tradition was so strong that in the late period, when the organs were returned to the body cavity after being treated, dummy or imitation jars were still included in the burial.

By the Fourth Dynasty, the techniques of mummification had advanced so far that they may be studied in detail. That the process took a considerable time is suggested by the lack of well-preserved evidence from the ear-

lier dynasties. A single foot found in the burial chamber of the Step Pyramid at Saqqara, tentatively identified as once a part of the mummy of Zoser, offers no evidence about the techniques of mummification, but it does suggest, from the layers of linen wrapping, that the corpse was padded out in some semblance of a lifelike form.

The number of preserved bodies from the Fourth Dynasty on (and, of course, the number of tombs that have been identified) makes it clear that the preservation process was used for the nobility as well as for royalty. One well-known example found at Medum by W. M. F. Petrie in 1891 was provisionally dated by Elliot Smith and Dawson to the Fifth Dynasty, but they also stated that "the exact age of this mummy is uncertain. On archaeological evidence, it may be as early as the IIIrd Dynasty, but the extended position and the great advance in technique which it displays would seem to indicate a somewhat later date, probably Vth Dynasty" [2450–2290 B.C.]. Petrie's description, made at the time of the mummy's discovery, is worth quoting:

The mode of embalming was very singular. The body was shrunk, wrapped in a linen cloth, then modelled all over with resin, into the natural form and plumpness of the living figure, completely restoring all the fullness of the form, and this was wrapped around in a few turns of the finest gauze. The eyes and eyebrows were painted on the outer wrapping with green." [Petrie 1892]

Elliot Smith and Dawson examined this specimen at the Royal College of Surgeons in London, where it had been deposited by Petrie, and they described it as being wrapped in large quantites of linen with the outer layers soaked in resin and modeled to resemble the fine details of the body. Even the genitals were so treated, with such care as to allow the investigators to determine that circumcision had been practiced. They also observed that the body cavity had been packed with resin-impregnated linen. This mummy, found by Petrie at Medum and identified by him as a man named Ranofer, is now dated to the

Fourth Dynasty. The descriptions of it give a concrete idea of the attempt that had been made to create a lifelike appearance by modeling and wrapping. The mummy is no longer available for further examination, as it was destroyed in an air raid in World War II (Lucas 1962).

The fully developed intention at the height of the Old Kingdom seems to have been to effect the most lifelike suggestion possible of the original appearance of the body before death. It is a pity that there are not more and better preserved examples of mummification that span the time between the beginning of the dynastic period and the pyramid age. Nevertheless, the conclusion is the same: The practice of preservation was accompanied by a desire to create of the dead body a resemblance to the deceased as he had been in life. One additional example from the Fifth Dynasty adds support to this assertion. The mummy of a man named Nefer, found at Saqqara, is described in *X-Raying the Pharaohs* as looking like a man asleep. The wrappings of this specimen were soaked in an adhesive and molded to suggest the shape of the body, "the genitalia were particularly well modeled. Eyes, eyebrows and mustache were carefully drawn in ink on the moulded linen" (Harris and Weeks 1973). From the description, this mummy seems to provide an almost exact parallel to the one from Medum, now destroyed.

The desire to preserve the outward appearance of the deceased took another direction, in addition to the coating of the body with resin and the modeling of the features in that material. Masks of plaster applied over the face are known from as early as the Fourth Dynasty. By the time of the Middle Kingdom, the facial features were often modeled in cartonnage, a combination either of cloth and glue or of papyrus and plaster (Figure 1.3). In the Middle Kingdom, the entire body was sometimes covered with cartonnage as a final layer of the wrapping process. The face seems naturally to have been the most important part of the body for realistic treatment. The technique varied from the plaster masks of the Old Kingdom to the flat, painted portraits of the Roman period (Figure 1.7) and includes such notable examples as the solid gold face mask of Tutankhamun. Like the coverings of the face, the style of wrapping in linen bandages varied. At its best-developed stage in the New Kingdom, every individual part, including each finger and toe, was wrapped separately. After this, each larger unit was covered, and finally the total mummy was enwrapped. Single sheets as long as 13 or 17 m have been recorded.

Changes in the technique of embalming were progressive and continuous, but not until the time of the New Kingdom can the complete sequence of steps in the process be detailed. Working on the basic studies carried out by Lucas, and with continued experimentation, Zaki Iskander (Mokhtar et al. 1973) outlined what he considered the complete method employed at its fully developed stage:

1. Putting the corpse on the operating table
2. Extraction of the brain
3. Extraction of the viscera
4. Sterilization of the body cavities and viscera
5. Embalming the viscera
6. Temporary stuffing of the thoracic and abdominal cavities
7. Dehydration of the body
8. Removal of the temporary stuffing material
9. Packing the body cavities with permanent stuffing material
10. Anointing the body
11. Packing the face openings
12. Smearing the skin with molten resin
13. Adorning and bandaging the mummy

The following is a commentary on the 13 steps.

1. The body of the deceased was taken to the place of mummification soon after death. The clothing was removed, and the body was placed on a work table

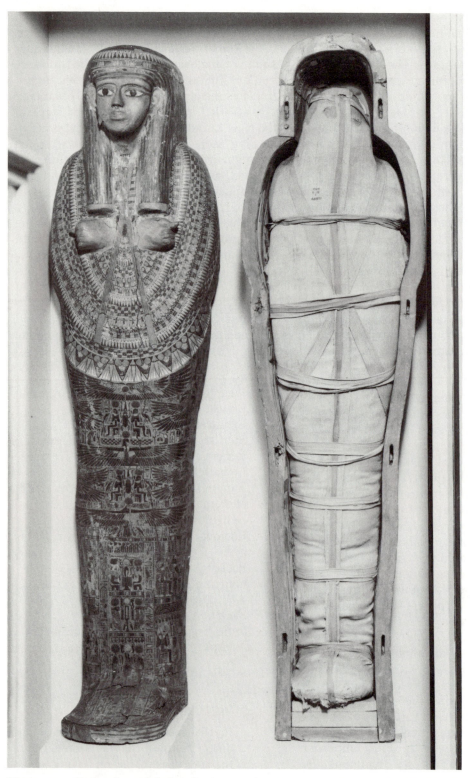

Figure 1.3.   *Body of an adult female, Twenty-first Dynasty, 1080–946 B.C. British Museum 48971. The well-preserved outer wrapping of this mummy is in the typical arrangement for its period. The large outer cloths have been tied in place with a simple but decorative strapping, which is also well preserved.*

for the succeeding processes. Embalmers' tables have been found and recognized as such. Little other comment is needed for what would have been the most obvious first stage of the working procedure.

2. The brain, one of the organs most subject to rapid putrefaction, was probably removed first; this is verified by Herodotus' account and seems practical. A passage was opened, through the nose usually, and the cerebral matter taken out with a hooked metal rod. Implements have been identified as possibly the types used for this operation. The brain was apparently not preserved. There is no mention on any container connected with the mummification process or on burial material of their use for the brain, but there are certainly many mummies in which it can be demonstrated that the brain is absent.

3. An incision was made in the abdomen, usually on the left side, but it may be found in other locations as well. The abdominal organs were extracted except for the kidneys, but this exception was not consistently observed; the kidneys are also missing sometimes. Next, the diaphragm was cut out and the contents of the thorax, except the heart and usually the aorta, were removed. This is the usual condition of well-prepared mummies. In mummification of the less expensive types, there is no incision and the removal of the organs is less consistent. The necessity for this stage in the preservation of the body needs little comment, for the extraction of the soft organs, particularly the intestines, would greatly aid the preservation of the body. The heart was usually left in place because it was considered the "seat of the mind." This may help to explain why the brain seems not to have been preserved. The heart, in

any case, is muscle and would not be as apt to decay as the organs that were removed.

4. After the removal of the internal organs, the thorax and the abdomen were cleansed, probably with palm wine, which would have had some sterilizing effect. Diodorus mentions the cleansing of the viscera with palm wine, and it is natural to assume that this would have also been done to the body cavities. The operation would have left no detectable trace, but it is a natural assumption that some sort of internal cleansing was carried out.

5. The viscera were separated, emptied, cleansed, and dried. They were then treated with molten resin, wrapped in separate linen packages, and placed in containers. The so-called canopic jars or chests took different forms at different times, as will be discussed elsewhere. This stage could have been carried out concurrently with the next.

6. After the cleaning mentioned in step 4, the thorax and abdomen were stuffed with temporary packing material to ensure the complete desiccation of the body. There is evidence from refuse material examined by Iskander that such temporary packing existed. Although this step has been doubted by some authorities, it would have been practical and useful, not only for the drying effect, but also for the maintenance of the shape of the corpse. Herodotus mentioned packing the cavities before the complete desiccation, but he did not specifically indicate that it was of a temporary nature.

7. The complete desiccation of the body could now be accomplished. Exactly how this was done has been the subject of considerable debate, but the general conclusion reached in modern scholarship indicates that the process

involved the use of dry natron. The body, probably on a slanting bed, was completely covered with natron. This had the effect of removing any remaining body liquid and consequently ensuring against any further putrefaction. The drying-out process lasted 40 days; the total embalming process, 70 days. There is a good deal of evidence to support this time scheme.

8. After the drying-out process, the temporary packing material was removed. It was not discarded, because it had come into contact with the body. Caches of embalmers' material have been found in sufficient quantity to make it clear that the temporary packing was buried near the tomb.

9. Resin or resin-impregnated cloth was put into the cranium. This is often evident in X rays of the skull, in which the resin can be seen as having reached its own level while liquid and then solidified. The body cavities were stuffed with linen cloth and bags of other materials including natron, sawdust, earth, and occasionally a few onions. The incision was closed with resin, wax, or linen and covered with a plate of metal or wax. The embalming incision is seldom found actually to have been stitched together.

10. The body was presumably anointed at this point with fragrant materials.

11. The orifices of the head were packed with wax or resin-soaked linen, and pads of linen were placed over the eyeballs.

12. Liquefied resin was smeared over the whole body. This acted as a preventative against the reentry of moisture and tended to strengthen the skin.

13. Amulets and other jewelry were placed on the mummy. The amount and quality of such materials depended on the wealth and position of the deceased. In a royal mummy, such as that of Tutankhamun, the quantity of objects was very large, including bracelets, rings, necklaces, pectorals, finger and toe coverings, as well as amuletic devices prepared especially for the burial. The mummy was then wrapped in linen bandages, sometimes with resin between the layers. The most complex wrapping began with the individual fingers and toes, proceeded to the limbs, and ultimately encased the total corpse in many layers of linen.

These 13 steps outline the most complete manner of preparing the body for the tomb in the New Kingdom. A mummy such as this would have stood a good chance of being completely preserved (Figures 1.4 through 1.7). There were, undoubtedly, many variations on this model program, but the principal operations of desiccation, washing with palm wine (which contained alcohol), and anointing with resin all resulted in the desired end of rendering the physical remains incorruptible.

One of the most complex arguments about the mummification process has centered around the chemical material used in the desiccation of the body. The principal ingredients that have been considered are salt and natron. To the earlier investigators, salt seemed the most likely desiccating agent employed, probably from actual experience with salted meat and fish. Considerable investigation and study have proved that salt appears only as an adulterant and was not the principal means of preserving the body. For a considerable time, natron was believed to have been used in a solution, mainly because of faulty translations of the description of the mummification process in Herodotus. Lucas and others have proved satisfactorily that the body was packed in dry natron, not soaked in a solution. Lucas made a series of experiments in which he treated the bodies of pigeons by four possible methods: salt in solution; dry salt packing; natron in solution; and dry natron packing. The conclusion he

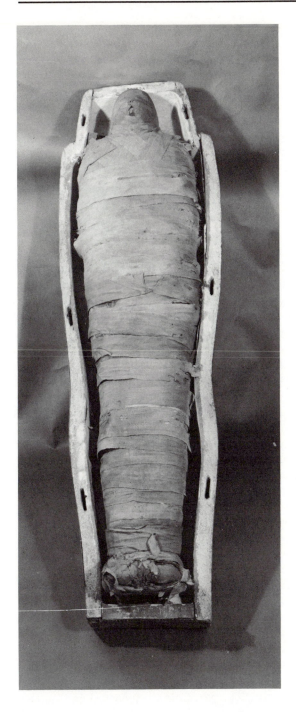

reached was that the mummification process depended for its success on the use of dry natron. Zaki Iskander treated a group of ducks using the principle suggested by Lucas. After 30 years, in 1973, he stated that they were "still in a very good state." Iskander had kept the mummified ducks in a laboratory under normal conditions of atmosphere and humidity. It can be generally assumed that the packing of the mummy in dry natron, a material abundant in ancient Egypt, was the simplest and most practical method of desiccation. The physical problem of obtaining containers of sufficient size to hold a human body should have long ago ruled out the possibility of a bath, whereas the dry method could have been employed by arranging the remains on a table or matting and simply heaping the natron around it.

Three other arguments for the use of a "pickling" solution have been propounded. The fact that mummies have been found with separate limbs that did not belong to them suggested that parts had become detached in a soaking process and had been incorrectly reassembled. In fact, it is more likely that such cases were the result of a later rewrapping of vandalized bodies. The purpose of finger and toe stalls was, at one time, explained as being to keep the fingernails and toenails in place during soaking. In actuality, these objects were probably more decorative than useful. The third argument for the use of a soaking bath was the apparent lack of epidermis in examples inspected; the theory was that the epidermis had soaked away. The lack of epidermis can usually be explained by its having come away with the wrapping or actually having been present but not recognized as such. The physical state of well-preserved mummies, taken together with accurate translations of the ancient texts, makes the use of a liquid bath and prolonged soak-

Figure 1.4.   Body of an old man, Ptolemaic period, 332–30 B.C. British Museum 20650. The somewhat rough and wide outer wrapping strips suggest that some further decoration is missing, such as additional bandings, a shroud, or other

elements. In the catalog, Mummies and Human Remains, *of the British Museum there is mention of beads found in the wrapping; this may indicate that the missing element is a bead netting.*

ing seem unlikely. The use of dry natron for complete packing of the body seems, at present, to offer the most understandable explanation of how desiccation was carried out.

From the earliest time for which there is evidence, the process of preservation was accompanied by a decided attempt to create a lifelike appearance of the mummy. In the Old Kingdom, this was accomplished mainly by wrapping with sufficient linen to restore the natural contours of the body. Special mention should be made of the practice followed in the Twenty-first Dynasty. Modern taxidermists would find the techniques of the embalmers in this period similar to their own work, for the basic steps outlined above as typical of the New Kingdom were augmented by a process designed to produce an even more natural effect. Stuffings of various materials, principally linen cloth, were inserted under the skin through incisions made for that purpose. The body cavity was filled and the arms and legs rounded out either from inside the trunk or through minor openings made in the limbs. The loss of body mass was made up wherever needed, and the face was stuffed from inside the mouth. Elliot Smith and Dawson suggest that this elaborate treatment of the body occurred at a time of, and may have been responsible for, less emphasis on substitute images of the deceased as alternate dwelling places for the spirit. It is true that during this period there are fewer examples of the *ka* statues made in the likeness of the dead. In any case, mummies from this time exhibit a definite attempt to restore an appearance of life and can be easily recognized as belonging to this period.

The evolution of the mummification process was accompanied by a development of the necessary funerary ''furniture,'' such as containers for the body and the viscera. The early pit burial of the predynastic age required no container except for the simple wrapping

Figure 1.5. *Body of an old woman, Ptolemaic to Roman period, date uncertain. British Museum 6665. This example illustrates the use, even at a late date, of a modeled face mask on the mummy. The other objects that embellish the front of the body may not belong, and as a consequence, the actual date of the mummy is difficult to determine.*

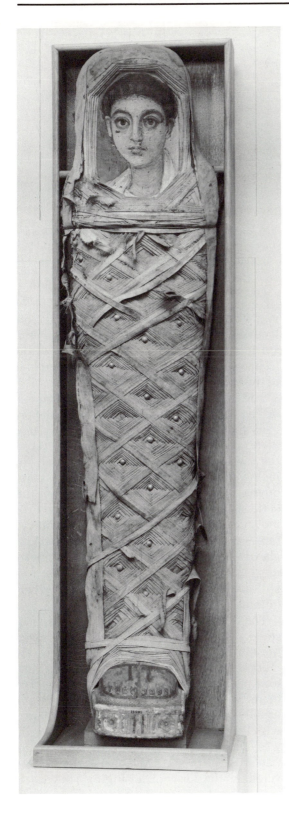

of the body in cloth, reed matting, or hide. Because the pit or hole was sometimes lined with brick, boards, or matting, it may be considered that this acted as a substitute for a portable container. In the early dynastic period, the notion of a miniature house for the deceased was suggested by the use of small paneled chests or boxes, suitable only for contracted burials. In form, these were imitative of lower Egyptian houses with paneled walls and arched roofs. As religious ritual developed, these small containers gave way to larger rectangular sarcophagi of wood or stone (limestone, granite, or alabaster). As the burial of the remains of Queen Hetepheres has already received some comment above, her sarcophagus can serve as an example of the beginning of Dynasty Four. Made of fine alabaster with a close-fitting lid, Hetepheres' sarcophagus was of a proportion that indicates it was made to accommodate an extended rather than a contracted body. When found by excavators in the twentieth century, it was, unfortunately, empty.

A rectangular container for the body was used throughout the Old Kingdom, but it is in the painted wooden coffins of the Middle Kingdom that the form reached its height as a decorated object. A typical coffin of the Eleventh and Twelfth dynasties was decorated with painted architectural motifs on the outside, which resemble the so-called palace facade design. The left, or east, side was usually decorated with some hieroglyphic texts and with a false door and a pair of eyes to allow the spirit the means by which he could communicate with the outside world. The interior of the coffin was decorated with paintings in registers or horizontal bands.

Figure 1.6. Body of an adolescent boy, Roman period, probably first to second century A.D. British Museum 13595. The typical crossed outer wrapping of narrow strips with gilded metal buttons common on mummies of the Roman period is shown here. The use of a flat, painted portrait is a Greco-Roman contribution to the manner of decorating the mummy.

Figure 1.7.   Body of an adult male, Roman period. British Museum 6704. An unusual (for its time) treatment of the final wrapping is illustrated here. The limbs are wrapped separately, and the face has had the features painted, a technique going back to the Old Kingdom but no longer common in later Egyptian history.

The uppermost of these contained a carefully painted invocation on behalf of the occupant; the middle register, a series of depictions of funerary offerings and necessities for the next life; and the lower areas, a series of finely written prayers, spells, and amuletic sayings drawn from a larger body of religious literature known as the Coffin Texts.

The anthropoid coffin makes its first appearance in the Middle Kingdom. It is probable that the notion of designing the complete container for the body in such a way that it resembles a human figure developed directly from the Old Kingdom tradition of covering the face of the deceased with a lifelike mask. Although the long-hallowed use of a rectangular coffin persisted into the New Kingdom, particularly for royal burials, the body at that time was first enclosed in an anthropoid coffin or a series of nested coffins of such shape. The notion, probably, was that the coffin helped to ensure the preservation of the shape of the body, while the stone sarcophagus served as a house or a shrine within which to contain it. Throughout the history of the anthropoid coffin the face was nearly always modeled in relief (Figure 1.5). The hands, arms, and breasts also were sometimes treated as relief decoration. Wooden examples could be elaborately painted inside and out with a combination of religious texts and

vignettes illustrating the funerary ritual, protective divinities, and the progress of the spirit in the next life. Wooden coffins could be items kept in stock, with the name and title of the individual added at the time of use.

The elaborate protection for the mummified body was extended to the internal organs that had been removed from it. They were considered with the same care because they were, in effect, part of the human remains and had to be treated with the same degree of respect. As said above, one of the earliest pieces of solid evidence for the removal of the viscera as a part of mummification was the canopic box of Hetepheres. The alabaster box was divided into four compartments, was sealed with a tight-fitting lid, and still contained the embalmed viscera when found.

The division of the viscera, as it was later standardized, was into four parts: the liver, the stomach, the lungs, and the intestines. At most times in the history of mummification, four containers, or symbolic substitutes for them, were provided. These containers are usually called canopic jars because their form, with the lid or stopper in the shape of a head, was thought to resemble the burial of Canopus, the priest of Menelaus, who was revered in the form of a bulging jar with a human head.

During the Old Kingdom, the canopic jar was typically a rough-hewn, slightly bulging limestone jar with a convex lid. There is preserved in the Metropolitan Museum a set of jars of this description found in the burial chamber of the tomb of Pery-neb of the late Fourth Dynasty. Although these four containers are identifiable as to their intended purpose, they were clean inside and were never used. By the beginning of the Middle Kingdom, the identification of the viscera as part of the body was reinforced by the shape of the jar lid or stopper, which was modeled in the shape of a human head. That the four jars had human heads as late as the end of Dynasty Eighteen is attested to by the four stoppers from the canopic chest of Tutankhamun. As a complete example of the treatment of the viscera in a royal burial, the canopic chest of this king should be described. Inside a gilt wooden chest was found an alabaster chest of similar shape. This was divided into four interior compartments, each of which was plugged with a stopper fashioned in a likeness of the king's head. In the four compartments were four miniature inlaid gold coffins that actually contained the visceral packets.

In the Eighteenth Dynasty, a second treatment of the four canopic lids developed. One continued to be made in the form of a human head, but the other three were fashioned as the heads of a jackal, a baboon, and a falcon. The four heads identified the viscera as being protected by four genii (called the four sons of Horus). When it became customary to package the organs that had been removed and return them to the body cavities, the tradition of the canopic containers was continued, but the jars were false or imitation, often solid, the body and lid carved from the same piece of stone.

The materials from which the canopic containers were made were extremely varied. Clay, limestone, alabaster, wood, faience, and cartonnage were all employed. The canopic jar could be a carefully designed work of art or a crude, roughly fashioned receptacle. As is the case with all aspects of the preparation for burial, the social status and ability to pay of the deceased or his family were the key factors in the choice of the methods and materials employed. This has resulted in a wide variety of tomb goods and, naturally, the method of embalming and wrapping during any one period. What had begun as a necessary precaution during the early dynastic times for the protection and preservation of the king's body had gradually become available to any who could pay the price. The number of objects – coffins, papyrus scrolls of the *Book of the Dead*, heart amulets – that have been found with the name of the deceased left blank attest to the common practice of producing standard funerary objects to be sold at a price. The place in the text appropriate for the name was intended to be filled in at the time of purchase. In some instances, this was not done, for what reason we shall probably never know.

The religious basis of the mummification process was rooted in the necessity of preserving the physical remains as a resting place for the spirit. What had been accomplished accidentally in the predynastic period was done by a gradually developed process over the centuries. The techniques and procedures, which became more and more complicated through the course of Egyptian history, served this single purpose: the preservation of the human form, and particularly the features of the face, from decay. With the embalming process there grew up attendant aids for the protection of the spirit. The ritual decoration of the mummy, coffin, and sarcophagus, and the amuletic devices placed on and around the body served this end. The mummy has become a symbolic touchstone that conjures up the mysteries of ancient Egypt for modern man. What the physical remains of the ancient Egyptians can tell us through scientific techniques is only now becoming evident.

REFERENCES

Diodorus Siculus. 1935. *History*. Translated by C. H. Oldfather. Cambridge, Mass.: Harvard University Press.

Elliot Smith, G. and Dawson, W. R. 1924. *Egyptian mummies*. New York: Dial Press.

Goyon, J. C. 1972. *Rituels funéraires de l'ancienne Egypte*. Paris: Cerf.

Harris, J. E., and Weeks, K. R. 1973. *X-raying the pharaohs*. New York: Scribner

Herodotus. *History*. Translated by G. Rawlinson. 1910. London: Dent.

Lucas, A. 1962. *Ancient Egyptian materials and industries*, 4th ed., revised and enlarged by J. R. Harris. London: Edward Arnold.

Mokhtar, G.; Riad, H.; and Iskander, Z. 1973. *Mummification in ancient Egypt*. Cairo: Cairo Museum.

Petrie, W. M. F. 1892. *Medum*. London: David Nutt.

Pettigrew, T. J. 1834. *A history of Egyptian mummies*. London: Longmans.

Reisner, G. A. 1927–32. Articles on Queen Hetepheres. *Bulletin of the Museum of Fine Arts* (Boston). 25 (1927), 26 (1928), 27 (1929), 30 (1932).

2

Diseases in ancient Egypt

A. T. SANDISON
Formerly of Department of Pathology
Western Infirmary
Glasgow, Scotland

All men and women share certain experiences. All are born (and during birth may injure their mothers); all suffer illnesses during their lives; and all must sooner or later die, whether from disease, degenerative process, accident, or violence. The historian's overall view of ancient peoples is incomplete if he fails to take into account these phenomena of states of health or disease.

The major lines of study of ancient diseases comprise examination of literary sources by scholars in collaboration with physicians, study of artistic representations in sculpture and painting, and study of skeletal remains and mummies by macroscopic examination, supplemented by radiography and by histological examination using light, polarizing, and electron microscopes.

The major literary sources for our knowledge of disease processes in Egypt are the Ebers, Edwin Smith, and Kahun papyri (Dawson 1953). The first deals with medical diseases and includes, among many others, descriptions of urinary disorders, virtually certainly including schistosomiasis and parasitic gut infestations. The second is surgical and contains accurate prognostic comments on traumatic and certain inflammatory diseases. The third concerns obstetrical and gynecological disorders. Precise diagnoses are, in many instances, difficult to make from the symptoms listed. Nevertheless, the papyri will continue to engage scholars and medical historians for many years. From these, as well as other literary sources, specialist scholars have adduced evidence of trachoma, seasonal ophthalmia, skin diseases, hernia, hemorrhoids, and so on.

Studies of artistic representations have yielded clear evidence of achondroplastic dwarfism and highly probable diagnoses of such states as bilateral dislocation of the hips, postpoliomyelitic limb atrophy, and pituitary disorder (Aldred and Sandison 1962; Wells 1964). Macroscopic examination of ancient Egyptian skeletons has revealed a wealth of pathological changes. These have been reviewed by Brothwell and Powers (1968) and Sandison (1968) with regard, respectively, to congenital abnormalities and acquired disease. Among the congenital lesions are included achondroplasia, acrocephaly, talipes equinovarus, Klippel-Feil syndrome, hip-joint dysplasia, hydrocephaly, and cleft palate. Bilateral parietal bone thinning has also been observed and must be differentiated from osteoporosis symmetrica. This has been noted in the mummies of Meritamen and Tuthmosis III as well as in Khety of the Twelfth Dynasty.

Acquired diseases include such common conditions as osteoarthritis, nonspecific osteitis, middle ear infection, and rarer lesions such as tuberculous and leprous osteitis, osteoma, osteochondroma, possible chondrosarcoma of the pelvis, cranial changes attributable to meningioma and possible nasopharyngeal cancer, gout, and osteoporosis. Satinoff (1968) described examples of osteoarthritis, otorhinolaryngologic disease, osteoma, possible metastatic tumors of the skull, and most interestingly, the recently recognized basal cell nevus syndrome in the Egyptian skeletal collection at Torino. Salib (1967) has considered fractures in ancient Egyptians.

In the macroscopic examination of bones, artifacts are troublesome in producing pseudopathological changes; these are fully discussed by Wells (1967), and I have summarized them elsewhere (Sandison 1968). Such pseudopathological changes may be caused by depredation by insects and rodents, effects of plant roots, high winds, pressure of overlying soil or matrix, and impregnation by chemical substances.

The study of actual mummies by dissection (Ruffer 1921; Elliot Smith and Dawson 1924), band-saw cutting and slab radiography (Sandison 1968), and histological examination (Ruffer 1921; Sandison 1955, 1970) has yielded much interesting information. If dissection is not possible macroscopic examination of mummies may be supplemented by radiography. Gray has carried out extensive surveys of mummies in several European museums and has discovered evidence of arthritis, arterial calcification, cholelithiasis, and possible bone infarction. It is now clear that artifacts must be carefully excluded; earlier radiographic diagnoses of alkaptonuric arthropathy are now known to have been erroneous (Gray 1967). However, Lee and Stenn (1978) have shown a homogentisic acid polymer in material from an Egyptian mummy of 1500 B.C.; this appears to be a proved case of ochronosis. In spite of this, the majority opinion today is against the presence of ochronosis and in favor of postmortem artifact.

If tibial bones are subjected to X-ray examination, transverse (so-called Harris's) lines may be seen. They have been thought to indicate episodes of intermittent disease or malnutrition. There is no way of telling what condition was causal, and lines may become absorbed. Nevertheless, the fact that about 30 percent of Egyptian mummies show Harris's lines suggests a generally poor state of health in childhood and adolescence in ancient Egypt.

Organisms are seen in abundance in many microscopic sections of mummy tissues, but they are putrefactive in type and have multi-plied in the tissues during the period between death and effective dehydration of the corpse. That putrefaction was a problem in Egyptian mummification is indicated by the fact that "stench" is implied in some of the names for the place of embalming.

After this preamble, we shall look at the evidence of disease in ancient Egypt.

INFECTIVE DISEASES

Ruffer's (1910b) identification of calcified ova of *Schistosoma (Bilharzia) haematobium* in the kidneys of two mummies of the Twentieth Dynasty is unquestioned. Hematuria was probably common in ancient Egypt. Schistosomiasis has certainly been very common in Egypt in the twentieth century. Ferguson (1910) reported that 40 percent of over 1,000 Egyptian males between the ages of 5 and 60 years who came to necropsy at the Kasr Aini Hospital in Cairo showed evidence of schistosomiasis. Larrey (1812–1817) reported frequent examples of hematuria, presumably of bilharzial origin, in French troops during the campaign of Napoleon Bonaparte in Egypt in 1799–1801. The parasite is small and was not recognized until 1851 by Bilharz, so it is unlikely that the ancient Egyptians ever identified it. Recently, in Toronto, mummy ROM I has been shown to harbor not only a tapeworm (*Taenia*) with eggs but also ova of *Schistosoma haematobium* and to display changes in the liver that may have resulted from the schistosomal infestation. It may be useful to mention also at this point that *Ascaris* eggs have been identified in mummy PUM II. We thus have positive identification of *Schistosoma haematobium*, *Ascaris*, and *Taenia* in Egyptian mummies. Ruffer tentatively diagnosed malaria in some Coptic bodies with splenomegaly, but this is not good evidence in a warm country.

The case of leprosy in a Coptic Christian body discovered by Elliot Smith and Derry (1910) at El Bigha in Nubia and redescribed by Elliot Smith and Dawson (1924) is unquestioned. This case was reviewed macroscopically by Rowling (1960) and macroscopically and radiologically by Møller-Christensen (1967); both accepted the diagnosis. I have examined skin, subcutaneous tissue, and nervous tissue from this specimen. Using modifications of the Ziehl-Neelsen method, it was impossible to demonstrate acid-fast bacilli. This is not surprising, as it is known that, even in paraffin block, tissues containing numerous *Mycobacterium leprae* may, after a few years, appear to be free of bacilli.

Møller-Christensen (1967) has also described a female skull from the same cemetery as the El Bigha body that shows the facies leprosa. So far these are the only acceptable cases of leprosy found in all the thousands of carefully examined mummies, dried bodies, and skeletons from ancient Egypt and Nubia. Leprosy is thus unlikely to have been a common disease.

If we turn now to the other important mycobacterial disease – tuberculosis – we find that Morse (1967) and Morse et al. (1964) have discussed the evidence for its presence in ancient Egypt. Their conclusions, which were derived from a critical survey of all the available evidence, both artistic and pathological, are completely acceptable. The famous mummy of the priest Nesperehan of the Twenty-first Dynasty has been unreservedly accepted as a case of typical spinal tuberculosis with characteristic psoas abscess. Morse et al. conclude that in all there are 31 acceptable cases of skeletal and mummy tuberculosis. Of these, 16 were culled from the literature and 15 were reported for the first time. The dates for these 31 cases are not all certain, nor is the provenance of the mummies absolutely clear, but probably the dates range from 3,700 to 1,000 B.C. Morse et al. accept that the fibrous adhesions and collapsed left lung found in a Byzantine Nubian female body from the Island of Hesa (Elliot Smith and Wood Jones 1908) are good evidence of pulmonary tuberculosis. This diagnosis is perfectly tenable, but other conditions might lead to similar appearances. I believe that these 31 acceptable cases probably represent only a part of those found in Egyptian sites. Doubtless many have been discarded unrecognized and others may languish in museums unrecognized and undescribed. Probably some form of granulomatous tuberculosis has infected man since Neolithic times and may have resulted from closer contact with livestock, presumably bovine, following the Neolithic Revolution. The contemporary domestic dog may suffer from pulmonary or, less commonly, renal tuberculosis, but this is attributable to a human form of bacillus and is probably derived from contact with the owner. The dog is therefore *not* likely to have been the source of origin of Neolithic human tuberculosis.

Another important granulomatous disease is syphilis caused by *Treponema pallidum*. Other treponemal diseases include yaws, pinta, and bejel, and some workers have concluded that all these disease processes may be caused by variants of one organism. This may explain the present obscurity of the origin of syphilis, and it seems to me there is no likelihood of a convincing early resolution of the problem. There is, however, *no* clear evidence of syphilis in the vast amount of material examined in Egypt and Nubia from the ancient period, although venereal syphilis is not uncommon in Egypt at the present time.

The interpretation of changes in the temporal bone of the skull is difficult. Although the ancient medical papyri give prescriptions for what must be middle ear infection, there is no literary evidence of surgical intervention. An early dynastic skull from Tarkhan shows the appearance of mastoiditis, but a fairly well healed trephined opening is situated some distance directly above the mastoid region and may have been of magicomedical significance. Some authors have claimed that mastoid disease was very common in ancient Egypt and Nubia, but only 6 acceptable cases appear to have been noted in a total of at least 10,000 individual remains examined. Apart from the Tarkhan skull, there is a predynastic case of probable acute mastoiditis, another case of predynastic or early dynastic date,

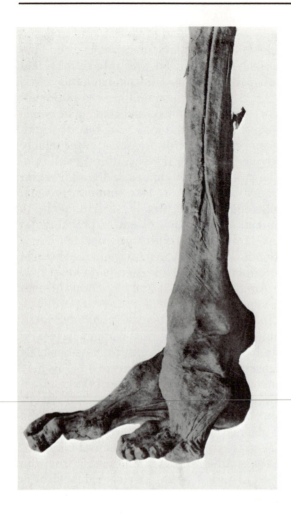

Figure 2.1.   Probable clubfoot of Pharaoh Siptah. (Courtesy of Service of Antiquities)

another in a New Kingdom female, another in a Coptic female, a further Nubian case dated to the first millennium A.D., and one of Meroitic date. Schultz (1939) reported 3 cases of maxillary sinus infection in 35 adult chimpanzees. Maxillary sinus infection is common in contemporary man, and it is probable that cases must have occurred in ancient Egypt.

Polymyelitis is a virus affection of the anterior horn cells of the spinal cord, and its presence can be deduced only by a deformity in persons who have survived the acute stage. Mitchell (1900) noted in an early Egyptian

body from Deshasheh shortening of the left leg, which he interpreted as evidence of poliomyelitis. The clubfoot of the Pharaoh Siptah (Elliot Smith 1912) (Figure 2.1) is more probably attributable to congenital abnormality than to poliomyelitis, so also is the deformity of Khnumu-Nekht of the Twelfth Dynasty (Cameron 1910). Some authorities, however, believe that the deformities in the last two individuals may be postmortem artifacts.

I think it possible that smallpox may have existed in ancient Egypt and that unrecorded epidemics occurred. The changes described by Ruffer and Ferguson (1911) in the skin of a male mummy may well have been those of variola, despite criticism of this diagnosis by Unna. So also the Pharaoh Rameses V (Figure 2.2) may have been the victim of lethal smallpox (Elliot Smith 1912). It would be of interest to submit to electron microscopy material from these and any other possible cases that come to light in the future. Other examples of skin conditions are hyperkeratosis of the skin and senile acne (Figure 2.3).

I have discussed elsewhere (Sandison 1967c) the evidence for infective ocular disease in ancient Egypt. Seasonal ophthalmia may have occurred. The evidence for ocular disease is, however, purely literary, and no paleopathological evidence is available. Blindness certainly is portrayed in ancient Egyptian art.

Rowling (1967) has surveyed the evidence for respiratory disease and accepts Ruffer's (1910a) cases of pneumonia (two of which are Twentieth Dynasty and one Greco-Egyptian), as well as that of Shaw (1938). However, I believe these should be considered with some reservation because of the possibility of artifacts of fungal nature that may simulate a cellular reaction. Rowling believes from literary evidence that bronchiectasis and pulmonary tuberculosis may have occurred; both are possible, but not certain.

Gallstones were illustrated in a Twenty-first-Dynasty mummy by Elliot Smith and Dawson (1924), and Gray has noted

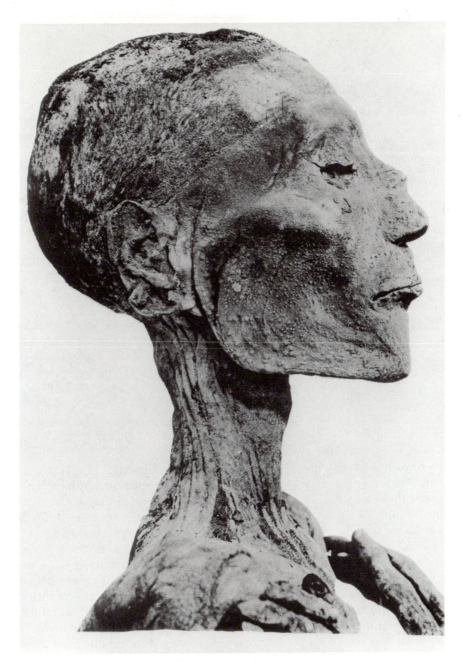

Figure 2.2.   *Head of Pharaoh Rameses V, showing probable smallpox vesicles. (Courtesy of Service of Antiquities)*

gallstones in radiography of a female mummy. However, cholelithiasis may well be the result of metabolic abnormality or stagnation of bile, and chronic cholecystitis need not necessarily be associated with stone formation, although it sometimes is. Renal stones also have been rarely discovered in association with ancient remains in Egypt and

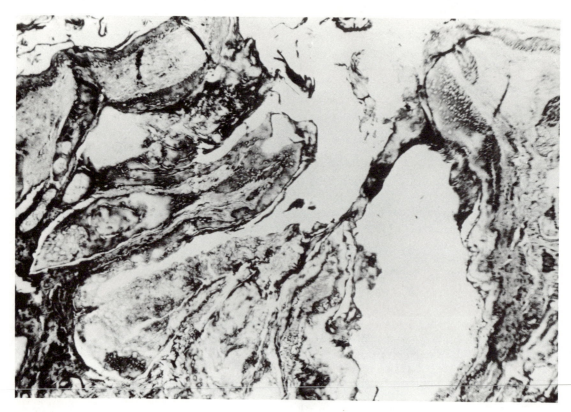

Figure 2.3.   Senile acne of the face in an old New Kingdom mummy. Phosphotungstic acid–hematoxylin.

Nubia. Renal lithiasis is not necessarily associated with infection, although this may occasionally be the case, either as a primary or as a secondary phenomenon.

More convincing as evidence of abdominal inflammation are the appendicular adhesions noted in a Byzantine body from Hesa by Elliot Smith and Wood Jones (1910). These probably followed resolving acute appendicitis, although the topography of the adhesion, which crosses the pelvis, is somewhat unusual.

BONE DISORDERS

Nonspecific bone inflammation is not rare in human remains from older societies. The evidence for this is overwhelming, and the phenomenon is of interest in view of the opinions formerly held by some morbid anatomists that the inflammatory reaction may have been a late evolutionary acquisition. Similar inflammatory processes also are seen in fossil animals as far back as the Mesozoic period, but their causes are likely to remain obscure. It has been suggested that many specific infections were probably rare or absent before the gregariousness permitted by the Neolithic Revolution. Nonspecific infections might, however, have been possible without close personal contiguity and might have been caused by a wide range of organisms. Such nonspecific changes are of significant frequency in early cemeteries, but are difficult to interpret.

It is customary to divide bone inflammation into periostitis, osteitis, and osteomyelitis, depending on whether periosteum, bone proper, or bone marrow is most obviously involved. This is to some extent artificial, because bone is a biological unit and not a series of distinct tissue entities. These phenomena may lead one to another; all three may be present together. When confronted with evidence of periosteal reaction in an ancient bone, it is difficult to say with any confidence whether the cause was infection or trauma. It must, however, be conceded that site is important, particularly the tibia, which has a large subcutaneous area. Even here we are on uncertain ground; the subcutaneous tibia is vulnerable to trauma, but also to extension of infection from the skin to the periosteum. Wells (1964) noted that one in six of a group of Saxon agriculturists had tibial periosteal reactions. Compared with Anglo-Saxons, ancient Egyptians show a lower fracture rate for the leg, and yet periosteal reaction is as common in ancient Egyptians. Wells (personal communication, 1970) found that among 92 ancient Egyptian tibiae (dating from predynastic to Coptic times) 14 (15.2 percent) had "well-marked" periostitic changes. Wells, therefore, suspects that something other than trauma may be operating, and suggests that in ancient Egypt infection of insect bites or simple abrasions may have been causal.

There are no recent incidence figures for ancient Egypt other than those of Wells, but there are isolated reports. Derry (1940–1941) noted only dental infection and osteoarthritis in the bones of Pharaoh Psusennes I of the Twenty-first Dynasty; Derry (1942) only arthritis in Pharaoh Amenenopet and no abnormality in Har-Nakht; Derry (1947) no disease in Prince Ptah-Shepses of the Fifth and Sixth dynasties; Batrawi (1947) some evidence of dental and maxillary sinus infection in a middle-aged male and possible postfracture sepsis of the radius in a middle-aged female from Shawaf, but no disease in Pharaoh Djed-Ka-Re of the Fifth Dynasty; Batrawi (1948) possible dental and air sinus infection of Akhet-Hetep, but only arthritis in

his wife; and Batrawi (1951) no evidence of infection in remains from the Northern Pyramid of Sneferu of the Fourth Dynasty. Apart from such isolated reports, we must fall back upon the *Archaeological Survey of Nubia* (Elliot Smith and Wood Jones 1910).

Among this enormous mass of material, although occasional bodies gave clear evidence of the cause of death, a very large proportion did not. Elliot Smith and Wood Jones (neither of whom was a pathologist) were therefore left in ignorance of the factors causing death in the vast majority of persons buried in ancient Nubia. They reached some important conclusions, in that they believed that examination of 6,000 bodies revealed no evidence of tuberculosis, syphilis, or rickets. As we have seen, however, this view had to be revised with regard to tuberculosis. They also believed correctly that malignant disease must have been exceptionally rare. Where the actual cause of death was clear to them, the death had usually resulted from violence. Although some remains showed evidence of disease, it was impossible even to guess at the precise cause of death. Elliot Smith and Wood Jones concluded that inflammatory diseases of bone were rarely seen in ancient Egyptian skeletons. Even when fractures had been severe and necessarily compound, sepsis rarely seems to have followed. Well-healed fractures are also commonly seen in wild apes. They postulate, in contrast to contemporary experience in surgical practice, that there must have been a remarkable resistance to infection in ancient Nubia.

An alternative explanation might, of course, be that organisms were of lower virulence. Elliot Smith and Wood Jones (1910) found that neglected dental disease accounted for practically all septic conditions of the facial bones, but in one female skull there were traces of chronic inflammation around the margin of the nares and destruction of the turbinates and part of the nasal septum. There was a direct communication through the hard palate posteriorly between nasal and oral cavities. The remainder of the skeleton was unexceptional, and a diagnosis of long-standing nasal infection was made. The cause of this must remain obscure.

Elliot Smith and Wood Jones (1910) also illustrated two examples of cranial disease, one in the parietal bone and the other in the frontal bone; these showed peripheral reaction and central necrosis, which were attributed to extension of scalp infection. The appearances are certainly not those of syphilis. An isolated humerus of a child of New Kingdom date showed necrosis of the lower half of the shaft, with a line of heaped-up reactive bone running down the middle of the anterior surface and a more superficial reaction over the lateral area of this line. The internal bone was necrotic and constituted a sequestrum. This appears to have been severe osteomyelitis. Sepsis following fracture appears to have been rare, even in apparently compound fractures. This is especially notable in skull wounds in which the scalp must surely have been severely affected. Nevertheless, in two New Kingdom scapulae there was evidence of reaction in transverse fractures, where there must have been severe soft tissue injury, but death occurred before healing took place.

Of 65 fractures of the upper limb, only one showed evidence of sepsis. This was in a woman of the Christian period, both of whose forearms were fractured; the right ulna had united, but the left showed periostitis. Another skeleton of this period from Hesa showed inflammation and necrosis following fracture of the clavicles, and there were two other ununited clavicular fractures. Of 38 fractures of the lower limb, only 2 showed septic changes. One early dynastic male with a right-sided fracture of tibia and fibula showed malunion and much inflammatory bone extending as periostitis over the bone shafts below the area of injury. The right femur of a male of the same period had an inflammatory reaction around the fractured lower portion.

Peter Ker Gray (1967) has discovered what appears almost certainly to be an old infarct of bone in a mummy from the Horniman Museum, and Campbell Golding (1960) a further example in a Ptolemaic female mummy from the same museum. Caution is necessary in accepting these findings. Very similar radiographs from clinical cases have been published and in these the lesions have been attributed to arteriosclerosis. I have shown that Ruffer's conclusion that arterial disease occurred in ancient Egypt is tenable and have published photographs of arteriosclerotic change (Sandison 1962); thus, a possible etiological factor is not lacking.

Healed fractures are not rare, and splints have been described. The mummy of Pharaoh Seknenre of the Seventeenth Dynasty shows that he was attacked by at least two men armed with ax and spear, possibly while asleep, and suffered severe wounds (Elliot Smith 1912). Wood Jones described judicial hanging and decapitation in Roman Egyptian skeletons.

One of the most common diseases found in ancient bones is arthritis. There are numerous accounts from many prehistoric and historical periods by many authors. Arthritis in animal fossils is discussed at length by Moodie (1923). Ankylosed vertebrae have been noted in animal remains over a wide span of time, from fossil reptiles to cave bears and even to domesticated animals from ancient Egypt. Arthritic changes have also been noted in human remains during the whole of Egyptian history from predynastic to Coptic times (Elliot Smith and Wood Jones 1908, 1910; Ruffer 1912; Bourke 1967). Zorab (1961) examined by radiography eight British Museum bodies of the New Kingdom and Roman period from Egypt. No cases of ankylosing spondylitis were found, but osteoarthritic lipping of the vertebrae was noted in four instances.

Rowling (1960) drew attention to specimen number 178A in the Nubian Collection. Hyperplastic new bone on the femora represented the adductor muscles and was more marked on the right side. Some new bone was also formed on the pelvis. There was ossification of the interosseous ligament between radius and ulna. The humeri were normal. There was a small spina bifida with a defect in the first and second sacral vertebrae. The appearances are not those of osteomyelitis or myositis ossificans. Rowling interprets these strange findings as ossification attributable to partial paraplegia consequent on the spina bifida. The forearm changes are, however, difficult to explain, and Rowling suggests that the patient supported himself on his hands. Brothwell believes this is an example of osteogenesis imperfecta and points out the similarity to cases illustrated by Fairbank (1951).

A metabolic disorder that produces recognizable changes is gout. There is a classic case reported by Elliot Smith and Dawson (1924): an old Coptic male from Philae on the Nile. The radiographs are characteristic, and analysis of tophi by W. A. Schmidt showed uric acid and urates. Rowling (1960) reviewed this specimen and entirely agreed with the diagnosis. Because of the intense sunlight, rickets is never seen in Egyptian material.

VASCULAR DISEASE

With regard to vascular disease, we are on firm ground and have direct evidence. Blood vessels are often well preserved in Egyptian mummies and dried bodies. Czermack (1852) described aortic calcification, and Shattock (1909) made sections of the calcified aorta of Pharaoh Merneptah. Elliot Smith (1912) noted this change in his macroscopic description of the royal body, and also described calcification of the temporal arteries in Rameses II. Ruffer (1910a, 1912) described histological changes in Egyptian mummy vessels from the New Kingdom to the Coptic period. Long (1931), examining the mummy of Lady Teye of the Twenty-first Dynasty described degenerative disease of the aorta and coronary arteries, with arteriosclerosis of the kidney

and myocardial fibrosis. Moodie (1923) described radiological evidence of calcification of superficial vessels in a predynastic body. It is often difficult to assess the older descriptions that are unaccompanied by photographs; Sandison (1962, 1967a) examined and photographed mummy arteries (Figures 2.4 to 2.6) using modern histological methods. Arteries were tapelike in mummy tissues, but could readily be dissected. Arteriosclerosis, atheroma with lipid depositions, reduplications of the internal elastic lamina, and medial calcification could readily be seen. Atheromatous lesions in mummy arteries tend to form sectoral clefts: This should not be interpreted as dissecting aneurysm. It is evident that the stresses of highly civilized life are not, at any rate, the sole causes of degenerative vascular disease.

TUMORS

With regard to tumors there is a marked paucity of evidence, possibly because the expectation of life in earlier times was short. Moreover, most examples are to be found in the skeleton, with a few exceptions. Elliot Smith and Dawson (1924), for example, suggested carcinoma of the ethmoid and of the rectum as being causal in the production of erosion of the skull base and sacrum in two Byzantine bodies; this is slender evidence, but may be correct. Other cases of primary carcinoma are evidenced by destructive changes in bone. These include Derry's case (1909) of probable nasal carcinoma in a pre-Christian Nubian. Elliot Smith and Derry's case (1910) of sacral erosion in a Nubian male may have been attributable to rectal cancer or chordoma. In all these, a prima facie case can certainly be made.

Evidence of primary malignant tumors in ancient bones is rare. This is not entirely surprising, because even at the present time primary malignant tumors of bone are not common; deaths from them constitute less than 1 percent of all deaths caused by malignant disease. On the other hand, many carcinomas

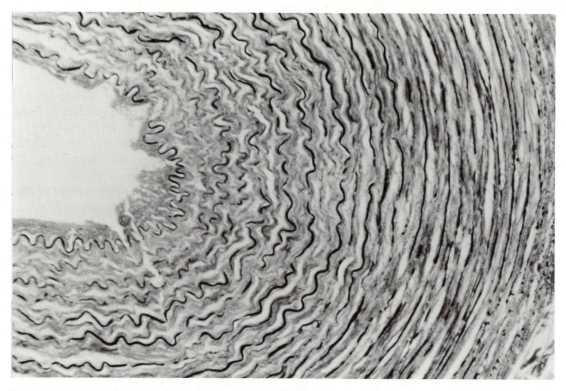

Figure 2.4.   Carotid artery of a male mummy showing fibrosis. Verhoeff elastic–van Gieson.

metastasize to bone in the terminal phase of the disease, and secondary cancer in bone is common in the necropsy room. Osteocartilaginous exostosis or osteochondroma is not uncommon in clinical practice, and cases are known in ancient material. Perhaps the best known is the celebrated specimen of the Fifth-Dynasty ancient Egyptian femur illustrated by Elliot Smith and Dawson (1924) and wrongly diagnosed as osteosarcoma. The contour, absence of periosteal reaction at the base, and lack of spiculation suggest that it is osteochondromatous and quite simple. It is not possible to comment on the two further alleged examples from Fifth-Dynasty graves (Elliot Smith and Dawson 1924), as these are neither described nor illustrated. A Roman pelvic tumor from Alexandria, described by Ruffer and Willmore (1914), was of large size and thought by them to be an osteosarcoma. This must remain in doubt. Rowling (1960) thought that osteosarcoma was possible but not certain. Brothwell (1967) considers the tumor may have been chondromatous. Certainly cartilage-forming tumors do occur in the pelvis, but are often malignant.

Intracranial meningioma may induce hyperostotic change in the cranium. This has long been known to radiologists. Such a reaction was postulated by Lambert Rogers (1949) in two Egyptian skulls of the First and Twentieth dynasties.

Possibly the most convincing evidence of neoplasm of soft tissues came from Granville, who diagnosed (without histological confirmation) cystadenoma of the ovary, possibly malignant, in a mummy now known to be Ptolemaic. The writer has noticed a small squamous papilloma of the skin in a mummy (Figure 2.7). There are no examples of breast cancer.

KIDNEY DISEASE

Kidney lesions noted by Ruffer (1910a) included unilateral hypoplasia of the kidney; in

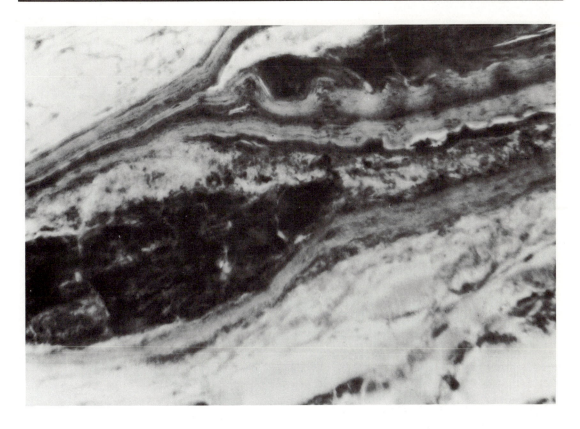

Figure 2.5.   Frozen section of tibial artery of an elderly female mummy showing lipid in an atheromatous plaque. Sudan black.

another Eighteenth- to Twentieth-Dynasty mummy, the kidney showed multiple abscesses with gram-negative bacilli resembling coliforms. Long (1931) described arteriosclerosis in the kidneys of Lady Teye of the Twenty-first Dynasty. Shattock (1909) described and analyzed renal calculi from a Second-Dynasty tomb; oxalates and conidia were noted. A vesical calculus found in the nostril of a Twenty-first-Dynasty priest of Amun contained uric acid covered by phosphates. Ruffer (1910a) described three mixed phosphate–uric acid calculi from a predynastic skeleton.

DISORDERS OF THE ALIMENTARY TRACT

Elliot Smith and Dawson (1924) also refer to the finding of multiple stones in the thin-walled gallbladder of a Twenty-first-Dynasty priestess. Shaw (1938) noted in the canopic preserved gallbladder of an Eighteenth-Dynasty singer that spaces resembling Aschoff-Rokitansky sinuses were present: This suggests chronic cholecystitis. Ruffer (1910a) mentions fibrosis of the liver in a mummy and equates this with cirrhosis, but insufficient evidence is given to evaluate this diagnosis. Little has been written about alimentary disease in mummies. Elliot Smith and Wood Jones (1908) report appendicular adhesions in a Byzantine period Nubian body: These are almost certainly the result of appendicitis. Ruffer (1910a) describes what may well be megacolon in a child of the Roman period and prolapse of the rectum in Coptic bodies. Elliot Smith (1912) mentions two probable cases of scrotal hernia – Rameses V shows a bulky scrotum now empty

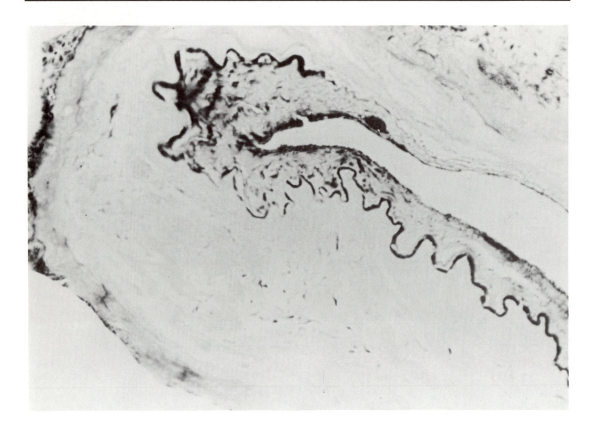

Figure 2.6.   Duplication of internal elastic lamina of tibial artery of an elderly female mummy. Heiden-hain's iron hematoxylin.

after evisceration, and the scrotum of Mer-neptah was excised after death by the embal-mers, possibly because of the bulk of a hernia. Anorectal problems seem to have been com-mon, as some of the royal physicians were regarded as shepherds of the royal anus.

RESPIRATORY DISORDERS

Some interesting studies of the lung have been published. Anthracosis in Egyptian mummy lungs was described by Ruffer and by Long (1931). Shaw (1938) reported an-thracosis in the lungs of Har-mose of the Eighteenth Dynasty, but Har-mose had also suffered from emphysema and lower lobe bronchopneumonia. Ruffer (1910a) reported pleural adhesions and diagnosed pneumonia in two mummies, one Twentieth Dynasty and

the other Ptolemaic; the latter may have been pneumonic plague, although the evidence is far from complete. Long (1931) reported caseous areas in the lung of a Twenty-first-Dynasty lady. As already indicated, these diagnoses must be accepted with some re-serve in view of the possible confusion of molds as leukocytes. With regard to an-thracosis, this seems to enhance lung preser-vation. More recently, silicotic lesions, pos-sibly attributable to inhaled sand, have been noted in mummy lungs.

ACROMEGALY

A fairly rare disease that should be readily recognized is acromegaly. This produces characteristic bone changes. Brothwell (1963) illustrates an ancient Egyptian skull

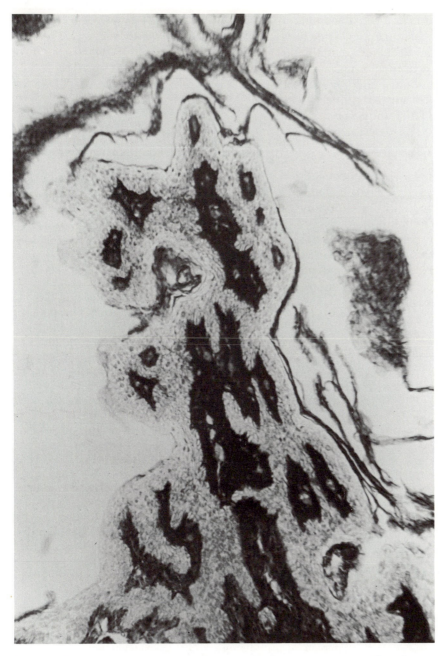

Figure 2.7.   Small squamous papilloma of the skin in a mummy. Phosphotungstic acid–hematoxylin.

that may represent this disease. Aldred and Sandison (1962) gave reasons for their belief that Akhenaten suffered from endocrine disorders. Statues and reliefs show ac-

romegaloid facies and eunuchoid obesity. Cameron (1910) describes the bones of two brothers from the Middle Kingdom of ancient Egypt and concludes that the skeleton of

Nekht-Ankh shows eunuchoid changes but also a curious penile appearance suggesting a subincisional operation. It is not certain, however, if this is a genuine lesion. Male Egyptian mummies show circumcision throughout the dynasties until the practice was abandoned in the Christian period.

GYNECOLOGICAL CONDITIONS

Elliot Smith (1912) described lactating breasts in the recently delivered Queen Makere. Williams (1929) reported an observation by Derry that Princess Hehenhit of the Eleventh Dynasty had a narrow pelvis and died not long after delivery with vesicovaginal fistula. Elliot Smith and Dawson (1924) described violent death in an unembalmed 16-year-old pregnant ancient Egyptian girl and postulated illegitimate conception. The *Archaeological Survey of Nubia* revealed a deformed Coptic negress, who died in childbirth as a result of absent sacroiliac joint contracting the pelvis. Vaginal prolapse was also noted in a Nubian specimen by Wood Jones (1908).

CONCLUSION

It will be seen from the reports mentioned in this chapter that many diseases of the present day occurred also in ancient Egypt. There is one notable exception: leprosy, which has not been found before Roman times. Apart from this, the Egyptians before Christ suffered many of the ailments of modern civilized persons.

REFERENCES

Aldred, C., and Sandison, A. T. 1962. The Pharaoh Akhenaten: a problem in Egyptology and pathology. *Bulletin of the History of Medicine* 36:293–316.

Batrawi, A. 1947. Anatomical reports. *Annales du service des antiquités de l'Egypte* 47:97–109.

– 1948. Report on the anatomical remains recovered from the tombs of Akhet- Hetep and Ptah-Irou-ka and a comment on the statues of Akhet-Hetep. *Annales du service des antiquités de l'Egypte* 48:487–97.

– 1951. The skeletal remains from the northern pyramid of Sneferu. *Annales du service des antiquités de l'Egypte* 51:435–40.

Bourke, J. B. 1967. A review of the palaeopathology of the arthritic diseases. In *Diseases in antiquity*, D. Brothwell and A. T. Sandison (eds.). Springfield, Ill.: Thomas.

Brothwell, D. 1963. *Digging up bones*. London: British Museum (Natural History).

– 1967. The evidence of neoplasms. In *Diseases in antiquity*, D. R. Brothwell and A. T. Sandison (eds.). Springfield, Ill.: Thomas.

Brothwell, D., and Powers, R. 1968. Congenital malformations of the skeleton in earlier man. In *The skeletal biology of earlier human populations*, D. Brothwell (ed.). Oxford: Pergamon Press.

Cameron, J. 1910. Report on the anatomy of the mummies. In *The tomb of two brothers*, M. A. Murray, (ed.). Manchester: Sherrat & Hughes.

Czermack, J. 1852. Beschreibung und mikroskopische Untersuchung zweier ägyptischer Mumien. *Akademie der Wissenschaften Wien*. 9:427–69.

Dawson, W. R. 1953. The Egyptian medical papyri in *Science, medicine and history*, E. A. Underwood (ed.). London: Oxford University Press.

Derry, D. E. 1909. Anatomical report. *Archaeological Survey of Nubia*, Bulletin 3.

– 1938. Pott's disease in ancient Egypt. *Medical Press* 197:1.

– 1940–1. An examination of the bones of King Psusennes I. *Annales du service des antiquités de l'Egypte* 40:969–70.

– 1942. Report on the skeleton of King Amenenopet and Har-Nakht. *Annales du service des antiquités de l'Egypte* 41:149–50.

– 1947. The bones of Prince Ptah-Shepses. *Annales du service des antiquités de l'Egypte* 47:139–40.

Elliot Smith, G. 1912. *The royal mummies*. Cairo: Cairo Museum.

Elliot Smith, G. and Dawson, W. R. 1924. *Egyptian mummies*. London: Allen & Unwin.

Elliot Smith, G. and Derry, D. E. 1910. Anatomical report. *Archaeological Survey of Nubia*, Bulletin 6.

Elliot Smith, G., and Ruffer, M. A. 1910. Pott'sche Krankheit an einer Aegyptschen Mumie aus der

Zeit der 21 Dynastie (Um 1000 V. Chr.). In K. Sudhoff (ed). *Zur historischen Biologie der Krankheitserreger*, Heft 3. Leipzig: Giessen.

Elliot Smith, G. and Wood Jones, F. 1908. Anatomical report. *Archaeological Survey of Nubia*, Bulletin 1.

– 1910. Report on the human remains. *Archaeological Survey of Nubia*, Bulletin 2.

Fairbank, T. 1951. *An atlas of general affections of the skeleton*. Edinburgh: Livingstone.

Ferguson, A. R. 1910. Bilharziasis. *Cairo Society Science Journal* 4.

Golding, F. C. 1960. Rare diseases of the bone. In *Modern trends in diagnostic radiology*, J. W. McLaren (ed.). London: Butterworth.

Granville, A. B. 1825. An essay on Egyptian mummies. *Philosophical Transactions of the Royal Society* O: 269.

Gray, P. H. K. 1967. Calcinosis intervertebralis, with special reference to similar changes found in mummies of ancient Egyptians. In *Diseases in antiquity*, D. Brothwell and A. T. Sandison (eds.). Springfield, Ill: Thomas.

Larrey, D. J. 1812–17. *Mémoires de chirurgie militaire et campagnes*.

Lee, S. L. and Stenn, F. F. 1978. Characterization of mummy bone ochronotic pigment. *Journal of the American Medical Association* 240:136–8.

Long, A. R. 1931. Cardiovascular renal disease: report of a case of 3000 years ago. *Archives of Pathology* 12:92–6.

Mitchell, J. K. 1900. Study of a mummy affected with anterior poliomyelitis. *Transactions of the Association of American Physicians* 15:134–6.

Møller-Christensen, V. 1967. Evidence of leprosy in earlier peoples. In *Diseases in antiquity*, D. Brothwell and A. T. Sandison (eds.). Springfield, Ill.: Thomas.

Moodie, R. L. 1923. *Palaeopathology: an introduction to the study of ancient evidences of disease*. Urbana: University of Illinois Press.

Morse, D. 1967. Tuberculosis. In *Diseases in antiquity*, D. Brothwell and A. T. Sandison (eds.). Springfield, Ill: Thomas.

Morse, D; Brothwell, D; and Ucko, P. J. 1964. Tuberculosis in ancient Egypt. *American Review of Respiratory Diseases* 90:524–30.

Rogers, L. 1949. Meningiomas in pharaoh's people: hyperostosis in ancient Egyptian skulls. *British Journal of Surgery* 36:423–6.

Rowling, J. T. 1960. Disease in ancient Egypt: evidence from pathological lesions found in mummies. M. D. thesis, University of Cambridge.

– 1967. Respiratory disease in Egypt. In *Diseases in Antiquity*, D. Brothwell and A. T. Sandison (eds.). Springfield, Ill: Thomas.

Ruffer, M. A. 1910a. Remarks on the histology and pathological anatomy of Egyptian mummies. *Cairo Scientific Journal* 4:1–5.

– 1910b. Note on the presence of "Bilharzia haematobia" in Egyptian mummies of the Twentieth Dynasty (1250–1000 B.C.) *British Medical Journal* 1:16.

– 1911a. Histological studies on Egyptian mummies. *Mémoires sur l'Egypte: Institut d'Egypte* 6(3).

– 1911b. On arterial lesions found in Egyptian mummies (1580 B.C.–525 A.D.). *Journal of Pathology and Bacteriology* 15:453–62.

– 1921. *Studies in the palaeopathology of Egypt*. Chicago: University of Chicago Press.

Ruffer, M. A., and Rietti, A. 1912. On osseous lesions in ancient Egyptians. *Journal of Pathology and Bacteriology* 16:439.

Ruffer, M. A. and Willmore, J. G. 1914. A tumour of the pelvis dating from Roman times (A.D. 250) and found in Egypt. *Journal of Pathology and Bacteriology* 18:480–4.

Salib, P. 1967. Trauma and disease of the postcranial skeleton in ancient Egypt. In *Diseases in antiquity*, D. Brothwell and A. T. Sandison (eds.). Springfield, Ill.: Thomas.

Sandison, A. T. 1955. The histological examination of mummified material. *Stain Technology* 30:277–83.

– 1967a. Degenerative vascular disease. In *Diseases in antiquity*, D. Brothwell and A. T. Sandison (eds.). Springfield, Ill.: Thomas.

– 1967b. Diseases of the skin. In *Diseases in antiquity*, D. Brothwell and A. T. Sandison (eds.). Springfield, Ill.: Thomas.

– 1967c. Diseases of the eyes. In *Diseases in antiquity*, D. Brothwell and A. T. Sandison (eds.). Springfield, Ill: Thomas.

– 1967d. Sexual behaviour in ancient society. In *Diseases in antiquity*, D. Brothwell and A. T. Sandison (eds.). Springfield, Ill.: Thomas.

– 1968. Pathological changes in the skeletons of earlier populations due to acquired disease and difficulties in their interpretation. In *The skeletal biology of earlier human populations*, D. Brothwell (ed.). Oxford, Pergamon Press.

– 1970. The study of mummified and dried

human tissues. In *Science in archaeology*, 2nd ed., D. Brothwell and E. Higgs (eds.). London: Thames & Hudson.

–   1972. Evidence of infective disease. *Journal of Human Evolution* 1:213–24.

Sandison, A. T. and Macadam, R. F. 1969. The electron microscope in palaeopathology. *Medical History* 13:8.

Satinoff, M. J. 1968. Preliminary report on the palaeopathology of a collection of ancient Egyptian skeletons. *Rivista di Antropologia* 55:41–50.

Schultz, A. H. 1939. Notes on diseases and healed fractures of wild apes. Reprinted in *Diseases in antiquity*, D. Brothwell and A. T. Sandison (eds.). Springfield, Ill.: Thomas, 1967.

Shattock, S. G. 1909. A report upon the pathological condition of the aorta of King Merneptah. *Proceedings of the Royal Society of Medicine* (Pathological Section) 2:122–7.

Shaw, A. F. B. 1938. A histological study of the mummy of Har-Mose, the singer of the Eighteenth Dynasty (c. 1490 B.C.). *Journal of Pathology and Bacteriology* 47:115–23.

Wells, C. 1964. *Bones, bodies and disease.* London: Thames & Hudson.

–   1967. Pseudopathology. In *Diseases in Antiquity*, D. Brothwell and A. T. Sandison (eds.). Springfield, Ill.: Thomas.

Williams, H. U. 1929. Human paleopathology. *Archives of Pathology* 7:839.

Wood Jones, F. 1908. The pathological report. *Archaeological Survey of Nubia*, Bulletin 2.

Zorab, P. A. 1961. The historical and prehistorical background of ankylosing spondylitis. *Proceedings of the Royal Society of Medicine* 54:415.

3

Dental health in ancient Egypt

JAMES E. HARRIS
Professor and Chairman,
Department of Orthodontics
University of Michigan
Ann Arbor, Michigan, U.S.A.

PAUL V. PONITZ
Clinical Professor,
Department of Orthodontics
University of Michigan
Ann Arbor, Michigan, U.S.A.

Teeth are the most indestructible of human tissue, and intense interest in them has resulted from two facts: (1) they are often the only biologic record of man and (2), just as important, they are extremely complex morphologically and represent a sophisticated genetic model. Because of the arid climate in Egypt and because of mummification, biologists, anthropologists, and dentists are able to examine not only the teeth but the entire craniofacial skeleton. Further, because soft tissues are well preserved, much has been learned about the tissue directly related to the function of the jaws as well as the tissue that supports the teeth, the periodontium. Dental disease and pathology can be readily interpreted through examination of the immense number of Egyptian mummies available, and an excellent understanding can be obtained of what was the usual state of dental health for these people.

The annual Michigan expeditions since 1965 have examined most of the mummy collections in Egypt, including the Old Kingdom nobles at Giza (3000 B.C.), the New Kingdom nobles and priests at Luxor (1200 B.C.), and the pharaohs and queens of the New Kingdom period at the Egyptian Museum (1500–1000 B.C.).

In addition, the investigation of oral health and disease in ancient Egypt has been greatly enhanced by studies of modern Egypt, especially Nubia (Harris et al. 1970). Not only have the ancestral records of Gebel Adda, Old Nubia (representing almost 2000 years) been studied, but modern Nubian people living in New Nubia at Kom Ombo have been examined over the past 10 years (Holden et al 1970).

From the dental viewpoint, what did the ancient Egyptian look like compared with the people of today? Basically, there has been little change as far as dental disease is concerned. In ancient Egypt, the greatest single problem was attrition, or wear (Figure 3.1). The teeth were rapidly worn down throughout life by the consumption of a coarse diet. Interestingly enough, the pharaohs of Egypt exhibit this wear just as do the farmers of both modern and ancient Egypt. In time, this wear becomes so extensive that the enamel and dentin are eroded away until the pulp is exposed. The living tissue inside the tooth dies, and the empty root canals become a source of chronic infection and abscess. The teeth of Rameses II are excellent examples of the effects of old age, attrition, and ultimate abscesses (Figure 3.2). Ghalioungui and El Dawakhly (1965) concluded that the dental surgeon had drained these abscesses through a hollow reed.

The second greatest problem from the viewpoint of both ancient and modern Egyptians was periodontal, or gum, disease. This disease results in loss of the bony support of the teeth and is often associated with calculus, or tartar, deposits on the teeth. Calculus was often so extensive in the skulls of the ancient Nubians that this deposit frequently held the teeth in place 2,000 years after death. Whereas calculus deposits of any consequence are rarely seen in Americans below 20 years of age, they have been observed in Nubian children in elementary

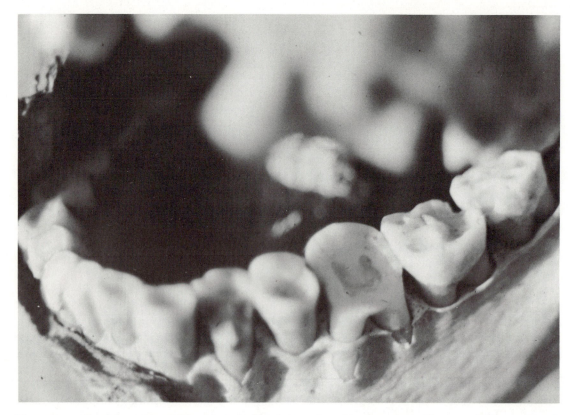

Figure 3.1.   *Dental wear or attrition typical of ancient and modern Egyptians. This mandible was found in a Nubian cemetery of A.D. 250.*

school (Holden et al. 1970). The ultimate result is loss of bony support, loose teeth, and deep periodontal pockets or even exposed root bifurcations. This in turn leads to infection, abscesses, and loss of teeth.

Dental caries, or cavities, were far less frequently seen in ancient Egyptians or Nubians, until the latter population was moved to New Nubia near Kom Ombo and the great sugarcane fields. Neither ancient kings, nobles, nor commoners exhibited much dental decay, and where observed, the decay was of the pit-and- fissure variety (top of the tooth) rather than the decay between the teeth so frequently seen in modern civilization. There are two major environmental causes that, one

may speculate, may have resulted in the lack of extensive dental decay. The first is the absence from the diet of refined carbohydrates such as sugar. The second, and equally important, is the extreme wear mentioned earlier, for wear occurs not only on the occlusal surface (top of the teeth), but between the teeth (interproximally) as well. It is between the teeth that dental decay is often initiated in modern Western society. The extensive wear provides a more difficult environment for decay to begin.

A brief comment must be made on dental occlusion or malocclusion and facial types. In general, perhaps owing to extreme wear, the dentition of the ancient Egyptians (Old King-

Figure 3.2.   *Lateral cephalogram of the mummy of Rameses II. This pharaoh was very old at death, and the extreme wear of the teeth may be noted with resulting exposure of the pulp chambers and periapical abscesses. Periodontal disease, or loss of bone support of the dentition, is also apparent.*

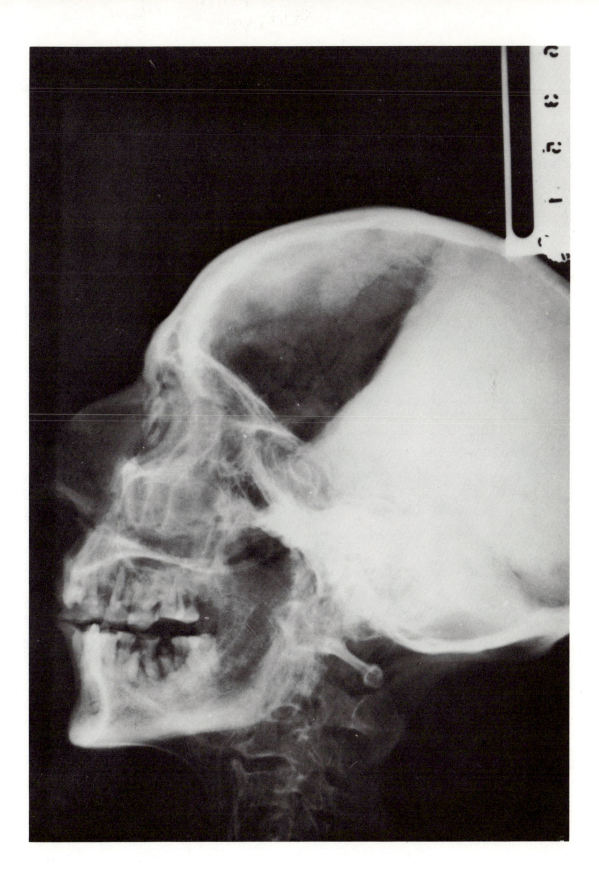

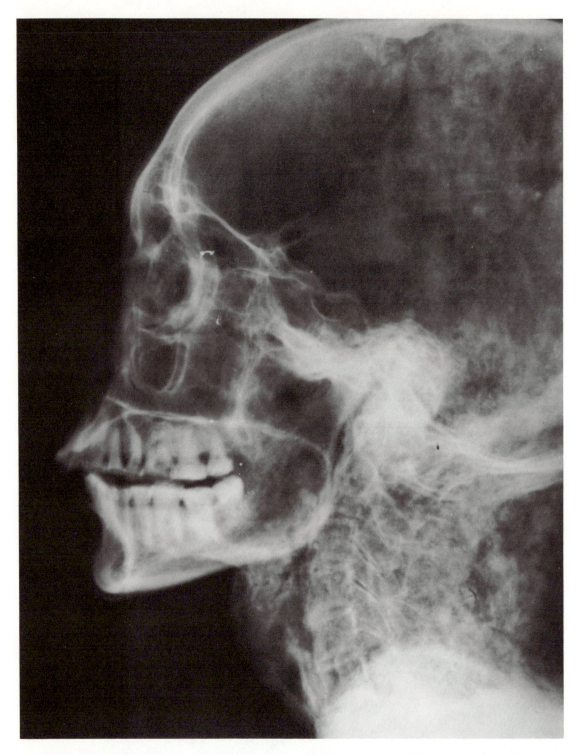

Figure 3.3.   X ray of the mummy of Ahmose Nefertiry illustrating the maxillary prognathism character-istic of the queens of the early Eighteenth Dynasty.

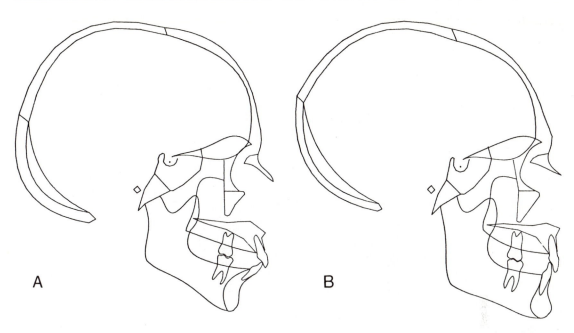

A   B

Figures 3.4.   Computerized tracings of the X rays of the mummies of (a) Tuthmosis I and (b) Tuthmosis IV of the Eighteenth Dynasty. These two facial profiles and anterior dentition demonstrate the remarkable heterogeneity among the pharaohs of the New Kingdom.

dom) and ancient Nubians rarely exhibited the dental crowding or abnormal molar relationships that are frequently observed throughout the world today. Most modern Egyptians have good molar relationships with moderate to severe crowding. However, if the queens of the New Kingdom period (early Eighteenth Dynasty) are examined by X-ray cephalometry, many resemble modern Europeans or Americans, with maxillary, or upper jaw, prognathism. This condition may be either hereditary or environmental – that is, the result of thumb sucking or other oral habits. Queen Ahmose Nefertiry is an excellent example of this type of occlusion (Figure 3.3). In Nubia, this same condition has been observed, but as the result of tongue thrusting or thumb sucking, not as an inherited phenomenon.

The kings of Egypt had little similarity in appearance, contrary to their portrayals by contemporary artists. Computer tracings of X-rays of the mummies of Tuthmosis I and Tuthmosis IV show the considerable heterogeneity in the mummies of the New Kingdom period as far as craniofacial complex is concerned (Figure 3.4). From the viewpoint of the orthodontist or anthropologist, there is abundant biologic evidence that the pharaohs of the New Kingdom period of Egypt were quite heterogeneous – as variable as any American population. This assumption may be supported by historical records, which indicate that during the New Kingdom period the Egyptian royal family brought princes from many conquered nations into its court, where they were accepted as equals and hence potential consorts (Iskander and Badawy 1965). Except for Tuthmosis I, II, and III, most of the pharaohs of the New Kingdom period had class I (i.e., normal) molar relationships with straight profiles, but neither their craniofacial skeletons nor their soft tissues suggested homogeneity of appearance. In contrast, the nobles of the Old Kingdom studied at Giza and those of the New Kingdom examined at Deir el-Bahri seem quite homogeneous.

Figure 3.5. *Ancient dental bridge from the Old Kingdom consisting of artificially prepared natural teeth and gold wire.*

Finally, a brief mention of the *dental profession* in ancient Egypt. Ghalioungui and El Dawakhly (1965) recall: "Hesy-Re, the oldest person in history who ever carried the title of physician, even in the time of Imhotep, two thousand years before the war of Troy, called himself Chief of Dentists." The time would date back to the Old Kingdom, and there are many medical papyri, such as the famous Ebers papyrus (Ebell 1937), that prescribe medicines to relieve dental pain and even describe how to fix loose teeth. Recently, there has been considerable debate about whether a restorative dental profession existed before the time of the Ptolemaic or Greek period, as no dental prosthesis has been found in a mummy, royal or otherwise (Leek 1967). However, in 1975, Harris, Iskander, and Farid reported the discovery of a dental bridge from the Fourth Dynasty of the Old Kingdom, about 2500 B.C. (Figure 3.5). This bridge consisted originally of four teeth and replaced an upper left lateral incisor and a central incisor. The bridge consisted of prepared natural teeth, which had very fine holes drilled through them, and gold wire, which was used in a skillful manner to attach the substitute teeth to the abutment teeth. This find, together with the written evidence of the medical papyri, suggests that Ghalioungui and El Dawakhly (1965) were correct when, speaking of the remarkable specialization of medicine, they cited "Men-kaou-Re-ankh who was called a maker of teeth (iry-ibh), to distinguish him from Ni-ankh-Sekhmet who figures on the same stele as a tooth physician."

In short, Egypt has the best recorded

biologic record, documented by history, of any country in the world. Comparisons of the ancient Egyptians with modern Egyptians suggest that attrition and periodontal disease are common to both populations. Only in recent times, with the development of refined sugars, has dental decay become a major problem in urban areas of Egypt. The ancient pharaohs and queens of Egypt show in their dental occlusion and craniofacial skeleton, as revealed by X-rays, the diversity and heterogeneity one might assign to modern Western communities with a history of racial admixture; the Egyptian nobles and the Nubian people present a much more homogeneous facial skeleton with good occlusion, sometimes associated with dental crowding. Except in cities such as Cairo and Alexandria, the types of dental malocclusion seen commonly in the Western world, such as maxillary prognathism, are not inherited, but are associated with oral habits.

REFERENCES

Ebell, E. 1937. *The Papyrus Ebers, the greatest Egyptian medical document* (translation), chapter 89, p. 103. Copenhagen: Levin & Munksgaard.

Ghalioungui, P. and El Dawakhly, Z. 1965. *Health and healing in ancient Egypt*, p. 12. Cairo: Egyptian Organization for Authorship and Translation.

Harris, J. E.; Iskander, Z.; and Farid, S. 1975. Restorative dentistry in ancient Egypt: an archaeologic fact. *Journal of the Michigan Dental Association* 57:401–4.

Harris, J. E.; Ponitz, P. V.; and Loutfy, M. S. 1970. Orthodontic's contribution to save the monuments of Nubia: a 1970 field report. *American Journal of Orthodontics* 58(6):578–96.

Holden, S.; Harris, J. E.; and Ash, M. 1970. Periodontal disease in Nubian children. *International Association of Dental Research Program and Abstract of Papers*, p. 65. Chicago: American Dental Association.

Iskander, Z., and Badawy, A. 1965. *Brief history of ancient Egypt*, 5th ed., p. 207. Cairo: Madkour Press.

Leek, F. 1967. The practice of dentistry in ancient Egypt. *Egyptian Archaeological Journal* 53:51.

4

A classic mummy:PUM II

AIDAN COCKBURN
President, Paleopathology Association
Detroit, Michigan, U.S.A.

WILLIAM H. PECK
Curator of Ancient Art
Detroit Institute of Arts,
Detroit, Michigan, U.S.A.

ROBIN A. BARRACO
Associate Professor of Physiology
Wayne State University School of Medicine
Detroit, Michigan, U.S.A.

THEODORE A. REYMAN
Director of Laboratories
Mount Carmel Mercy Hospital
Detroit, Michigan, U.S.A.

The traditional Egyptian mummy is one on which all the arts of embalming have been employed, the organs have been preserved, the body is wrapped in linen, and everything is contained in a highly decorated sarcophagus. Such was mummy PUM II. It belongs to the Philadelphia Art Museum and was lent to the Paleopathology Association for dissection and study through the courtesy of David O'Connor of the Pennsylvania University Museum – thus the name PUM II, this being the second mummy from that museum. PUM II is now on loan to the National Museum of Natural History, Smithsonian Institution, Washington, D.C., and can be seen there complete with its sarcophagus, and photographs illustrating the autopsy and the finds made during subsequent studies (Figure 4.1).

Little is known of the provenance of this mummy (Figure 4.2). It was probably brought to America about the turn of the century and has been in the possession of the Philadelphia Art Museum since that time, but its origins in Egypt are unknown. The sarcophagus was highly decorated, but lacked the name and any details of the person inside (Figures 4.3 and 4.4).

This chapter gives an overall picture of the autopsy and the findings made during the following years. The work is by no means completed and, indeed, is likely to continue for several more years. This is because new techniques are continually being devised and applied to the tissues, wrappings, and resin.

The unwrapping and the autopsy took place on 1 February 1973, as part of a symposium, "Death and Disease in Ancient Egypt," that was held at Wayne State University Medical School, Detroit, Michigan (Cockburn 1973). Radiographic examinations had been made a week earlier at Mount Carmel Mercy Hospital and Hutzel Hospital, Detroit. Specimens of the radiograms and xerograms are presented in Chapter 17. It was seen that the mummy was in good condition. The brain had been removed and replaced with resin, which had formed a pool in the skull before it solidified, appearing in the X ray as a "water level." A diagnosis of fractured skull was also made; this frequently occurs with X rays of mummies that are still wrapped. When the skull was exposed, it was found that these "fractures" were merely scratches in the scalp that appeared as linear defects in the bone on the X ray. Let this be a warning to anyone trying to make a diagnosis on a mummy that is still in its wrappings.

Four packages were seen in the body cavities. No amulets were visible. There was a transitional or sixth lumbar vertebral body that might have made stooping painful and difficult during life. The right fibula and adjoining tibia had a pathological thickening resembling periostitis.

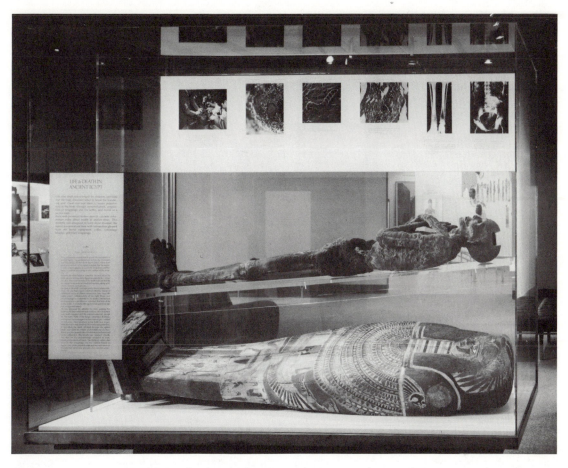

Figure 4.1.   Mummy PUM II on display in the National Museum of Natural History, Washington, D.C. (Photograph by Victor Krantze, Smithsonian Institution)

After the autopsy, more radiographs were taken of the right leg, and polytomographs were made of the skull and temporal bone regions. The polytomographs showed the hole punched through the cribriform plate for the removal of the brain: This had been missed, although it was looked for, in earlier radiological studies.

REMOVAL OF WRAPPINGS AND GENERAL EXAMINATION

There proved to be about 12 layers of linen wrapping of varying qualities of cloth. The outer layers were generally larger sheets or strips of fine weave. Hot liquid resin had been poured liberally over the body at many of the stages, so that most of the wrappings had been converted into a hard, solid mass, which could be removed only with a hammer and chisel or cut through, several layers at a time, with a Stryker saw. After the general broad wrapping had been removed, it was found that limbs and even individual fingers and toes were wrapped separately. As many as nine people worked simultaneously, but it still required almost 7 hours to strip away all the bandages completely.

At a later date, the wrappings were examined by Meryl Johnson (1974). As expected,

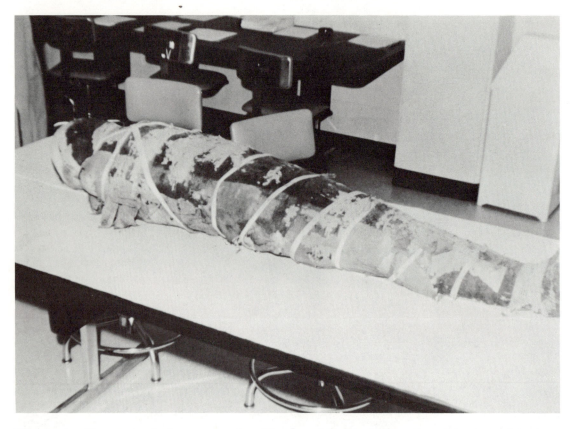

Figure 4.2.   The mummy before unwrapping. (Photograph by Nemo Warr, Detroit Institute of Arts)

the cloth was linen, with a simple weave, but a complete surprise was the discovery of a ball of cotton wrapped between two pieces of linen. It was adherent to the linen and was partially coated with some nondescript material that could have been unguent or tissue juice. This material has not yet been identified (Figure 4.5).

Cotton has not been recorded in the Western World before Christ, the earliest find being from a Roman grave about A.D. 200, though cotton has been found in cultures of the Indus Valley dating back to about 2000 B.C. The interesting question is: How did cotton arrive in Egypt by 200 B.C.? By the time of the Romans, there was considerable trade with India, and indeed the Romans had several trading posts in southern India (Miller 1969). Until the secrets of the monsoon were discovered, sea traffic hugged the coast, with

most traffic taking the route up the Persian Gulf and across the desert to Palestine via Petra. Were the Egyptians using some similar route to import cotton as early as 200 B.C? Perhaps cotton was so rare and valuable that the ball found in PUM II was, as Meryl Johnson has speculated, included as a form of amulet.

THE GENERAL AUTOPSY

The skin and tissues were as hard as plastic and were cut with the Stryker saw. When the saw cut through the resin, the resin burned and gave off a most fragrant odor. The anterior abdominal wall and the incision made by the embalmers in the left side were cut out and removed (Figure 4.6). Inside the abdominal and thoracic cavities there were four packages. Hot resin had been poured in, cov-

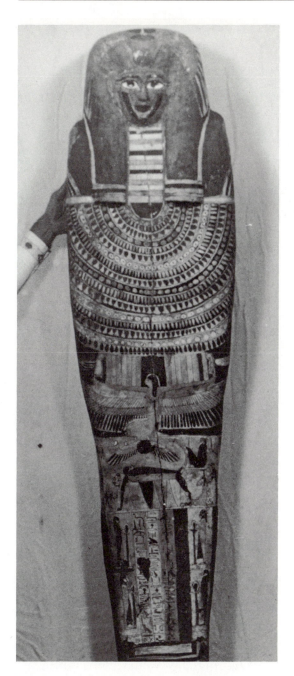

Figure 4.3.   Coffin of PUM II. (Photograph by J. Lawrence Angel, Smithsonian Institution)

ering both the packages and the floors of the thorax, abdomen, and pelvis. The packages were removed with a chisel and were found to be covered with insect pupae (Figures 4.7 and

4.8) preserved by the resin; further study showed that one package contained spleen and some intestine, and the three others contained lung. Some of the aorta and a piece of heart tissue were found in situ, coated with resin. The kidneys and urinary bladder were not seen.

The penis was intact, held in an upright position with support from a small piece of wood (Figure 4.9). There had been no circumcision. The testes were missing, probably having been removed via the pelvis. The right leg was abnormal (Figure 4.10) and is discussed later in this chapter. The feet and hands were in excellent condition. The nails were painted red with henna, and the soles of the feet were white with lime (Figures 4.11 and 4.12).

Radiograms taken before the autopsy had shown a fluid level in the skull, so a window was cut in the cranium above this level. It was found that resin had been poured into the skull through a hole punched through the base of the skull by a tool forced up the left nostril. Presumably, the brain had been removed by a small hook through this same hole and replaced by the resin. Originally, we had supposed that the brain would liquefy and could be drained away. However, this does not happen: Brain tissue, if undisturbed, simply retains its general shape and shrinks to about one-third its volume, as was the case in mummies ROM I, PUM I, PUM III, and PUM IV.

The eyes were intact and on removal appeared well preserved (Figure 4.13). At a later date the temporal bones containing the ears were removed with a circular Stryker saw and taken out through the window in the skull (Figure 4.14). Also at a later date, the anterior part of the lumbar vertebral column was removed in order to search for the spinal cord. The cord had vanished and been replaced by resin trickling down from the skull through the foramen magnum.

Tissues were collected from the location of the thyroid and parathyroids, but later studies failed to reveal these glands. Lewin

Figure 4.4.   *Detail from coffin. The Apis bull carrying the mummy. (Photograph by J. Lawrence Angel, Smithsonian Institution)*

noted that the color of the mummy changed from a light brown to a darker brown within 24 hours. At the present time, the skin is almost a black brown. On the basis of anatomical studies, Angel estimated the age of the individual as between 35 and 40 years, and his height as approximately 162 cm (5 ft 4 in.).

SPECIAL STUDIES

There has been much speculation regarding the length of time organisms such as seeds or bacterial spores can survive in a dormant state and still become active again. There are reports from the Antarctic of bacteria 10,000 years old recovered in a living state from deep in the frozen soil. It was, therefore, decided to look for living bacteria or fungi inside this mummy. There were two objections to this project: (1) any fungi found might be modern ones that had grown through the mummy from the outside; and (2) the act of cutting open the mummy would contaminate the interior.

In spite of these drawbacks, cultures were taken as soon as the abdominal cavity was opened from areas remote from the opening. All the specimens proved sterile. In two previous mummy autopsies, Reyman had found almost all tissues to be riddled with fungi; in

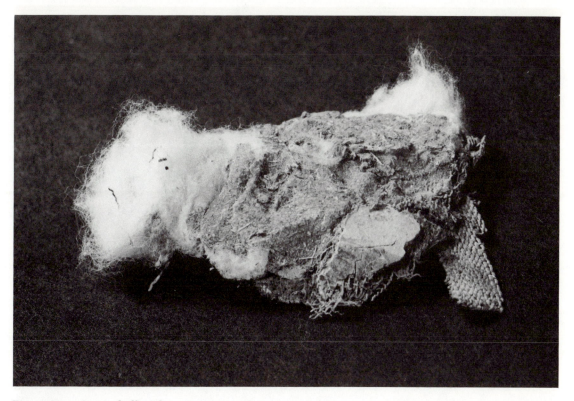

Figure 4.5.   Cotton ball with incrustations that are probably unguents. (Photograph by Nemo Warr, Detroit Institute of Arts)

this case, fungus was absent. The explanation is probably the abundant use of resin. This was obviously very hot and fluid when applied, for it penetrated not only into large cavities, but also into the mastoid air cells via the foramen of the eighth nerve and into the middle ear through a perforation in the eardrum, and even trickled from the skull down the whole length of the spinal canal.

THE RESIN

Specimens of the resin have been distributed to a number of laboratories, and some reports are now available. One scientist was intrigued by the observation that it burned with a most fragrant odor when cut with the Stryker saw and wanted to test this fragrance in his studies of smell. However, when a sample was set on fire in Detroit, the resin melted and burned, giving off a thick black smoke that was most unpleasant!

An analysis of trace elements was undertaken by Nunnelley and his colleagues (1976). Their report, given later in this chapter, indicated that the resin had penetrated all the tissues of the body (Table 4.1).

Another analysis of the resin was made by Coughlin (1977). Using mass spectroscopy, she found that the PUM II resin, or mummy fluid, had completely polymerized into one vast and continuous molecular form. This polymerization is attributable to a combination of aging and the electromagnetic properties of natural botanical products. The result is a kind of organic glass, an intermediate with respect to amber. This condition of being a "glass" has been confirmed by X-ray diffraction. The known use of natron (sodium salts) in later Egyptian glass-making processes – natron is the chemical used for desiccation of the body during the mummification process – suggests that the development of a

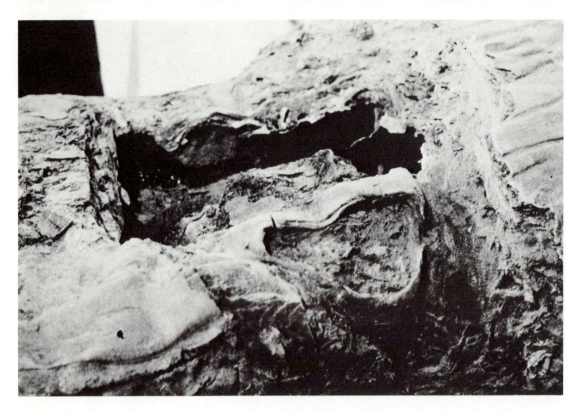

Figure 4.6.   The embalmers' incision. The abdomen has been opened, and the layers of wrappings, congealed into one mass, can be seen. (Photograph by Nemo Warr, Detroit Institute of Arts)

Figure 4.7.   Package containing lung covered with fly pupae, which are covered with resin. (Photograph by Nemo Warr, Detroit Institute of Arts)

Figure 4.8.   Embalmed pupa visualized with a scanning electron microscope. × 80. (Courtesy of Peter Lewin, University of Toronto)

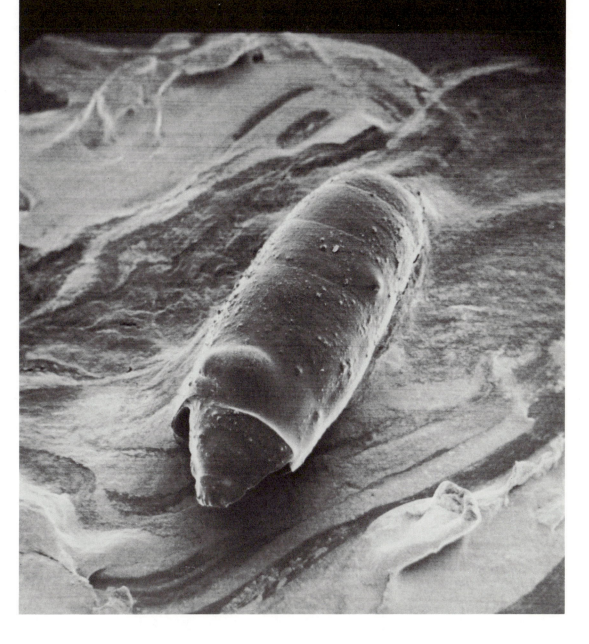
500μm

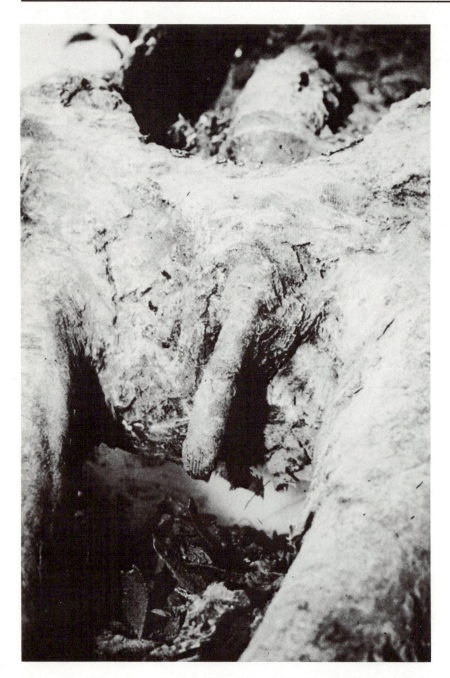

Figure 4.9.   Penis. (Photograph by Nemo Warr, Detroit Institute of Arts)

Figure 4.10.   Lower part of the legs. The right leg is swollen and shows the marks of the bandages. (Photograph by Nemo Warr, Detroit Institute of Arts)

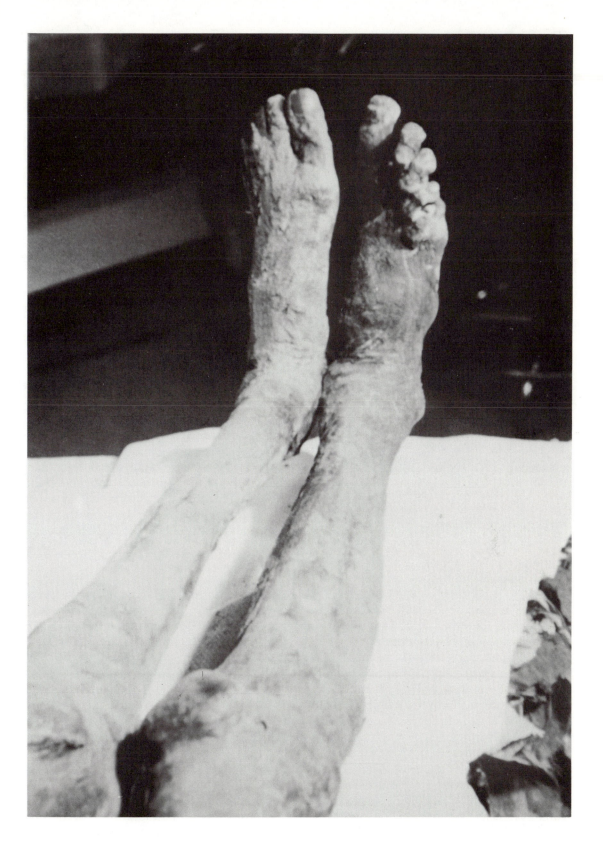

Figure 4.11.   *Hands. The nails are painted red.*
(Photograph by Nemo Warr, Detroit Institute of Arts)

technology of glass making may have occurred as an offshoot of the mummification process.

The major constituent of PUM II mummy fluid or resin identified by X-ray diffraction techniques is the oil of a coniferous evergreen tree, Coniferae, *Juniperus* (Linnaeus). This genus, *Juniperus*, comprises approximately 35 species of evergreen trees or shrubs whose distribution ranges from the Arctic Circle to Mexico, the West Indies, the Azores, the Canary Islands, North Africa, Abyssinia, and the mountains of tropical East Africa, China and Formosa, and the Himalayas. *Juniperus* is one of the few northern forms that has distributed into the southern hemisphere. These juniper trees have a fragrant wood, and a red to reddish-brown oil is expressed from the

wood, leaves, and shoots. This oil is the major constituent of the PUM II mummy fluid, resin, or glass.

Two additional, although minor, components were separated from the major constituent by means of an organic extraction and filtration technique. One of the additional components identified by thin-layer chromatography 3 is an oil from an aromatic tree, Lauraceae, *Cinnamomum camphora* (Nees & Eberm). This is the camphor tree, a stout, dense-topped tree capable of reaching a height of about 13 m. Its enlarged base, twigs, and bruised leaves have a marked camphor odor. The tree is distributed geographically in Ceylon and Asia. The second additional component is myrrh, the fragrant gum resin exuded from special resin ducts in the bark of the myrrh tree, Burseraceae, *Commiphora myrrha*. This tree ranges in height from 3 to 12 m, and is native to only two parts of the world: southern Arabia and northern Somaliland.

Although minute quantities of other botanical products, such as spices or flowers, may be additional unidentified components, the three components identified as oils of juniper and camphor and the gum resin myrrh are the essential constituents of the PUM II mummy resin.

THE PACKAGES

Peck has described (Chapter 1) how the Egyptians preserved certain organs either in canopic jars or by wrapping them in linen and replacing them in a mummy's abdominal cavity. The process of extracting water with natron shrank the organs considerably, some being only one-tenth their natural weight. Traditionally, organs treated in this way were the lungs, liver, stomach, and intestine.

PUM II had the four customary packages, but Reyman discovered that three of them contained only lung and the fourth spleen plus a tiny piece of intestine. This lent support to the opinion that although the form of mummification had followed traditional lines, it had suffered some debasement. The

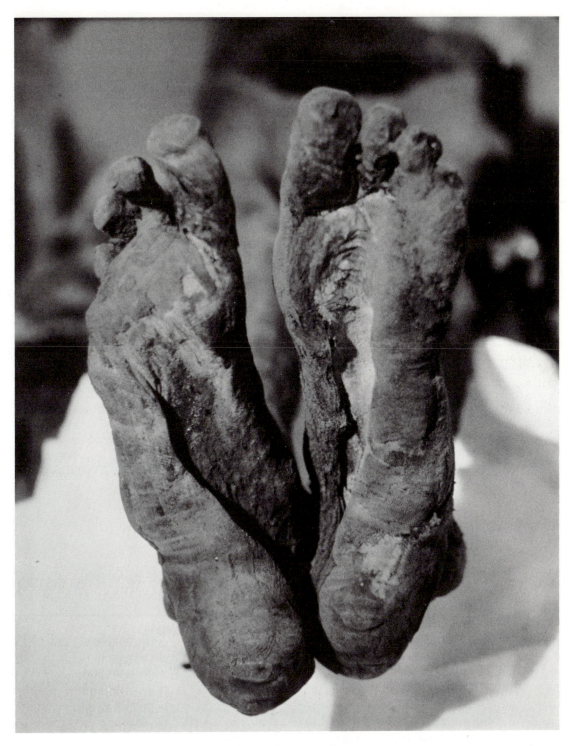

Figure 4.12. Feet. The feet are painted white with lime. The distortion is postmortem and caused by the wrappings. (Photograph by Nemo Warr, Detroit Institute of Arts)

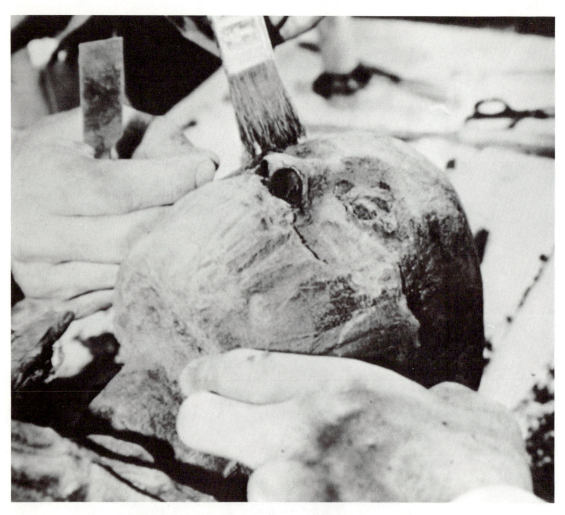

Figure 4.13.   *Face emerging. (Photograph by Nemo Warr, Detroit Institute of Arts)*

embalming was obviously expensive, yet the embalmers had handled the organs in a slip-shod way.

Some of the pupae found embalmed on the packages have been studied by the U.S. Department of Agriculture at its Systematic Entomology Laboratory, Washington, D.C. The entomologists at this laboratory pointed out that certain insects have specialized in breeding on decaying flesh and that Motter, in his studies in 1898, found a wide range of genera in human graves. Indeed, in PUM IV, a child 6 to 8 years of age autopsied in Detroit in 1976 (Chapter 6), the insect larvae within the wrappings had been so numerous that they had penetrated to all parts of the body, including the brain, and had left large holes in the bones and tissues.

In the case of PUM II, the process had not progressed to that point. The insects had certainly laid their eggs on both body and packages, larvae had hatched out and eaten their fill, and some had turned into pupae; but at that point, the embalmers had poured in hot liquid resin, which killed and embalmed them all in an instant (Figures 4.7 and 4.8). Chapter 18 describes the finding of a larva on an eardrum.

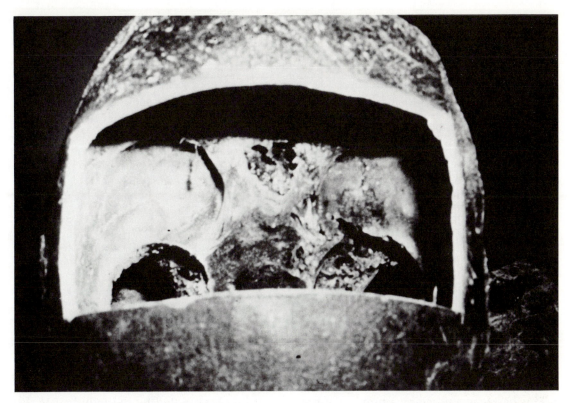

Figure 4.14.   Skull. The openings in the base are two circular ones made by the Stryker saw; the foramen magnum is between; and the opening above this was made by the embalmers. (Photograph by Aidan Cockburn)

The insects from PUM II so far identified (Cockburn et al. 1975) are: *Dermestes*, probably *frischii*; *Piophila casei*; *Atheta* sp.; and *Chrysomya* sp.

GENERAL HISTOLOGY
The histological report is given in Chapter 15. In brief, it can be said that tissue from PUM II, such as bone, cartilage, and muscle, was found to be in good condition. The skin was preserved and showed intact glandular structure (but without nuclei), hair follicles, and an intact basal layer of epithelium with ghost forms of nuclei and melanin pigment.

The lung tissue from the visceral packages contained intact bronchi and bronchioles with normal cartilage and connective tissue. The pulmonary parenchyma had areas of diffuse and nodular fibrosis. In some sections,

the alveolar septa appeared normal. Within the fibrotic areas, there were anthracotic (carbon) and silicotic (silica) deposits. The silica content of the lung was 0.22 percent; the normal value has an upper limit of 0.20 percent and is usually less than 0.5 percent. These findings indicate that the man had pneumoconiosis, probably from inhaling sand during desert dust storms. Whether he had symptoms of this pulmonary disease is difficult to assess.

One of the visceral packages housed spleen and a small portion of intestine. The spleen, with recognizable capsule and trabeculae, was normal. The intestinal tissue contained a single fragment of partially digested but recognizable meat (muscle) fiber with residual striations. Also present within the tissue was a single parasite egg.

Table 4.1. *Trace element concentrations of PUM II tissues and resin (parts per million dry weight)*

Element	PUM II muscle	PUM II skin	PUM II tendon	PUM II resin	Modern muscle	Mammalian muscle
K	1,500 ± 300	3,500 ± 1,000	1,400 ± 300	580 ± 160	11,600 ± 1,800	10,500
Ca	500 ± 90	83,000 ± 16,000	520 ± 90	760 ± 170	570 ± 80	105
Mn	2.1 ± 0.6	<8	2.9 ± 0.4	7.4 ± 1.3	<1.7	0.21
Fe	145 ± 8	27 ± 4	111 ± 6	600 ± 50	110 ± 30	140
Ni	3.0 ± 0.3	<3	2.6 ± 0.2	7.3 ± 0.7	—	0.008
Cu	4.1 ± 0.3	<2	3.4 ± 0.3	5.8 ± 0.4	1.8 ± .8	3.1
Zn	86 ± 3	37 ± 2	56 ± 2	4.9 ± 0.3	170 ± 30	180
As	0.12 ± 0.006	<0.5	0.06 ± 0.03	0.31 ± 0.08	<0.3	0.16
Se	0.29 ± 0.04	—	0.25 ± 0.03	0.04 ± 0.03	—	2.5
Br	13.9 ± 0.3	6.0 ± 0.3	12.1 ± 0.3	8.9 ± 0.3	—	4
Rb	2.0 ± 0.1	0.6 ± 0.2	1.34 ± 0.08	0.82 ± 0.06	9 ± 5	24
Sr	4.3 ± 0.1	78 ± 2	4.3 ± 0.1	10.1 ± 0.3	0.13 ± 0.006	0.05
Y	0.04 ± 0.03	—	0.08 ± 0.02	0.27 ± 0.4	—	—
Zr	0.36 ± 0.03	<0.9	0.32 ± 0.03	1.82 ± 0.08	—	<0.3
Nb	0.03 ± 0.02	—	0.019 ± 0.016	0.82 ± 0.04	—	—
Mo	1.64 ± 0.05	<0.3	1.32 ± 0.03	4.0 ± 0.1	0.06 ± 0.01	<0.2
Sn	0.57 ± 0.06	<1.6	0.68 ± 0.04	1.37 ± 0.08	—	<0.2
Pb	0.33 ± 0.06	<1.2	0.41 ± 0.04	3.4 ± 0.2	0.8 ± 0.5	<0.2

Dash indicates concentration not measurable.

This has been studied by a number of helminthologists, who are agreed that it probably is *Ascaris*; some state definitely that it is *A. lumbricoides*. This finding was not a complete surprise, for *Ascaris* has already been reported from seven locations in antiquity in Europe. Sometimes, there were millions of ova in the feces, as in the prehistoric salt mines at Hallstatt in Austria.

Both eyes were collected, and the whole section of one revealed the lens to be present, although the cornea had disappeared. The choroid and the ciliary body were intact and contained melanin pigment, but there were no traces of the retina. Large nerves, probably those to the extrinsic eye muscles, were well preserved in the retrobulbar fat and muscle. Portions of the aorta and other vessels were found within the visceral packages; large and small arterioles and arteries also showed areas of intimal fibrous thickening, typical of arteriolar sclerosis. In some of the vessels, partially and completely intact red blood cells could be seen (Chapter 15).

It had been noted by the radiologists that the right leg was abnormal in that there appeared to be periostitis of the fibula and the adjoining part of the tibia. This abnormality was confirmed when the leg was unwrapped, for the right leg was swollen compared with the left. The bandages wrapped around the leg had left distinct marks, suggesting that the leg had been edematous at the time of mummification. The fact that the right toes were curled back led to some dispute, but it was finally agreed that this was a postmortem effect caused by the tightness of the wrappings.

A piece of the affected fibula was removed and sectioned. It was found that a good deal of new but unorganized bone had been laid down in the distal half of the fibula (Chapter 15). The cause of this pathology is unknown.

BIOCHEMICAL STUDIES
It is well known that amino acids are stable for immense periods of time. It is, therefore, not surprising that various workers have re-

ported amino acids and even peptides from Egyptian mummies. However, it had usually been assumed that proteins would break down into component parts over any significant length of time. Cockburn (1963) suggested that this might not necessarily be the case and that gamma globulin and even antibodies might persist under favorable conditions. It was to test this speculation that Barraco set out to isolate proteins from the tissues of PUM II.

Biochemistry is complex and no field for the beginner. The technical details are given step by step in Chapter 19 for those with the learning to follow them. Here it is enough to say that Barraco did indeed succeed in extracting what appeared to be pure protein of a molecular weight of 150,000 (which is the same as for gamma globulin), but that testing indicated it to be biologically inactive. Trace amounts of intact immunoreactive albumen were identified by Reyman.

Another problem to be tackled was the question of whether any given mummy had been treated with natron. Mummies DIA I and PUM II quite obviously had been so treated, but with the remainder in doubt. They just might have been wrapped up in linen without preliminary dehydration. Barraco found that the salt content of the tissues of PUM II was very high, perhaps 10 times that of normal tissues, but the salt content of the uncertain mummies was the same as in normal living tissues. This provides a future test for natron. It also incidentally demonstrated that the natron, like the resin, had penetrated into the tissues all through (Chapter 19).

DATING

Several techniques are available for dating a mummy. First, carbon-14 dating was done by Stuckenrath (1974), using linen from the wrappings. The date he obtained was 170 B.C. ± 70 years.

The coffin should give valuable information for dating, but Strouhal (personal communication, 1973) reported that about 10 percent of the 180 mummies he examined in Czechoslovakia appeared to be in coffins not originally intended for them. Angel measured PUM II and concluded that his size was consistent with the assumption that the coffin was made for him. Photographs of the coffin taken by Angel were studied by Fischer (1974), who described it as Greco-Roman. The Apis bull carrying the dead man (Figure 4.4) is a late motif. Fischer also noted that the slight garbling of the hieroglyphs and the absence of any name for the dead man suggest a "stock" coffin rather than one that was custom-made.

An estimate based on cultural features was given by Strouhal (personal communication, 1973). At first sight it appeared that the methods of mummification (packaging the organs, removing the brain, painting the nails with henna and the feet with lime, crossing the arms) indicated a mummy of the Third Intermediate period, perhaps about 700 B.C. However, later evidence showed that the organs were packed carelessly, with three packages containing lung and one spleen and some intestine, instead of the lungs, liver, intestines, and stomach being placed in separate packages. Also circumcision had not been performed. These facts suggested that the methods were a debased form of those used in an earlier period.

The linen wrappings were examined by Johnson (1974), who believed them to be Ptolemaic. In short, all the evidence points to the Ptolemaic period, about 170 B.C.

TRACE ELEMENTS

Tests were made to see whether the concentrations of metals in bone from a vertebra could be estimated by using neutron activation and atomic absorption techniques. It seemed possible that the overwhelming amount of calcium might interfere with the measurements of other metals present in only trace amounts, and this proved to be the case with the neutron activation test; of the 20 metals sought, only the calcium could be measured.

Smith (1974) tested for lead and mercury by

using atomic absorption and found a lead concentration of 0.6 part per million (ppm) and a mercury concentration of 0.43 ppm (dry weight). According to Kehoe (1961), the lead content of modern flat bone averages 6.55 ppm and that of long bone 18.0 ppm, so PUM II had only a fraction of the lead load of modern man. The mercury level in bone from PUM II, however, is about the same as that in modern bone, which ranges from 0.03 to 1.04 ppm with a mean of 0.45 ppm (Goldwater 1972).

Using atomic absorption, Reyman obtained similar results from mummy PUM I. His heavy metal values for soft tissue were (in parts per million): lead, 1.3; copper, 1.9; arsenic, 6.2; and mercury, 0.3. The values for long bone were: lead, 2.5; copper, 2.3; mercury, 0.1; and arsenic, none detected.

Nunnelley and colleagues (1976) reported on the trace elements in PUM II. Specimens of muscle, tendon, and skin were identified visually and separated from a gross sample of mummy tissue. Trace elements were concentrated by ashing the tissue and resin samples at 410°C for 48 hours. Some elements such as arsenic, mercury, and selenium tend to form volatile compounds, and therefore the concentrations of these elements should be regarded as lower limits. Modern tissue samples were dried before ashing and otherwise treated in the same way. The samples were analyzed by X-ray fluorescence. The samples were placed in the collimated X-ray beam from a 3-kW, 60-kV X-ray tube. The characteristic X rays emitted from the samples were detected with a lithium drifted silicon detector. The X-ray intensities were corrected for absorption within the samples and compared with standards to calculate concentrations. X-ray fluorescence is well suited for a trace element scan, as many elements are detected simultaneously.

The results are shown in Table 4.1. Many elements are more concentrated in the resin than in the tissues. This complicates the interpretation of the tissue concentrations. The more exotic elements in muscle and tendon, such as yttrium, zirconium, and niobium, are possibly attributable entirely to contamination from the resin. Because the resin is so rich in trace elements, it may be possible to develop trace element profiles of other resins to help distinguish the origin or treatment of different resin samples. The skin of PUM II is rich in calcium and strontium (a chemical homolog of calcium). This may be the result of postmortem calcium soap formation in the subcutaneous fat. Skin has a different trace element profile from either muscle or tendon, whereas muscle and tendon have very similar trace element concentrations. This may be because they had similar environments in relation to the resin and that of the skin was different.

Also shown in Table 4.1 are the average results from three modern human muscle samples. These samples were analyzed in the same way as the PUM II samples. Included for comparison in Table 4.1 are typical values for mammalian muscle as reported by Bowen (1966). Compared with modern values, PUM II tissues appear to be low in potassium. Because potassium is an essential component of tissue, the depression in PUM II tissue suggests some removal process – possibly something that occurred during the preparation of the mummy. The modern value for zinc concentration in muscle is about 170 ppm. The zinc concentration in PUM II muscle is about half the modern value. This suggests that PUM II could have had a deficiency in this essential element. However, much caution should be used in describing endemic zinc deficiencies in ancient populations until a larger number of mummies has been studied and the effect of long-term storage on trace element concentrations has been investigated.

Many disease states are correlated with trace element abnormalities. Examples include anemia caused by iron deficiency and vitamin B_{12} deficiency caused by the lack of cobalt porphyrin in the diet. In modern Egypt, retarded growth and the failure of adolescent males to reach sexual maturation have been associated with endemic zinc deficiency.

Trace element analysis of mummy tissues may offer an opportunity to study long-term trace element body burdens. Studies may also help delineate possible disease states of a given individual before mummification.

DISCUSSION OF THE FINDINGS

Discoveries made during the autopsy of PUM II cover a broad variety of disciplines. Some merely confirm what had been reported earlier, but others are new.

The presence of silica in the lungs was surprising only because it had not been reported before. At certain times of the year, in many areas of Egypt, it is almost impossible to avoid breathing in sand; the air is full of it and so, inevitably, are the mouths and nostrils of the people living there. Shortly after the first report on PUM II appeared, Israeli workers recorded finding sand in the lungs of Bedouins in the Negev, a condition now known as Negev desert lung (1976). A similar condition was reported from a mummy in Manchester, England (1976).

Anthracosis, or carbon particles, in the lung has been reported from most mummies whose lungs have been examined. Air pollution is not a modern development. It was just as severe in antiquity and must have followed quickly after the discovery of fire making, for man would take fire with him into his home, whether cave, tent, hut, or igloo. As none of these had proper chimneys, they would fill with smoke almost to the point of asphyxiation.

Atheromatous disease of the arteries is also a common finding in mummies. Nowadays, a great deal of emphasis is placed on the stress of modern life or on modern diet as factors in the high incidence of this disorder in our present-day industrialized civilization, but the etiological influences were certainly there in the ancient world, and this fact should be taken into account in any theorizing regarding causation.

At the time the autopsy was performed, the perforated eardrum and the disease of the temporal bone in PUM II were the earliest known records of these conditions. Since then, additional finds have been reported by Benitez and Lynn (Chapter 18) and by Horne et al. (1976) in Egyptian mummies, and the same condition was discovered in the Chinese princess described in Chapter 13. In certain areas of the world, temporal bone disease was apparently not uncommon.

Barraco's recovery of protein with a molecular weight of 150,000 is a major step forward in biochemical studies of ancient tissues. It raises the possibility and practicality of demonstrating many large molecules such as gamma globulins and hemoglobins in well-preserved bodies from the past, particularly frozen ones. Once this is done, a whole new frontier of science will open up.

The periostitis of the right fibula and tibia poses a problem that has not yet been solved, though the radiologists suggest that it may be attributable to a chronic condition like varicose veins.

Trace elements were studied by Nunnelley et al. (1976) and by Smith (1974). No conclusions can be derived from examination of a single body, but the pointers for future work are valuable. First, the trace element analysis showed that the resin had penetrated not only the body cavities of PUM II but also the tissues themselves. Smith found that the lead level was only one-tenth that of today, whereas the mercury was at modern concentrations. This suggests that our present-day environment may be polluted with lead, compared with Egypt 2,000 years ago.

The low zinc level in PUM II's muscle may be significant, for it is not uncommon in modern Egypt. Obviously one should not use a single mummy as a basis for conclusions regarding a whole population. Still, the data are interesting.

The cotton ball was a startling discovery. Cotton was grown and used by 2000 B.C. both in South America and in the Indus Valley of India, but it was unknown in the Mediterranean world and Persia until after the time of Christ. Was this cotton ball imported as a valuable object from India or was it grown in Egypt? The find poses a whole series of new questions regarding trade routes and agriculture for which there are as yet no answers.

The analysis of the resin by Coughlin (1977) is another striking piece of work, for she has not only named the components of the fluid by tree, but has even located their sources with some accuracy. In addition, her identification of the resin with glass is a fascinating observation. The idea that the Egyptians' development of glass may have resulted from their experiences in heating together natron and other substances for the purpose of mummification is a new concept and is worth a follow-up study by someone interested in the history of glass making.

Finally, the superb condition of PUM II's tissues is a tribute to the skills and techniques of the Egyptian embalmers. There is little sign of decay. Embedded in "glass," which has perfused every tissue, there is no reason why this body, as long as it is kept in either a dry warm or a cold place, should not continue to survive to the end of time. For a parallel, we can look at insects embalmed in amber from the Baltic Sea: They have been preserved for 30 million years already and could easily survive another 30 million. PUM II, if left undisturbed, could do the same.

REFERENCES

Bowen, H. J. M. 1966. *Trace elements in biochemistry*. New York: Academic Press.

Cockburn, T. A. 1963. *The evolution and eradication of infectious diseases*. Baltimore: Johns Hopkins University Press.

Cockburn, A. 1973. Death and disease in ancient Egypt. *Science* 181:470.

Cockburn, A.; Barraco, R. A.; Reyman, T. A.; and Peck, W. H. 1975. Autopsy of an Egyptian mummy. *Science* 187:1155–60.

Coughlin, E. A. 1977. Analysis of PUM II mummy fluid. *Paleopathology Newsletter* 17:7–8.

Fischer, H. 1974. Quoted in A. Cockburn, R. A. Barraco, T. A. Reyman, and W H. Peck. Autopsy of an Egyptian mummy. *Science* 187:1155–60, 1975.

Goldwater, L. J. 1972. *Mercury: a history of quicksilver*. Baltimore: Fork.

Horne, P. D.; Mackay, A.; John, A. F.; and Hawke, M. 1976. Histologic processing and examination of a 4,000 year old human temporal bone. *Archives of Otolaryngology*. 102:713–15.

Johnson, M. 1974. Quoted in A. Cockburn, R. A. Barraco, T. A. Reyman, and W. H. Peck. Autopsy of an Egyptian mummy. *Science* 187:1155–60, 1975.

Kehoe, R. A. 1961. The metabolism of lead in man in health and disease. *Journal of the Royal Institute of Public Health and Hygiene* 24:1–40.

Miller, J. I. 1969. *The spice trade of the Roman Empire*. London: Oxford University Press.

Nunnelley, L. L.; Smythe, W. R.; Trish, J. H. V.; and Alfrey, A. C. 1976. Trace element analysis of tissue and resin from Egyptian mummy PUM II. *Paleopathology Newsletter* 12:12–14.

Smith, R. G. 1974. Quoted in A. Cockburn, R. A. Barraco, T. A. Reyman, and W. H. Peck. Autopsy of an Egyptian mummy. *Science* 187:1155–60, 1975.

Stuckenrath, R. 1974. Quoted in A. Cockburn, R. A. Barraco, T. A. Reyman, and W. H. Peck. Autopsy of an Egyptian mummy. *Science* 187:1155–60, 1975.

5

ROM I: mummification for the common people

NICHOLAS B. MILLET
Curator, Egyptian Department
Royal Ontario Museum,
Toronto, Ontario, Canada

GERALD D. HART
Physician-in-Chief
Toronto East General Hospital,
Toronto, Ontario, Canada

THEODORE A. REYMAN
Director of Laboratories
Mount Carmel Mercy Hospital,
Detroit, Michigan, U.S.A.

MICHAEL R. ZIMMERMAN
Associate Professor,
Departments of Anthropology and Pathology
University of Michigan,
Ann Arbor, Michigan, U.S.A.

PETER K. LEWIN
Hospital for Sick Children
Toronto, Ontario, Canada

Herodotus mentions that the least expensive form of mummification was that where no treatment was given and the body was simply wrapped in linen. ROM I, autopsied in Toronto in August 1974, was just such a mummy, and it proved to be one of the most interesting studied by our group. The name is shorthand for the Royal Ontario Museum, to which the mummy belongs. The autopsy was an international operation, a demonstration in cooperation among the Toronto Academy of Medicine, the Royal Ontario Museum, and the Detroit group of the Paleopathology Association, with literally dozens of workers involved. The participants are named in reports published elsewhere (Hart et al. 1977; Millet et al. 1978), and those playing major roles are listed at the end of this chapter. The study arose as the result of a lecture on PUM II given by Aidan Cockburn and Theodore A. Reyman in February 1974 at the Academy of Medicine in Toronto. The following day, Eve Cockburn suggested a joint Canadian – United States project, and the day after that Nicholas B. Millet offered to lend a mummy from the collection of the Royal Ontario Museum.

The examination was carried out in a laboratory at the anatomy department in the Medical Sciences Building, University of Toronto. The proceedings were recorded by means of still photography, 16-mm color film,

and videotape. The body was unwrapped by Millet and the museum staff in August 1974, and the autopsy was directed by Reyman, Zimmerman, and Lewin. Radiology studies by D. F. Rideout had been completed some days before the unwrapping.

After the autopsy, the tissue specimens were divided among those participants who were interested. This had the advantage of ensuring greater coverage in the search for abnormalities. For example, Lewin reported Schistosoma haematobium ova in the liver; Zimmerman found them in the kidney as well as red cells in the bladder; and Reyman discovered ova in the intestine and cirrhosis in the liver. All these related findings gave a fairly clear picture of a single disease that would not have been obtained by a solitary worker.

THE MUMMY

In the winter of 1904–1905 Dr. C. T. Currelly, founder of the Royal Ontario Museum, was attached to the Egypt Exploration Fund's expedition at Deir el-Bahri, across the river from modern Luxor, where he assisted at the excavation of the funerary temple of Menthuhotep II, a king of the Eleventh Dynasty (ca. 2010 B.C.). All the tomb chambers in the temple area had been robbed in antiquity, and

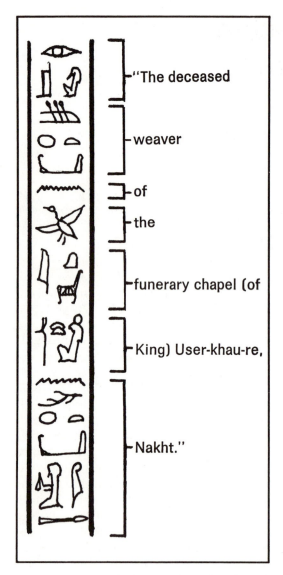

"The deceased

weaver

of

the

funerary chapel (of

King) User-khau-re,

Nakht."

Figure 5.1.   Hieroglyphics on the coffin, describing Nakht. (From Hart et al. 1977)

ner, with planks and small pieces of wood, probably sycamore. The lid, which is carved in anthropoid shape, shows the deceased wearing a long wig striped in blue; his forearms and clenched hands are executed in relief. The whole exterior of the coffin, except the bottom, is covered with a thin coating of gypsum plaster and gaily painted with the usual scenes and inscriptions. Time and the excreta of bats have eroded much of the lid's surface, but the scenes on the box itself are well preserved. The texts inscribed on it (Figure 5.1) tell us that the owner was a male named Nakht, invariably described as "weaver of the kny-temple of User-khau-re." User-khau-re was the throne name of the king Setnakht, the first ruler of the Twentieth Dynasty, who died about 1198 B.C. after a brief reign, leaving the throne to his son, the great Pharaoh Rameses III. The latter established a funerary cult for his dead father on the west bank at Thebes, which was carried on in a mortuary chapel of the type called kny, a word meaning both "armchair" and "carrying chair" or "sedan chair." The name seems to refer to either a statue of the deceased god-king in a palanquin or an empty thronelike chair over which the spirit of the dead ruler was thought to hover. The chapel's staff of priests and laymen and the regular food offerings for the dead pharaoh's spirit depended on the income from the land with which it was endowed. The fact that the establishment of King Setnakht's chapel included weavers suggests that some of the land was used to grow flax, linen being the common cloth of Egypt in those days. Setnakht's funerary chapel was still being maintained as late as the second regnal year of Rameses IV, about 1164 B.C., and may have continued in being for a century more. The style of Nakht's coffin suggests that it was made in the first half of the twelfth century B.C.

From the historian's point of view, Nakht's mummy was a natural choice for autopsy; there is a good account of its discovery and

many had been used in later times by humbler people. It was in one of these that the coffin of Nakht was found. Although the date the mummy was acquired by the museum is not known, we must assume that its acquisition was directly attributable to Dr. Currelly's presence at the time of the excavation.

The coffin was built in the traditional man-

excavation, and the texts and the style of the coffin provide unusually clear evidence of its date. The simple title "weaver" shows that Nakht was a person of the laboring class and was far more representative of the great mass of the ancient population than most mummies, which tend to be of persons from the middle classes or the aristocracy, because these persons were better able to afford the considerable expense of a traditional Egyptian burial. Finally, we are probably better informed about Nakht's times – the last century of the New Kingdom, whose imperial glories had by this day faded and given way to dreary years of political confusion, moral uncertainty, and spiraling inflation – than we are about any other period of Egyptian history.

Nakht's lower-class family apparently had been able to afford a relatively fine coffin because he had not undergone the expensive process of mummification that included removal of the viscera, but had simply been washed and wrapped in linen (the good preservation of his body was owing entirely to the peculiarly dry and stable Egyptian climate). By omitting mummification, his family had been able to spend more of their presumably slender resources on the coffin itself. The records of this time note that workmen were sometimes given time off to construct the coffin of a deceased member of their guild or group, so cooperative effort may have reduced some of the expense. The cost of decorating such a coffin in Nakht's day was approximately 31 g of silver, representing as much as 10 percent of a working family's yearly income, so his grieving parents must have been willing to sacrifice a great deal to see their young son suitably interred.

Although the body had been carefully wrapped in linen in the traditional manner, the amount of linen used was noticeably less than in many mummies of the period. The bandages were in very good condition and came away easily, chiefly because none of the usual sacral oils had been poured over the body. The manner in which the bandages and filling pads had been arranged suggests familiarity with ritual custom and hints at a professional hand, but the poor people of western Thebes in the twelfth century B.C. may have attained a certain expertise in wrapping their own dead simply from necessity. The wrappings were well preserved in all parts of the mummy except the head, where they had broken through entirely, probably more as a result of the collapse of the cranial vault beneath them than from interference by tomb robbers (Figure 5.2). Several of the pads contained in the wrappings proved to be more or less complete garments; two large, sleeveless tuniclike robes of a type familiar to us from wall paintings and sculpture of the period represent the characteristic male costume (Figure 5.3). Their size is about right for Nakht himself, and his family probably contributed some of his clothing to provide wrapping material. Each piece of cloth was carefully scrutinized for laundry or owner's marks, but none was found.

Surviving records of the community, labor rolls and fragments of official day books, tell us something of the physical conditions under which Nakht lived during his short life. Nakht's house was probably not at Deir el-Medina but nearer his place of burial, in the Asasif valley below the Deir el-Bahri temples, and nearer the cultivation on the east. Since he was in his middle teens when he died, he was probably what the official records of his day describe as a *mnh* or "stripling," a youth of employable age but still unmarried and living in his parents' home and drawing a smaller ration allowance (wages being paid in kind) than the head of a family. The house in which he lived was probably similar to excavated samples, consisting of two or three rooms of mud brick with a flat roof of earth on rafters of palm logs, plus a small courtyard. His diet and general standard of living would have been better than those of most of the peasant cultivators who composed the bulk of the population, and by any reckoning he must have been in the upper

Figure 5.2. *Mummy before unwrapping. Note the broken skull.*

ranks of the working class. In addition, he enjoyed the security derived from being attached to a permanent and prestigious institution, which may have exempted him from conscription for military service or forced labor and may have protected him from the economic troubles that afflicted the kingdom in his time.

RADIOLOGIC FINDINGS

The subject was a male teenager, but more exact determination of age was difficult because desiccation had widened some epiphyseal lines and narrowed others, so that the hip joints suggested age 18 and the knees age 14. The left knee showed unfused epiphyses and Harris's lines suggesting episodes of infection or malnutrition during life. The hands were not well shown because they overlapped the pelvis. As far as could be seen, they corresponded with a modern standard of age 14 years, so it was reasonably certain that Nakht was between 14 and 18 years of age at the time of his death. The wisdom teeth were

well developed but unerupted. All the other teeth were accounted for and in good condition, although the upper incisors had fallen into the wrappings postmortem.

The pelvis was of male configuration, but appeared to show protrusio acetabuli. As there was no other evidence of rickets or osteomalacia, this change was probably caused by postmortem bending of an unfused Y-cartilage in the acetabulum. This conclusion was confirmed by a xeroradiograph, which showed the cartilage space where the conventional film did not. It was also later confirmed at autopsy.

X rays of the chest showed a mass in the center and to the right that was too large for a desiccated heart and was assumed to represent the heart and liver adhering together. Patchy opacity in both hemithoraxes suggested the remains of lung tissue adhering to the posterior chest wall. Tomography confirmed the position of these masses within the body cavity and also showed linear opacities – an intact diaphragm – between abdomen and thorax.

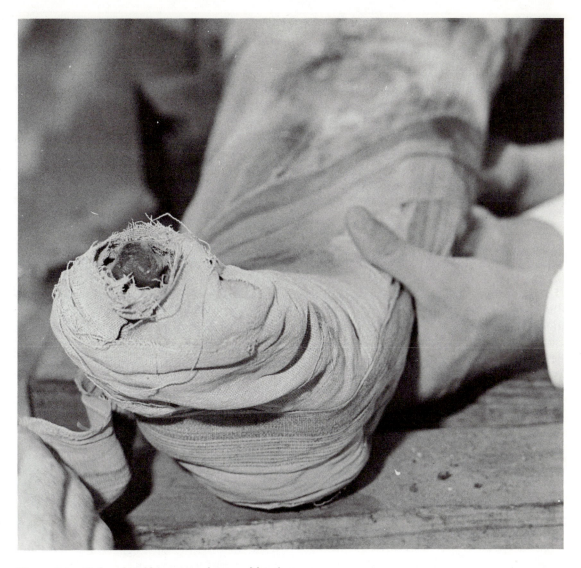

Figure 5.3. Robe of Nakht wrapped around his feet.

Between the shrunken tissues and the wrappings there was an air-containing gap up to 4 cm across. This indicated that desiccation occurred after wrapping. Harris's lines in the lower 1.5 cm of the distal femoral metaphyses suggested recurrent severe illness in the last 2 years of his life.

Radiological examination gave no evidence that Nakht had been eviscerated or even embalmed. He had desiccated naturally in the dry, hot air of Thebes. Apart from the rather doubtful evidence of Harris's or growth arrest lines, there was no radiological clue to the cause of death.

GROSS ANATOMY

A general study showed that the wrappings of the head had been removed earlier and that the skull had been damaged (Figure 5.2). In addition, the cranial sutures had not united, and the skull bones had collapsed inwardly and the facial features disintegrated. This gave a first impression of decapitation. However, the pieces of broken bone were recovered from the wrappings.

The body showed no evidence of artificial preservation by means of natron, oils, or bitumen. The body, which was firm, demonstrated an atypical rigor mortis (it could be lifted like a board). The intact body weighed only 5.13 kg, and the overall length was 143.1 cm.

Circumferential measurements of upper and lower extremities before and after unwrapping revealed a shrinkage of 17 cm at the midarm level and of 16.8 cm at the knees. This shrinkage, which could also be seen on the X-ray plates, indicated that the dehydration that had preserved the body had occurred after it had been wrapped.

The skin was a light café-au-lait color and had a tough, leathery consistency. At areas of fissuring, the muscles were visible and had a crumbly, friable consistency. The whorls and ridges on the fingers and toes were preserved. The toeprints were very well preserved and easy to see. The fingernails and toenails were also well preserved.

The autopsy began with a special study of the remnants of the head and neck area. The disturbed wrappings acted as a receptacle to contain the various structures. The skull bones were carefully retrieved and the skull was subsequently reconstructed. On some areas of the frontal and parietal bones the scalp, with hairs 2 mm long, was still adherent. The imprint of the ears was present in the head wrappings, where many loose hairs were also found. The left eye socket was covered with a thin, translucent film on which eyelashes were identified. The teeth showed some wear, but were well preserved and did not show evidence of caries. Three teeth had become dislodged and were later retrieved from under the wrappings of the back and lower extremities.

The cerebral hemispheres were found lying in the base of the skull (Figure 5.4). The left hemisphere weighed 61.6 g and measured 9 by 7 by 2.5 cm. The right hemisphere weighed 66.15 g and measured 8 by 6 by 2.5 cm. The hemispheres were dark brown, firm in consistency, and had a soapy feel. The convolutions were preserved and best seen on the inferior surface. The sigmoid sinus was identified, and dark rusty brown material suggesting dried blood was adherent to the internal lining. The mandible remained in position supported by the cervical structures. There was a postmortem transverse fracture of the neck of the mandible just below the left condyle.

The thorax was opened with the assistance of a Stryker saw. This cut through the leathery skin and the anterior lateral rib margins so that the anterior chest wall could be removed in toto. This gave a unique anatomical demonstration of the pericardium and its attachments (Figure 5.5). The ligaments had been preserved, but the fat had disappeared. The pericardium appeared as a tent tethered between the sternum and the thoracic spine. The lungs had collapsed posteriorly, and it was not possible to distinguish the upper and lower lobes. They were grey black and of a powdery consistency. The aortic arch was transected, and the heart and mediastinum were removed. The heart with the great veins and arteries weighed 17.7 g.

The trachea was identified and removed with the thyroid cartilage. The intact diaphragm was dark brown and its consistency was firm and leathery. It was cut around its periphery and removed. The anterior abdominal wall was then removed in toto. Internally, the wall was connected to the liver by the round ligament. The liver was shrunken, but had retained its shape and had a sharp lower border. It measured 12.5 by 7.5 by 3 cm and weighed 106.3 g. Portions of the gallbladder were removed.

The spleen was present and, taking into account the amount of shrinkage of other organs, was enlarged. It was crumbly and so could not be weighed in toto. The posterior

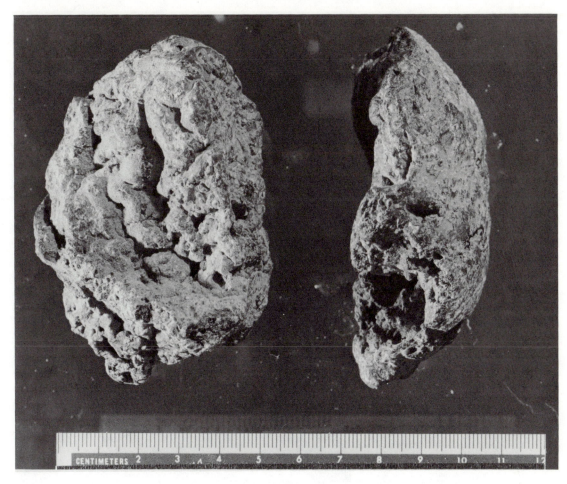

Figure 5.4.   *Cerebral hemispheres showing some of the convolutions well preserved.*

and lateral walls of the splenic bed showed a dark discoloration, possibly representing hemorrhage from a splenic rupture. The intestines were paper-thin and collapsed. The bladder was a saclike hollow structure measuring 6 cm at its widest point. The prostate was not identified. The rectum passed through the pelvic cavity; it was desiccated and very fragile. Removal of the posterior pelvic peritoneum displayed the anatomical details of the sacral plexus excellently preserved. The penis was noncircumcised. The scrotum could be identified, but testicular material was not found.

HISTOLOGIC FINDINGS

The heart and brain were not processed in detail, because they had to be retained for permanent display. The other tissue specimens were rehydrated in modified Ruffer's solution and processed in the same way as fresh tissue. Sections were stained with hematoxylin and eosin, Masson's trichrome, periodic acid–Schiff, acid-fast, Grocott's methenamine silver, elastic tissue, and alizarin red staining techniques, and examined with polarized light (Chapter 15). Histological detail of the tissues was preserved to a

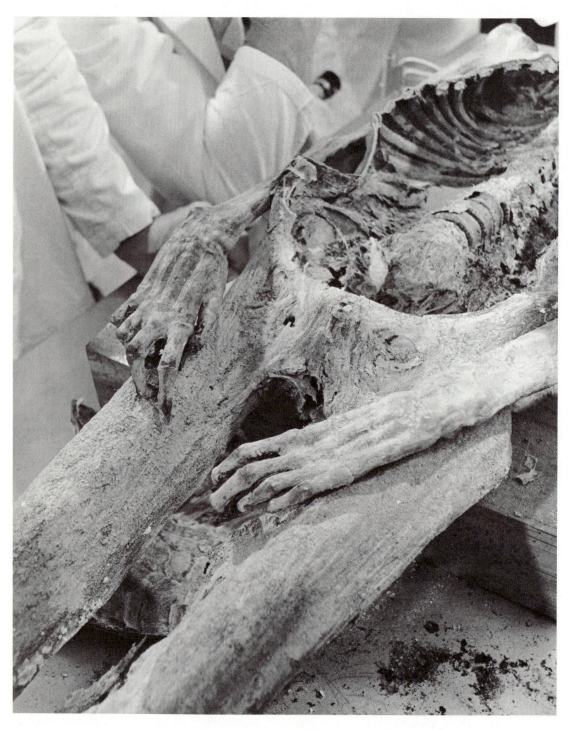

Figure 5.5   Trunk and hands after removal of the organs.

variable degree, although distinct cellular outlines were generally lost. The tissues were infiltrated with numerous saprophytic invaders, both bacterial and fungal, but these organisms could not be cultured.

In the lungs the alveolar architecture was partially preserved, and there was marked deposition of anthracotic pigment within connective tissue. Throughout the tissue, bright birefringent particles were noted; however, the results of silica analyses on lung tissue were normal. Electron microscope microprobe diffraction analysis at University College, Cardiff, Wales, by Dr. E. Pooley, suggests that these particles are granite.

The muscle coats of the intestinal tract at various levels were well preserved. The lumens of both large and small intestines contained numerous ova of both *Schistosoma* spp. and *Taenia* spp. (Chapter 15). Some of the *Schistosoma* ova had large terminal spines. No adult worms of either type were seen, but the *Taenia* ova were clumped together, suggesting the site of degenerated proglottids.

The liver showed preservation of cords of indistinct hepatic parenchyma and a fibrous pattern of early cirrhosis. Thick and thin fibrous septa were common, and the organ contained occasional small nodules of parenchyma. Portal areas contained calcified *Schistosoma* ova with terminal spines similar to those noted in the intestinal lumen. The spleen was poorly preserved and showed heavy postmortem microbial contamination. No malarial pigment was seen. Sections of the gallbladder were poorly preserved. Histologically, the brain was poorly preserved as well. Sections from the myocardium, a coronary artery, and an aortic valve were normal. The various components of the kidney were not well preserved, but several *Schistosoma* ova were seen. The bladder revealed remnants of epithelium. We found no ova or changes suggesting inflammation, but a few well-preserved red blood cells on the mucosal surface suggested hematuria during life.

Postmortem examination of this 3,200-year-old mummy of a teenage Egyptian boy revealed a variety of disease processes. He had at least two types of parasitic infestation, both of which may have produced severe complications.

Numerous ova of *Taenia* spp. were found within the intestinal tract. As the ova of *T. solium* and *T. saginata* cannot be differentiated and no scolex was found, no final decision can be made concerning the type of infestation.

Many schistosomal ova were also found, several with the large terminal spines diagnostic of *S. haematobium* and others without obvious spines. These ova may be degenerated forms or may be *S. mansoni*. Both forms of schistosomiasis are endemic in modern Egypt, and *S. haematobium* has been reported in other Egyptian remains. There was evidence of early cirrhosis of the liver and congestive splenomegaly, possibly with terminal rupture. Schistosomal ova were found in the liver, suggesting that the cirrhosis was secondary to hepatic schistosomiasis. Though *S. mansoni* is the commonest offending parasite, *S. haematobium* may give the same picture in the liver. The calcified ova in the kidney and the presence of blood within the urinary bladder also indicate involvement of this system with *S. haematobium*.

Finding tapeworm ova is also of interest, implying as it does that Nakht ate meat, and probably meat that was not well cooked. Meat fibers have been found in the intestine of another mummy, so ancient Egyptians were probably not strict vegetarians. In any case, the associated malnutrition probably contributed to the youth's demise. The presence of Harris's lines in the leg bones supports this thesis.

An incidental finding, present in almost all ancient remains, is pulmonary anthracosis, which is attributable to environmental pollution from cooking and heating fires and from oil lamps in small rooms. It is also possible that this boy had pulmonary silicosis resulting from inhalation of sand during a sandstorm.

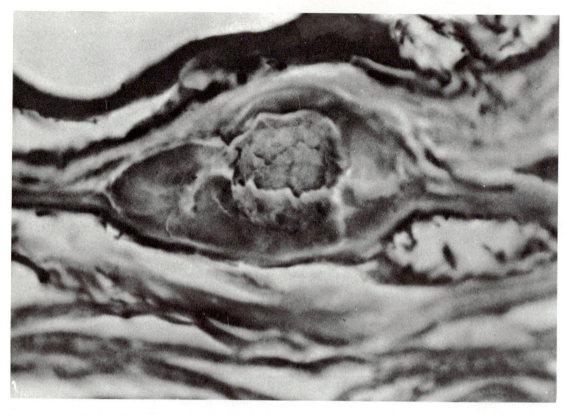

Figure 5.6.   Trichinella *cyst found in intercostal muscle.*

Near the subcutaneous border of an intercostal muscle a small cyst was found, just visible to the naked eye (Figure 5.6). This cyst has the appearance of a parasite. At first, *Cysticercus cellulosae* (the larva of *Taenia solium*) was considered, but these cysts are about 5 mm in diameter and much larger than the muscle fibers. The cyst is small to be that of *Trichinella spiralis*, but it is appropriate when compared with the muscle fibers. The small size could be the result of shrinkage during drying. *Trichinella* infestation, like cysticercosis, is caused by eating inadequately cooked pork, and the finding of this cyst suggests that Nakht ate pork.

EXAMINATION OF TEMPORAL BONES

The temporal bones were examined (Lynn and Benitez 1977) by means of polytomog-

raphy and studied under the operating microscope to determine whether ear disease that might have occurred during his lifetime could still be identified (Chapter 18).

The foramen of Huschke was an obvious defect in the temporal bone. As noted by others, its pathological significance is unknown. The ossicles in both temporal bones were dislodged from their normal position in the middle ear cavity. However, they were normally formed and showed no signs of the destructive effects of chronic middle ear disease or mass lesions. It would therefore appear that such ossicular dislocations represented a postmortem artifact. As X rays with polytomography revealed normal air cell system throughout the mastoid regions and no increased density attributable to sclerosis in the area of the oval windows, it seems certain that Nakht did not suffer from chronic middle ear disease or otosclerosis in either ear during

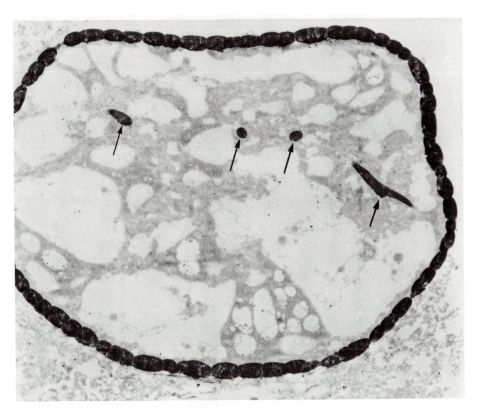

Figure 5.7.   *Electron micrograph showing* Taenia sp. *ova. Three of the hooklets have been cut in cross section; the fourth is seen in full view.* × 5,800. *(Courtesy of Patrick Horne, Banting Institute.)*

his lifetime. Furthermore, no bony changes were evident in the inner ears or internal auditory canals, thus indicating the absence of such destructive lesions as neoplasm or congenital malformations.

Examination of each temporal bone with the Zeiss operating microscope confirmed the abnormal position of the ossicles that had been observed radiographically. Although the three ossicles in the right ear were grossly displaced in position, they were normal in form and showed no signs of erosion or destruction, as would have been the case if Nakht had suffered from chronic otitis media, cholesteatoma, or other destructive lesions of the middle ear.

ELECTRON MICROSCOPIC FINDINGS

Tissue samples were taken from the sole of Nakht's right foot and rehydrated in buffered 10 percent formalin. Dry, dustlike intestinal contents were spun in normal saline to obtain a button of material and were rehydrated in Sandison's modification of Ruffer's solution consisting of two parts 5 percent sodium carbonate (aqueous), three parts 96 percent ethyl alcohol, and five parts 1 percent formalin. The epidermis of the skin was well preserved, and cellular components were easily recognized. The intestinal contents contained several ova of *Taenia* spp., which at the ultrastructural level demonstrated in great detail the striated embryophore of an egg with its hooklets (Figure 5.7). Figure 5.8 shows a red cell found in the intestinal contents as visualized with a scanning electron microscope. These observations confirm earlier reports that Egyptian mummified material contains preserved cells with recognizable cytoplasmic organelles.

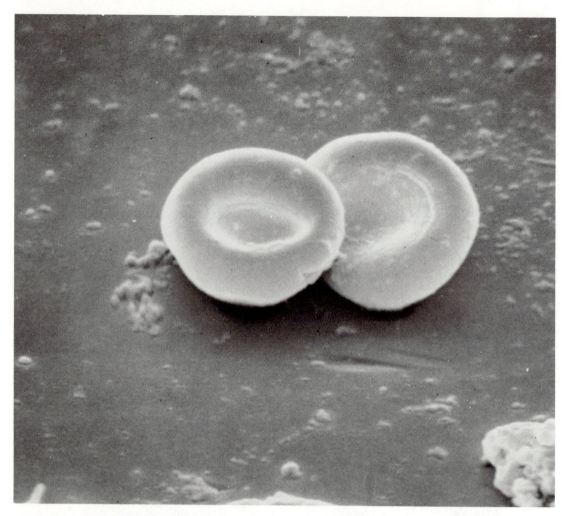

Figure 5.8.   Scanning electron micrographs of red cells. × 23,700.
(Courtesy of Patrick Horne, Banting Institute.)

BLOOD GROUP TESTING

Splenic material and a dark brown substance from the inside of the sigmoid sinus of the boy Nakht were tested with both the serological micromethod (SMM) and the inhibition agglutination tests (IAT). Repeated testing of the splenic material using SMM produced no agglutination, and the procedure was complicated by hemolysis of the absorbed group O cells. However, when splenic material was used in the IAT, a positive result for blood group B was obtained. The sigmoid sinus material showed a positive reaction for blood group B with both SMM and IAT.

There was no explanation for these results until histological sections of the spleen and the sigmoid sinus were studied. The splenic material was heavily contaminated by bacterial and fungal spores, which were hemolytic to the group O test cells. Hence, the presence of B antigen in the splenic material could not be demonstrated by absorption into group O cells, but was detectable by the IAT. Histological sections of the sigmoid sinus showed excellent preservation of red cells and absence of bacterial spores. When tested, this material gave a good source of blood group antigen and the tests were not negated by contaminating hemolytic spores.

The preservation of intact red cells for many centuries is not unique. Zimmerman (1971) has reported preservation of intact red cells in the pulmonary vein of a naturally preserved 2,000-year-old American Indian mummy. At this time, the red cells isolated from Nakht are the oldest known preserved human blood cells. The histological findings make us confident that our testing techniques are bona fide and that Nakht's blood group was B.

ANALYSIS OF PROTEIN EXTRACT

Attempts were made to extract, fractionate, and identify proteins and other macromolecular components in the tissues of Nakht. The prime objective was to detect gamma globulins and the antibodies against infectious agents they may contain. In addition, an attempt was made to identify certain lipids, particularly neutral lipids, to determine the dietary milieu of the young weaver. The following paragraphs describe the degree of preservation of proteins in Nakht's tissues and the nature of the process by which he was mummified.

Because it is known that natron and other salts were used for chemical mummification by the ancient Egyptian embalmers (Lucas and Harris 1962), we studied the relationship of Na and other cation levels in Nakht's tissues to the molecular weight distribution (a measure of degradation) of extracted protein from the same tissues. Desiccated aliquots were weighed, ashed, and solubilized in a $SrCl_2$–HCl solution for analysis of Na, K, Ca, and Mg by atomic absorption spectrophotometry (see Table 19.2).

Figure 19.3B shows the chromatographic pattern for protein (extracted by the same procedures) from freshly autopsied human skeletal muscle and for the extracted protein from Nakht. Peak I represents the high-molecular-weight protein (ca. 150,000 daltons); peak II represents proteins of intermediate molecular weight (ca. 60,000); and peak III represents low-molecular-weight protein (ca. 20,000 or less). In Table 19.2 the various tissue cation levels for Nakht and for freshly autopsied human skeletal muscle are represented as micromoles of cation per gram of dry weight of tissue (gdw). Table 19.2 makes it apparent that Nakht was not natronized or chemically treated with other salts, as tissue cation levels approximate closely those of the freshly autopsied specimen. Further, from Figure 19.3 it is apparent that much of the high-molecular-weight protein from Nakht's tissues has undergone degradation, as can be seen by the shift in chromatographic profile toward the lower-molecular-weight region. Of interest here is a previous report (Barraco 1975) that the degree of preservation of extracted protein from mummified tissue is enhanced with increasing levels of Na in the tissues (natron). The percent amino acid composition of extracted protein from Nakht closely approximates that of myoglobin, the major small-molecular-weight protein (ca. 17,000) in skeletal muscle that may be resistant to degradation.

OTHER STUDIES

When nuclear medical techniques were applied to Nakht, whole-body examination of the intact mummy before unwrapping indicated a high concentration of manganese present in the soil and other contaminants adherent to the wrappings. Various samples were cultured aerobically and anaerobically, without significant results. Electron microscope studies of liver tissue did not demonstrate virus particles. Radioimmunoassay of liver tissue was negative for hepatitis B antigen. Studies of craniofacial characteristics and dentition were also carried out at the faculty of dentistry, University of Toronto.

Computerized transaxial tomography (CTT scan) done on the intact brain at the Hospital for Sick Children showed that the gray and white matter had been preserved and that the lateral ventricles were intact. This procedure made destructive examination of the brain unnecessary. Calcified cysts suggesting cerebral cysticercosis were not demonstrated, and therefore a needle biopsy of affected areas was not carried out. This is the first time CTT has been used in paleopathology.

The findings reported here are now part of a teaching exhibit on disease in ancient times, sponsored by the Royal Ontario Museum and the Academy of Medicine. The mummy itself is on display at the academy.

DISCUSSION

The importance of ROM I is that the mummy can be located accurately in time and place. To have actual facts like these is a rare luxury when dealing with antiquity, so the data are priceless. We can now state that in the twelfth century B.C., on the bank of the Nile opposite present-day Luxor, there existed a focus of infection of the parasite *Schistosoma haematobium*. This has been proved: Speculations about the epidemiology of the infection in Egypt can begin with this firm base.

The identity of the tapeworm is less certain, for it could be either the pork or the beef parasite. However, the cyst of *Trichinella spiralis* is definitely pork-related, so the tapeworm is probably the same. This raises the interesting subject of eating pork. In the Middle East today, eating the flesh of the pig is taboo, but many people think that in these cases, as with the cow in India, the animal in question was once regarded as sacred. According to Fraser, in his *Golden Bough*, the pig in Egypt was the totem animal of Osiris. Osiris was killed, rose from the dead, reigned over life after death, and was represented as a mummy. The flesh of the pig was forbidden year-round except on the holy day of Osiris. On that day, everyone ate pork, and even the poor who could not afford meat made cakes resembling pigs and ate them instead. Certainly, the findings from ROM I indicate that 3,000 years ago at least one Egyptian ate pork on at least one occasion.

The most likely explanation for the pork taboo is a religious prohibition, probably going back long before Moses to the dawn of Egyptian history. A modern explanation linking it with hygienic reasons and trichinosis can be dismissed. The parasite *Trichinella spiralis* was not discovered until 1834, and its linking with pigs came two decades later. The human disease was not recognized before that time, nor was its association with pigs. The hygienic theory is probably a modern rationalization for an otherwise inexplicable taboo.

ACKNOWLEDGMENTS

Special sections were contributed by the following persons: radiology, D. F. Rideout; trichinosis, U. de Boni, M. M. Lenczner, and John W. Scott; temporal bones, George E. Lynn and Jaime T. Benitez; electron microscopy, Peter K. Lewin and Patrick Horne; blood group testing, Gerald D. Hart, Inge Kvas, and Marja Soots; analysis of protein extract, Robin A. Barraco; nuclear medical techniques, B. N. Ege and K. G. McNeil; electron microscopy, L. Spence; dentition, Arthur Storey and D. W. Stoneman; computerized transaxial tomography, Derek Harwood-Nash.

REFERENCES

Barraco, R. A. 1975. Preservation of proteins in mummified tissue. *Paleopathology Newsletter* 11:8.

Hart, G. D.; Cockburn, A.; Millet, N. B.; and Scott, J. W. 1977. Autopsy of an Egyptian mummy
– ROM I. *Canadian Medical Association Journal* 117:461–73.

Lucas, A., and Harris, J. 1962. *Ancient Egyptian materials and industries*. London: Edward Arnold.

Lynn, G. E., and Benitez, J. T. 1977. Examination of ears: Autopsy of an Egyptian mummy. *Canadian Medical Association Journal* 117:461–73.

Millet, N. B., and Reyman, T. A. *Nakht: the weaver of Thebes. An archeologic and autopsy study*. Toronto: Royal Ontario Museum. To be published.

Zimmerman, M. R. 1971. Blood cells preserved in a mummy 2,000 years old. *Science* 180:303.

6

Egyptian mummification with evisceration per ano

THEODORE A. REYMAN
Director of Laboratories
Mount Carmel Mercy Hospital
Detroit, Michigan, U.S.A.

WILLIAM H. PECK
Curator of Ancient Art
Detroit Institute of Arts
Detroit, Michigan, U.S.A.

The Egyptian embalmers were masters of their art. The arduous trial-and-error method they employed for 2,000 years resulted in a scientific discipline for preserving bodies (Mokhtar 1973). This embalming technique required long hours of toil, expensive medicants, and fine linen wrappings. The costs were necessarily high. Because the majority of people who were mummified in the early dynasties were royalty or were the rich and influential of the time, this had little importance. However, when the poorer segments of the population were finally allowed the privilege of mummification, these costs were prohibitive. For this reason and perhaps others, a significant number of modifications were made in the classical mummification process, most of which appeared to be designed to reduce the cost and the time involved. Although the external form and appearance of the mummy remained the same, the fact is that mummification for the poor became less a preservative and more a symbolic exercise. The rich were given the specialized care demanded by their wealth; the poor were given only what they could afford. With PUM II, we have seen mummification similar to the classical method. In this chapter, two examples will be presented of a common alternative method of embalming: mummification with evisceration per ano. Both mummies were provided by Dr. David O'Connor, Department of Egyptology, Pennsylvania University Museum, and neither had known provenance or coffin. The first mummy, an adult, was designated PUM

III; the second, a child, PUM IV. They will be described separately.

PUM III

RADIOGRAPHY

Before the unwrapping, the mummy was examined radiographically. The body arrived with the head unwrapped and separated from the body at the level of the fifth cervical vertebral body. This separation appeared to have occurred postmortem.

There was a healed fracture of the second left rib. Harris's, or growth arrest, lines were present in the distal femora. A slight dorsal scoliosis was noted.

The chest cavity showed air contrast, and there were central densities that had the general positions of the heart and mediastinal tissue and collapsed lungs. The hemidiaphragms clearly defined the chest cavities inferiorly. In the lower portion of the right hemithorax, lying on or near the diaphragm, was an irregular density with speckled opaque areas.

The contents of the abdominal portion of the trunk were less well defined. There was a density in the right upper quadrant suggesting the liver, conforming to the smooth outline of the diaphragm. Overlying this and present within the remainder of the abdominal cavity were numerous speckled opacities and irregular densities without pattern or identifiable characteristics. In the pelvis, a double shadow contour centrally suggested the urinary bladder with a central air contrast

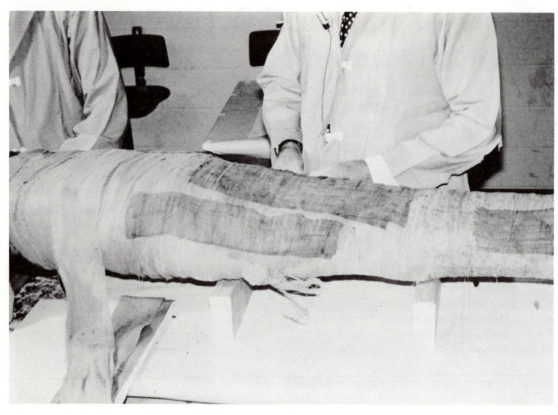

Figure 6.1.   *Dark linen noted in the deeper layers of PUM III's wrappings, used to fill out the body contour. (Photograph by Nemo Warr, Detroit Institute of Arts)*

lumen; uterine shadow was visible directly behind it. Pelvimetry was indeterminate, but the pelvic soft tissue shadows strongly suggested that the mummy was a female. There were numerous irregular wavy air contrast lines within the muscle groups of the thighs, suggesting fissuring of the tissue.

THE WRAPPINGS
The next step was the unwrapping of the mummy. Because the head was already separated from the body and the greater part of the head bandaging was gone, there was no way of knowing how the head had been wrapped. The outer layers of the body wrapping were without decoration and consisted of a medium quality linen apparently torn from larger sheets. Most of these outer bandages were complete strips with a straight woven end and a fringed end that had been torn from a sheet originally 6 or 7 m long. Whenever possible, these individual linen strips were wrapped around rectangular cardboard as they were removed and labeled according to anatomical site and the layer of the wrapping. With care, it was possible to reconstruct whole sheets or parts of sheets from the strips. Intermixed with the first few layers of outer wrappings were small folded pads of a darker and slightly finer linen (Figure 6.1). These were torn from larger pieces, but to no apparent standard. When unfolded, they were generally rectangular, and some could be matched with others to re-form the original larger pieces. The function of these pads, which were generally on or near the front of

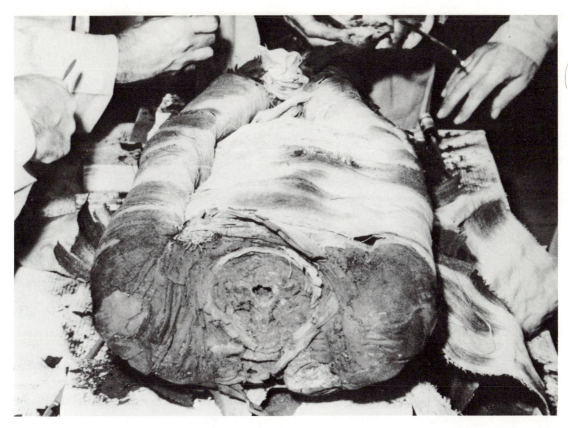

Figure 6.2.   Mummy PUM III viewed from above. The circular bandages around the body enclose the right arm, but not the left. Note the trachea (hole) in the area of the neck from which the head had become separated. The body tissues were so severely degenerated that the arms also became detached inadvertently during the unwrapping. The dark-stained areas on the cloth are the result of chemicals used during the embalming, not of the body fluids. The irregular pieces of cloth between the circular wraps were used to fill out the body contour. (Photograph by Nemo Warr, Detroit Institute of Arts)

the lower body and legs, was to increase the finished size of the body as well as to regularize its outline.

By the fifth layer, the linen material began to show signs of deterioration, possibly from the body fluids, but more likely from liquids used in the wrapping process. After about 10 layers of transverse wrappings, the size of the bandages increased to large sheetlike strips that appeared to have been laid on lengthwise to cover the entire body. At various stages, wood chips, reeds, and fibers were found, all of which were probably accidental inclusions during the wrapping process. Under the large

lengthwise coverings, the wrapping became very irregular, as did the nature of the packing. The spaces between the arms and the body were filled with linen wadding. The legs were bound together with a figure-of-eight continuous bandage, probably to keep the legs together and also to reduce the amount of wadding material necessary. The right arm was bound to the body by a continuous layer of circular bandages; the left arm, at the same stage of wrapping, was not (Figure 6.2). The limbs were individually wrapped, but the fingers and toes were not. The layer of wrapping immediately next to

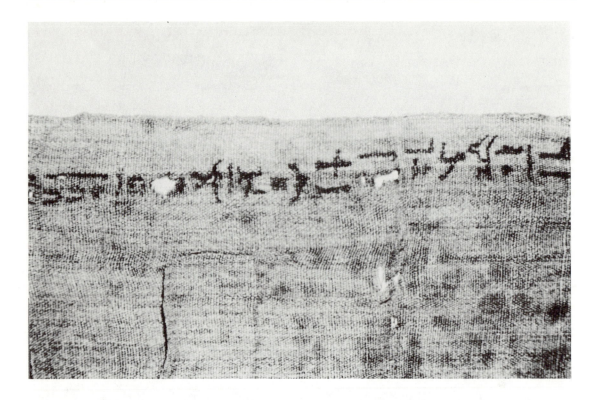

Figure 6.3.   The larger of the two hieroglyphic inscriptions on PUM III's wrappings. See text. (Photograph by Nemo Warr, Detroit Institute of Arts)

the body was crossed over the shoulders and through the pubic area, having been wound around the body from top to bottom. The layers nearest the body were in good condition, suggesting that the intermediate layers, which had partially decomposed, were not affected by body fluids.

The most remarkable part of the wrapping consisted of two pieces of linen that had ink inscriptions (Figure 6.3). The translation of the writing indicates that the owner of the linen was the priest Imyhap, son of Wah-ib-Re. These inscriptions appear not to pertain to the subject mummy, and the wrappings were probably reused fabric. Linen from other areas of the wrapping revealed evidence of wear that seemed to be the result of repeated use.

A disturbing feature was that the ink-inscribed fabric disintegrated within a few days of exposure to air, leaving only holes in

the linen where the inscriptions had been. It was fortunate that several photographs were made of these hieroglyphics.

The time of the mummification has been estimated by Robert Stukenrath of the Carbon Dating Laboratory of the Smithsonian Institution, Washington, D.C., as 835 B.C. (2785 B.P. ± 70 years), following analysis of the cloth wrappings.

GENERAL AUTOPSY FINDINGS

The autopsy was started with some misgiving because of the poor preservation of the body. There was extensive degeneration of the skin of the head, with most of the external parts of the ears missing. Although the external auditory canals appeared normal, there was a perforation of one eardrum, discovered by Lynn and Benitez and described in Chapter 18. The eyes had been either removed or were so severely degenerated that they could not be identified within the orbits, which contained granular packing. The external nasal bones were deformed, with the tip of the nose pushed posteriorly. The teeth were intact. There were no other apparent fractures. The calvarium was removed, and an irregular 2-cm hole was noted in the cribriform bone communicating with the left ethmoid sinus and left nostril. A small plaquelike mass of brown granular tissue was adherent to the inner aspect of the occipital bone and was thought to represent residual brain. When processed by Jeanne Riddle, intact red and white blood cells were discovered within the degenerated tissue. Her findings are discussed in Chapter 16.

The skin of the body was generally poorly preserved. Numerous large and small fissures were noted that extended into the underlying muscles, particularly over the thighs, buttocks, and lower abdomen. A 7- by 4-cm irregular defect was present in the anterior chest wall that communicated with the right chest cavity and appeared to be postmortem in nature. Flattened, discoid breasts were present on the chest wall, but no nipples could be identified. The external genitalia were female, with poorly preserved labia. Large fragments of the labial, perineal, gluteal, and upper thigh tissue broke away from the body with slight manipulation. The arms were inadvertently separated from the body at the shoulder joints during the unwrapping, owing to very poor tissue preservation. The legs were loosely held at the hip joints. The overall configuration of the body was normal. No flank or abdominal incision was noted. The fingernails were slightly discolored and reddish brown.

The chest plate was removed; the heart, mediastinal connective tissue, and thoracic aorta were intact and were removed en bloc. The lungs were collapsed and adherent to the posterior thoracic wall and to the anterior and lateral aspects of the middle thoracic vertebral bones. They were black, brittle, and fragmented easily during removal. The tissue had a honeycomb appearance, and discrete holes

in the tissue suggested bronchi. Each lung measured approximately 10 by 6 by 1 cm.

The superior surface of the diaphragm was covered by a thin layer of black material, and the right hemidiaphragm contained a central defect through which protruded a piece of irregularly folded cloth that was impregnated with black resinous material. When the abdominal skin was removed, the entire abdominal cavity was found to be packed full of large wads of resin-soaked linen. The liver was displaced and flattened upward and laterally (Figure 6.4). The surface was irregular and the tissue itself was hard and black and without detail. The liver measured approximately 20 by 10 by 4 cm.

The remainder of the abdominal tissue was flattened posteriorly, and no organs could be identified. Tissue was removed from the areas normally occupied by spleen and kidneys. In the pelvis, the urinary bladder and the uterus were removed. The ovoid bladder contained a central lumen, the entire structure measuring 6 by 4 cm. The uterus measured 5 by 3 cm and had tissue on the lateral aspects that ran to the lateral pelvic walls in the position of the broad ligaments. Deep in the pelvis, there was a large defect in the area of the rectum and anus. No intestinal tissue could be identified. Apparently the defect in the area of the anus was the passage used to stuff the linen wads into the abdominal and pelvic cavities. The vertebral column and the spinal canal were normal. No spinal cord was present.

EXAMINATION OF THE HEAD

Following the completion of the autopsy, the head of PUM III was examined in detail by Drs. Richard K. Wesley and Edwin Secord, School of Dentistry, University of Detroit. Their report reads:

Cephalometric analysis of the skull indicated that PUM III exhibits a slight protrusion of the maxilla, compared with modern Caucasian standards, and that the mandible is in a normal relationship to the cranial base. This results in protrusion of the maxilla relative to the mandible – a class II skeletal

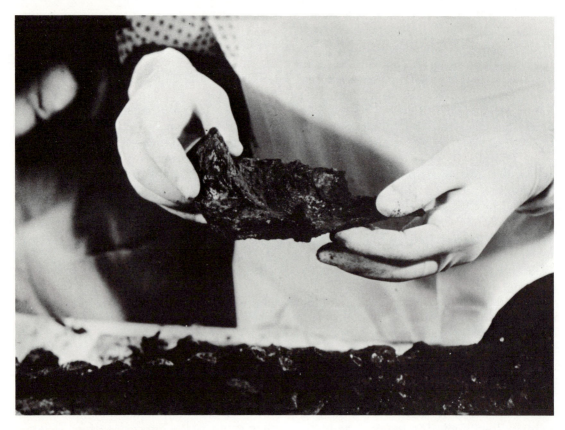

Figure 6.4.   *The liver of PUM III as it was being removed. It has the appearance of being carbonized. (Photograph by Nemo Warr, Detroit Institute of Arts)*

relationship. Morphology of the body and ramus of the mandible is normal. The vertical relationship of the body of the mandible to the cranial base is also normal. The upper and lower incisors are in an upright position relative to the mandibular and maxillary arches as well as to each other. The molars are in an end-to-end, or class II, relationship. A 6-mm overbite of the incisors is a result of this class II dental relationship. The facial profile, estimated on the basis of the underlying skeletal and dental pattern (Figure 6.5), includes the well-formed bony chin and prominent nasal bones typical of the eastern Mediterranean people.

Clinical and radiographic evaluation of the dentition indicates severe occlusal attrition as well as significant interproximal wear. Normal cusp morphology is lacking on all teeth, especially the molars. Severe wear is especially noticeable on the first mandibular and maxillary molars, which usually are larger than the second molar, but in this case are smaller in mesiodistal size. The severe occlusal attrition of the dentition is attributable primarily to a coarse and gritty diet consumed over a prolonged period of time, not to bruxism from contraction of the muscles of mastication. This is evidenced by the lack of antegonial notching of the mandible. A moderate degree of alveolar bone loss is present around all teeth, and no calculus was found. We theorize that this loss of alveolar bone must be secondary to occlusal trauma. There is

Figure 6.5.   a. *Soft tissue detail of the facial profile of PUM III, estimated from the bony structure.* b. *Profile of the head. (a, courtesy of Dr. R. Wesley, University of Detroit Dental School; b, photograph by John Levis, Mount Carmel Mercy Hospital)*

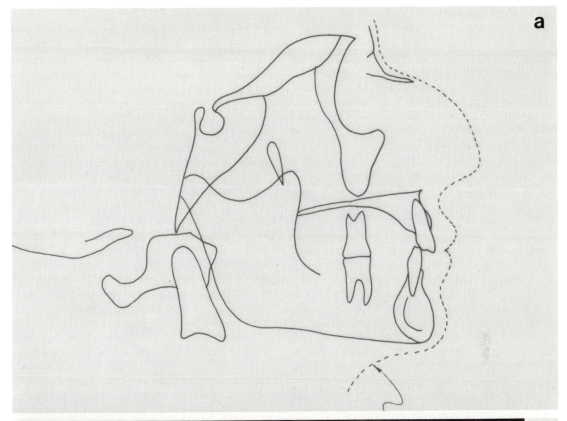

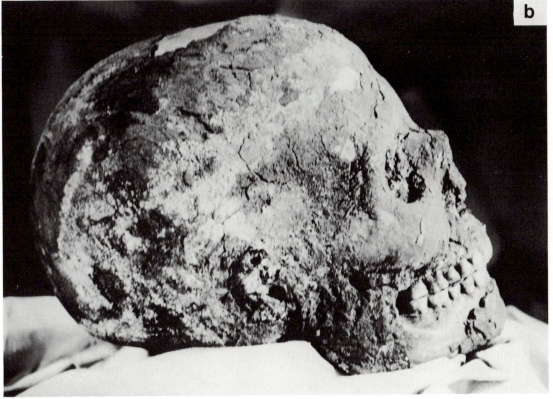

congenital absence of all third molars, and no caries or dental restorations are present. The morphology of the cervical vertebrae indicated that the individual had completed skeletal maturation, and the attrition of the dentition suggested that PUM III was in the third or fourth decade of life at the time of death.

EXAMINATION OF THE BONES

Dr. Michael Finnegan, Osteology Laboratory, Kansas State University, Manhattan, Kansas, submitted this report:

Sex. Recent experiences with mummies have proved interesting in terms of assessing the sex of the individual. Even after the unwrapping is complete, the sex may not be obvious in terms of the soft parts remaining. For example, do we have a penis and a scrotum flattened up against the pelvis or do we have the two labia minora elongated and flattened up against the pelvis? Under such conditions, it is best to look at the bony skeleton to determine the sex of the individual.

The width of the greater sciatic notch was utilized to ascertain the sex of this individual on the basis of X-ray examination of the skeleton before the unwrapping. The greater sciatic notch of the innominate bone was extremely broad, suggesting female. Care must be used in taking many of the angular measurements for skeletal determination of sex from radiographs because the exact position of the skeleton during X-ray examination is not always known. When the greater sciatic notch is seen as extremely broad, it is a very good indicator of femaleness, even in an X ray. The converse of this, however, cannot be used alone to determine maleness. On the basis of width of the greater sciatic notch, the mummy was judged to be female. The width of the subpubic arch is also a reliable indicator of sex, but the angle of the pelvis hinders such an approach in a radiograph. A well-developed preauricular sulcus was noted in the X rays on both sides of the sacrum, and in each case the sulcus was eroded, suggesting femaleness.

The skeleton in general suggests a female individual. Once the skeleton was unwrapped and autopsied, the subpubic angle was found definitely to be female. Based on Phenice's criteria (1969), the fine morphology of the pelvis was also female. The left femur head diameter was 40.5 mm, which would suggest a female individual.

Age. At the time of the autopsy, I had suggested that the appearance of suture closures suggested an age of 25 to 30 years, based on the limited amount of sutures that could be seen on the cranium owing to covering of soft tissue. However, as Brooks (1955) has pointed out, suture closure is relatively unreliable as an age indicator. At the end of the autopsy, the pubic symphyses were cut away and returned to our laboratory so that we could assess age based on the pubic symphysis. Also, a section of the right femur was taken for use in determining age by thin-section techniques. Examination of the pubic symphyses placed them in Todd's (1921) phase 7, suggesting an age of 35 to 39 years. Thin sections and microradiographs produced and read by Dr. D. J. Ortner of the Smithsonian Institution suggested an age at death of 42 years, but Dr. Ortner feels that this estimate may be a little high.

Stature. The stature of the individual was calculated by measuring from the heel up to the farthest extent of the vertebrae and combining that length with the head and neck height measured from the detached head of the mummy. This totaled 153 cm. However, because of the dehydration and subsequent shrinking of the mummy, primarily at the loci of the intervertebral discs, we measured the left femur physiological length (412 mm) in order to apply stature formulations to reconstruct possible live stature. Using the Trotter and Gleser (1958) formula for white females, a stature of 155.86 cm is obtained.

Those measurements considered reliable are listed in Table 6.1.

WEIGHT ESTIMATION

Applying Dr. Finnegan's data to what is known regarding the water content of the human body, the living weight of the mummy was calculated. The estimated length of the body was 156 cm. The normal range of weight for a nonobese female of this height is between 43.2 and 52.3 kg (95 and 115 lb). The dry weight and the mummified weight would be very nearly the same. The dry weight of the human body has been calculated to be 25 to 30 percent (Sunderman and Boerner 1949). The weight during life then would be approximately 37.8 to 45.4 kg (83.2 to 99.8 lb). Again, assuming a degree of caloric malnutri-

Table 6.1. *Measurements and indices of PUM II (in millimeters)*[a]

Head length	182
Head breadth	142
Minimum frontal breadth	93
Bizygomatic breadth	130
Total face height	110
Nose height	55
Cephalic index	78.02
Frontoparietal index	65.49
Total facial index	84.62
Left femur physiological length	412
Left femur maximum head diameter	40.4
Right femur midshaft diameters	
Mediolateral	23.6
Anteroposterior	23.3

[a] These are standard measurements used in physical anthropology.

tion and considering the weight lost with the removed organs, this calculation is certainly reasonable.

HISTOLOGICAL EXAMINATION
An insect larva was found within the body cavity during the autopsy, and electron micrographs were taken by Dr. Jeanne Riddle (Chapter 16). These photographs were sent to G. C. Steyskal and J. M. Kingsolver of the Systematic Entomology Laboratory at the U.S. National Museum, Washington, D.C., who identified the larva as *Thelodrias contractus* Motschulsky, family Dermestidae, a cosmopolitan species.

The tissues obtained during the autopsy were processed using the methods outlined in Chapter 15. Unfortunately, the poor preservation noted grossly was even more evident microscopically. Even those organs that were identifiable at the time of the autopsy were virtually without histological detail. A single exception was a small sample taken from the lateral aspect of the left breast. The tissue was very friable and crumbled during the processing. However, within this disintegrated specimen, there was a rounded, 1-cm nodule that remained intact (Figure 6.6). The nodule was composed of connective tissue – not fat,

which would be more typical of normal breast tissue. Within the connective tissue, there were irregular cystlike spaces, some of which contained large, partially preserved cuboidal cells with recognizable nuclei. These had the appearance of epithelial cells. The overall configuration and residual microanatomy strongly suggested that this was a fibroadenoma of the breast. The woman's age, the size of the tumor, and its lateral position in the breast supported this thesis.

SUMMARY: PUM III
PUM III was a female with an estimated age of 35 years at the time of death in approximately 835 B.C. She was 156 cm tall and weighed approximately 41 (± 4) kg. The wrappings were modest and parts were reused linen. Two small hieroglyphic inscriptions were present within the wrappings. She had sustained a fracture of the left second rib that had healed. All third molars were absent congenitally. Partial evisceration had been performed per ano, and the brain had been extracted through the left nostril. The body tissues were poorly preserved with the exception of a small fibroadenoma, a benign tumor of the left breast.

PUM IV

RADIOGRAPHY
From its size, the second mummy was obviously a child. Before the unwrapping, the mummy was studied radiographically. As with PUM III, the study was performed by Dr. Karl Kristen and is considered in more detail in Chapter 17. His report follows:

The skeleton appears to be normally developed. Within the wrappings, posteriorly, there is a body-length opaque, slatlike inclusion that has the density of wood. There are bilateral basal and inferior occipital fractures without evidence of healing. The nature of the skull fractures is not apparent and may represent postmortem artifact or damage. There are no visible healed fractures and no developmental anomalies. No Harris's lines are visible. The epiphyses are open and there are several unerupted teeth, including some of the central incisors. The age of the child is estimated to be 8 years.

THE WRAPPINGS

The exterior condition of the mummy made it obvious that great care would be needed in the removal of the bandaging. A loose, ropelike cord was wrapped around the body from neck to feet, concentrated around the ankles. When removed, this proved to be a net, probably a fishnet, made of string in a square-knot pattern (Figure 6.7). The purpose or significance of this is not known. The outside wrapping consisted of a painted covering that would normally be termed a shroud, except that it did not completely cover the body, but extended from the top of the head to the ankles and did not meet in the back. It was made of coarse linen, assembled from several pieces in a neat patchwork, an unusual feature for the last decorated piece placed on a mummified body. The area of the textile that had covered the face was completely destroyed, so no painted portrait remained. The rest of the covering was in a badly damaged and fragmentary condition, but traces of paint remained. These were interpreted as geometric patterning and, in the lower left-hand corner, a figure of a seated Anubis jackal. This covering was stitched to the lower sides of the torso and across the top of the head with a thin strip of twisted linen cloth.

Under the net and the painted covering, the first layer of wrapping consisted of narrow linen strips that crossed the body at right angles to the trunk (horizontal). This was thinly applied and did not conceal the next layer, which was composed of thin strips running from the feet to the neck (vertical). Then the pieces of linen became larger, almost random in their application, of no standard size, and of varied quality. Some had been torn roughly

from large shapes, and some showed obvious signs of wear, as if they had been used for cleaning or other rough work. Little attempt had been made to pad out the mummy to a lifelike shape, with the exception of a small concentration of material below the rib cage. Some additional folded material had been applied to the sides of the head to round it out. Interspersed with the partial layers of this wrapping were loose cord ropes. These had been applied in a diagonal spiral to the body and seem to have been used to hold the wrappings in place.

After the "random" wrapping had been removed, the body was found to have been tied to a full-length board. The board was broken at its midportion about the level of the pelvis. Linen strips had been used at the neck and at the sides, probably to straighten the body out. It was now seen to have been dressed in a short tunic, a simple flat garment with a neckhole cut in the middle, placed over the head of the mummy and extending down the front and back of the body to about waist level. The neckline of this garment had been rolled and stitched. It was decorated with two vertical bands of near black color, which extended completely down the front and the back, passing over the shoulders on either side. These bands were not part of the original weaving of the linen material, but had been added to the fabric in a tapestry weave. Near the two edges of this simple garment were borders of the same color as the solid bands, but the borders were composed of four threads with space left between them.

Beneath the decorated tunic, the body was enveloped in what appeared to be a shroud but proved to be three complete full-length garments with neckholes. These may have been made expressly for the burial, as the edges of the front and back were not hemmed, the neckholes were crudely stitched, and the

Figure 6.6.   *Round, 1-cm piece of tissue from breast of PUM III, consisting of connective tissue without fat (a). Elastic tissue. Within small spaces are cells that resembled epithelial cells (b). The tissue is thought to be a fibroadenoma. Elastic tissue. (Photographs by John Levis, Mount Carmel Mercy Hospital)*

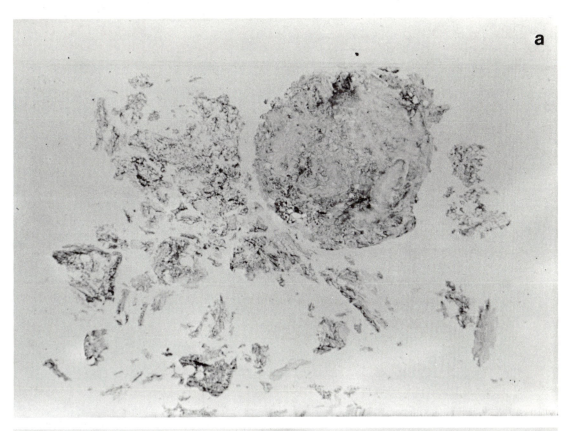

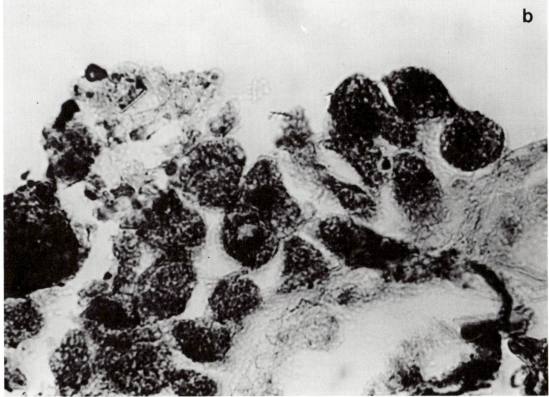

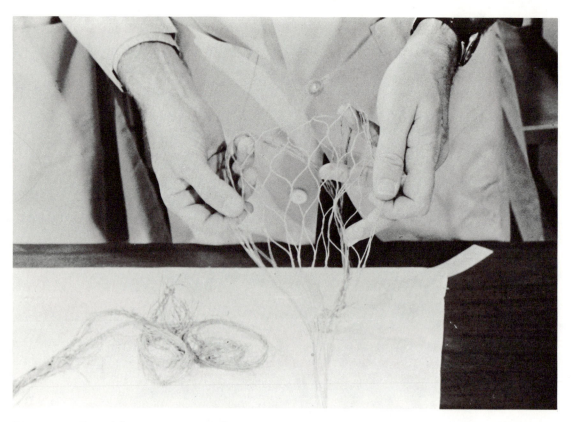

Figure 6.7.   Part of the outer wrapping of PUM IV, consisting of a knotted net. (Photograph by Nemo Warr, Detroit Institute of Arts)

fabric rather narrow. In contrast, the decorated tunic could well have been used in life. Around the neck and wrists, next to the body, knotted cords of one strand were found. A small fragment of plaster cartonnage was discovered in the "random" wrapping, located deep enough inside to suggest that it was not part of the original decoration. The paint preserved on it suggested it may have been a sliver from the eye decoration of a face mask. The general impression was that the mummy had been prepared from the contents of the embalmer's scrap bag, and the cartonnage fragment swept up with the other material.

On the basis of this examination, the mummy was dated as Roman period, probably in the first or second century A.D.

GENERAL AUTOPSY FINDINGS

At the time of autopsy, the body weighed approximately 3.5 kg and measured 106 cm from crown to heel and 65 cm from crown to rump; the head circumference was 50.7 cm (Figure 6.8). The body length of 106 cm, even considering some shrinkage owing to dehydration, is small by modern standards for an 8-year-old. Calculation of the weight was not possible, as total evisceration had been performed and the body tissue was so severely degenerated. The skin, which was very dark brown, was poorly preserved and full of holes varying in size from 1 mm to 1 cm. There were numerous small beetles and insect larvae present on almost all areas of the skin. These were scarab beetles, similar to those found

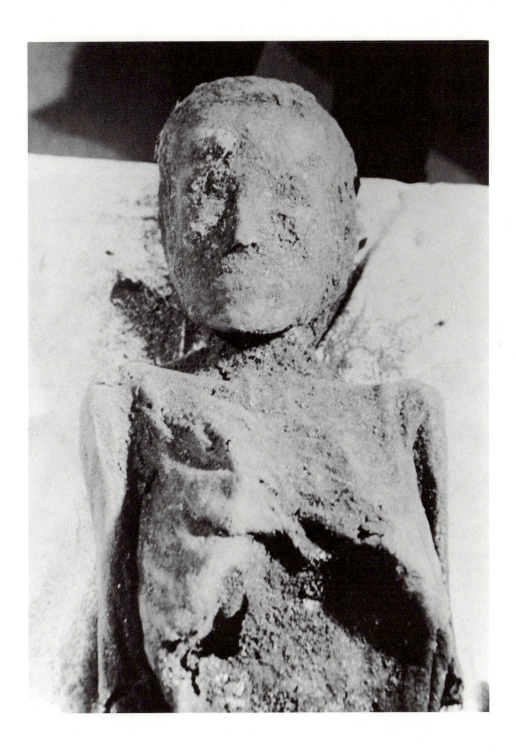

Figure 6.8.   Upper part of the body of PUM IV, showing the granular packing material and the extensive degeneration of the tissue. (Photograph by Nemo Warr, Detroit Institute of Arts)

Figure 6.9.   Abdominal and chest cavities of PUM IV, packed with granular material that had the appearance of sawdust. (Photograph by Nemo Warr, Detroit Institute of Arts)

during previous mummy autopsies. The mummy's eyes were depressed into the orbits by cloth packing and a black tarry substance; they had assumed a cup-shaped configuration, but appeared to be otherwise intact. The external ears were poorly preserved, but the external canals appeared normal. The visible teeth were well preserved, with no recognizable caries, and the anterior incisors appeared to be milk, or baby, teeth. The head was partially covered by dark hair, thickly matted with a dark brown to black material. There were no specific skin lesions or other external abnormalities. The external genitalia were those of an immature male: The penis measured 5 by 1 cm and was uncircumcised. The scrotum was present, but it was not certain whether the testes were also there. There was

a large defect in the rectal area that contained a moderate amount of granular packing material and a wad of cloth, 5 cm in diameter, which partially sealed the defect, implying mummification per ano.

The anterior trunk wall and then the anterior chest wall were removed; no flank or abdominal incision was present. There were no recognizable organs in the body cavities. Instead, the cavities were filled with large masses of granular packing material, which may be sawdust (Figure 6.9). This was similar to that noted on the skin, under the wrapping and between the legs, and in the anal defect. Large numbers of dried insect larvae were also found. Sections through the neck revealed residual structures resembling the esophagus and/or trachea. The spinal canal

Figure 6.10.   Two cerebral hemispheres found loose within the cranial cavity of PUM IV when the calvarium was removed. (Photograph by Nemo Warr, Detroit Institute of Arts)

was opened, but no trace of the cord or other structures was seen. When the calvarium was removed, two large brown granular masses were found within the posterior fossae (Figure 6.10). These appeared to be the cerebral hemispheres, measuring approximately 10 by 4 cm each, and markedly desiccated. The posterior and inferior portions of both occipital bones were fractured, probably after death. The temporal, parietal, and frontal bones appeared normal, although there was slight separation of the sagittal suture posteriorly. Small fragments of spinal ligaments were found on the odontoid process. During the dissection, the tissue had degenerated so severely that virtually every bone of the thoracic cage, spinal column, and pelvis became loose and separated. There was no evi-

dence of trauma or other pathologic process, and determination of cause of death was not possible.

The tissue removed during the autopsy was so severely degenerated that processing for histological examination was not successful. When placed in the rehydrating solution, it crumbled into amorphous sediment in the bottom of the container. No detail was observed in the cell block preparations of this material (see Chapter 15).

SUMMARY: PUM IV
The data on the mummified body of a male child indicated that he was 8 to 10 years of age at the time of death, probably in the first century A.D. His height was approximately 106 cm, short by modern standards for a child of

this age. The wrappings and filler were crude. The body had been eviscerated per ano, although the brain had not been removed. The body was so severely degenerated that little gross and no microscopic detail persisted.

SUMMARY: PUM III AND PUM IV

The mummification of these two bodies was less than classical – indeed, was haphazardly done. Both bodies had been eviscerated per ano, but to varying degrees. PUM III had partial abdominal evisceration and removal of the brain, but no organs had been removed from the chest. PUM IV had total abdominal and thoracic evisceration, but the brain had not been removed. In both instances, the wrapping had been done in much the same manner. The outer wrappings were circular bandages around the body, and the deeper layers consisted of larger sheets or pieces of clothing. Various artifacts and assorted fragments of unrelated wrapping and decorative material had been included in the deeper wrappings. PUM III had been treated sparingly with resin and the cavities packed with resin-soaked linen wads. PUM IV had been packed with what appeared to be sawdust mixed with a colorless oily substance. Both bodies had apparently been poorly dehydrated, with subsequent severe tissue degeneration. PUM III had been mummified in approximately 835 B.C. and it appeared that more care had been taken with the preparation of the mummy. PUM IV perhaps demonstrated the ultimate debasement of the mummification process. Both bodies were small for their age and may reflect poor nutrition or the effects of disease. This may have been a result of their low socioeconomic status, which is suggested by the method of mummification employed.

REFERENCES

Brooks, S. T. 1955. Skeletal age at death: the reliability of cranial and pubic age indicators. *American Journal of Physical Anthropology* 13:567–90.

Mokhtar, G.; Riad, H.; and Iskander, Z. 1973. *Mummification in ancient Egypt.* Cairo: Cairo Museum.

Phenice, T. W. 1969. A newly developed visual method of sexing the os pubis. *American Journal of Physical Anthropology* 30:297–301.

Sunderman, E. W., and Boerner, F. 1949. *Normal values in clinical medicine,* p. 649. Philadelphia: Saunders.

Todd, T. W. 1921. Age changes in the pubic bone: II, The pubis of male Negro-white hybrid; III, The pubis of the white female; IV, The pubis of the female Negro-white hybrid. *American Journal of Physical Anthropology* 4:1–70.

Trotter, M., and Gleser, G. 1958. A re-evaluation of estimation of stature based on measurements taken during life and of long bones after death. *American Journal of Physical Anthropology* 16:79–123.

PART II
Mummies of the Americas

7

Mummies and mummification practices in the southwestern and southern United States

MAHMOUD Y. EL-NAJJAR
New Mexico State University
Las Cruces, New Mexico, U.S.A.

THOMAS M. J. MULINSKI
University of Idaho
Moscow, Idaho, U.S.A.

The origin of mummification practices is not precisely known. It appears, however, at least among American Indian tribes, that they may have resulted from the belief in a future life. Grave offerings and the various cultural and personal artifacts recovered indicate that such beliefs did exist. Mummification practices, both in Egypt (Chapter 1) and in the Americas, were of two types: artificial and natural. Artificial mummification flourished and was more prevalent in ancient Egypt. Natural mummification, on the other hand, is the predominant kind in the dry areas of the New World. In North America, almost all desiccated bodies recovered thus far are from rock shelters, caves, and overhangs. Mummies found in these localities are usually in a sitting position, tightly flexed, with the arms and knees drawn to the chest and the head bent forward.

In the New World, mummification is known to occur in three main regions: the southern and southwestern United States, the Aleutian Islands, and Peru. This chapter is limited to a discussion of mummification practices and a tabulation of the whereabouts of mummies in the southern and southwestern United States (Figure 7.1).

SOUTHWESTERN UNITED STATES

Most of our information regarding mummification practices comes from the study of bu-rial techniques and of the extensive mortuary offerings made by the prehistoric natives of the New World. In the American Southwest, these natives are known to anthropologists as *Anasazi*, which is the Navajo word for "ancient people" and is applied to the prehistoric inhabitants of the plateau area of the American Southwest; this includes the drainage of the Rio Grande, and the San Juan, Little Colorado, Upper Gila, and Salt rivers, much of Utah, and some of eastern Nevada. Southwestern American mummies come from three main localities: northeastern, east-central, and southern Arizona. From northeastern Arizona, mummies have been recovered from Canyon de Chelly and Canyon del Muerto, Vandal Cave, and Painted Cave.

Canyon de Chelly and its major tributary, Canyon del Muerto, have yielded some of the best preserved desiccated bodies in the New World. The majority of these (n = 10) is housed at the American Museum of Natural History, New York City. No studies, either histological or anthropological, have been done on them. Four of these mummies are being studied at Case Western Reserve University, Cleveland, Ohio. A partial mummy is at the Human Variation Laboratory, Arizona State University, Tempe, and the naturally desiccated body of a Pueblo child is now being examined further at the Department of Anthropology in the same university.

The earliest of the Anasazi are known as the

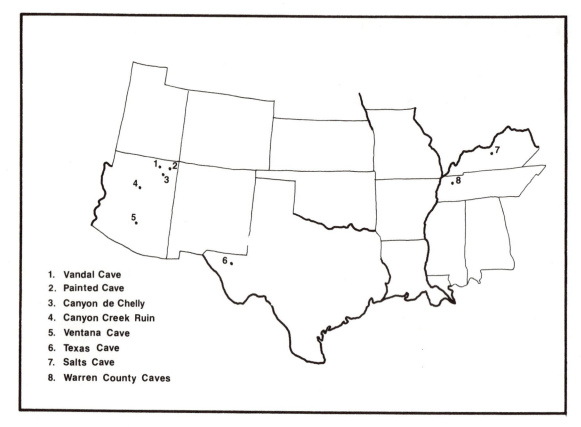

1. Vandal Cave
2. Painted Cave
3. Canyon de Chelly
4. Canyon Creek Ruin
5. Ventana Cave
6. Texas Cave
7. Salts Cave
8. Warren County Caves

Figure 7.1.   Sites where mummies have been found in the southern and southwestern United States. (Map by Timothy Motz, Detroit Institute of Arts)

Basket Makers, a seminomadic group of hunters and gatherers who lived in the caves and rock shelters of the area between A.D. 100 and 700. The Basket Makers survived in an unusually harsh environment. They had no cotton, no wool, no pottery, and no draft animals. Their diet consisted mainly of corn and squash, though hunting small game animals and gathering nuts and seeds provided enough in the way of food supplements to ensure their biological survival. The Basket Makers were short and had coarse, black hair with a tendency to be wavy, little body hair, and brown skin (Wormington 1973).

In general, the desiccated bodies of these inhabitants were placed in pits or stone-lined cists that had originally been constructed for storage. Occasionally, however, a body was left in a corner on the floor of a cave or was placed in a crevice. This was probably done immediately after death occurred, before the body had stiffened. It is possible that the small size of the cist led to the custom of flexing, in which the knees are drawn up to the chest and the arms are extended at the side. The desiccated bodies were usually wrapped in fur blankets, but occasionally tanned deerskins were used. Bodies of infants and small children were wrapped in a padlike mass of soft fiber made from the leaves of yucca plants and shrouded either in fur, skin, or feather-cloth blankets (Figures 7.2 through 7.4). Mortuary offerings included baskets, sandals, beads and ornaments, weapons, digging sticks, cone-shaped pipes, and a variety of personal possessions.

In her discussion of mummification among the Basket Makers, Wormington concludes:

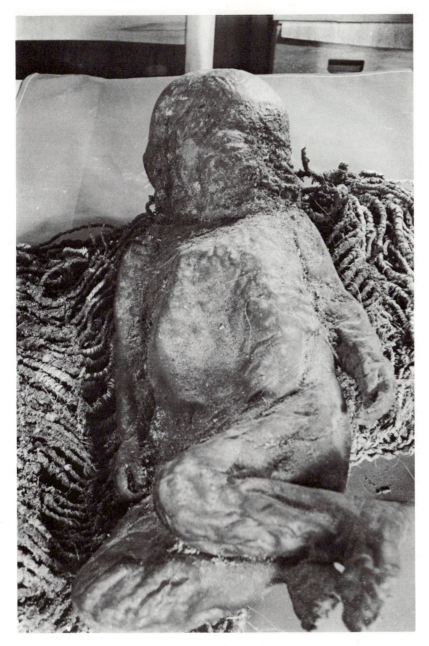

Figure 7.2.   *Mummy of a 1-year-old child from Canyon de Chelly, Basket-Maker period No. 2, A.D. 300–500.*

Almost every body is found wrapped in a blanket of fur and it is probable that these served as wraps and blankets for living as well as shrouds for the dead. The manner in which these coverings were constructed is most ingenious. Strings were made of yucca fibers, then tied together in close parallel rows, producing a light warm climate. Sometimes they were ornamented with borders made of cords which had been wrapped with strips of bird skin. Some mantles of tanned deer skin were also made

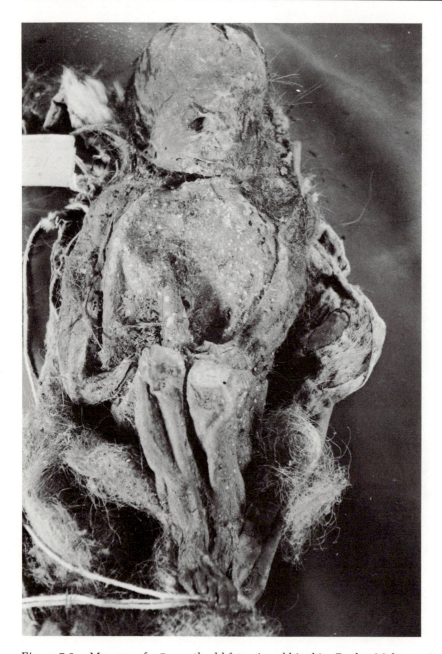

Figure 7.3.   Mummy of a 7-month-old fetus in rabbit skin, Basket-Maker period No. 2, A.D. 300–500.

and it may be that there were some woven robes, for a few fragments of woven cloth have been found. [Wormington 1973]

Reporting on mummies from Ventana Cave, southern Arizona, Haury (1950) found two types of burial practices: flexed and ex-tended. In flexed bodies, the arms are folded across the chest; in extended bodies they lie at the sides or rest on the abdomen. Haury fur-ther states that the degree of flexure varies, from doubling up the legs without drawing them up to the chest to tight flexing, the latter

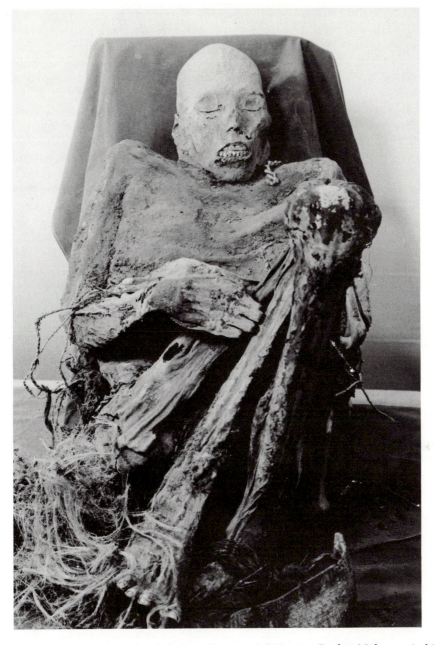

Figure 7.4.   *Young male adult from Canyon del Muerto, Basket-Maker period No. 2, A.D. 300–500.*

being more common. In the former cases, there is a binding about the legs. Here, as elsewhere in the Southwest, the mummies were entirely the result of natural desiccation. The author concludes: "There is no evidence whatever that evisceration or other artificial means of preserving were known."

Among the unique finds associated with Basket-Maker mummies is a pair of unworn sandals. Apparently, these ancient nomads believed that the dead person required a new pair of sandals for the time when he would rise again and walk. These sandals were woven of cord made from the fibers of yucca and apocyum, a plant related to the milkweed. They were double-soled, somewhat cupped at the heel, had a square toe, and were usually ornamented with a fringe of buckskin or shredded juniper bark (Wormington 1973).

One of the most unusual mummies recovered from the American Southwest is a young Pueblo child approximately 3 years of age. The Pueblos were the agriculturist descendants of the Basket-Makers and lived in large communal houses in the same area between A.D. 700 and 1300. The child died during the eleventh century (El-Najjar et al. 1975). Its desiccated body was laid flat on an elaborate cradleboard with a cottonwood-bark sunshade in place around the head. There was also a worn textile fragment round the neck and a bracelet round the right wrist. This burial contrasts markedly with other burials recovered from the same site. None of the others had a grave cover or had as many or as elaborate grave goods. The child's death has been attributed to severe anemia (El-Najjar and Robertson 1976). The diagnosis was based on macroscopic, radiographic, and histochemical analysis. In the earlier paper, El-Najjar et al. conclude:

Of particular interest is the fact that this apparent three-year-old child was still on a cradleboard. If we interpret the association correctly, the child was unable to walk, perhaps even unable to participate in normal infant behavior, and may well have been mentally retarded. We noticed no evidence of fractures or broken bones, nor did we see any other pathological features. [El-Najjar et al. 1975]

Four mummies from Canyon del Muerto are now being examined at the Department of Anthropology and Institute of Pathology, Case Western Reserve University, Cleveland. These are an adult male, an adult female, a young child, and a fetus. They are dated around A.D. 100–300. Autopsies have been performed on two of these mummies, and bone and soft tissues are being processed.

The mummies from Vandal Cave and Painted Cave, northeastern Arizona, as well as those from east-central and southern Arizona are all stored at the Arizona State Museum, Tucson. Pertinent information on each mummy is provided in Tables 7.2 through 7.8. Before each site and its mummies are discussed below, it is necessary to point out two things. First, when the burial number of a mummy is not known, the Arizona State Museum (ASM) catalog number of the specimen is used in its place in order to distinguish individuals. The catalog number always appears in parentheses. Second, the age and sex of each mummy were estimated by T. M. J. Mulinski and Dr. Walter H. Birkby, physical anthropologist at the museum.

Of the 43 mummies listed in Table 7.1 only 18 (41.9 percent) are complete. The rest are partial mummies of varying degrees of completeness. There are 29 (69.4 percent) subadults and 14 (32.6 percent) adults. Of the latter, 4 are definitely or probably males, 6 are definitely or probably females, and 4 cannot be sexed. With regard to dating, it can be safely assumed that all mummies are from prehistoric times, although none is older than 2,000 years. In fact, the oldest ones that can be dated with some degree of assurance are only 1,500 years old.

All the dehydrated remains at the ASM collection have become mummified through natural desiccation. These individuals were buried in either caves or rock shelters, where the extremely dry conditions allowed the soft tissues to dry out before putrefaction could destroy them. In connection with this, it is interesting to note that the integument of the head is usually the first to disintegrate. For example, more than one mummy in the collections has generally intact skin on the torso and extremities, but the covering of the head, especially of the face, has not been preserved or has a significantly lesser percentage of skin still intact. This phenomenon is undoubtedly

Table 7.1. *Sites with mummies in the collections of the ASM*

Site name	Site number[a]	Total number of burials	Number of mummies in ASM collections	Time period[b]	Cultural affiliation[b]	Archeological reference
Vandal Cave	Ariz. E:7:1	11	8	A.D. 500–700 A.D. 1150–1250	Anasazi	Haury (1936)
Painted Cave	Ariz. E:7:2	3	2	A.D. 1150–1250	Anasazi	Haury (1945)
Canyon Creek Ruin	Ariz. V:2:1	40	5	A.D. 1300–1350	Anasazi	Haury (1934)
McCuen Cave	Ariz. W:13:6	21(?)	10	Undoubtedly prehistoric	?	None
Ventana Cave	Ariz. Z:12:5	39	11	A.D. 1000–1400[c]	Hohokam	Haury (1950)
Texas Cave	Texas 0:7:3[d]	2(?)	2	?	?	None
Miscellaneous	Various places in Arizona and Colorado	?	5	Probably prehistoric	?	None

[a] Except when noted, sites are designated according to the system employed by the Archeological Survey of the ASM (Wasley 1964).
[b] Information on the time period and cultural affiliation of Vandal Cave, Painted Cave, Canyon Creek Ruin, and Ventana Cave comes from Haury (personal communication).
[c] Ventana Cave was occupied off and on for thousands of years, beginning more than 10,000 years ago. However, all the burials except three (nos. 20, 35, and 36), and all the mummies, date from the period A.D. 1000–1400.
[d] This designation is according to the system employed by the no-longer-existing Gila Pueblo Archeological Foundation.

related to differences in the thickness of the soft tissues surrounding the skull and post-cranium.

Vandal Cave (Table 7.2), 8 mummies. The site had two main occupations, a Basket-Maker III (A.D. 500–700) and a Pueblo III (A.D. 1150–1250). Burials 7, 9, and 10 are from the earlier occupation; burial 2 is from a later level. The exact provenance of the other 4 mummies is not known. They are, however, from the same general area of the site. The Vandal Cave mummies are among the best preserved at the ASM collection.

Painted Cave (Table 7.3), 2 mummies. Both Painted and Vandal caves are located some 30 km north of Canyon de Chelly. The major occupation of the site was during Pueblo III times (A.D. 1150–1250), which is when the burials took place. Another mummy recovered from Painted Cave is on permanent loan to the Amerind Foundation, Dragoon, Arizona.

Canyon Creek Ruin (Table 7.4), 5 mummies. Canyon Creek Ruin is located in the western half of the Fort Apache Indian Reservation in east-central Arizona. The site is from the period A.D. 1300–1350.

McCuen Cave (Table 7.5), 10 mummies. Mc-Cuen Cave is located in the southern half of eastern Arizona. The site is prehistoric, although little information is available on its exact date of occupation.

Ventana Cave (Table 7.6), 11 mummies. Although some are incomplete, preservation of these mummies is very good. Ventana Cave is located in the Castle Mountains of southern Arizona in the Papago Indian

Table 7.2. *Mummies from Vandal Cave*

Burial number	Burial position	Condition of mummy	Sex	Age (yr)	Comments
2	Flexed	Complete, but no nails or hair present	Female(?)	Old adult, (>40)	Part of shroud still covering legs
7	Flexed	Complete, but no nails present; small amount of hair present	?	Infant (1–2)	Bracelet still in place on right wrist
9	Flexed	Complete, but no nails present; very small amount of hair present	Male(?)	Adult	Part of burial blanket still covering lower torso
10	Semiflexed	Apparently complete; nails and fair amount of hair present	?	Adult	Body still almost entirely covered with burial blanket and encrusted with soil
?(0–485)	Flexed/semiflexed	Complete; nails, but only very small amount of hair present	?	Infant (0.5–1.0)	Buried on flexible cradleboard
?(0–487A)	Flexed	Complete, although head detached from rest of body; some nails and very small amount of hair present	?	Infant (1.5–2.5)	Cranium with occipital deformation
?(0–487B)	?	Partial; only right forearm and hand and right leg and foot present	?	Infant (0.5–1.5)	
?(0–487C)	?	Partial; only lower part of left leg and foot present	?	Infant (birth–0.5)	

Reservation. This cave has a long history of interrupted use from over 10,000 years ago to the present century. All the mummies recovered, however, date from A.D. 1000–1400.

Texas Cave (Table 7.7), 2 mummies. Texas Cave is located roughly 80 km northwest of Toyah, Texas, at the western end of the state. Little information is available from this site. Of the two mummies, one is complete and one partial.

Other localities (Table 7.8). In addition to the above, 5 other mummies at the ASM come from various places in Arizona and Colorado. No exact provenance is known. The only noteworthy feature is a rather extreme example of lambdoid deformation exhibited by the cranium from Slab House Ruin.

Very few biological studies on the mummies in the ASM collections have been carried out. The only known published report on any of this material is by Gabel (1950), who examined the human remains from Ventana Cave but made no specific studies of the mummies. On the other hand, two unpublished studies on the Ventana Cave mummies are mentioned by Haury (1950). One of these was concerned with paleopathology:

The recovery of the mummies in Ventana Cave aroused considerable interest among some of the personnel of the Indian Service as to the possibility of tracking down diseases. Dr. Joseph D. Aronson, then special investigator in tuberculosis for the service, and engaged in research on valley fever (coccidioidomycosis), arranged to have the mummies x-rayed. The incidence of valley fever among Papago is very high and it was hoped that some

Table 7.3. *Mummies from Painted Cave*

Burial number	Burial position	Condition of mummy	Sex	Age (yr)
?(0–514)	Semiflexed(?)	Partial: left leg and foot missing, part of right foot missing; anterior walls of thoracic and abdominal cavities almost completely disappeared; nails absent; some hair present	?	Infant (0.5–1.5)
?(0–515)	Flexed	Complete, but skin rather worm-eaten in appearance; nails and some hair present	Male	Child (3.5–4.5)

Table 7.4. *Mummies from Canyon Creek Ruin*

Burial number	Burial position	Condition of mummy	Sex	Age (yr)	Comments
13	Extended(?)	Indeterminate, but no skin left on exposed part of head	?	Infant (1–2)	Body still wrapped in shroud(s); buried on cradle-board
20	?	Partial: only bones of right leg and both feet present, with some tissue also present	?	Adult	Osteitis observable on tibia and fibula; both feet in sandals
22	Extended(?)	Indeterminate, but does not appear to be much tissue left	?	Probably infant	Body still wrapped in shroud(s)
32	?	Partial: skeleton disarticulated; very little tissue remaining	?	Infant (birth–0.5)	Body still wrapped in shroud(s); buried on cradle-board
33	?	Partial: skeleton disarticulated and incomplete; with no skull and very little postcranium remaining; very little tissue left	?	Fetal–newborn	

evidence might be found to show whether or not the earlier residents in the area were afflicted, too. The findings were negative, at least to the extent that no trace of the disease was revealed if it was present and nothing significant appeared from a pathological standpoint either. [Haury 1950)

A second study involved a search for ABO antigens in tissue samples:

In 1947, Mr. Edward L. Breazeale, then with the Division of Laboratories, Arizona State Department of Health (now Assistant Agricultural Chemist, University of Arizona), undertook blood group tests of Ventana Cave mummy tissue. Samples from ten mummies were examined by two different methods: (1) by absorption and cross agglutination studies, and (2) by extracting the tis-

sue with normal saline and using the extracted fluid as the antigen against known type A and B cells. The results produced by these two methods are in perfect agreement. Of the ten samples analyzed, nine were type "O" (burials 2, 3, 5, 6, 8, 9, 11, 15, 31) and one was type "AB" (burial 16). [Haury 1950]

One other research project should be mentioned. Birkby has undertaken an examination of the head hair from several mummies for ectoparasites. His results, which are unpublished, are presented in Table 7.9. Out of 18 individuals with a sufficient amount of hair to be analyzed, 8 (44.4 percent) had head lice (*Pediculus humanus capitis*). In all instances, only the nits were found.

Table 7.5. *Mummies from McCuen Cave*

Burial number	Burial position	Condition of mummy	Sex	Age (yr)	Comments
Mc:1–4	?	Partial: body jumbled mass, but some tissue present	?	Fetal–newborn	
?(0–483)	Extended	Complete, although head detached from rest of body; a few strands of hair present	?	Infant (1–2)	Body still somewhat covered by shroud(s)
?(0–493)	?	Partial: only some lumbar vertebrae, pelvis, and lower extremities present; only small amount of tissue present	Male	Adult	
?(0–494)	?	Partial: head, upper extremities (except for left humerus), and feet missing; fair amount of tissue still remaining	Female	Adult	
?(0–500)	Extended	Complete; abundant amount of hair present	?	Infant (birth–0.5)	Body still wrapped in shroud(s); buried on cradleboard
?(0–502)	Flexed	Complete, although head detached from rest of body and skin not well preserved; no hair present	?	Infant (1–2)	
?(0–503)	Extended	Complete; some hair present	?	Fetal–newborn	Body still wrapped in shroud(s); buried on cradleboard
?(0–512)	?	Partial: only head, some vertebrae, and rib fragments present; some tissue preserved, but no hair present	Female	Adult	Cranium exhibits lambdoid deformation
?(0–750A)	?	Partial: only both legs and feet present; some tissue preserved	?	Adult	Feet in sandals
?(0–750B)	?	Partial: only left leg and foot present; some tissue preserved	?	Adult	Foot in sandal

SOUTHERN UNITED STATES

Another collection of naturally mummified prehistoric American natives comes from Kentucky. The best known of these is Little Alice. Little Alice's desiccated body was recovered by two local men in 1875 near what is now known as Mummy Valley. On the limestone slab where the body was found, the following inscription appears:

Sir I have found one of the Grat wonder of the World in this cave Whitch is a muma "Can All Seed hear after" found March the 8 1875

T.E. lee J l lee "an Wd Cutliff" discuvers [*sic*, Robbins 1971]

Of the original discovery, Watson cites the following published account, which appeared in a newspaper clipping:

It was lying on the ledge up against the wall of the cave with a pile of ashes and half-burned sticks in front. A bowl, pipe, several pairs of moccasins made of grass and bark, some pieces of an exceedingly light wood, flints and arrow points, etc., were all about. [Watson 1969]

Table 7.6. *Mummies from Ventana Cave*

Burial number	Burial position	Condition of mummy	Sex	Age (yr)	Comments
3	Flexed	Complete, although right upper extremity disarticulated at elbow; some hair present	Female	Old adult (>50)	Most of head hair present is gray; calculus present on anterior mandibular teeth; periodontal disease evident
5	?	Partial; skeleton fairly complete, but disarticulated; some tissue remaining, including very small amount of hair	?	Young child (5–6)	
6	Extended	Complete, although left upper extremity disarticulated at elbow; some hair present	Female	Young child (4–5)	Wooden block wrapped with textiles placed under head of this individual when buried
9	Extended	Complete; small amount of hair present, but no nails	Male	Adult	Nose plug and earrings still present; most of torso and upper extremities covered with shroud; grave goods included skin quiver containing cord with attached shell, nose plug, projectile points, four bone awls, human-hair wig, cactus-spine needle, and several fragments of preserved sandals, and miscellaneous cotton cloth fragments
11	Extended	Complete; nails and hair absent	Female	Adult	Body covered with cotton robe when buried
15A	?	Partial: skeleton fairly complete, but disarticulated; very little tissue remaining; extremely small amount of hair present	?	Infant (1.5–2.5)	
15B	?	Partial: only left forearm and hand present; some tissue remaining	?	Young child (5–6)	
16	?	Partial: only skull, some cervical vertebrae, and right talus present; some tissue remaining, including very small amount of hair	Male(?)	Old adult (>40)	
24	?	Partial: skeleton fairly complete, but somewhat disarticulated; some tissue remaining	?	Infant (0.5–1.5)	Body placed in twined bag and buried in grass nest
25	Semiflexed	Complete; fair amount of hair present	?	Probably infant/young child	Body still almost entirely covered with shroud
29	Semiflexed	Complete, although head detached from rest of body; fair amount of tissue remaining; very small amount of hair remaining	?	Infant (1.0–1.5)	Body buried in fur robe shroud

Table 7.7. *Mummies from Texas Cave*

Burial number	Burial position	Condition of mummy	Sex	Age (yr)	Comments
?(0–740)	?	Partial: skeleton fairly complete, although somewhat disarticulated; some tissue remaining	?	Infant (birth–0.5)	
?(0–759)	Extended	Complete; large amount of hair present	?	Infant (birth–0.5)	Body still covered with burial blanket; buried on mat

Table 7.8. *Mummies from several localities in the Southwest*

Location	Burial position	Condition of mummy	Sex	Age (yr)	Comments
Slab House Ruin, Duggagei Canyon, Arizona (0–200)	?	Partial: legs and feet missing; no skin left anteriorly and only small amount remaining posteriorly	?	Infant (1–2)	Cranium exhibits rather extreme lambdoid deformation
Yellow Jacket Canyon, Colorado (0–245)	?	Partial: skeleton fairly complete, but almost completely disarticulated; some tissue remaining	?	Infant (1.5–2.5)	
Cliff House, Tonto Basin, Arizona (0–498)	?	Partial: skeleton fairly complete, but for most part disarticulated; some tissue remaining	?	Infant (birth–0.5)	
Cottonwood area, Arizona (0–501)	?	Partial: most of face and lower extremities missing	?	Infant (birth–1)	
Duggagei Canyon, Arizona (0–511)	?	Partial: only skull, some cervical vertebrae, and innominates present; small amount of tissue present	Female	Adult (15–20)	

Little Alice was bought by a man named Morrison, who described her as follows:

The little girl turned to stone, the most interesting and wonderful of all cave phenomena; a little girl, petrified or mummified by the action of the cave air; a mummy that was found in Salts Cave in 1875; that during the 47 years since the discovery, it was exhibited in the Smithsonian Institution and at various other places. [Watson 1969]

Little Alice was displayed in commercial caves for many years after the original discovery. In 1958 she was brought to the University of Kentucky, where detailed studies were made. The presence of external genitalia showed the desiccated body to be that of a young male about 9 to 10 years of age! Little Alice is now known as Little Al. According to Robbins (1971), the body is in an excellent

Table 7.9. *Findings of examination of head hair from certain North American Indian mummies in ASM collections for head louse*, Pediculus humanus capitis

Site	Number of mummies with lice	Number of mummies without lice
Vandal Cave	0	3 (burials 7, 9, 10)
Painted Cave	2 (0–514, 0–515)	0
McCuen Cave	0	3 (Mc:2, 0–500, 0–503)
Ventana Cave	6 (burials 3, 5, 9, 15A, 16, 25)	2 (burials 6, 29)
Texas Cave	0	2 (0–740, 0–759)
Total	8	10

Source: W. H. Birkby (unpublished data).

state of preservation, except for slight fungus as a result of its exposure to the outside atmosphere. Radiocarbon dating using abdominal and lower thoracic tissue produced an age of 1,960 ± 160 years. On the basis of cultural and physical anthropological data, Robbins concluded that Little Al may have belonged to a group of Woodland Indians who were the recent human occupants of the cave.

Several other desiccated bodies have been found in the Mammoth Cave area. Most of these were discovered by saltpeter miners early in the nineteenth century in Short Cave. Between 1811 and 1815, at least four mummies were found (Meloy and Watson 1969). The Mammoth Cave mummy known as Fawn Hoof was found in Short Cave in 1813. She was sitting in a stone box grave, of the kind commonly found in Tennessee and neighboring counties in Kentucky to the south of Short Cave. Physically, the body was well preserved; the flesh dry, hard, and dark in color. According to Robbins (1974), Fawn Hoof was dressed in several finely fashioned skin burial garments and was accompanied by a variety of grave goods. Fawn Hoof is the only one of the mummies that definitely seems to have been accompanied by grave goods (Watson 1969). According to Watson (1969), Fawn Hoof and several items found with her were given to the American Antiquarian Society in

Worcester, Massachusetts, about 1817. She was then exhibited at the U.S. National Museum in 1876. Her body has been dissected, and the clean bones are stored at the Division of Physical Anthropology, Smithsonian Institution.

Another mummy, known as Scudder mummy, was also recovered from Short Cave. Deerskin wrappings on the body and deerskin items found with it indicated that it was from the same population as Fawn Hoof (Robbins 1974). According to Robbins, the Scudder mummy, thought to be an adolescent boy, showed evidence of a fracture of the occipital bone which may have contributed to his death.

The remains of a mummy known as Lost John were recovered from Mammoth Cave in 1935. The desiccated body was found lying partially crushed under a boulder. Apparently, Lost John was the victim of a prehistoric mining accident. Neumann (1938) believes that the miner was kneeling when the boulder fell, its impact forcing him to fall on his right side. The cultural items found near the body indicate that this individual was involved in mining activities at the time of death (Robbins 1974).

According to Robbins, the body is well preserved, with flesh and internal organs present except for areas where rodent activities are evident. Lost John was a male in his forties. Textile material, evidently some sort of a blanket or robe of open twined weave, was tied with a braided cord around the body, and a mussel-shell pendant was suspended from the neck by a piece of two-strand twisted cord. A crude limestone hammer, bundles of reeds tied with grass, sticks, parts of gourds, a fragment of bagging, a stout pole which probably was used as a ladder, some hickory nuts, and human excrement are the only other materials in the cave (Neumann 1938). On the basis of cultural and geological evidence, Neumann suggests a date of about 500 years since John's death. Lost John has not been studied since the work of Neumann, but detailed analysis, including histologic and radiographic examination, are now being made by Dr. Louise Robbins of the University of North Carolina, Greensboro.

Mummies have also been found in caves in Tennessee. Holmes (1891–1892) reported on two mummies found in "a copperas cave" in Warren County, West Tennessee. The bodies, a male and a female, were discovered in 1810. Both had been placed in large cane baskets and buried in the cave floor. The female, like the bodies in Short Cave, was wrapped in a succession of materials, including hides, a feather cloak, and a piece of plain textile. According to Holmes, a scoop net, a moccasin, and a mat–all made of bark thread–were also found. In addition, Holmes states: "She had in her hand a fan formed of the tail feather of a turkey."

According to Robbins (1974) the interment of the Short Cave mummies exhibits a pattern similar in some ways to mummies found in Tennessee, though it is different in others. In both areas mummies were wrapped in deer-skin and accompanied with grave goods. Robbins further suggests that the Tennessee mummies differ in that some were disarticulated at the hips before being wrapped or dressed. She states:

Following the wrapping, they were placed upright in woven baskets. Wrapping the body before bu-

rial, and the kind of wrapping used, implies that the Short Cave and Tennessee mummies have come from one population occupying a broad geographic area. . . . If the Short Cave mummies were part of the Tennessee population, it is curious that the former were not disarticulated at the hips before burial. Why particular members of the population were selected for burial in caves is another interesting question that leads to speculation concerning the social structure of the people, a question that the existing evidence is quite inadequate to answer. [Robbins 1974]

CONCLUSION

As already stated, the origin of mummification practices among New World natives remains unknown. Why particular individuals were placed in caves and others buried in an open shelter is an unanswered question. It is possible that only persons of high social and/or economic status or warriors were left to dry. Wrapping the bodies may have been done to protect them or because the dead would need the wrappings in a future life. For example, the contemporary American natives (Navajos) who inhabit Canyon de Chelly and Canyon del Muerto never venture close to these caves, which are known to them as *chindi*, or "haunted houses." It is common practice among these people to abandon the house when an individual dies. In the New World, grave offerings may have had more than one purpose. In addition to the belief in a future life, the dead man's possessions may no longer have been used by other members of the community because of magicoreligious practices. Regardless of these questions, however, New World mummies offer a rich resource for future research to scholars in many disciplines. Only a small number of studies have been done, most of them long before the present revival of interest in human paleopathology and the utilization of advanced analytical techniques. The mummies at the Arizona State Museum and the American Museum of Natural History will be excellent subjects for future autopsies.

REFERENCES

El-Najjar, M. Y.; Morris, D. P.; Turner, C. G.; and Ryan, D. 1975. An unusual pathology with high incidence among the ancient cliff-dwellers of Canyon de Chelly. *Plateau* 48:13–21.

El-Najjar, M. Y., and Robertson, A. 1976. Spongy bones in prehistoric America. *Science* 193:141–3.

Gabel, N. E. 1950. The skeletal remains of Ventana Cave. In *The stratigraphy and archeology of Ventana Cave*, E. W. Haury (ed.), pp. 473–520. Tucson: University of Arizona Press.

Haury, E. W. 1934. *The Canyon Creek ruin and the cliff dwellings of Sierra Ancha*. Medallion Papers, No. 14. Globe, Ariz.: Gila Pueblo.

– 1936. Vandal Cave. *Kiva* 1(6):1–4.

– 1945. *Painted Cave, northeastern Arizona*. Dragoon, Ariz.: Amerind Foundation.

– 1950. *The stratigraphy and archeology of Ventana Cave*. Tucson: University of Arizona Press.

Holmes, W. H. 1891–2. Prehistoric textile art of the eastern United States. In *Thirteenth annual report of the Bureau of American Ethnology*, pp. 3–55. Washington, D.C.: Smithsonian Institution.

Meloy, H., and Watson, P. J. 1969. Human remains: "Little Alice" of Salts Cave and other mummies. In *The prehistory of Salts Cave, Kentucky*, P. J. Watson (ed.), pp. 65–9. New York: Academic Press.

Neumann, G. K. 1938. The human remains from Mammoth Cave, Kentucky. *American Antiquity* 3:339–53.

Robbins, L. M. 1971. A woodland "mummy" from Salts Cave, Kentucky. *American Antiquity* 36(2):201–6.

– 1974. Prehistoric people of the Mammoth Cave area. In *Archeology of the Mammoth Cave area*, P. J. Watson (ed.), pp. 137–62. New York: Academic Press.

Wasley, W. W. 1964. *The archeological survey of the Arizona State Museum*. Tucson: University of Arizona Press.

Watson, P. J. 1969. *The prehistory of Salts Cave, Kentucky*. Reports of investigation no. 16. Springfield: Illinois State Museum.

Wormington, M. 1973. *Prehistoric Indians of the Southwest*. Colorado Museum of Natural History, Series 7. Denver: The Museum.

Aleutian and Alaskan mummies

MICHAEL R. ZIMMERMAN
Associate Professor of Pathology and Anthropology,
The University of Michigan, and
Pathologist, Wayne County General Hospital,
Detroit, Michigan, U.S.A.

Mummies from Alaska are unique in several respects, owing to the climatic extremes of this area. The frigid climate of Alaska proper has resulted in the production of frozen mummies with remarkable preservation of histologic detail. In contrast, the cool damp climate of the Aleutian Islands would seem to be poorly suited to natural mummification. Cultural practices have supervened in this area to produce mummies.

A 1,600-YEAR-OLD FROZEN ESKIMO MUMMY

In October 1972 the frozen body of a woman washed out of a low beach cliff at Kialegak Point on Saint Lawrence Island in the Bering Sea. The Kialegak site is on the Southeast Cape of Saint Lawrence Island, which is about 60 km from Russia and 200 km from mainland Alaska. Occupation of the island can be traced back more than 2,000 years.

The body was found by three Eskimo hunters, the Gologergen brothers of the village of Savoonga. They felt that the body would be of interest to scientists and reburied it in the tundra, below the permafrost level, which in that area is 5 to 10 cm below the surface (Collins 1933). In the summer of 1973, visiting National Park Service anthropologist Zorro Bradley was notified of the find and taken to the burial site. With the permission of the Eskimos of the island, Bradley and the Gologergens exhumed the body, placed it in a bag, and transported it to Northeast Cape. From there it was flown to Nome and on to Fairbanks, where it was stored in the freezer facilities of the federal Arctic Health Research Center (no longer in operation).

Using the facilities of the research center (as arranged by Dr. Robert Rausch), the author and George S. Smith, of the National Park Service and the Anthropology Department of the University of Alaska, performed a complete autopsy (Zimmerman and Smith 1975). The body was thawed at room temperature, the process taking 24 hours. Tattooing noted on the arms indicated some degree of antiquity, as this practice had been discontinued on Saint Lawrence Island by the 1930s (Geist 1928). Tissue from psoas and quadriceps femoris muscle was radiocarbon dated at two separate institutions. The Smithsonian Institution Laboratory date was A.D. 405 ± 70 years (SI-1656) and the University of Pennsylvania Laboratory date was A.D. 370–390 ± 90 years (P-2090, I-7584). This dating placed the body in the Old Bering Sea Phase on Saint Lawrence Island (A.D. 200–500) (Birket-Smith 1959).

Examination of the tattoos (Smith and Zimmerman 1975), which were confined to the arms, was undertaken in an effort to provide an archeologic date. The tattooing on the right forearm, much clearer than on the left, was visible on the dorsal aspect of the forearm, hand, and fingers, starting 90 mm below the elbow. The tattooing on the right forearm consisted of rows of dots with alternating lines (Figure 8.1). The dots measured approximately 1 mm across and the solid lines were approximately 3 mm in width. The total length covered by the forearm tattooing was about 100 mm.

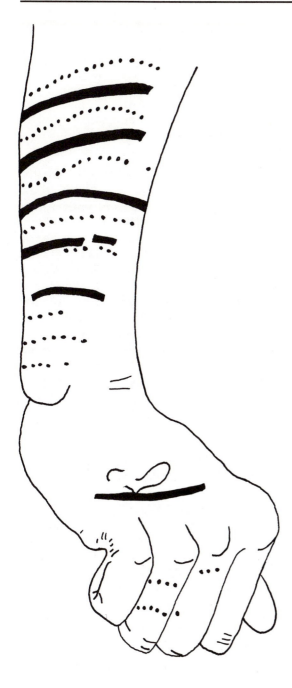

Figure 8.1.   Pattern of tattooing on the right fore-arm of a 1,600-year-old frozen body from Saint Lawrence Island, Alaska. (Drawing courtesy of George S. Smith, University of Alaska)

Tattooing on the dorsal aspect of the right hand was at first too faint to be clearly seen. Upon examination with infrared film, it was seen to be a "flanged heart" shape attached to a horizontal line. There were also two rows of dots on the second and third fingers. The coloration of the tattooing was dark blue to black.

The tattooing on the left arm was more elaborate than that found on the right (Figure 8.2). Its coloration was the same. The left arm was more desiccated than the right, making observation more difficult. The most prox-imal solid line had attached to it four designs that resembled the "flanged heart" seen on the right arm, but smaller. Each of these de-signs was attached to the main line by a verti-cal line. The tattooing on the dorsal aspect of the left hand was very difficult to distinguish, even with the use of infrared photography. Piecing together the many photos taken, the design on the back of the left hand seemed to consist of an oval, which may or may not have been complete, with a line extending laterally from its proximal border. Within the oval there may have been another oval, but this could not be verified (Figure 8.2). There was also tattooing on the second and fourth fin-gers consisting of two rows of dots. The tat-tooing on the forearm started 80 mm below the elbow and was 146 mm in length.

The process of tattooing on Saint Lawrence Island is described by Otto Geist in a letter to Dr. Charles Bunnell dated 1928, a portion of which follows:

Some of the St. Lawrence Island Eskimo women and girls have beautifully executed tattoo marks. These are made free hand although sometimes an outline is traced before the tattooing takes place. The pigment is made from the soot of seal oil lamps which is taken from the bottom of tea kettles or similar containers used to boil meat and other food over the open flame. The soot is mixed with urine, often that of an older woman, and is applied with steel needles. Two methods of tattooing are prac-ticed. One method is to draw a string of sinew or other thread through the eye of the needle. The

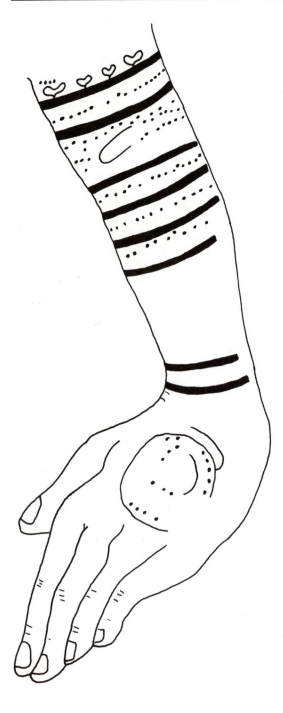

thread is then soaked thoroughly in the liquid pigment and drawn through the skin as the needle is inserted and pushed just under the skin for a distance of about a thirty-second of an inch when the point is again pierced through the skin. A small space is left without tattooing before the process is again repeated. The other method is to prick the skin with the needle which is dipped in the pigment each time. [Geist 1928]

Collins (1937), in illustrating decorative motifs of Old Bering Sea Style 2, has a drawing of a gorget-like ornament with a motif very similar to the tattooing design found here (Figure 8.3). Collins also shows four designs that could be along the same lines as the "flanged hearts" (Figure 8.4). These are also from the Old Bering Sea Phase. Collins also states that a similar design occurs on a dart socket piece (Okvik) which he bought on Little Diomede Island and which is illustrated on Plate 14-5 of "Archaeology of St. Lawrence Island, Alaska."

Thus the artistic motifs of the tattooing correlate with the radiocarbon dates in placing this individual within the Old Bering Sea Phase of Alaskan prehistory.

The body (Figure 8.5) appeared to be quite well preserved. As is usual with bodies long dead, the skin was dark brown. The subject appeared to have been an elderly woman; no external male genitalia were visible, and the breasts were atrophic. The unclothed body weighed about 25 kg and showed mild scoliosis. No incisions, scars, or decubitus ulcers were seen. Some brown hair was found on the vertex of the scalp. The right side of the face was partly crushed. Several teeth were missing, as was the left lower leg. No pathological changes were seen in the protruding distal left femur.

Standard Y-shaped and intermastoid incisions were made. The internal organs were somewhat desiccated, but were generally comparable in appearance to those of cadavers used for anatomical dissection. The body was that of a postmenopausal woman; atrophic female internal genitalia were identified. Gross pathological changes were

Figure 8.2.   Pattern of tattooing on the left forearm of a 1,600-year-old frozen body from Saint Lawrence Island, Alaska. (Drawing courtesy of George S. Smith, University of Alaska)

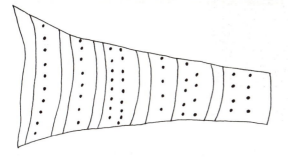

Figure 8.3.   Decorative motif of the Old Bering Sea Style 2 type, as found on a gorget-like ornament. (From Collins 1937:82)

found in several viscera. There was a moderate degree of coronary atherosclerosis, but no evidence of myocardial infarction, acute or healed. The lower lobes of both lungs showed fibrous adhesions to the chest wall and diaphragm, and the lungs contained heavy deposits of anthracotic pigment. The smaller bronchi of both lungs were packed with moss (later identified as *Meesia triquetra*), forming casts of the bronchi. A calcified carinal lymph node was found. Moderate scoliosis and aortic atherosclerosis were present. The brain was a crumbling brown mass.

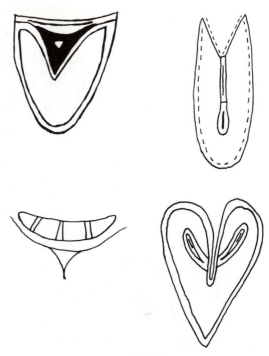

Figure 8.4.   Decorative designs of the Old Bering Sea Style 2 type that are similar to the "flanged heart." (From Collins 1937:82)

The tissues were somewhat desiccated, a process which continues even in the frozen state. The tissues were rehydrated with Ruffer's solution, embedded in paraffin, and sectioned as any fresh tissue would be.

Sections of the coronary arteries clearly showed the atheromatous deposits that had been seen grossly (Figure 8.6). The myocardium was less well preserved; striations and, as is usual in mummified tissue, nuclei were not seen. The lungs showed the patchy deposition of anthracotic pigment observed in modern patients with centrilobular emphysema (Figure 8.7). The alveolar architecture was generally preserved; many of the alveoli appeared to be coalescent, although some of this change may be postmortem artifact. Some moss fibers were seen in the bronchi and were associated with hemorrhage (Figure 8.8). The liver showed clearly the distinction between the parenchymal

cells and the portal triads, particularly with the trichrome stain. The cells contained a brown pigment that failed to stain for iron and bile. This almost certainly represents lipofuscin. The thyroid contained well-preserved follicles, and the colloid took the specific iron stain.

The calcified carinal lymph node contained numerous concentric areas of fibrosis with central calcification (Figure 8.9). These were interpreted as healed granulomas; identical lesions were seen in the spleen and possibly in the meninges, where the calcified lesions were much smaller and may represent phleboliths. Examination with polarized light revealed only minute and insignificant amounts of silica, and results of staining for acid-fast bacilli were negative. Stains for fungi revealed many weakly staining budding yeast cells and hyphal filaments. The morphology was that of a *Candida* species. A screening conjugate reagent for *Candida* sp.

Figure 8.5. *The frozen body of an Eskimo woman. The scoliosis is clearly visible.*

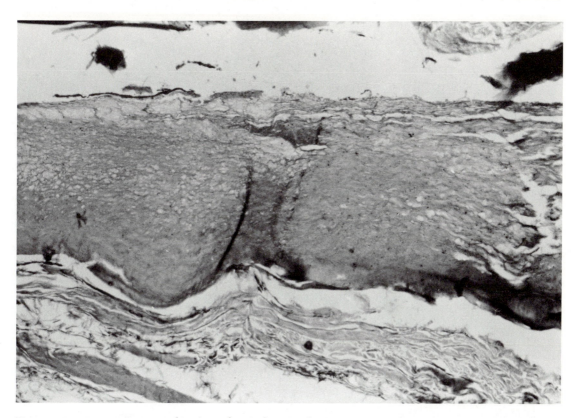

Figure 8.6.   Coronary artery showing atherosclerotic plaque. Hematoxylin and eosin. × 95.

stained the hyphae, but not the yeast cells. The same fungi were found in other tissues, such as the diaphragm. Fluorescein-labeled *Histoplasma capsulatum* antiglobulins that had been absorbed with cells of *Candida albicans* did not demonstrate *H. capsulatum*.

Examination of the feces revealed the ova of a fish trematode, *Cryptocotyle lingua* (Figure 8.10). The ova of this parasite have been reported in modern Eskimos by Rausch et al. (1967), but the adult helminth has not been identified in man.

The conclusion from the gross findings was that this elderly woman had been trapped in her semisubterranean house by a landslide or earthquake, and had been buried alive and asphyxiated. This conclusion was based on several facts. The body was unclothed, and Eskimos are unclothed only in their houses; when burial is deliberate, they are clothed. In view of the preservation of the body, one would have expected any clothing to have been preserved also.

Aspiration of foreign material into the bronchi is known to occur in accidental inhumation and has been demonstrated in persons buried in heaps of coal (Gonzalez et al. 1954). The microscopic finding of hemorrhage associated with the moss fibers in the bronchi is consistent with asphyxiation. It is not unusual for red blood cells to be preserved for extended periods. Preserved erythrocytes have been reported in the tissues of Peruvian (Allison 1975) and North American Indian (Zimmerman 1973) mummies. Microscopic fracture of the right temporal bone was also seen, with associated hemorrhage indicating that this was a true antemortem fracture, thus confirming the role of trauma in this woman's death (J. Benitez, personal communication).

Paleopathology includes an interest in the

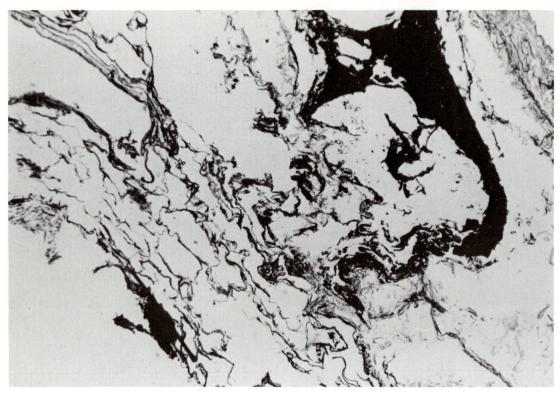

Figure 8.7.   Centrilobular deposition of anthracotic pigment in the lungs. Hematoxylin and eosin. × 37.5.

history of disease processes. This Eskimo woman, far removed from the stresses of modern technological society, suffered from coronary artery disease – a process that has been well documented as far back as dynastic Egypt, by both historical (Breutsch 1959) and anatomical (Sandison 1970) evidence. The present case not only confirms the antiquity of the process of coronary atherosclerosis, but also exhibits its occurrence in a preliterate society.

The finding of severe anthracosis can be attributed to a lifetime spent around open cooking and heating fires. Similar findings have been reported in several mummies (Brothwell et al. 1959; Sandison 1970; Zimmerman et al. 1971). Air pollution, at least on a local level, is not a recent phenomenon.

Several of the organs also showed a healed granulomatous process. Tuberculosis is considered to have been nonexistent in Alaska prior to its introduction by the Russians in the early eighteenth century. Of the fungi pathogenic for man that produce a granulomatous reaction, only histoplasmosis is thought to occur in Alaska, but information on its distribution is far from complete (Comstock 1959). Less than 1 percent of modern Eskimos have a positive cutaneous reaction to histoplasmin (Sexton et al. 1949; Comstock 1959). *Histoplasma capsulatum* was not demonstrated in the tissues of this woman. However, the distribution of the granulomas is most consistent with the diagnosis of healed histoplasmosis. The *Candida* species that was found, both in the granulomas and elsewhere in the body, undoubtedly is a postmortem invader. The weak staining of the fungi indicates that the contamination occurred some considerable time in the past, probably shortly after death.

In summary, this elderly woman is thought

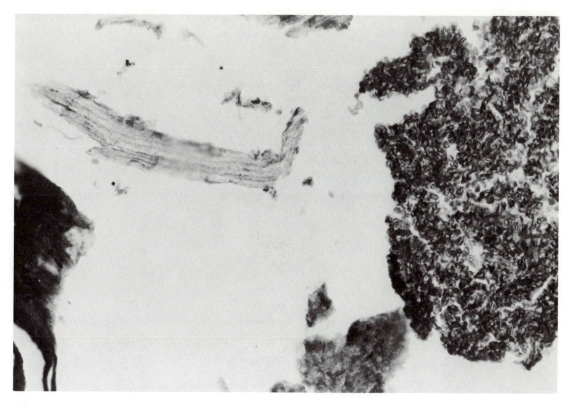

Figure 8.8.   Aspirated moss fiber associated with hemorrhage in bronchial lumen. Masson's trichrome. × 95.

to have suffered a traumatic death some 1,600 years ago. There was gross and microscopic evidence of skull fractures, and the finding of aspirated moss in the bronchi associated with hemorrhage suggests that accidental burial and suffocation played a significant role in her death. Other pathological changes documented included coronary atherosclerosis, scoliosis, anthracosis, and emphysema, and probable healed histoplasmosis. Radiocarbon dating and archeologic evaluation of tattoos on the body correlated in giving an approximate date of A.D. 400.

AN ALEUTIAN MUMMY

The mummy reported on in this section was collected in 1938 from Kagamil Island, in the central part of the Aleutian chain, by Dr. Aleš Hrdlička of the Division of Physical Anthropology, U.S. National Museum (1945). The individual was an Aleut, probably of the immediate pre-Russian era (prior to 1740). There were insufficient archeologic data for more precise dating, and the material was too recent to be dated by the radiocarbon method (Willis 1970).

The cold and damp climate of the Aleutian Islands would appear ill suited to the practice of mummification, which is generally based on desiccation. Hrdlička (1945) attributes the development of mummification by the Aleuts to a reluctance to part with the deceased; Laughlin (n.d.) points to the anatomic interests of the Aleuts in conjunction with their desire to preserve and use the spiritual power residing in the human body. The Aleuts studied comparative anatomy, using the sea otter as the animal most like man, conducted autopsies on their dead, and had an extensive

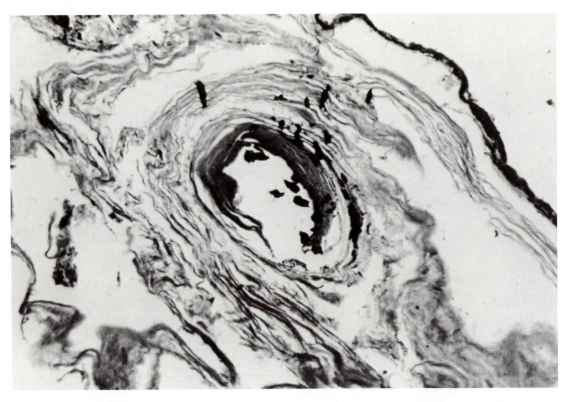

Figure 8.9. Fibrocalcific granuloma in a carinal lymph node. Hematoxylin and eosin. × 95.

anatomic vocabulary. Mummification as an Aleut funerary practice was an extension of their pragmatically oriented culture.

The technique of mummification varied with the social status of the deceased (Jochelson 1925; Veniaminov 1945; Dall 1945). The bodies of hunters and tribal leaders were eviscerated through an incision in the pelvis or over the stomach. No chemicals were used, but fatty tissues were removed from the abdominal cavity, which was stuffed with dry grass. The body was then put in running water, which completed the removal of fat, leaving only skin and muscle. The body was then bound with the hips, knees, and elbows flexed. This position has been variously explained as an imitation of the fetal position, an attempt to economize on space, or an effort to prevent the dead from returning and harming the living. Jochelson (1925) rejects these interpretations in pointing out that the flexed position was the habitual leisure posture of the Aleuts. The binding of the mummy bundle is properly considered an effort to maintain the deceased in a comfortable position.

The flexed body was then air-dried by carefully and repeatedly wiping off exuded moisture. When drying was complete, the cords were removed and the mummy was wrapped in its best clothes, usually a coat of aquatic bird skins. It was encased in a waterproof coat of sea lion intestines and then various layers of seal, sea lion, or otter skins and perhaps some matting. The entire bundle was then tied with a braided sinew cord and removed to a burial cave. There the mummies were placed on platforms or suspended from the ceiling to avoid contact with the damp ground. The cave in which the mummy described in this chapter was found was heated by a volcanic vent, creating a preservative warm, dry atmosphere.

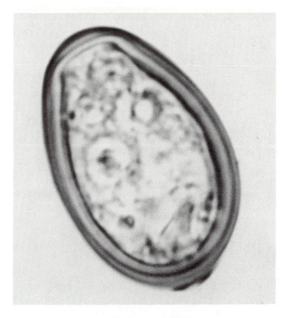

Figure 8.10.   Ovum of Cryptocotyle lingua, a fish trematode, found in the feces. × 600.

These caves were probably used only for a few hundred years before the Russian contact of the early eighteenth century. An Aleut tale (Jochelson 1925), explaining the use of the warm cave, tells of a rich headman, Little Wren, who lived near the cave on Kagamil Island. His young son was accidentally killed by his brother-in-law. In the subsequent funeral procession, the boy's pregnant sister slipped on a rock and suffered a fatal miscarriage. As the season was snowy and cold, the chief decided to place the bodies in the nearby cave, which had been used previously for storage. The chief declared that the cave would become a mausoleum for his entire family, and when he died of grief shortly afterward, he was interred there with all his possessions.

Dr. Hrdlička removed some 50 mummies from the warm cave in 1938 (it is thought that the body of Little Wren had been removed in 1874 by Captain E. Hennig of the Alaska Commercial Company). Except for blood group determinations (Candela 1939), the mummies remained undisturbed at the Smithsonian until a group directed by the author examined one in 1969. It was fortunate that the mummy selected for study was apparently that of a common man, as it had not been eviscerated.

Radiologic examination of the 112-cm-long, coffin-shaped, fur-wrapped bundle revealed the outlines of the heart and lungs. The brain appeared as an occipital opacity. Pathologic changes were limited to minimal arthritic changes in the vertebral column and evidence of dental attrition and periodontal disease. A number of radiopaque masses were seen in the left side of the abdomen.

The wrappings were removed sequentially. The outer five were animal skins, probably sea otter. The innermost layer was an eiderdown parka, composed of numerous birdskins sewn together with the feathers on the inside, with a spotted fur collar. No incision was seen in the body.

The individual was an adult male of indeterminate age. The weight was approximately 10 kg, and the overall length of the body was 165 cm. The skin was dark brown, dry, and leatherlike. The body was flexed as shown in Figure 8.11.

The face was partially covered by a birdskin, probably a cap that had slipped down. There was some balding, and the hair appeared singed, suggesting the body had been suspended over a fire for desiccation. A mustache and full beard were present.

There was a full complement of teeth, in normal occlusion. Except for the shrinkage of mummification, the neck, chest, abdomen, and genitalia were unremarkable. No skin incisions were seen. Lodged between the left forearm and left side of the abdomen was an empty birdskin pouch.

A relatively standard postmortem examination was possible, using a Stryker electric autopsy saw to remove the rigid tissues of the anterior chest and abdominal wall. The thoracic viscera were found to be intact and were removed. Gross pathologic change was limited to a few pleural adhesions and consolidation of the lower lobe for the right lung.

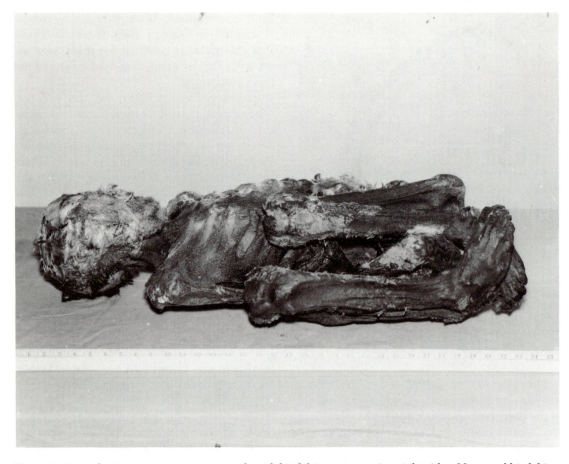

Figure 8.11. Aleutian mummy, unwrapped, with birdskin cap covering right side of face and birdskin pouch between left forearm and abdomen.

The abdominal viscera were poorly preserved, only the distal large intestine remaining intact, being filled with coprolites.

The rectum was slightly dilated; it measured 7 cm in diameter and was filled with fecal material. The abdominal aorta and iliac vessels were well preserved and easily identified. A firm yellow plaque measuring 2 by 1 cm was noted in the right iliac artery, but there was no other gross evidence of atherosclerosis.

The skull was examined after removal of the calvarium. The bone and the dura were found to be intact. The latter was thin and transparent in the frontal area and thicker and opaque elsewhere. Upon removal of the dura, the brain tissue was found to be shrunken into the posterior fossa of the cranial cavity, the major portion of which was empty (Figure 8.12). The brain was roughly rectangular; it measured 14 by 10 by 5 cm, and was covered with a fine crystalline material.

The upper left maxillary dentoalveolar process was removed en bloc. Extreme dental attrition was present to a point slightly beyond the interdental contacting tooth surfaces. Heavy dental calculus and periodontal bone loss were evident.

The pulmonary architecture was generally well preserved, although cellular detail was lost. A moderate amount of interstitial black anthracotic pigment was noted throughout.

Figure 8.12. *Position of brain in posterior midline, as seen after removal of the calvarium.*

Microscopic examination of the aorta revealed preservation of the three layers of the wall and of the elastic tissue. There was no calcification or atheromatosis, but cellular detail was absent. There was excellent preservation of the general architecture of the iliac artery and vein, including the elastic tissue and a venous valve. The single atherosclerotic plaque noted on visual inspection was composed of cholesterol crystals and contained minute calcific foci.

Sections of skin from the abdominal wall, eyelid, ear, and lower lip showed only connective tissue, a few structures suggestive of blood vessels, hair follicles and shafts, and in the ear, well-preserved cartilage. The inferior labial artery was partially collapsed and exhibited a poorly stained plaque that was considered to be consistent with atherosclerotic intimal changes. A section from the right thigh showed connective tissue, skeletal muscle, and a few areas of pigmented epidermis. Multiple hair shafts were noted in each of several follicles.

The Schneiderian membrane of the antral floor consisted of connective tissue covered by a thin (12μ) amorphous basophilic layer of epithelium. Polarized light elucidated the perivascular connective tissues and the perpendicular fibers (Sharpey's) of the periosteum.

The dental pulp chambers were thoroughly desiccated and contained only scattered strands of unrecognizable filamentous elements. No odontoblasts were seen. Nonetheless, the hard tooth structures were in an excellent state of preservation. Ground tooth sections revealed complete histologic properties of enamel and dentin. The Hunter-Schreger bands and the incremental lines of Retzius were clearly visualized in the enamel. The tubular nature of the dentin was perfectly preserved, and the incremental lines of Von Ebner and Owen were seen. Secondary dentin was present, measured about 350μ in thickness, and was separated from the reparative (tertiary) dentin by a prominent basophilic line. The reparative dentin was 1 to 2 mm in thickness under the worn cuspal areas where the attrition had abraded through the enamel into the dentin of the teeth. In spite of the severe attrition, structurally sound enamel remained in the intercuspal areas. Because of the excellent reparative response to attrition and the absence of periapical dental disease, it was assumed that the teeth were vital.

Several special studies were performed.

The blood group, determined on cancellous bone of the femoral head by a modification of the agglutination-inhibition test described by Springer et al. (1957) was O.

Cultures of the lung tissue failed to reveal viable organisms.

Analysis of skin, heart, kidney, brain, and muscle revealed almost total preservation of protein content. Enzyme analyses showed absence of activity of lactic dehydrogenase, creatine phosphokinase, glutamic pyruvic transaminase, glutamic oxalacetic transaminase, and alkaline dehydrogenase. The analyses were done on homogenates of dry tissue (20 mg per milliliter of normal saline).

Neutron-activation analysis of lung, hair, fingernails, skin, and retroperitoneal tissue revealed no unexpected nuclides. The sodium activity in all the samples was greater than anticipated from previous studies of dried human tissues (H. B. Gardner 1969, personal communication), and the right lower lobe showed some increase in ^{82}Br as compared with the remainder of the lung.

The crystalline areas were subjected to X-ray crystallographic analysis, which revealed them to be composed of acid-ammonium-sodium-phosphate-hydrate and apatite, a calcium–phosphate compound.

Examination of the coprolites was negative for parasites and the ova of parasites. Chemical analysis revealed the coprolites to be composed of ammonia and phosphates; as there was no calcium, their radiopacity was a function of density. The coprolites were soluble in a wide range of organic and inorganic solvents, including chloroform, acetone, ethanol, water and dilute acids, and alkalis.

The reduction of the lower lobe of the right lung to a consolidated mass was the most remarkable gross pathologic change in the mummy. Histologic examination confirmed the destruction of the parenchyma in this area and revealed the presence of free gram-negative bacilli and clumps of material that took a red color with the Brown-Hopps stain. Multiple small aggregates of crystalline material, often containing gram-negative bacilli, were found, not only in the right lower lobe, but in the other lobes of both lungs, the heart, the trachea, and the retroperitoneum.

There are several possible explanations for the appearance of the right lower lobe and the crystalline areas. A component of postmortem change is indisputable; the question is one of degree. Do these areas represent antemortem disease or are they attributable entirely to postmortem change?

The posterior midline position of the remains of the brain indicates that the body was in the supine position during the postmortem period of liquefaction and subsequent desiccation. Although the condition of the lower lobe of the right lung could be a manifestation of postmortem autolysis, one would expect, given the supine position of the body, that a change of this nature would involve the posterior portions of both lungs. The mummification of the other lobes is evidence against autolysis. Conversely, the failure of one lobe to mummify implies a predisposing factor, such as antemortem disease.

Analysis of crystalline material present in the lungs and viscera revealed it to be inorganic, and not to be confused with adipocere. No adipocere was seen grossly, although the foggy and hazy conditions common in the Aleutians are said to favor the formation of adipocere (Evans 1963). Adipocere results from the postmortem autolysis of body fats and consists primarily of palmitic, stearic, and hydroxystearic acids (Mant 1957). Evans (1962) notes that the crystals of adipocere are found only in tissues containing fat and not in such structures as the lung and trachea. It is apparent that the crystalline material under discussion is not adipocere, but probably represents postmortem mineralization of areas containing discrete aggregates of gram-negative bacilli.

There are two possible explanations for the presence of the bacteria in the crystalline foci. One is that the bacilli were present throughout the tissues and were preserved only in the areas of mineralization. Many gram-negative and gram-positive cocci were scattered throughout the tissues, and it is difficult to imagine a process that would preserve bacilli selectively in one area and cocci in another. The more plausible explanation is that the crystalline foci represent antemortem bacterial abscesses. The preservation of bacteria for 300 years is not unusual; bacteria have been stained in the intestinal contents of a 4,000-year-old Egyptian mummy (Ruffer 1921). The bacteria may have had a role in the process of mineralization by invoking a mechanism similar to that which results in adipocere (Evans 1963). Proteolytic bacterial enzymes may produce a localized acidic environment conducive to the deposition of calcium salts, especially if supersaturation resulted from desiccation. However, in the absence of experimental studies, a discussion of the process of mineralization remains speculative.

The distribution of the crystalline areas also suggests antemortem abscesses. As the bacteria in these foci appear to be the same as the gram-negative bacilli in the right lower lobe, one can infer that the terminal illness was lobar pneumonia (possibly caused by *Klebsiella pneumoniae*), with septicemia and multiple visceral abscesses.

Postmortem changes have altered the picture considerably. Although they might have caused all the changes described, this appears to be improbable for the reasons already given. The involvement of the tracheal cartilage can be explained by postmortem invasion by the bacilli.

Anthracotic pigment found in the lungs can be attributed to the culinary habits of the Aleuts. Until recently they prepared their food over an open seal-oil fire, which filled their homes with smoke. Indeed, ocular changes in the Aleuts, noted by early visitors, were attributed to the smoke (Petroff, quoted in Hrdlička 1945), and modern visitors have found it impossible to live in Aleut houses for the same reason (T. D. Stewart, personal communication). The lungs showed changes consistent with moderate emphysema and bronchiectasis, probably of the same origin. Tobacco may be ruled out as a cause, as the use of tobacco was unknown before the advent of the Russians.

Severe masticatory dental stresses must have existed, because of the marked dental attrition, the increased thickness of the lamina dura, the prominent hypercementosis of the tooth roots, and the significant deposits of tertiary dentin.

The presence of periodontal disease was manifested by deposits of heavy dental calculus, periodontoclastic bone changes, and migratory protrusion of the anterior teeth.

There was no evidence of impacted teeth, supernumerary teeth, missing teeth, dental caries, or malocclusion disorders. Similarly, the maxillary bone and antrum exhibited no pathologic changes. A possible atheromatous plaque was noted in the inferior labial artery.

Sections of the major blood vessels showed only mild focal atherosclerosis of the iliac vessels. This finding, combined with the roentgen evidence of mild arthritic changes, enabled us to estimate the age of the subject at the fourth or fifth decade.

There were two interesting incidental findings. Chondrocytes appeared to be well preserved, even at the ultrastructural level (Yeatman 1971). An inexplicable finding was the presence of several hair shafts in single follicles in a section of skin (a nonhuman characteristic). As the cadaver was separated from the fur wrappings by an eiderdown parka, this section could not be one of adherent animal skin.

The negative findings are also noteworthy. There was no evidence of trauma, and no foreign material or organisms were seen in the pulmonary alveoli; this evidence ruled out accidental death by drowning. No poisons were found in the tissues analyzed by neutron activation. Results of staining fungi and tubercle bacilli were negative.

The blood group, determined on bone from the femoral head, was type O. The science of paleoserology is still in a state of evolution (Lengyl 1975), but blood groups have been successfully determined in varied mummified material (Boyd and Boyd 1939; Candela 1939; Thieme et al. 1956). Candela (1939) typed 30 of the Aleutian mummies when they arrived in Washington, D.C., by use of vertebral bone corings. The blood group distribution was: 11 O, 11 A, 6 B, and 2 AB. These results are in contrast to the prevalence of type O in Eskimos and American Indians (although some type A is found among Northwest Coast Indians). Candela noted that the Aleuts have an almost identical blood type distribution to that of Eastern Siberian tribes, but he felt that the number of individuals typed was too small to draw any valid conclusions regarding the origin of the Aleuts.

In summary, examination of a 200- to 300-year-old Aleutian cadaver mummified by desiccation suggested that the cause of death was lobar pneumonia caused by a gram-negative bacillus, possibly complicated by septicemia and diffuse metastatic abscesses. The abdominal viscera were not preserved, and the role of intraabdominal disease in the death of the subject could not be assessed. Other findings included pulmonary anthracosis and mild atherosclerosis. Severe masticatory dental stresses were attested to by marked dental attrition, increased thickness of the lamina dura, prominent hypercementosis of the dental roots, and significant deposits of tertiary dentin. Periodontal disease was manifested by deposits of heavy dental calculus, periodontoclastic bone changes, and migratory protrusion of the anterior teeth. No adipocere was seen, and there was no evidence of death from trauma, drowning, or poisoning.

On 7 October 1978 another Aleutian mummy dated about 1700 was examined at the Peabody Museum at Harvard. It had been in the museum for about 100 years, having been in the group removed by Captain Hennig from Kagamil Island in 1874. The body was covered with the original wrappings of sea lion skin lined with sea otter fur. The mummy was that of a woman in the sixth decade of life. Preliminary studies have suggested healed pleuritis and renal tubular necrosis. She also suffered from middle ear disease and head lice. Other studies are in progress (Zimmerman 1979).

REFERENCES

Allison, M. A.; Klurfeld, D.; and Gerszten, E. 1975. Demonstration of erythrocytes and hemoglobin products in mummified tissue. *Paleopathology Newsletter* 11:7–10.

Birket-Smith, K. 1959. *The Eskimos*, 2nd ed. London: Methuen.

Boyd, L. G., and Boyd, W. C. 1939. Blood group reactions of preserved bone and muscle. *American Journal of Physical Anthropology* 25:421–34.

Breutsch, W. L. 1959. The earliest record of sudden death possibly due to atherosclerotic coronary occlusion. *Circulation* 20:438–41.

Brothwell, D. R.; Sandison, A. T.; and Gray, P. H. K. 1959. Human biological observations on a Guanche mummy with anthracosis. *American Journal of Physical Anthropology* 30:333–47.

Candela, P. B. 1939. Blood group determinations upon the bones of thirty Aleutian mummies. *American Journal of Physical Anthropology* 24:361–83.

Collins, B. 1937. Archeology of St. Lawrence Island, Alaska. *Smithsonian Institution Miscellaneous Collections* 96(1).

Collins, H. B. 1933. Prehistoric Eskimo culture of Alaska. In *Explorations and field work of the Smithsonian Institute in 1932*. Washington, D.C.: Smithsonian Institution.

Comstock, G. W. 1959. Histoplasmin sensitivity in Alaskan natives. *American Review of Tuberculosis and Pulmonary Disease* 79:542.

Dall, W. H. 1945. Quoted in *The Aleutian and Commander islands and their inhabitants*, A. Hrdlička (ed.), pp. 184–91. Philadelphia: Wistar Institute.

Evans, W. E. 1962. Some histological findings in spontaneously preserved bodies. *Medicine,*

Science and the Law 2:153–64.

–   1963. Adipocere formation in a relatively dry environment. *Medicine, Science and the Law* 3:145–53.

Geist, W. W. 1928. Diary. University of Alaska archives.

Gonzalez, T.; Vance, M.; Helpern, M.; and Umberger, C. J. 1954. *Legal medicine: pathology and toxicology*. New York: Appleton.

Hrdlička, A. 1945. *The Aleutian and Commander islands and their inhabitants*. Philadelphia: Wistar Institute.

Jochelson, W. 1925. *Archeological investigations in the Aleutian Islands*. Washington, D.C.: Carnegie Institute.

Laughlin, W. S. n.d. The use and abuse of mummies. Unpublished manuscript. University of Connecticut, Storrs.

Lengyl, I. A. 1975. *Paleoserology*. Budapest: Akademiai Kiado.

Mant, A. K. 1957. Adipocere: a review. *Journal of Forensic Medicine* 4:18–35.

Petroff, I. 1945. Quoted in *The Aleutian and Commander islands and their inhabitants*, A. Hrdlička (ed.), p. 174. Philadelphia: Wistar Institute.

Rausch, R. L.; Scott, E. M.; and Rausch, V. R. 1967. Helminths in the Eskimos in western Alaska, with particular reference to Diphyllobothrium infection and anemia. *Transactions of the Royal Society of Tropical Medicine and Hygiene* 61:351–7.

Ruffer, M. A. 1921. *Studies in the paleopathology of Egypt*. Chicago: University of Chicago Press.

Sandison, A. T. 1970. The study of mummified and dried human tissues. In *Science in archeology*, 2nd ed., D. Brothwell and E. Higgs (eds.), pp. 490–502. New York: Praeger.

Sexton, R. L.; Ewan, J. R.; and Payne, R. C. 1949. Determination of the specificity of histoplasmin and coccidioidin as tested on 365 Aleuts of the Pribilof Islands. *Journal of Allergy* 20:133–5.

Smith, G. S., and Zimmerman, M. R. 1975. Tattooing found on a 1600 year old frozen, mummified body from St. Lawrence Island, Alaska. *American Antiquity* 40:434–7.

Springer, G. F.; Rose, C. S.; and Gyorgy, P. 1957. Blood group mucoids: their distribution and growth-promoting properties for *Lactobacillus bifidus* var. Pen. *Journal of Laboratory and Clinical Medicine* 43:532–42.

Thieme, F. P.; Otten, C. M.; and Sutton, H. E. 1956. A blood typing of human skull fragments from the pleistocene. *American Journal of Physical Anthropology* 14:437–44.

Veniaminov, I. 1945. Quoted in *The Aleutian and Commander islands and their inhabitants*, A. Hrdlička (ed.), pp. 182–4. Philadelphia: Wistar Institute.

Willis, H. E. 1970. Radiocarbon dating. In *Science in archeology*, 2nd ed., D. Brothwell and E. Higgs (eds.), pp. 46–57. New York: Praeger.

Yeatman, G. 1971. Preservation of chondrocyte ultrastructure in an Aleutian mummy. *Bulletin of the New York Academy of Medicine* 47:104–8.

Zimmerman, M. R. 1973. Blood cells preserved in a mummy 2000 years old. *Science* 180:303–4.

Zimmerman, M. R. 1979. Harvard mummies: a preliminary report. *Paleopathology Newsletter*, 25:5–8.

Zimmerman, M. R., and Smith, G. S. 1975. A probable case of accidental inhumation of 1600 years ago. *Bulletin of the New York Academy of Medicine* 51:828–37.

Zimmerman, M. R.; Yeatman, G. W.; Sprinz, H.; and Titterington, W. P. 1971. Examination of an Aleutian mummy. *Bulletin of the New York Academy of Medicine* 47:80–103.

9

Mummies of Peru

JAMES M. VREELAND, JR.
Department of Anthropology
University of Texas, Austin, Texas, U.S.A.

AIDAN COCKBURN
President, Paleopathology Association
Detroit, Michigan, U.S.A.

ANTHROPOLOGICAL AND HISTORICAL PERSPECTIVES
JAMES M. VREELAND, JR.

Peruvian mummies have been the object of anthropological and historical interest for more than four centuries. In 1560, long before Egyptian pharaohs were put on public display in Cairo's Museum of Archaeology, curious Europeans had already been queuing up in Lima's San Andrés Hospital to view several of the marvelously preserved mummies of Peru's legendary Inca kings.[1] Struck by what seemed to them an idolatrous, but fascinating, custom, the early Spanish chroniclers of Andean culture noted that the practice of mummifying principal lineage heads and local chiefs was widespread in western South America. Today, studies of pre-Hispanic mortuary practices draw heavily on these richly detailed ethnohistorical accounts, as well as on the wealth of cultural and biologic materials preserved in the desertic coastal zone of Peru. Here, despite the absence of written history until the arrival of Pizarro in 1532, the archeologic record of mummification is now 6,000 years old.

Although the origins of this practice still remain unclear, naturally mummified bodies[2] occur in Peruvian graves before Andean societies became sedentary and stratified; they may well have provided models for subsequent experimentation with methods of artificially preserving human flesh. The importance of specialized techniques to retard decay of the remains of local secular and theocratic elite individuals probably increased with the emergence of complex

societies and clearly represents an intensification of the ancient Andean practice of ancestor worship (Trimborn 1969:116). Venerated as "living corpses," the mummified bodies of clan ancestors or chiefs often served as community or tribal fetishes, and in the case of the Inca rulers, as historical gods. By the end of the pre-Hispanic epoch, grave goods accompanying the mummy of a high-status figure often included the mummified bodies of his wives, retainers, and slaves (Steward 1948:10).

Although the term *mummy* is repeatedly used to describe the often extraordinarily well preserved human remains recovered from Peruvian cemeteries, there is in fact little agreement on what constitutes a Peruvian mummy and how it was actually produced. The term *mummification* will be used here to refer to all natural and artificial processes that bring about the preservation of the body or its parts. Such methods include drying by air, sun, or fire (with or without evisceration); covering with plastic materials (such as clay); filling body cavities with plant or other materials; and embalming with chemical or other substances (Dérobert and Reichlen, n.d.:8).

Three principal types of mummification can be identified in pre-Columbian America (Dawson 1928b; Comas 1974):

Type I. *Natural mummification,* caused by a number of factors (either singly or in combination) such as dryness, heat, cold, or absence of air in the burial unit or grave
Type II. *Intentional natural mummification,* brought about through the intentional exploitation or deliberate enhancement of

natural processes, such as those listed above

Type III. Artificial mummification, produced by a variety of techniques including evisceration, fire-and-smoke curing, and the application of such embalming substances as resins, oils, herbs, and other organic materials

In Peru, the combined archeologic and ethnohistorical evidence indicates that the large majority of mummies known are of types I and II.[3] The skin, when preserved, has generally been modified to a tough, almost leathery consistency. Although connective tissue frequently remains, most or all of the internal organs have disintegrated to a fine powder, often filling much of the abdominal cavity. However, mummified bodies with nearly intact intestinal tracts have been found in several coastal regions where natural preservation was particularly favorable (Stewart 1973:44; Allison et al. 1974).

PHYSICAL AND CULTURAL
ENVIRONMENT

Geographically, the Peruvian, or central Andean, cultural area consists of the coast and highlands of Peru and the adjacent highlands of Bolivia, southern Ecuador, and parts of the north coast and highland regions of Chile (Figure 9.1). The Peruvian littoral, a narrow desert zone crosscut at nearly regular intervals by fertile river valley oases, supported a number of densely populated regions, some of which grew to the status of large chiefdoms and states. Despite the periodic saturation of the surface air layer and occasional winter drizzles (*garúa*), precipitation is negligible and rarely penetrates more than a few centimeters into the ground. Not all areas are, however, equally conducive to the preservation of organic materials; some sites may have been specifically chosen as burial precincts because of their optimal conditions for preservation. The preservative effect of the uppermost soil horizon, when enriched with certain salts, has long been cited as an important additional factor in the mummification process (Rivero and von Tschudi 1854; Mead 1907).[4]

In contrast to the coast, the highland zone is far less homogeneous, characterized by a series of complex gradients of climate and vegetation. In the treeless high-altitude valleys and plateaus, or altiplano, a marked rainy season delivers as much as 800 mm of precipitation annually. Near- or below-freezing temperatures are recorded through much of the year, especially on the upper slopes (over 4,300 m), where frost is an almost nightly occurrence. Both the rarefied atmosphere and cool temperatures of the altiplano were doubtless key factors in mummification processes.

Any description of Andean mummification practices must move in two dimensions: time and space. Prehistoric Andean cultural chronology is customarily broken down into seven major periods, beginning with a long preceramic sequence dating back over 20 millennia and closing with the Spanish conquest of the Inca empire in 1534 (Table 9.1). The first ceramic period, beginning about 1800 B.C., also marks the emergence of the "Peruvian cultural tradition" (Bennett 1948), characterized by the appearance of widespread maize agriculture, irrigation, terracing, complex religious iconography, and marked ancestor worship (Willey 1971:88).

Following this so-called Initial period, a series of three Horizon styles developed, each typified by a complex of more or less homogeneous traits or features, separated by two Intermediate periods when regional cultures eclipsed and superseded the unifying Horizon styles (Rowe 1967). Most authorities generally agree that the three pan-Peruvian cultures evolved from three highland sites: Chavín de Huantar, Huari or Tiahuanaco, and finally Cuzco. From these centers, certain diagnostic styles are seen to have spread outward through most of the central Andean area. However, increasingly persuasive arguments supporting a tropical forest inception for the first of these highland cultural

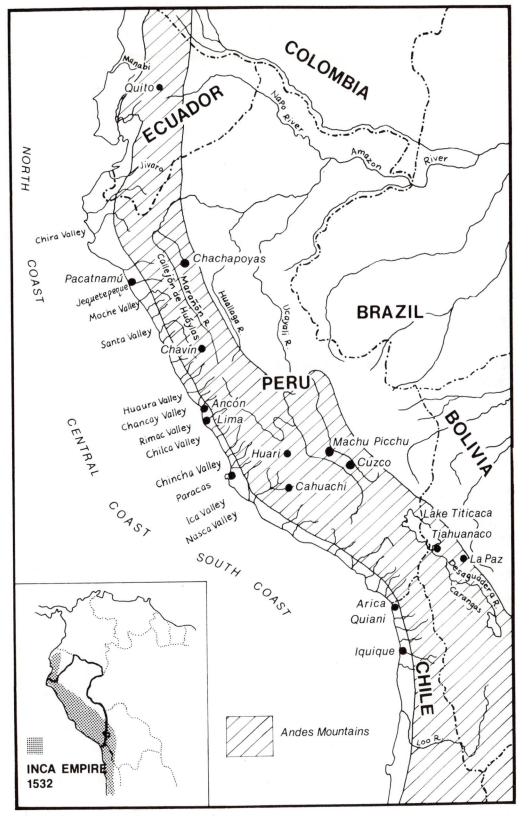

Figure 9.1. Central Andean cultural area.

Table 9.1. *Major cultural periods and phases for the Central Andes*

Period	Time	Culture
Colonial	A.D. 1534	Spanish Conquest
Late Horizon	A.D. 1476	Inca Empire
Late Intermediate	A.D. 1000	Ica, Chimú, Chancay
Middle Horizon	A.D. 600	Huari, Tiahuanaco
Early Intermediate	200 B.C.	Nasca, Moche, Paracas-Necropolis
Early Horizon	900 B.C.	Paracas-Cavernas, Chavín
Initial	1800 B.C.	Arica, Santo Domingo
Preceramic	10,000 B.C.	Tres Ventanas
	20,000 B.C.	Ayacucho

matrixes have induced some investigators to look east of the Andes for archeological evidence of the origins of Peruvian civilization in this moist lowland region (Lathrap 1974).

PRECERAMIC AND INITIAL PERIODS (20,000–900 B.C)

Although numerous burials containing skeletons wrapped in skins, hides, and vegetable-fiber fabrics have been described for the coastal regions, and to a much lesser extent for dry highland cave sites, little evidence of mortuary practices involving mummification occurs before the fifth millennium B.C. Engel (1970, 1977) recovered four naturally mummified bodies, two adults and two juveniles, from Tres Ventanas Cave in the upper Chilca Valley (4,000 m), dating from about 4000 to 2000 B.C. In contrast to the tightly flexed adult bodies, placed on their sides, the position of the subadults was semiflexed, lying on their backs. The bodies had been wrapped in camelid mantles or cloaks bearing traces of a red pigment and were found with fragments of netting and twined and looped fabrics. The skin and hair appear sufficiently well preserved by the high-altitude tomb matrix that we might justly term these individuals the oldest mummies so far reported from South America.

The earliest mummified remains from northern Chile are quite different and indicate that some coastal fishing societies 5,000 years ago practiced a variant of type III mummification (Figure 9.2; see Uhle 1918; Skottsberg 1924; Nuñez 1969; Munizaga 1974). Special attention had been given to the preparation of mummies of infants, described by Bird at the site of Quiani:

In all cases the viscera and brains appear to have been removed; the legs, arms and body reinforced by sticks inserted under the skin or in the flesh; the faces coated with thin clay and painted; a wig of human hair fastened over the head; and [frequently a] sewn leather casing wrapping the body. [Bird 1943:246]

The presence of several coats of paint on a similar mummy from Punto Pichalo suggests that the body had not been buried immediately following death, but may have been stored or displayed for a considerable time before final interment.[5] In 1917 Skottsberg, working at the preceramic cemetery of Los Gentiles in Arica, found a bundle containing the remains of two infants similarly mummified (Skottsberg 1924:32–37).

A second variety of mummification existed during this same period that appears to represent a form of secondary burial. The extended cadaver was flayed, and the skin was replaced with a thin coating of clay or "cement" and then wrapped in a reed matting. Bodman (in Skottsberg 1924) analyzed such

Figure 9.2. Detail of elaborately prepared (Type III) 5000-year-old mummy of child from Quiani, Chile. Body is coated with thin layer of clay and some paint, wrapped with birdskin "cloak," with wig of human hair over face. Twined reed matting and cordage is not shown. Specimen #41.1/5780, American Museum of Natural History, New York.

a brownish "cement" and found it to contain sand and a certain agglutinate, mixed with an unidentified material. Although Skottsberg reported that the mummy had been eviscerated, no clear evidence of evisceration or embalming was found by Alvarez Miranda in similar interments at Arica (Alvarez Miranda 1969:189).

EARLY HORIZON TO EARLY INTER-
MEDIATE PERIODS (900 B.C.–A.D. 600)
The abundant archeologic information from

the Paracas–Ica area of the south coast of Peru indicates that by the end of the Early Horizon period a major transformation in burial practices had taken place in that region. At least as early as 400 B.C., sedentary farming communities had developed a keen interest in enhancing the preservation of the dead, wrapped in an upright position inside "mummy bundles" up to 1.5 m in height. The most spectacular finds of this period include 429 mummy fardels recovered from the Necropolis at Paracas, of which approximately one-half have been opened (Tello 1929). Nearly all the bodies examined were elderly males showing a distinctive type of cranial deformation (Tello 1959, 1980; Vreeland 1978a).[6]

Seated in a coiled basket or gourd, the flexed cadaver was generally covered with a simple cotton shroud and wrapped with plain-weave cloth, often alternated with polychrome, patterned fabrics widely acclaimed for their intricately embroidered designs. Naturally mummified remains of parrots, cavies, foxes, dogs, cats, and deer have also been found in Paracas period mummy bundles. In the larger bundles, four discrete layers of ceremonial garments and wrapping cloths normally occur (Yacovleff and Muelle 1934; Bennett 1938; Tello 1959).

The subject of a heated debate for decades, convincing evidence of artificial mummification (type III) is generally indirect and exceedingly difficult to recognize in archeological contexts. Strong (1957:16) has argued that the presence of large areas of calcined earth and ashes at the temple complex of Cahuachi suggests that the site had been used as a massive mummy-processing area about 2,000 years ago. No mummies were recovered from Cahuachi, but bundles belonging to the same cultural period were found at the Necropolis by Mejía Xesspe in 1927–1928. Following his examination of the largest and best preserved units, Tello concluded:

After extracting the viscera and a great part of the muscles, the body has been subjected to a special mummifying treatment. At times the head has been removed from the body, the brain tissue being extracted through the foramen magnum. The thorax is opened nearly always across the sternum and the lungs and heart pulled out. . . . In certain cases they have made incisions in the extremities to pull out the muscles. . . . The body is [then] subjected to a process of mummification through the use of fire and perhaps various chemical substances, as indicated by the carbonized appearance of certain parts of the body, and by the salty efflorescences of the chemical substances employed. [Tello 1929:131–135]

Unfortunately no large intact bundles are now available against which to check Tello's findings. Unable to determine ABO blood groups from muscle tissues extracted from Paracas mummies opened by Tello, Candela (1943) attributed the negative results to the presence of some gummy, resinous substances, which, he suggested, had served as preservatives. In an independent study, Yacovleff and Muelle argued that mummification of the Paracas cadavers had been caused by natural desiccation (type II) without any artificial treatment:

To explain the preservation of these mummies, it is not necessary to revert to an hypothesis involving the use of fire and certain chemical substances, because the physical conditions of the place suffice to impede the decomposition of organic material. . . . The nearly complete absence of vegetation for twenty kilometers round about is due to the perpetual aridity; the rich salinity of the dry soil and the constant on shore wind; the relative height of the cemeteries above possible ground water; the constant action of the sun – all this makes special treatment for the preservation of the bodies unnecessary. [Yacovleff and Muelle 1932:48]

This view is also shared by Mahler and Bird (n.d.), who examined a single large Necropolis bundle in 1949. They found no evidence of foreign material inside the body cavity; the brain had not been removed, and no appreciable dehydration of the tissues appeared to have occurred before burial.

Recent examinations of smaller Necropolis cadavers also have failed to produce any convincing evidence of artificial preservation (Allison and Pezzia 1973; Rivero de la Calle 1975; Vreeland 1976). The leathery consistency and dark brown color of the skin, drawn tight over the upper portions of the skeleton, indicate that the bodies probably had been desiccated intentionally, at least in some cases. Nonetheless, sufficient body fluids or putrefaction products resulted from autolytic decomposition to have induced extensive rotting in the lower sections of the bundles. The internal soft tissues in most cases had been reduced nearly to powder, and only bits of fibrous connective tissues remained attached to the walls of the body cavities and extremities. Furthermore, the presence of large numbers of pupa cases of necrophagous insects attests to the lack of any immediate and complete mummification treatment, especially one requiring the use of fire and certain embalming substances such as those described by Tello. However, tissues taken from one small bundle recently opened and presently under microscopic examination show what appear to be artificially preserved, fire-dried, and in places, burned tissues, found in association with several small pieces of charcoal (Vreeland 1978a:41). Nevertheless, in the absence of further studies of large units, the theory that the presumably elite individuals wrapped in such bundles had in fact been accorded a complex, type III mummification must remain moot.

Little is known regarding mummification practices from other regions during the Early Intermediate period, but available archeological information suggests that a pattern distinct from that described for the south coast occurred in other areas. On the north coast, the Mochica buried their high-status dead in cane coffins placed in chamber tombs filled with diverse grave offerings (Larco Hoyle 1946:170). One exceptional (and very late) tomb excavated at the site of Pacatnamú yielded three mummies, all fully extended and placed on their backs (Ubbelohde-Doering 1966).[7] One of these, an 18-year-old woman, was found with skin "like fine old parchment and black hair" and tattooing on the right forearm. In contrast to the type

III treatment described during the previous period on the Chilean north coast, no evidence of artificial mummification has been reported from postceramic periods in that area.

MIDDLE HORIZON PERIOD
(A.D. 600–1000)

During this period, two highland kingdoms, emanating from the sites of Huari and Tiahuanaco, spread differentially through much of the central Andes, bringing with them significant changes in mortuary practices that, in some areas, persisted until 1534. Although no mummies clearly dating from this period have been reported in the damp altiplano region, several excellently preserved bundles have been found on the coast (Reiss and Stübel 1880–1887; Allison et al. 1974). Unfortunately, no comprehensive study of these remarkable fardels has yet been made, but recent examinations of several large coastal Huari bundles from the Ica–Nasca area provide a general conception of the mortuary treatment involved.

Tightly flexed and covered in a cloth shroud or poncho, the cadaver was generally seated on a firmly rolled and coiled cotton disc about 50 cm wide. A more or less cylindrical bundle was then built up around the body by alternating layers of lint cotton with plain-weave textiles and with tightly interworked cord superstructures. Other packing materials, such as grass, reeds, and leaves, were also used. Protruding from the top of the "body" was a slightly conical false head constructed of alternating fiber and fabric layers, frequently decorated with metal or shell "eyes," "nose," a human-hair wig, and a woven cap or sling headband. A tapestry tunic was then placed over the completed, bottle-shaped bundle (Vreeland 1977; Figure 9.3).

Examinations of the human remains from the central and southern Peruvian coast areas (Allison and Pezzia 1973; Vreeland 1976) and northern Chile (Le Paige 1964:56) showed no evidence of type III mummification. Desiccation by means of natural agents had probably been utilized in some cases. Preservation was also enhanced by the tightly wrapped and highly absorbent cotton layers, which would have helped draw off body decomposition fluids. This process is demonstrated in radiographs taken of the bundles before they were opened; the radiopaque oval areas below the skeleton correspond to the cotton discs, apparently hardened by the absorption of internal moisture (Vreeland 1976; Figure 9.4).

LATE INTERMEDIATE PERIOD
(A.D. 1000–1476)

Despite the decline of the Huari and Tiahuanaco cultural influences in the central Andes, throughout much of Peru numerous characteristics of Middle Horizon mortuary practices continued, with regional variations, until the Spanish Conquest. The most common form of interment continued to be the bundle burial, except in the eastern sierra, where the body was cut in sections or cremated (Tello 1942:120). In the western sierra the cadaver was wrapped in several ways: in a cactus fiber net, in twisted grass cords, or in a deer- or camelid-hide bag. The body was always tightly flexed in adult burials, with knees drawn up against the chest, hands opened flat over the face, and arms and legs bound in place with additional cords (Figure 9.5). The wrapping cords often covered the entire mummy, with the exception of a rectangular opening over the face and a smaller aperture for the toes (Figure 9.6). Although complete mummies are rarely preserved in the moist highland zones, hair, usually faded from its natural black to a reddish color, is often encountered. The hair of male mummies appears to have been kept relatively short, and louse eggs are quite common (Villar Córdoba 1935:227).

The mummy burial also predominated in the coastal areas, where the bundles were normally topped with false heads and masks in Middle Horizon style (Figure 9.7). Some of the larger units weigh over 100 kg (Waisbard

Figure 9.4.   *Composite print of radiograph taken of a Middle Horizon bundle similar to the one shown in Figure 9.3, showing tightly flexed mummy with metal offering in mouth (a), stone or metal bracelets on wrists (b), and seated on a cotton disc (c) heavily impregnated with radiopaque body decomposition fluids.*

and Waisbard 1965:82). In the northern sierra, the mummy bundle was covered with a layer of mud to form a conical structure and was crowned with a modeled and painted clay mask simulating the human head. Some of the larger mummy casings are from 1 to 1.5 m high, weighing over 125 kg (Savoy 1970:167).

Mummies on the north Peruvian coast were generally extended and fully clothed (as in the Early Intermediate period Mochica burials), in contrast to the flexed and shroud-covered mummies from other coastal regions (Figures 9.8 and 9.9).[8] Preparation of these large, plain-weave cotton shrouds required considerable amounts of energy and raw material. One large central coast bundle contained an estimated 265 km of single-ply yarn, requiring some 4,000 hours of spinning and plying time, used to weave the 60 m² of cotton wrapping shrouds alone. Another very large and well preserved unit from the Lima area, containing the remains of an 18-to-20-year-old woman, had been wrapped with over 150 kg of cotton cloth; one of these textiles, having a complete warp length of 40.40 m, is the longest single-web fabric known from prehistoric America (Vreeland 1978b).

LATE HORIZON PERIOD
(A.D. 1476–1534)
The final period of the Andean prehistoric sequence begins with the effective consolidation of the Inca empire and concludes with the destruction of its highland capital, Cuzco, by the Spanish in 1534 (Rowe 1946). Although the burial ritual accompanying the Inca elite appears to depart from preexisting patterns, mortuary practices evidenced throughout most of Peru show general regional variations characteristic of the preceding periods (Vreeland 1980). Supplementing the very limited available archeological data from the highlands is a rich corpus of

Figure 9.3.   *High-status Middle Horizon mummy bundle. Anthropomorphic features include false head and hair, face mask, cap, headband, necklace, and poncho shirt. Probably from Nasca area. Collection Museo Nacional de Antropología y Arqueología, Lima.*

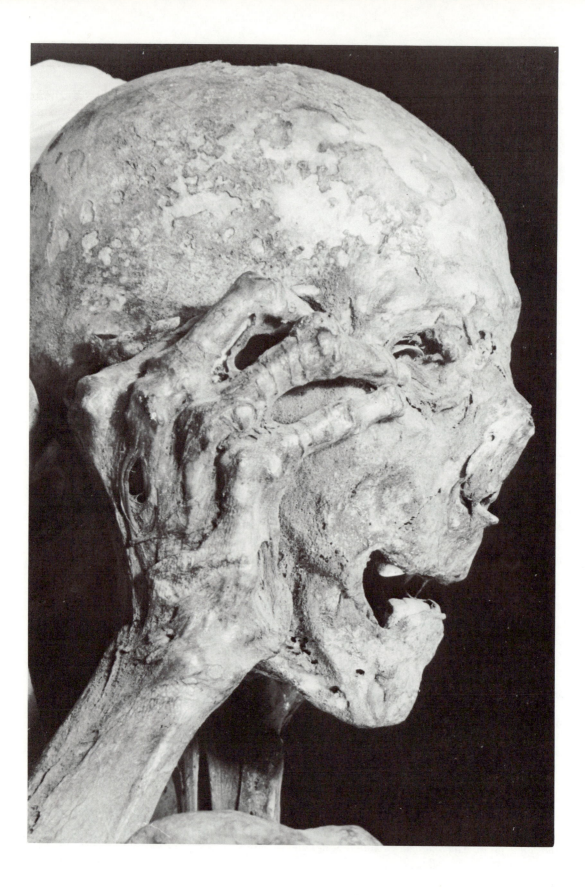

ethnohistorical information written during the early part of the Colonial period. These sources indicate that the practice of mummification was largely conditioned by two factors: local traditions and social rank or status of the deceased. One of the fullest accounts of this regional variation is provided by the Indian chronicler Guamán Poma, who not only described, but also illustrated at the beginning of the seventeenth century the prevailing customs of the four Inca *suyos* ("quarters") constituting the Inca empire (Guamán Poma [1613] 1956:451–456).[9]

In Condesuyo (i.e., the central highlands) the body of the deceased was placed either in a burial tower or in a sepulcher located on a high mountain ridge or peak. Guamán Poma noted that the cadaver was eviscerated and that certain balsamic substances were used to preserve it. In the Yungas (lowlands or coastal) regions, on the other hand, the body was covered with a simple cotton funeral shroud, then wrapped in cloth or cord ropes, forming a netlike superstructure. The upper portion of the mummy bundle was painted or decorated to suggest the human head and face. Apparently the viscera and sometimes even the flesh were removed from the bones and placed in freshly made ceramic vessels buried next to the mummy bundle.

An early account of type III mummification is also given in a document written about 1580, describing the mortuary ritual of the Pacajes, an ethnic group inhabiting the Bolivian altiplano region to the southwest of Lake Titicaca: "The manner in which these Pacajes bury their dead is to remove the viscera, and to throw them in a pot which they bury next to the cadaver, bound with ropes of straw. . . . The deceased was buried with the best clothing and plenty of food" (Jiménez de la Espada 1965:339). This practice is in part corroborated by Ponce Sanginés and Linares Iturralde (1966), who examined 10 mummies from the Bolivian province of Carangas.

Three had been eviscerated through an incision made in the abdominal wall. The cadavers were subsequently mummified by the naturally dry, cool atmosphere of the Bolivian altiplano, where it appears that this type of mummification may have been extensively practiced in the Late Horizon period and possibly earlier.

Social status also conditioned mortuary practices to a significant degree. According to the Jesuit chronicler Blas Valera, the common Indian was generally buried with the few possessions he owned in a simple grave in outlying community fields. In contrast, a member of the *kurakas*, or regional nobility, was often interred in a multiroom sepulcher with certain of his wives, servants, and others selected to serve him in the afterlife. These victims were sacrificed (some not unwillingly) and "embalmed" in the same fashion as the *kuraka* (Valera [1609] 1945:14–15). Guamán Poma ([1613] 1956:428) added that whereas gold or silver offerings were placed in the mouths of the *kurakas*, clay offerings were customarily used in the interments of common Indians.[10] In Chachapoyas, burial in conical clay casings apparently was reserved for the principal members of local descent groups; individuals of lower status were simply buried in the ground.[11]

Funeral ceremonies following the death of an Inca sovereign were probably the most elaborate rituals of their kind performed in prehistoric Peru (Figures 9.10 and 9.11). The combined ethnohistorical descriptions, though not uniform in detail, indicate that the cadaver of the king was placed on a special seat or throne in a flexed position, arms crossed over the chest, and head positioned over the tightly drawn-up knees. Bits of silver or gold were placed in the mouth, fists, and on the chest. The body was then dressed in the finest vicuña cloth and "wrapped in great quantities of cotton, and the face covered."[12]

One month after death, the body of the Inca

Figure 9.5.   Elderly male mummy, not eviscerated. Note cotton fiber in orbits and remains of string laced between fingers. No provenance; probably coastal Late Intermediate to Late Horizon period. Collection Museo Nacional de Antropología y Arqueología, Lima.

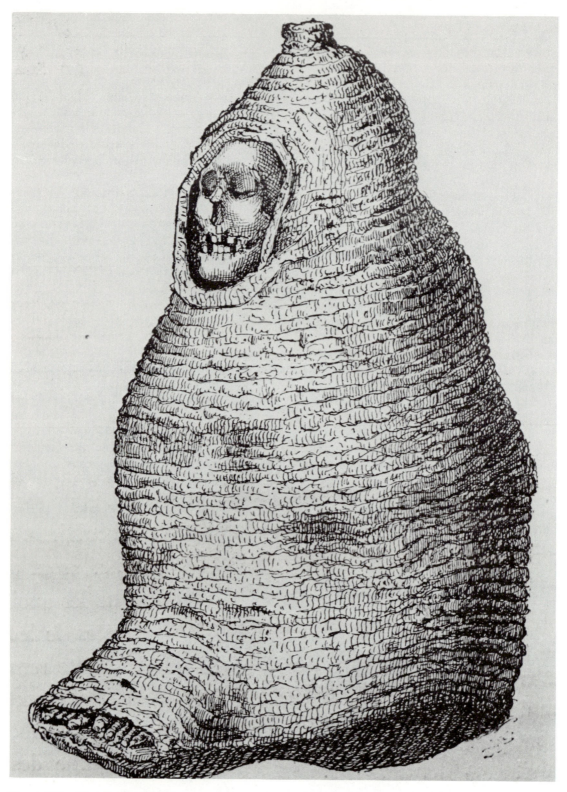

Figure 9.6.   Sketch of highland mummy wrapped in cords with apertures for hands and feet. Cuzco area, probably Late Intermediate or Late Horizon period. (After Wiener 1880)

Figure 9.7.   *Large mummy bundle from Lima area, Late Intermediate period. False head and face mask follow typical Middle Horizon pattern. Collection Museo Nacional de Antropología y Arqueología, Lima.*

was placed in the royal funeral sepulcher, or *pucullo*, along with great quantities of fine cloth, woven by special craft personnel expressly for the royal funeral. Tributed or bestowed from the four *suyos* of the vast empire, this exquisite cloth was either folded and placed next to the body or under the funeral shrouds, or burned. Food and drink were also

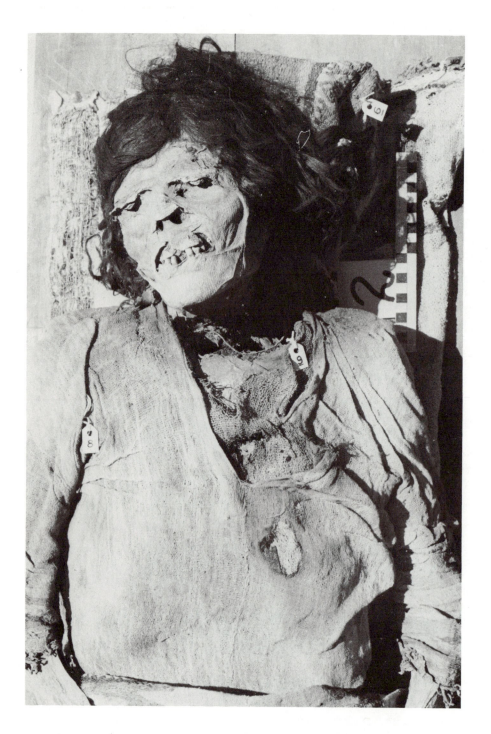

Figure 9.8.   Classic Lambayeque period (ca. A.D. 800–1200) mummy from Collus, Lambayeque Valley, north coast of Peru. Dressed with fabrics decorated in Middle Horizon style, the mummy was interred in extended position typical of mortuary practices on the coast prior to Middle Horizon influence there. Brüning Museum, Lambayeque.

Figure 9.9. Pottery vessel depicting funeral procession and extended mummy inside "coffin." North Peruvian coast, Late Intermediate period. Collection Museo Nacional de Antropología y Arqueología, Lima.

included with the dead ruler's armaments, symbols of power and office, and bags containing all his used clothing, nail parings, hair, and even the bones and corn cobs upon which he had once feasted. Llamas were sacrificed, as were some of the Inca's principal wives, concubines, and retainers.[13] Upon conclusion of the ceremonies in Cuzco, the royal mummies were reclaimed by the lineage groups of the dead king and were cared for by male and female attendants. These specially appointed custodians knew not only when to give food and drink to the king's mummy, but also acted as spokesmen

for the dead ruler's personal desire. They carried out routine chores such as whisking the flies from the mummy's brow, changing and washing its clothing, calling in visitors with whom the Inca wished to "speak," and lifting the bundle when its occupant needed to "urinate" (Polo de Ondegardo [1554] 1916a:124; Pizarro [1571] 1939:294–295; Imbelloni 1946:190). Ordinarily none but these professional cult personnel was permitted to look on the royal mummies, except when these relics were removed from their sepulchers and exhibited in Cuzco during certain religious and state ceremonies, such as the two solstice

festivals and the coronation of Inca rulers (Molina [1575] 1916; Estete [1535] 1938:54–56).

The earliest known account of an Inca royal mummy is that recorded by Pizarro's secretary, Pedro Sancho del la Hoz, who less than 10 years after the Conquest described the mummy of Huayna Capac (d. 1525) as being nearly intact, wrapped in sumptuous cloth, and "missing only the tip of the nose" (Sancho [1543] 1938:183). Garcilaso de la Vega, who saw several royal mummies collected by the Spanish licentiate Polo de Ondegardo in Cuzco in 1559, provides a more detailed description:

The bodies were so intact that they lacked neither hair, eyebrows nor eyelashes. They were in clothes just as they had worn when alive, with *llautus* ["bands"] on their heads but no other sign of royalty. They were seated in the way Indian men and women usually sit, and their eyes were cast down. . . . I remember touching the finger of Huayna Capac. It was hard and rigid, like that of a wooden statue. The bodies weighed so little that any Indian could carry them from house to house in his arms or on his shoulders. They carried them wrapped in white shrouds through the streets and plazas, the Indians dropping to their knees, making reverences with groans and tears, and many Spaniards removing their caps. [Garcilaso de la Vega [1609, pt. I, bk. V, chap. XX] 1963)

The bodies of at least three Inca kings and the ashes of another, as well as the bodies of two *coyas* ("queens"),[14] were sent to Lima in 1560 by Polo. Some 20 years later, the Spanish priest Acosta noted that they were still "wonderfully preserved, causing great admiration" among the people of that city (Acosta [1590, bk. V, chap. VI] 1954:146).

Despite these provocative accounts, little information on the actual mummification process employed by the Incas can be gleaned from the available ethnohistorical reports. Both Garcilaso de la Vega and Guamán Poma stated that the bodies of Inca rulers (and their principal wives) were embalmed, but except for the special properties of the natural highland environment, no preservation processes are mentioned. Blas Valera, on the other hand, specifically described a type III treatment, including both evisceration and embalming. This was effected with a variety of balsam brought from the province of Tolú.[15] When applied with some unspecified substances, Valera remarked, "the body thus embalmed lasted four to five hundred years" (Valera [1609] 1945:14). He further noted that when Tolú balsam was unavailable, the embalmers resorted to a kind of bitumen prepared with an unidentified material that preserved the flesh, apparently with some success. Acosta also reported that the bodies of the royal mummies had been "dressed with a certain bitumen" (see Imbelloni 1946:193). Father Cobo described a mummy that was "so well cured and prepared that it seemed to be alive, its face was so well formed and complexion full of color," and then went on to tell us how this was done: "The preservation of the face . . . was effected by means of a piece of calabash placed under each cheek, over which the skin had become very taught and lustrous, with false open eyes" (Cobo [1653, bk. XII, chap. X] 1964:65).

Unfortunately, the accounts of these three Jesuit fathers, Cobo, Acosta, and Valera, are all somewhat late to be completely reliable and may not in fact represent entirely independent sources. It is unlikely that Cobo ever saw a royal mummy. Garcilaso de la Vega's narrative was written in Spain some 40 years after he witnessed the mummies in Cuzco as a young man. Valera, like Acosta, may well have seen the Inca mummies brought back to Lima, where he began his novitiate in 1568. But his papers, lost in 1596, are known to us only through the writings of Garcilaso de la Vega, remarkable for their impressionistic detail rather than their veracity. Furthermore, the descriptions of Acosta and

Figure 9.10.   Inca period mummy being borne on a stretcher during November "festival of the dead." (From Guamán Poma [1613] 1956)

CONQVISTA
DEFVNTOGVAINACAPAC
INGA.   ILLAPA

lleuan ae enterrallo al cuzco —

Fesenel defunto dequito
aenterralle asu obedaxcal
del cuzco

al

Valera presumably refer to mummification procedures applied only to Inca nobility and are hardly confirmed by examinations of highland mummies recovered from the Cuzco area.

The use of certain herbs and plant materials in the embalming process, mentioned by the Augustinian friar Ramos Gavilán ([1621] 1976:73) in reference to Colla burial practices, has also been suggested by Cornejo Bouroncle (1939:108), who claims to have identified the remains of the fragrant plant muña[16] stuffed inside a number of "lower-status" Inca period cadavers in the Cuzco museum. Lastres (1953:73), after examining mummies in both the Cuzco and Lima archeology museums, found no evidence of evisceration and was of the opinion that mummification had been caused predominantly by natural agencies, with the occasional use of herbs and balsam applied to the skin. On the other hand, McCreery (1935) examined about 20 mummies in Cuzco and stated that they were all rather well preserved, of all ages and sexes, and that no evidence of artificial mummification could be found. From these conflicting reports it is clear that additional research is urgently needed to document adequately the nature and range of mummification practices in Late Horizon burials.

HUMAN SACRIFICE, TROPHY HEADS, AND HUMAN TAXIDERMY

Although ritual sacrifice and mummification appear to be closely related, especially in the later pre-Hispanic periods, space precludes all but the briefest review of human sacrifice and the practice of preserving the body or its parts. Types I and II mummification have been cited in reference to burials (usually of juveniles) in the 6,000-m and higher zones of the central Andes, in what clearly appear to be cases of human sacrifice. The most celebrated of such interments is that found at Cerro El Plomo in 1954, when the frozen body of an 8-

to 10-year-old boy, dressed in a camelid wool poncho, was recovered with several metal ornaments and figurines from an Inca period sepulcher (Medina Rojas 1958).[17] Mummies of several other subadults have been reported in similarly inaccessible high-altitude funeral cairns (Schobinger 1966), where the youths had probably been made intoxicated with the alcoholic corn beer *chicha* or with the narcotic coca leaf (*Erythroxylon coca*), and either sacrificed by strangulation or simply left there to die (Ramos Gavilán [1621] 1976:26).

On the Peruvian coast, mummy bundles containing the remains of dismembered bodies also suggest human sacrifice, possibly to obtain entrails for purposes of divination (Allison et al. 1974; Walter 1976). A different motive is indicated by the partial immolation found in a recently opened unit from the Lima area, dated to the Late Intermediate period. The bundle contained a pair of well-calloused, naturally mummified feet and lower legs, torn off at the knees (Vreeland 1978b). In a bundle from the same area Jiménez Borga found a mummified left foot (Waisbard and Waisbard 1965:82, pl. ix). Both bundles were relatively large and constructed in a manner identical to those containing entire mummified bodies.

Type III mummification of sacrificed individuals is amply documented for the late pre-Hispanic periods by several early ethnohistorical references. On the eve of the Spanish entry into northern Peru in 1531, Estete reported that in the coastal Ecuadorian village of Pasao (Manabí province), the Indians flayed the bodies of the dead and burned off the remaining muscle tissue. The skin was then "dressed like a sheep's hide" and stuffed with straw. Thus "crucified," the body, with arms crossed, was hung from the temple roof (Estete [1535] 1938:207–208). The Chanca Indians of the central Peruvian highlands, as well as the Incas, practiced a similar kind of human taxidermy, displaying the stuffed

Figure 9.11. *"Mummified" bodies of Inca king Huayna Capac, his queen, and a retainer carried on a litter from Quito to Cuzco for burial. (From Guaman Poma [1613] 1956)*

skins of their war captives in temples, making their stomachs into drums (Métraux 1949: 408). According to Estete ([1535]1938:208–209), the heads of the dead in Pasao were also mummified with certain balsamic substances and shrunken in a process similar to that described for the Jíbaro of the eastern Ecuadorian mountain slopes (Tello 1918; Figures 9.12 through 9.16).

SUMMARY AND CONCLUSIONS

Why Peruvian dead were artificially mummified is a question that cannot be comprehensively answered until more archeological and ethnohistorical information is made available. Based on the present evidence, one can tentatively state that religious, cult, and magical motives, some clearly derived from political and economic contexts, were all contributing factors in Andean mummification practices. As noted earlier, artificial enhancement of soft tissue preservation, which occurs naturally under proper conditions, and the desire to maintain the body in a more or less lifelike state, presumably represent an intensification of the mortuary cult and an extension of the widespread Andean custom of ancestor worship. The aperture over the face in the wrappings of many highland mummies, tubes leading from the tomb to the ground surface, washing and changing the ritual mummy clothing, and the false heads and face masks of the coastal bundles from the Middle Horizon period on, signify further elaboration of the concept of the "living dead," enabling, in effect, the deceased to participate in its own mortuary cult.[18] The mummified corpse thus represented a physical entity with "human" characteristics, and also served as an intermediary for symbolic communication between the worlds of the living and the dead. In some areas such active and periodic participation in ritual activity also presented a threat to the conservation of the mummy bundle and its contents. Mummification therefore may also have provided a solution to the problem of body disarticulation during transport and display.[19]

During the Late Horizon period, mummies of the Inca kings served an important state function. Preserved by royal privilege in sanctuaries on family estates, the mummies not only provided unequivocal testimony to the previous existence of those rulers, but also ensured their continued worship as semideified clan ancestors, whose cult was maintained by their descendants and specially appointed retainers. In a similar manner, possession of the mummified body of an important clan ancestor or of a political or religious figure constituted a powerful religious talisman that could often be exploited by the lineage or community owning it.

If the origins of Andean artificial mummification still remain obscure, it is nonetheless likely that natural mummification (Figure 9.17) may have directly inspired the prehistoric Peruvians to experiment with intentional mummification for a variety of cultural reasons, with motives growing more varied as complex societies emerged. The possibility that some forms of artificial preparation may have been introduced from the tropical lowlands to the east of the Andes should not be eliminated. A variant of type II treatment, appearing relatively early in the pre-Hispanic sequence on the north coast of Chile, frequently is mentioned in later periods, especially on the periphery of the central Andean area (northern Chile, the Bolivian highlands, parts of Ecuador and southern Colombia, and the Peruvian montaña), where contacts with tropical forest cultures apparently were more continuous and extensive. Whatever their origins, if complex embalming techniques had been utilized by the Cuzco elite for religious and political reasons, these practices soon fell into disuse and were forgotten as a result of the Spanish campaign to baptize Inca nobility quickly and forcibly.

In summary, the range of possible agencies or processes noted for each of the three types of mummification considered here are:

Type I. Natural mummification
1. Perpetually dry or frozen tomb matrix
2. Hot (coastal) or cold (highland) temperatures throughout much of the year

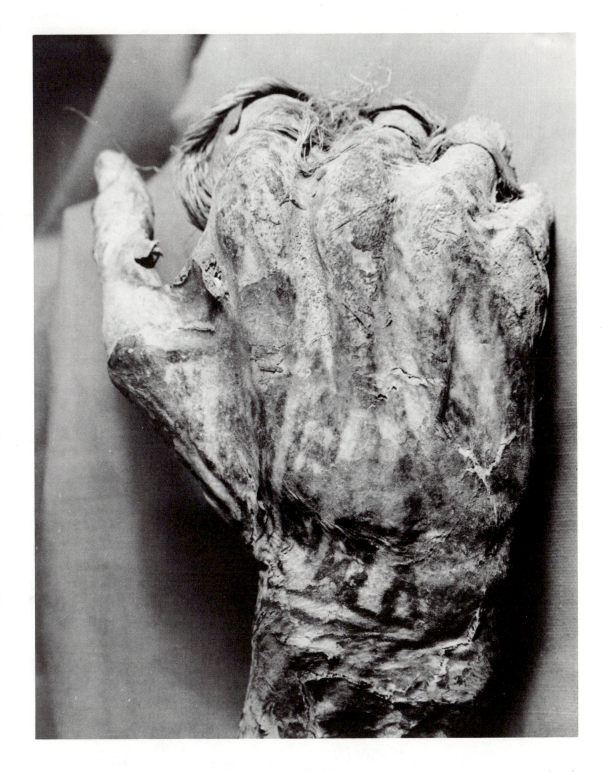

Figure 9.12.   Mummified hand showing tattooing. Probably central coast, Late Intermediate period. Collection Museo Peruano de Ciencias de la Salud, Lima.

3. Anaerobic tomb environment (e.g., direct burial in sand)
4. Local soil characteristics (salinity, alkalinity, etc.)
5. Highly absorbent substances (e.g., sand) in direct contact with the cadaver

Type II. Intentional natural mummification
1. Body intentionally dried by rarefied and/or cold sierra atmosphere
2. Body intentionally desiccated by warm coastal climate
3. Body intentionally wrapped with materials of highly absorbent nature (e.g., cloth, cotton fiber, leaves, grass)
4. Intentional location of cemeteries in areas having favorable natural conditions for preservation of organic materials

Type III. Artificial mummification
1. Evisceration of internal organs and/or other soft tissues
2. Replacement of soft tissues with plastic materials (e.g., clay)
3. Removal of all or parts of skeletal material and replacement with sticks, grasses, or other reinforcing materials
4. Fire desiccation
5. Smoke curing
6. Use of bitumen, balsam, or other resinous substances
7. Filling of body cavity with herbs or other materials having antiseptic chemical properties

DISEASES
AIDAN COCKBURN

In proportion to the number of its mummies, Peru has not been investigated in depth for evidence of disease in ancient populations. Most research on mummy bundles has been concentrated on the textiles, not on the human bodies inside. This is particularly true

of the grave robbers, so it is not uncommon to find an ancient cemetery plundered, with bones scattered unwanted on the desert surface. In Egypt there is a long history of careful dissection of bodies and diagnosis of pathologic conditions, but in Peru, investigation has been limited to the efforts of a handful of devoted scientists, who often worked under difficult conditions. Interest has sharpened within the past decade or two. In Lima, a group of physicians, disturbed at the lack of attention being given to the wealth of material available, founded the world's first museum of paleopathology. The museum, now renamed Museum of Health Sciences (Museo Peruano de Ciencias de la Salud) has an excellent building and a good collection. There are enormous possibilities for future research, although funds are badly needed for a sustained program. Under its new director, Dr. Fernando Cabieses, the future looks promising. In Ica, Marvin Allison and Alejandro Pezzia have been doing first-class work for a decade and have made some brilliant discoveries, with far-ranging implications.

Much of the data that follow are drawn from these sources.

TUBERCULOSIS
The antiquity of tuberculosis in the Old World has been well documented (Chapter 2). In the New World, the subject is more debatable, but there appears to be clear evidence that bone tuberculosis at least was present in pre-Columbian times (Morse 1961). A clear-cut case from Peru was described by Garcia Frias (1940), but the body, unfortunately, was not clearly dated: It was an Inca mummy, and these were prepared right into Colonial times.

Before discussing the antiquity of tuberculosis in the New World, it is necessary to analyze the meaning of the term. Basically, it refers to a condition in a person or an animal

Figure 9.13. Adult male mummy with cranial deformation. Note tattooing on wrist, cords used to bind cadaver in flexed position and textile impressions from mortuary shroud on right knee. Probably from coast, Late Intermediate to Late Horizon period. Collection Museo Nacional de Antropología y Arqueología, Lima.

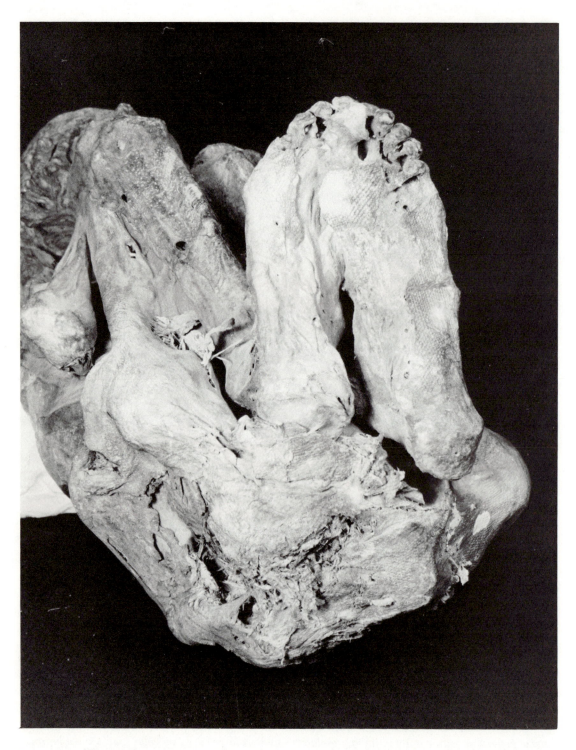

Figure 9.14. *Posterior view of adult male mummy showing no signs of evisceration. Probably coastal, Late Intermediate to Late Horizon period. Collection Museo Nacional de Antropología y Arqueología, Lima.*

caused by an acid-fast-staining mycobacterium, which produces a granulomatous tissue reaction. There are several mycobacteria that can cause lesions of this type, so the discovery of some granulomatous abnormality does not necessarily prove the presence of what today we call "tuberculosis." In man, granulomatous lesions in bone can be the result of infections by mycobacteria of man, cattle, birds, or even what appear to be free-living organisms from water and mud. Some forms of tuberculosis can also be caused by fish or snake pathogens. In addition to the variety of organisms that can cause "tuberculosis," the status of the human host can also alter the clinical picture. Populations exposed to human tuberculosis for the first time differ sharply in their reactions from those that have had centuries of saturation. After centuries of exposure, the urban dweller is apt to develop a chronic pulmonary form; the rural African or Eskimo, infected for the first time, suffers a rapidly progressive, often fatal, glandular type.

These points must be kept in mind when considering the case of tuberculosis reported by Allison and Pezzia (1973). The body was disinterred with its burial goods from the Nasca area in the department of Ica, and is dated to between A.D. 200 and 800; carbon-14 dating gave a time of around A.D. 700. The body, that of an 8-year-old child, was sitting in a hunched position on an adobe pad made to fit its body contours in life (Figure 9.18). Radiography showed Pott's disease (tuberculosis of the spine) involving the first, second, and third lumbar vertebrae. As so often happens in this condition, pus from the lesion had tracked from the spine down the psoas muscle, producing a psoas abscess and leaving a hollow sack about 5 cm in diameter. The abscess cavity contained a layer of dried caseous material. The organs of the throat and abdomen were removed, and it proved possible to identify, then rehydrate in Ruffer's solution, the heart, lungs, right kidney, liver, and spleen. On inspection with a hand lens, small white nodules resembling tubercles were found on the lung, pleura, and pelvis of the kidney. Histologically, little structure could be recognized at the cellular level. Staining by the Ziehl-Neelsen method revealed many clumps of acid-fast bacilli in those lesions.

We have here a clear-cut case of bone and miliary tuberculosis with a psoas abscess, which belongs to an era and location far removed from any Old World contact. Unfortunately, the source of the infection – whether human, mammal, bird, or other – cannot be determined, so the case cannot definitely be claimed as one of the "human" types found in both Old and New Worlds today.

HOOKWORM INFESTATION

A favorite game among medical historians is arguing about how infectious diseases spread. The battle over Columbus and the first outbreak of syphilis at Naples in 1493 has been progressing merrily almost ever since the epidemic. A similar debate, although less heated, has involved hookworm: Was it brought over from Africa by infested slaves, or was it already present in the Americas before the voyage of Columbus?

The matter has now been settled, for Allison et al. (1974b) found adult hookworms (Ancylostoma duodenale) in the small intestine of a Tiahuanaco mummy from a gallery burial in Peru dated between A.D. 890 and 950 (Figure 9.19). The mummy was opened in southern Peru in 1960, and pieces of intestine were studied. Examination with a 20-power dissecting microscope showed the worms attached to the intestinal lumen. They were subsequently photographed at 100 enlargement by scanning electron microscope. Details of the parasites' heads and buccal cavities were clearly visible, leaving no doubt about the identification. One worm had two large teeth and a rudimentary one, indicating that the species was A. duodenale.

It is highly probable that hookworms were also imported from Africa during the period of the slave trade, but the native Indians must have been infested long before this occurred. The parasites were probably carried to Peru

Figure 9.15.   a. Adult male mummy, not eviscerated. Note extensive insect damage and remains of cord bindings between fingers. b. Lateral view, showing trephined skull and cephalic material inside. Possibly

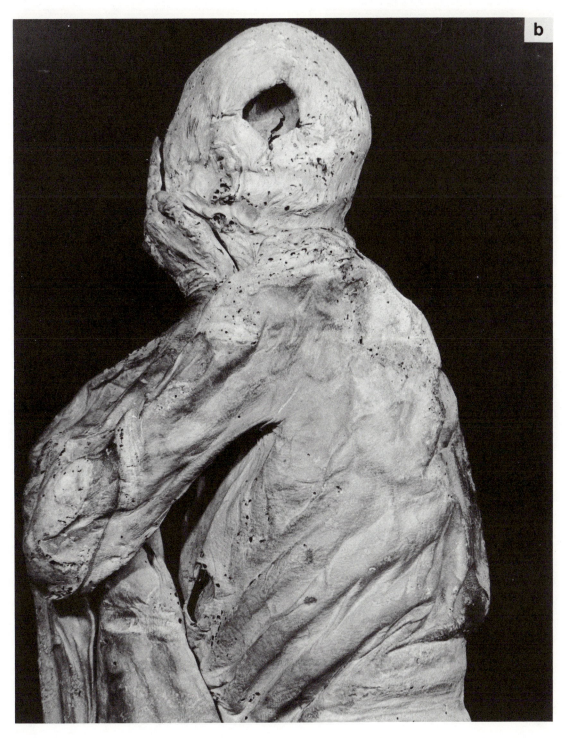

b

highland, Late Intermediate to Late Horizon period. Collection Museo Nacional de Antropología y Arqueología, Lima.

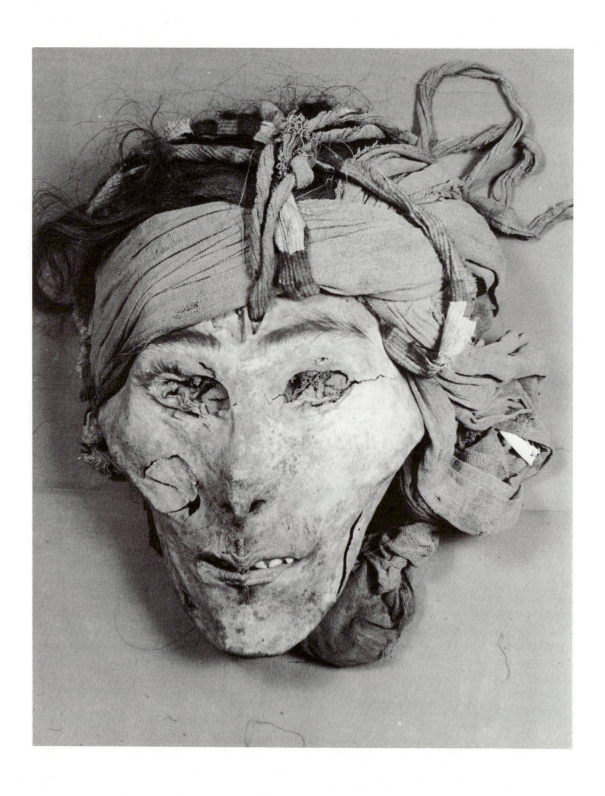

Figure 9.16.   *Mummified trophy head showing perforation in forehead and cactus spine pinned through lips. Nasca area, Early Intermediate period. Collection Museo Peruano de Ciencias de la Salud, Lima.*

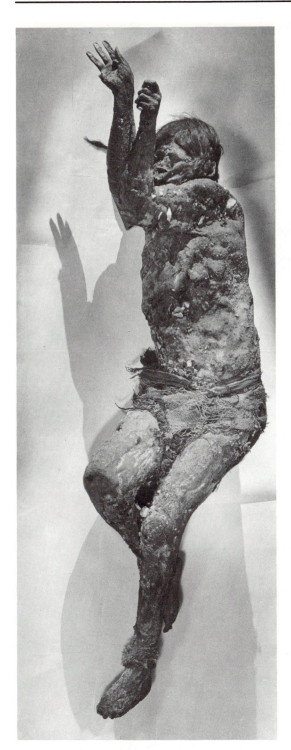

Figure 9.17.   *Four-century-old copper miner mummified naturally by copper salts. Chuquicamata, Chile. (Courtesy of American Museum of Natural History, New York)*

by the original migrants from Asia, who brought them over the Bering land bridge during their wanderings in the Ice Age.

VERRUGA, OR CARRIÓN'S DISEASE

Carrión's disease is confined to Peru and neighboring countries. It is caused by the microorganism *Bartonella bacilliformis*, is transmitted by sandflies, and is confined to certain valleys in the high mountains. It appears in two forms: The first is Oroya fever, an acute disease with destruction of the blood and a high mortality; the second is an unpleasant but not fatal skin infection, verruga, characterized by multiple fungating skin lesions. The disease is named after a medical student called Carrión, who showed that the two diseases were different forms of one infection by inoculating himself with crusts of verruga and afterward dying of Oroya fever.

A case of verruga was identified by Allison et al. (1974a) in a mummy found in the Nasca area. This is not in the area in which *Bartonella* infection is endemic, but the burial was of the Tiahuanaco culture and it is known that Nasca was invaded by Tiahuanaco people who would have had to pass through areas where the disease is endemic during the course of the invasion. The body had been sacrificed by being cut in half at the lower lumbar vertebrae: The bottom half was missing. The skin was found to have a rash on the back, arms, and legs, and was covered with small nodules varying from pinhead to pea size. On autopsy, the left part of the thoracic cavity proved to be empty, with no trace of the heart or lung. The left hand was severed at the wrist and restored to normal size by immersion in Ruffer's solution for a week. At the end of this time, a series of different types of skin lesion was readily seen. There were vesicles as well as pendulous tumorlike lesions, areas of healing as well as of excoriation. Evidently this was a process of long duration showing numerous stages of the disease. On section, some of the tumors proved granulomatous. Giemsa stain (but not Gram's) revealed clumps of organisms in the lesions and blood vessels. Pictures of 8,000 magnification by

Figure 9.18. Mummy of 8-year-old Peruvian with spinal and miliary forms of tuberculosis. Ica Museum.

the scanning electron microscope showed bacilli with a single polar flagellum. *Bartonella* stains badly with Gram's stain and well with Giemsa's and has one or more flagella at the tuft of one pole of the body. A diagnosis of Carrión's disease in the verruga stage was therefore made, based on the nature and distribution of the lesions and the identification of organisms similar morphologically to *B. bacilliformis*.

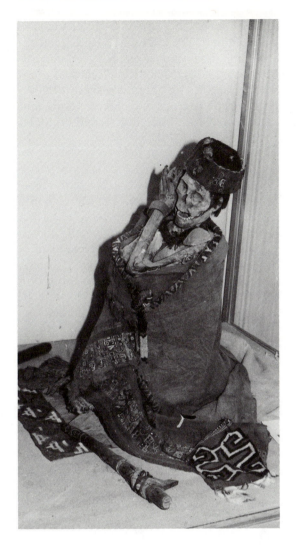

Figure 9.19 Mummy with hookworm infestation. Ica Museum.

TREPANATION

Trepanation is the removal of a piece of the skull while the individual is still living and without penetration of the underlying tissues. It was practiced until very recent times, and all the evidence shows that a large proportion of the patients survived, often undergoing repeated openings of the skull. The literature is reviewed by Lisowski (1967) and Margetts (1967). The practice was apparently worldwide, and many examples have been found in Peru. The modern operation, which uses an improved tool, is called trephination.

This is a surprising operation to be undertaken, and many guesses have been made about why it would have been done. These discussions and theories are beyond the scope of this section, but I can add from personal experience that the operation is perfectly practical. In 1934, as a final-year medical student, I worked as assistant to a brain surgeon in the north of England. One of my tasks was to remove the skull bone so the surgeon could tackle the tumor in the brain below. Providing the patient had a local anesthetic for incision of the skin, he felt little discomfort while I drilled four holes in his skull with a hand drill and burr, then cut the bone between them with a Gigli (fretwork) saw. Those were the days before antibiotics and modern technologies; all 15 patients died later – but from advanced brain tumors, not from my crude surgeries. My attempts were probably not too far removed from those of the trepanist of antiquity.

According to Allison et al. (1976), more than half of all the trepanned skulls in the world have been found in Peru. The list of finds is a long one, and an incomplete record of publications includes McGee (1894), Muñiz and McGee (1894), Hrdlička (1914), Moodie (1927), Rogers (1938), Quevedo and Sergio (1943, 1945a,b), Weiss (1949, 1958), Rocca (1953), Grana et al. (1954), Stewart (1956), Lastres and Cabieses (1960), Mac-Curdy (1970), and Allison et al. (1976).

Four main techniques were used in trepanation: scraping away the bone (Figure 9.20), boring a hole with a drill, making a circular hole with some cutting method, and making straight sawing cuts to outline an oblong hole. Allison et al. (1976) examined 288 skulls from the Ica area and found that 24 had been trepanned or treated surgically; 13 showed evidence of the fracture that had led to the trepanation. Of the 24, 11 died, but 13 survived the operation for at least 6 to 8 weeks. Obviously, this was a fairly common

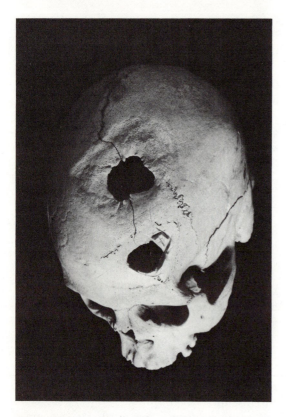

Figure 9.20. Trepanation. Peabody Museum, Harvard CL-1. One operation has been done by the scraping technique and has healed; the second was done by a groove-cutting method. (Courtesy of Peabody Museum)

operation in the Ica region and met with a fairly high rate of success.

THYROID DISEASE

Thyroid disease was discovered in a 30-year-old female of the Nasca culture in the Ica valley. Carbon-14 dating placed her death about 94 B.C. The possibility of thyroid disease was suggested before autopsy, when radiologic examination showed a 1-cm area of pathologic calcification in the thyroid region. The calvarium of the skull was twice the normal thickness and there was calcification of the aorta.

Dissection of the neck revealed the thyroid gland, which usually cannot be found in mummies. The gland contained two large calcified areas and several smaller focuses, surrounded by thick tissues. Histological examination disclosed occasional scattered follicles filled with thick colloid material.

The diagnosis of thyroid disease rests on the physical findings of the gland, skull, and aorta, which are common in hypothyroidism (Gerszten et al. 1976).

BLOOD GROUPS OF PERUVIAN MUMMIES

The blood groups of Peruvian mummies have long attracted considerable attention, mainly in the hope that light might be shed on the evolution and movements of people in antiquity. The work was first pioneered on a large scale by Boyd and Boyd (1933, 1937, 1959) using the agglutination-inhibition technique. Coombs introduced the mixed-cell agglutination technique, and this was used by Otten and Florey on Chilean mummies, as described in Chapter 20. Allison et al. (1976) tested 111 mummies with both methods plus induction of antibody. They found that all three techniques detected the presence of H(O) antigen. All blood groups (A, B, AB, and O) have now been identified in Peruvian mummies, but the distributions differ in various ages. The B and AB groups were present in early pre-Columbian Indians, but the B group became almost extinct in Colonial mummies and is very rare in more recent Indian populations. Boyd (1959) has suggested that the ancestors of modern Indians carried the B group with them in their wanderings over the Bering land bridge, but that this B group was gradually eliminated by natural selection. Allison et al. (1976) think there is merit in this suggestion. They also point out that the western cultures of South America probably originated with small family groups that were valley-oriented, so that examination of material from different valleys might help in tracing migration patterns.

POROTIC HYPEROSTOSIS AND CRIBRA ORBITALIS

These pathologic conditions of the cranium are commonly found in ancient bodies from many parts of the world, although they are rarely seen today. Porotic hyperostosis is primarily a hypertrophy of the bone marrow of the cranium that results from severe anemia in childhood. The vault is greatly thickened, and the true bone thinned, so that the marrow is visible. Cribra orbitalis is a particularly baffling manifestation of the upper plate of the orbital cavity, as bone marrow does not normally occur there. Because radiography reveals a "hair-on-end" picture that is typically seen in modern-day thalassemia, some physical anthropologists and physicians working on specimens from the eastern Mediterranean claim that the condition indicates severe falciparum malaria. According to current theory, the abnormality of the blood that produces thalassemia also protects against falciparum malaria and the disease is therefore common in highly malarious areas. However, as the presence of malaria in ancient Peru is highly unlikely (though the matter is debatable), the protective effect would not seem to have been a factor in that country.

Both porotic hyperostosis and cribra orbitalis were prevalent in pre-Columbian Peru. The average mummy autopsy does not reveal their presence unless a radiogram is made. Normally the skull is not scalped, nor are the eyeballs removed for examination of the socket. However, there are large numbers of skulls in collections as well as strewn over the desert around cemeteries, and these show without question that the ancient peoples of Peru suffered from severe anemias that resulted in the growth of their bone marrows and the pathologies known to us today as porotic hyperostosis and cribra orbitalis.

In October 1976, the Paleopathology Association held a symposium in Detroit to review the causes of these conditions (Cockburn 1977). Although the results were not altogether conclusive, it became clear that iron deficiency was the chief contributing factor. Other factors, such as inadequate protein in the diet, may have played a part, but the essential cause was a lack of iron. This brings us to diet: It is always people living on a vegetarian diet who are vulnerable. The Peruvians had few domestic animals, except for members of the camel family at high altitudes, and these could not survive successfully at lower levels. The plains people had an exceedingly good source of fish in the ocean, brought there by the Humboldt Current, and in addition hunted the sea lions ("sea wolves") along the coast. In general, though, animal protein provided only a small part of the ancient Peruvian diet. These nutritional deficiencies are recorded for us today as cases of porotic hyperostosis and cribra orbitalis.

Other conditions leading to lack of iron in the body include loss of blood. Such parasitic infestations as schistosomiasis, with its hematuria and/or melena, and hookworm, with its bleeding into the intestine, can cause severe iron deficiency and anemia, although in modern times these have not been related to any bone pathology resembling porotic hyperostosis. Vitamin deficiencies (e.g., scurvy and rickets) have also been suggested as causative factors, but this theory is now discredited. In Mediterranean countries thalassemia is a very possible cause, for it does produce a picture identical to porotic hyperostosis and is found even today. The matter is not yet settled. As far as Peru in antiquity is concerned, however, thalassemia was probably not a factor.

An example of a skull from Peru showing porotic hyperostosis is shown in Figure 9.21. The literature on porotic hyperostosis up to 1966 has been carefully reviewed by Angel (1967); the views he expresses tilt strongly in support of the thalassemia theory. Most probably the condition in Peru is the result of nutritional deficiencies and not malaria.

ACKNOWLEDGMENTS

Part of the research upon which the section "Anthropological and Historical Perspectives" is based was carried out with an Organization of American States research grant (No. 73-38/910) between 1974 and 1975, in Lima's Museo Nacional

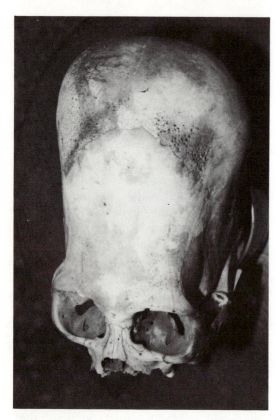

Figure 9.21.   Mummy with porotic hyperostosis. The skull was deformed deliberately in childhood. Museo Peruano de Ciencias de la Salud, Lima.

de Antropología y Arqueología. I would like to thank Dr. Luis G. Lumbreras, director of that institution, and the personnel of the departments of textile and physical anthropology, for the continued support that made this project possible. Valuable technical assistance during the first 2 years of study was provided by Prof. T. Mejía Xesspe, Dr. Germán Sánchez Checa, and Dr. Tamotsu Ogata. Many students, too numerous to name individually, helped in analyzing the textile materials recovered. Additional financial support was provided through the University Research Institute and the University of Texas Latin American Archaeology Program (Austin); scientific instruments and laboratory supplies were generously provided by Bausch & Lomb Corporation, Rochester, New York, and Hummel Chemical Company, South Plainfield, New Jersey.

Valuable substantive and editorial suggestions on previous drafts have been made by R. P. Schaedel, J. B. Bird, and N. Kaufman, whose critical observations are gratefully acknowledged here. I would also like to thank Dr. Fernando Cabieses, director of the Museo Peruano de Ciencias de la Salud, and Dr. Frédéric Engel, director of the Centro de Investigación de Zonas Aridas (Lima), for permission to examine and photograph mummies in those collections.

NOTES

1.   Acosta ([1590, bk. V, chap. VI] 1954:146); Riva-Agüero (1966:397).

2.   Naturally mummified individuals in non-burial contexts have also been reported from several areas in the central Andes. Sénechal de la Grange found the naturally mummified body of a woman in a pre-Columbian copper mine in Chuquicamata, Chile, where the body was accidentally preserved in part by the action of the copper salts (in Boman 1908:757). Imbelloni (1956:282) mentioned that a number of mummies of individuals who died in cave accidents are presently found in various Argentine museums. In 1903 a child was found buried in, and subsequently mummified by, a natural salt formation in the Argentine altiplano (Casanova 1936:264).

3.   Outside the central Andean area, evidence of artificial mummification is extensive (see in particular Steward 1949:721 and Linné 1929). Among the northern Andean and circum-Caribbean peoples, the body of the chief was desiccated, placed in a hammock and later cremated (Caquetío); disemboweled, desiccated, and kept as an idol or buried with several wives (Antillean Arawak); desiccated, temporarily buried, then roasted and reburied (Pititú). In southern Panama it was customary to bury the common people in the ground, but to desiccate and preserve the remains of the chief, which were slung in a hammock and mummified over a slow-burning fire (Lothrop 1948:147). The Ecuadorian Quijo eviscerated, smeared with tar, and smoked the bodies of their dead chiefs, and then filled the abdominal cavity with jewels (Steward and Métraux 1948:655). Dawson (1928a:73–74) examined two mummies from Colombia, both of which appeared to him to have been eviscerated – one via a perineal incision, the other through a cut in the abdominal wall – and then smoke-cured.

4.   In such arid zones almost anything buried in the sand will dry out to a naturally mummified state. For example, during the restoration of a series of Republican period forts constructed around Lima during the war with Chile, a number of Chilean soldiers were recovered from mass graves scooped in the sand. With buttons still shiny, documents intact, and soft external tissues remarkably preserved after nearly 100 years, the cadavers were sent back to Santiago, where they purportedly were returned to their families. Naturally mummified animal carcasses have even served as landmarks to travelers on old Peruvian roads (Rivero and von Tschudi 1854:209).

5. Bird (1943:246). This form of mummification (type III) appears to extend as far south as Iquique and may have continued briefly into the succeeding cultural phases (Schaedel 1957:21–25 and Appendix IV; cf. Nuñez 1969:130 ff.).

6. Tello (1929:120–125) posited that the slightly earlier Cavernas phase mummies at Paracas contained predominantly the remains of adult females and that all the mummies recovered had deformed crania (40 percent of them trephined) and probably had belonged to a single, stratified ethnic group.

7. Hollow cane tubes have been found leading from the tomb to the ground surface to permit, it is speculated, the passage of food and drink to the "living corpse" buried in the shaft tomb below (see Larco Hoyle 1946; Trimborn 1969:119–120). Similar tubes (ushnu) have been reported in ethnohistorical literature bearing on Late Horizon Inca burial practices (Zuidema, n.d.).

8. Extended burials are also reported from the far northern Chira Valley, as well as from the Huaura, Chancay, and Rimac Valleys on the central coast, and Chincha on the south coast of Peru (see Mead 1907:8; Williams 1927:1; Tello 1942:121; Reichlen 1950; Cieza de Leon [1553, bk. I, chap. LXIII] 1959:312; and Buse 1962:261).

9. Original dates for the ethnohistorical sources are given in brackets.

10. Gold palatal offerings in Peruvian mummies are found at least as early as the Salinar phase of the Early Intermediate period on the north Peruvian coast (see Larco Hoyle 1946).

11. This status distinction is perhaps no more graphically illustrated than in the case of the burial of a Chachapoyas chief named Chuquimis, who was convicted of regicide after allegedly having poisoned the Inca king Huayna Capac in 1525. Chuquimis died before the death sentence could be carried out, but desiring to desecrate the noble Chachapoyas lineage completely (and thereby set an example for other would-be assassins), the Incas ordered that the mummified cadaver of Chuquimis be exhumed from its clay casing and buried in the ground "like any other common Indian" (Espinoza Soriano 1967:246).

12. Acosta ([1590, bk. V, chap. VII] 1954:147); Garcilaso de la Vega [1609, pt. I, bk. V, chap. XXIX] 1963:190); Cobo ([1653, bk. XIV, chap. XIX] 1964:274–275.

13. Garcilaso de la Vega [1609, pt. I, bk. VI, chap. V] 1963:199). The burial of the Inca king Huayna Capac was supposed to have been accompanied by the sacrifice of no less than 1,000 individuals throughout the 80 Inca provinces (Polo [1567] 1916b:9). Polo also informs us that part of Atahualpa's ransom delivered to his Spanish captors at Cajamarca was obtained through the looting of jewels and precious metals from Huayna Capac's mummy in Cuzco (Polo [1561] 1940:154).

14. There is considerable confusion among the ethnohistorical sources regarding how many, and precisely which, of the royal mummies were actually discovered by Polo. Imbelloni (1946), after examining the various testimonies, tends to favor the version given by Garcilaso de la Vega, holding that the mummified remains of three kings (Huiracocha, Tupac Yupanqui, and Huayna Capac) and two queens (Mama Runtu and Mama Ocllo) were recovered from the villages around Cuzco, where they were still the object of great veneration in 1559. The identification and ultimate fate of the mummies will probably never be known, but informative and fascinating studies have been published by some of Peru's eminent historians, including Juan Toribio Polo (1877) and José de la Riva-Agüero (1966). It is certain, however, that the royal mummies brought to Lima were not provided Christian reburials (Von Hagen 1959:189, note 2). Rather, after some two decades of exhibition, they were probably unceremoniously buried in a patio or courtyard of the Hospital San Andrés, Lima, sometime after 1580 (see Riva-Agüero 1966:397).

15. "Tolú" probably refers to Santiago de Tolú, located in the archbishopric of Cartagena, Colombia (Bernal 1970), "donde se coge muy oloroso bálsamo, sangre de drago, y otras resinas, y licores medicinales" (Vázquez de Espinoza [1628] 1948: 294). Peruvian balsam probably originated in Colombia, where it is typed as Myroxylon balsamum or M. toluifera, known to have magnificent

antiseptic properties. It grows in the montaña and moist lowland regions of tropical South America and is also found in Peru at Tarapoto, Pozuzo, Húanuco, Loreto, Huallaga, Iquitos, and other regions (MacBride 1943:241–242). As early as 1887, Peruvian balsam was found interred with a mummy at the Necropolis at Ancón (Safford 1917:22), a sample of which is now in the National Museum of Natural History (catalog no. 132613), where spectrographic analysis has recently been conducted on it. However, it should be pointed out that the hardened, blackish resin had been stored inside a *crescentia* gourd container and was not recovered directly from the mummified bodies.

16. *Mithostachis mollis?* In the sierra of Huancayo, Lima, and Ancash, among other regions not high enough to permit the customary freeze-drying of potatoes, muña leaves are used as a preservative for these tubers. The plants are found between 2,400 and 3,700 m along permanent waterways where they grow in an uncultivated state (E. Cerrate, personal communication, Museo de Historia Natural, Lima, 1977).

17. The nematode *Trichuris trichiura* was found in the boy's intestine (Stewart 1973:46).

18. This concept is partially illustrated by an incident recorded by Bennett (1946:618) several decades ago. In the center of an underground family mausoleum used since pre-Hispanic times in northern Chile, a table had been set up, and around it the mummies of the family ancestors were arranged. A member of the family who was seriously ill was carried into the chamber, seated at the table, and surrounded by offerings of food and gifts. A ceremonial dance was then given by his relatives in order to help him "die well."

19. Perhaps such a situation is suggested in a pre-Hispanic north Peruvian coast myth of an important local *kuraka* who died en route to his homeland after an extended stay in Cuzco as an Inca prisoner. His corpse was mummified over a funeral pyre at Pacatnamú and borne home on a litter by his retainers (Kosok 1965:175–176).

REFERENCES

Anthropological and historical perspectives
Acosta, J. de. 1954. *Historia natural y moral de las Indias* [1590]. Madrid: Biblioteca de Autores Españoles.
Allison, M. J., and Pezzia, A. 1973, 1974. Preparation of the dead in pre-Columbian coastal Peru. *Paleopathology Newsletter,* 4:10–12; 5:7–9.
Allison, M. J.; Pezzia, A.; Gerszten, E.; and Mendoza, D. 1974. A case of Carrión's disease associated with human sacrifice from the Huari culture of southern Peru. *American Journal of Physical Anthropology* 41(2):295–300.
Alvarez Miranda, L. 1969. Un cementerio precerámico con momias de preparación complicada. *Rehue* 2:181–90.
Bennett, W. C. 1938. If you died in old Peru. *Natural History* 41(2):119–25.
– 1946. The Atacameño. In *Handbook of South American Indians,* vol. 2, pp. 599–618. Bureau of American Ethnology, Bulletin 143. Washington, D.C.: Smithsonian, Institution.
– 1948. The Peruvian co-tradition. In *A reappraisal of Peruvian archaeology,* W. C. Bennett (ed.), pp. 1–7. Menasha: Society for American Archaeology.
Bernal, S. 1970. *Guía bibliográfica de Colombia.* Bogotá: Universidad de los Andes.
Bird, J. B. 1943. Excavations in northern Chile. *Anthropological Papers* 38(4):173–318.
Boman, E. 1908. *Antiquités de la région andine de la République Argentine et du désert d'Atacama.* Paris: Imprimerie Nationale.
Buse, H. 1962. *Perú 10,000 años.* Lima: Colección "Nueva Crónica."
Candela, P. B. 1943. Blood group tests on tissues of Paracas mummies. *American Journal of Physical Anthropology* 1:65–8.
Casanova, E. 1936. El altiplano andino. *Historia de la nación Argentina* 1:251–75.
Cieza de Leon, P. de. 1959. *The Incas of Pedro de Cieza de Leon* [1553]. Edited by V. Von Hagen; translated by H. de Onis. Norman: University of Oklahoma Press.
Cobo, B. 1964. *Historia del Nuevo Mundo* [1653]. Madrid: Biblioteca de Autores Españoles.
Comas, J. 1974. Orígenes de la momificación prehispánica en America. *Anales de Antropología* 11:357–82.
Cornejo Bouroncle, J. 1939. Las momias Incas: Trepanaciones cráneas en el antiguo Perú. *Boletín del Museo de Historia Natural Javier Prado* 3(2):106–15.
Dawson, W. R. 1928a. Two mummies from Colombia. *Man,* no. 53 (May), pp. 73–4.
– 1928b. Mummification in Australia and in America. *Journal of the Royal Anthropological Institute* 58:115–38.

Dérobert, L., and Reichlen, H. n.d. *Les Momies.* Paris: Editions Prisma.

Engel, F. 1970. La Grotte du mégatherium à Chilca et les écologies de Haut-Holocène Péruvien. In *Echanges et communications*, J. Pouillon and P. Miranda (eds.). The Hague: Mouton.

– 1977. Early Holocene funeral bundles from the central Andes. *Paleopathology Newsletter* 19:7–8.

Espinoza Soriano, W. 1967. Los señores étnicos de Chachapoyas. *Revista Histórica* 3:224–332.

Estete, M. de. 1938. Noticia del Perú [ca. 1535]. In *Los cronistas de la Conquista*, H. Urteaga (ed.), pp. 195–251. Paris: Biblioteca de Cultura Peruana.

Garcilaso de la Vega, I. 1963. *Commentarios reales de los Incas*, part 1, vol. 133. [1609]. Madrid: Biblioteca de Autores Españoles.

Guamán Poma de Ayala, F. 1956. *Nueva corónica y buen gobierno* [ca. 1613]. L. F. Bustios Galvez (ed.). Lima.

Imbelloni, J. 1946. Las momias de los reyes cuzqueños. *Pachakuti IX, Humanior* (sección D) 2:183–96.

– 1956. *La segunda esfinge indiana.* Buenos Aires: Librería Hachette.

Jiménez de la Espada, M. (ed.). 1965. *Relaciones geográficas de Indias*, vol. I, pp. 183–5, Madrid: Biblioteca de Autores Españoles.

Kosok, P. 1965. *Life, land and water in ancient Peru.* New York: Long Island University Press.

Larco Hoyle, R. 1946. A cultural sequence for the North Coast of Peru. In *Handbook of South American Indians*, vol. 2, pp. 149–75. Bureau of American Ethnology, Bulletin 143. Washington, D.C.: Smithsonian Institution.

Lastres, J. B. 1953. El culto de los muertos entre los aborígenes Peruanos. *Perú Indígena* 4(10–11):63–74.

Lathrap, D. W. 1974. The moist tropics, the arid lands, and the appearance of great art styles in the New World. *Special Publications* 7:115–158. Museum of Texas Tech University, Lubbock.

Le Paige, G. 1964. El precerámico en la cordillera atacameña y los cementerios del período agro-alfarero de San Pedro de Atacama. *Anales de la Universidad del Norte*, no. 3.

Linné. S. 1929. *Darien in the past.* Göteborgs Kung. Vetenskaps-och Vitterherts, Samhälles Handlingar, Fjärde Földjen, Series A, Band 1(3). Göteborg.

Lothrop, S. K. 1948. The archeology of Panama. In *Handbook of South American Indians*, vol. 4, pp. 143–67. Bureau of American Ethnology, Bulletin 143. Washington, D.C.: Smithsonian Institution.

MacBride, J. F. 1943. The flora of Peru. In *Botany*, vol. 12, part 3, no. 1. Chicago: Field Museum of Natural History.

Mahler, J., and Bird, J. B. n.d. Mummy 49: A Paracas Necropolis mummy. Manuscript in possession of the authors, American Museum of Natural History, New York.

McCreery, J. H. 1935. The mummy collection of the University of Cuzco. *El Palacio* 39(22–4):118–20.

Mead, C. W. 1907. *Peruvian mummies and what they teach.* Guide leaflet 24. New York: American Museum of Natural History.

Medina Rojas, A. 1958. Hallazgos arqueológicos en el Cerro El Plomo. In *Arqueología Chilena.* Santiago: Centro de Estudios Antropológicos, Universidad de Chile.

Métraux, A. 1949. Warfare, cannibalism, and human trophies. In *Handbook of South American Indians*, vol. 5, pp. 383–409. Bureau of American Ethnology, Bulletin 143. Washington, D.C.: Smithsonian Institution.

Molina, C. de (of Cuzco). 1916. Relación de las fábulas y ritos de los Incas [1575]. In *Colección de libros y documentos referentes a la historia Peruana*, ser. I, no. 1, H. Urteaga and C. A. Romero (eds.), pp. 1–103. Lima.

Munizaga, J. R. 1974. Deformación craneal y momificación en Chile. *Anales de Antropología* 11:329–36.

Nuñez, A. 1969. Sobre los complejos culturales Chinchorro y Faldas del Morro del norte de Chile. *Rehue* 2:111–42.

Pizarro, P. 1939. Relación del descubrimiento y conquista de los reinos del Perú [1571]. In *Los cronistas de la Conquista*, ser. 1, no. 2, H. Urteaga (ed.), pp. 265–305. Paris: Biblioteca de Cultura Peruana.

Polo, J. T. 1877. Momias de los Incas. In *Documentos Literarios del Peru*, 10:371–8.

Polo de Ondegardo, J. 1916a. Errores y supersticiones de los indios [1554]. *Colección de libros y documentos referentes a la historia del Perú*, ser. 1, no. 3, H. Urteaga and C. A. Romero (eds.). Lima.

– 1916b. Instrucción contra las ceremonias y ritos que usan los indios conforme al tiempo de su gentilidad [1567]. *Colección de libros y documentos referentes a la historia del Perú*, ser. 1, no. 3, H. Urteaga and Romero (eds.). Lima.

– 1940. Informe . . . al licenciado Briviesca de Muñatones . . . [1561]. *Revista Histórica* 13:125–96.

Ponce Sanginés, C., and Linares Iturralde, E. 1966. *Comentario antropológico acerca de la determinación paleoserológica de grupos sanguíneos en momias prehispánicas del altiplano boliviano*. Publication no. 15. La Paz: Academia Nacional de Ciencias de Bolivia.

Ramos Gavilán, A. 1976. *Historia de nuestra señora de Copacabaña* [1621]. La Paz: Academia Boliviana de la Historia.

Reichlen, H. 1950. Etude de deux fardeux funéraires de la côte centrale du Pérou. *Travaux de l'Institut Français d'Etudes Andines* 1:39–50.

Reiss, J. W., and Stübel, M. A. 1880–7. *The necropolis of Ancón in Peru: A contribution to our knowledge of the cultures and industries of the empire of the Incas, being the results of excavations made on the spot*. Translated by A. H. Keene. Berlin: Ascher.

Riva-Agüero, J. de la. 1966. *Obras completas de José de la Riva-Agüero: vol. V, Sobre las momias de los Incas*. Lima: Pontífica Universidad Católica del Perú.

Rivero, E. M., and von Tschudi, J. J. 1854. *Peruvian antiquities*. Translated by F. Hawks. New York: Barnes.

Rivero de la Calle, M. 1975. Estudio antropológico de dos momias de la cultura paracas. In *Ciencias*, ser. 9, Antropología y Prehistoria no. 3. Havana.

Röseler, P. 1975. Huac'a und mallqui-Röntgenanatomische und pathologische Studien zum präspanischen Peru. *Röntgenstrahlen* 32.

Rowe, J. H. 1946. Inca culture at the time of the Spanish Conquest. *Handbook of South American Indians*, vol. 2, pp. 183–330. Bureau of American Ethnology, Bulletin 143. Washington, D.C.: Smithsonian Institution.

– 1967. Introduction. In *Peruvian archaeology: selected readings*, J. H. Rowe and D. Menzel (eds). Palo Alto: Peek.

Safford, W. E. 1917. Food-plants and textiles of ancient America. In *Proceedings of the 19th International Congress of Americanists* (1915), pp. 12–30. Washington, D.C.: The Congress.

Sancho, P. 1938. Relación para SM de lo sucedido en la conquista y pacificación de estas provincias de la Nueva Castilla y de la calidad de la tierra [1543]. In *Los cronistas de la Conquista*, ser. 1, no. 2, H. Urteaga (ed.), pp. 117–193. Paris: Biblioteca de Cultura Peruana.

Savoy, G. 1970. *Antisuyo*. New York: Simon & Schuster.

Schaedel, R. P. 1957. Informe general sobre la expedición a la zona comprendida entre Arica y La Serena. In *Arqueología Chilena*, R. P. Schaedel (ed.). Santiago: Universidad de Chile.

Schobinger, J. (ed.). 1966. La "momia" del Cerro El Toro. *Anales de Arqueología y Etnología* (Suppl.) 21.

Skottsberg, C. 1924. Notes on the old Indian necropolis of Arica. *Meddelanden fran Geografiska Forenningen i Göteborg* 3:27–78.

Steward, J. H. 1948. The circum-Caribbean tribes. In *Handbook of South American Indians*, vol. 4, pp. 1–41. Bureau of American Ethnology, Bulletin 143. Washington, D.C.: Smithsonian Institution.

– 1949. South American cultures, an interpretive summary. In *Handbook of South American Indians*, vol. 5, pp. 669–772. Bureau of American Ethnology, Bulletin 143. Washington, D.C.: Smithsonian Institution.

Steward, J. H., and Métraux, A. 1948. Tribes of the Peruvian and Ecuadorian montaña. In *Handbook of South American Indians*, vol. 3, pp. 535–656. Bureau of American Ethnology, Bulletin 143. Washington, D.C.: Smithsonian Institution.

Stewart, T. D. 1973. *The people of America*. New York: Scribner.

Strong, W. D. 1957. Paracas, Nazca and Tiahuanaco cultural elements. *Memoirs of the Society for American Archaeology* 13.

Tello, J. C. 1918. Es uso de las cabesas humanas artificialmente momificadas y su representación en el antiguo arte peruano. *Revista Universitaria* 1:477–533.

– 1929. *Antiguo Perú*, part 1. Lima: Excelsior.

– 1942. *Orígen y desarrollo de las civilizaciones prehistóricas andinas*. Lima: Librería Gil.

– 1959. *Paracas*, part 1. Lima: Empresa Gráfica Scheuch.

– 1980. *Paracas*, part 2, *Cavernas y necrópolis*. Lima: Universidad Nacional Major de San Marcos.

Trimborn, H. 1969. South Central America and the Andean civilizations. In *Pre-Columbian*

American religions, E. O. James (ed.). History of Religion Series. New York: Holt.

Ubbelohde-Doering, H. 1966. *On the royal highways of the Inca*. New York: Praeger.

Uhle, M. 1918. Los aborígenes de Arica. *Revista Histórica* 6:5–26.

– 1975. La momia peruana. *Indiana 3*. [1898]. Ibero-Amerikanisches Institut, Berlin: Preussischer Kulturbesitz, 189–97.

Valera, B. 1945. Las costumbres antiguas del Perú y la historia de los Incas [ca. 1590]. In *Los pequeños grandes libros de historia americana*, ser. 1, vol. 8, F. Loayza (ed.). Lima: Miranda.

Vázquez de Espinosa, A. 1948. Compendio y descripción de las Indias Occidentales [1628]. *Smithsonian Miscellaneous Collections* 108 (whole volume).

Villar Córdoba, P. E. 1935. *Arqueología del departamento de Lima*. Lima.

Von Hagen, V. (ed.). 1959. *The Incas of Pedro de Cieza de Leon*. Norman: University of Oklahoma Press.

Vreeland, J. M. 1976. Second Annual Report: Proyecto de investigación textil "Julio C. Tello." Research report presented to the Secretariat for Technical Cooperation, Organization of American States, Washington, D.C.

– 1977. Ancient Andean textiles: clothes for the dead. *Archaeology* 30(3):166–78.

– 1978a. Paracas. *Américas* 30(10):36–44.

– 1978b. Prehistoric Andean mortuary practices: a preliminary report from central Peru. *Current Anthropology* 19(1):212–14.

– 1980. Prácticas mortuorias andinas: perspectivos teóricas para interpretar el material textil prehispánico, vol. 3. Lima: Actas del Tecer Congreso del Hombre y de la Cultura Andina.

Waisbard, S., and Waisbard, R. 1965. *Masks, mummies and magicians*. Edinburgh: Oliver & Boyd.

Walter, N. P. 1976. A child sacrifice from pre-Inca Peru. Paper presented at the annual meeting of the Southwestern Anthropological Association, San Francisco, April 1976.

Weiner, C. 1880. *Pérou et Bolivie: récit de voyage*, Paris: Librairie Hachette.

Willey, G. R. 1971. *An introduction to American archaeology*, vol. 2, *South America*. Englewood Cliffs, N.J.: Prentice-Hall.

Williams, H. U. 1927. Gross and microscopic anatomy of two Peruvian mummies. *Archives of Pathology and Laboratory Medicine* 4:26–33.

Yacovleff, E., and Muelle, J. C. 1932. Una exploración de Cerro Colorado. *Revista del Museo Nacional* 1(2):31–102.

– 1934. Un fardo funerario de Paracas. *Revista del Museo Nacional* 3(1–2):63–153.

Zuidema, R. T. n.d. Shaft tombs and the Inca empire. Manuscript in possession of the author. University of Illinois, Urbana.

Diseases

Allison, M. J., and Pezzia, A. 1973. Documentation of a case of tuberculosis in pre-Columbian America. *American Review of Respiratory Diseases* 107:985–91.

Allison, M. J.; Pezzia, A.; Gerszten, E.; and Mendoza, D. 1974a. A case of Carrión's disease associated with human sacrifice from the Huari culture of southern Peru. *American Journal of Physical Anthropology* 41:295–300.

Allison, M. J.; Pezzia, A.; Hasega, L.; et al. 1974b. A case of hookworm infestation in a pre-Columbian American. *American Journal of Physical Anthropology* 41:103–5.

Allison, M. J.; Houssaini, A. A.; Castro, N.; Munizaga, J.; and Pezzia, A. 1976. ABO blood groups in Peruvian mummies. *American Journal of Physical Anthropology* 44:55–62.

Angel, L. J. 1967. Porotic hyperostosis or osteoporosis symmetrica. In *Diseases in antiquity*, D. Brothwell and A. T. Sandison (eds.). Springfield, Ill.: Thomas.

Boyd, W. C. 1959. A possible example of action of selection in human blood groups. *Journal of Medical Education* 34:398–9.

Boyd, W. C., and Boyd, L. G. 1933. Blood grouping by means of preserved tissues. *Science* 78:578.

– 1937. Blood grouping tests on 300 mummies. *Journal of Immunology* 32:307–9.

Cockburn, E. (ed.). 1977. *Porotic hyperostosis: an inquiry*. Monograph no. 2. Detroit: Paleopathology Association.

Garcia-Frias, J. E. 1940. La tuberculosis en los antiquos Peruanos. *Actualidad medical peruana* 5:274.

Gerszten, E.; Allison, M. J.; Pezzia, A.; and Klurfeld, D. 1976. Thyroid disease in a Peruvian mummy. *Medical College of Virginia Quarterly* 12:52–3.

Grana, F.; Rocca, E. D.; and Grana, L. R. 1954. *Las trepanaciónes craneanas en el Perú en la época prehispánica*. Lima: Imprenta Santa Maria.

Hossaini, A. A., and Allison, M. J. 1976. Paleoserology studies: ABO and histocompatibility antigens in mummified American Indians. *Medical College of Virginia Quarterly* 12:67–73.

Hrdlička, A. 1914. Anthropological work in Peru in 1913 with notes on the pathology of the ancient Peruvians. *Smithsonian Miscellaneous Collection* 61(12).

Lastres, J. B., and Cabieses, F. 1960. *La trepanación del cráneo en el antigua Perú.* Lima: Imprenta de la Universidad Nacional Major de San Marcos.

Lisowski, F. P. 1967. Prehistoric and early historic trepanation. In *Diseases in antiquity,* D. Brothwell and A. T. Sandison (eds.). Springfield, Ill.: Thomas.

MacCurdy, C. G. 1970. Surgery among the ancient Peruvians. *Art Archeology* 7:381–94.

Margetts, E. L. 1967. Trepanation of the skull by the medicine-men of primitive cultures. In *Diseases in antiquity,* D. Brothwell and A. T. Sandison (eds.). Springfield, Ill.: Thomas.

McGee, W. J. 1894. Primitive trephining illustrated by Muñiz Peruvian collection. *Bulletin of the Johns Hopkins Hospital* 5:1–23.

Moodie, R. L. 1927. Injuries to the head among pre-Columbian Peruvians. Studies in paleopathology, 21. *Annals of Medical History* 9:91–102.

Morse, D. 1961. Prehistoric tuberculosis in America. *American Review of Respiratory Diseases* 85:489.

Muñiz, M. A., and McGee, W. J. 1894–5. *Primitive trephining in Peru.* Bureau of American Ethnology, Annual Report 16, pp. 7–72. Washington, D.C.: Smithsonian Institution.

Quevedo, A., and Sergio, A. 1943. La trepanación incan en la región del Cuzco. *Revista del Museo Nacional* 12:1–18.

– 1945a. La trepanación incan en la región del Cuzco. *Revista del Museo Nacional* 13:1–7.

– 1945b. La trepanación incan en la región del Cuzco. *Revista del Museo Nacional* 14:1–10.

Rocca, E. 1953. *Traumatismos encefalocraneanos.* Lima: Imprenta Santa Maria.

Rogers, S. L. 1938. The healing of wounds in skulls from pre-Columbian Peru. *American Journal of Physical Anthropology* 23:321–40.

Stewart, T. D. 1956. Significance of osteitis in ancient Peruvian trephining. *Bulletin of the History of Medicine* 30:293–320.

Weiss, P. 1949. *La cirugía del cráneo entre los antiguos Peruanos.* Lima: Imprenta Santa Maria.

– 1958. *Osteológica cultural prácticas cefálicas,* part 1. Lima: Imprenta Universidad Nacional Major de San Marcos.

PART III
Mummies of the world

10
Bog bodies of Denmark

CHRISTIAN FISCHER
Director, Silkeborg Museum
Silkeborg, Denmark

Translated by KIRSTINE THOMSEN

In general, bog bodies are considered a northwestern European phenomenon reflecting special forms of sacrifice or punishment common among Germanic peoples around the time of the birth of Christ. The German researcher Dieck (1965) has shown that from Norway in the north to Crete in the Mediterranean and from Ireland in the west to Russia in the east bog bodies number more than 1,400 (that is the 1968 figure; today the number is closer to 2,000) and cover a period from 9000 B.C. to World War II.

If we consider this large distribution area as one, the bodies can be seen as a natural phenomenon and not as the practice of a special, culturally influenced group. Of more than 1,400 known bog bodies or parts thereof (20 percent of the finds consist of isolated legs, arms, and heads), less than one-third can be dated. About 100 may be dated to the Stone Age and the older Bronze Age (5000–1000 B.C.) and a similar number to the period up to A.D. 400. From the period A.D. 400–1500 about 100 are known. From A.D. 1500 until today, about 50 have been recorded (Lund 1976).

THE PRESERVATIVE QUALITIES OF THE BOG

The reason for the preservation of the bog bodies (and of other organisms also) lies in the special physical and biochemical makeup of the bog, above all the absence of oxygen and the high antibiotic concentration. The manner in which the body was deposited is also of great importance – for example, placed in the bog in such a way that air was rapidly excluded. It is important not only that the bog water contained a high concentration of antibiotics but also that the weather was cold enough (less than 4°C) to prevent rapid decomposition of the body. If the body had been deposited in warm weather, one can assume that the presence of anaerobic bacteria in the intestinal system would have had a destructive effect on the interior of the corpse before the liquid of the bog could penetrate the body.

The bogs in which bodies are found can be roughly divided into three types: raised bogs (acid), fens (containing lime), and transitional types. The raised bog holds the greatest interest for us because the bodies found there are so well preserved that they are hardly different from when they were deposited; in the fen and the transition areas all the soft parts have generally disappeared, and the body is found as skeleton or adipocere.

The flora of the raised bog is sparse and dominated by peat moss (sphagnum), the leaves of which are constructed in a special manner. Only a few of the cells contain chlorophyll and are able to carry out the process of photosynthesis. The other cells, which lie among those containing chlorophyll, are dead and empty. They are constructed of cellulose and connected with one another and their surroundings through pores. These "empty" cells have an extraordinary ability to absorb water; for this reason, the raised bog feels wet to walk on even in dry summers. It is a widely held misconception that the raised bog acts as a sponge that sucks up groundwater. This is not true. The deepest lying peat layers are so compressed that they totally prevent the passage of any water. In addition, it has been shown by laboratory experiments that the height to which water can be raised by capillarity is here only 40 to 50 cm.

The water of the raised bog is therefore not mineral-containing groundwater, but rainwater. The raised bog holds water because of its ability to absorb surface water and the ability of the underlying peat to retain it. In addition, the surface of the bog is dotted with mounds so that rainwater does not run off. The nutrient bases that the peat moss requires – Ca, Mg, Na, and K – come from atomized seawater, which is carried into the atmosphere; the amount of nutrient salts therefore increases the closer one gets to the sea.

Measurements have shown that the true annual growth of the raised bog amounts to approximately 15 mm, but pressure from the layers above results in the bog's profile showing only 6.4 mm growth per year. This compression is the causative factor preventing oxygen from reaching the underlying layers, and the oxygen lack is the reason the peat and the organisms in it cannot be destroyed by oxygen-dependent bacteria. In addition, raised peat is one of the most acid soil types one can find: The sphagnum produces sulfuric acid in very small quantities, and in the peat humic acid is produced by the action of anaerobic bacteria on lignin. Because the acids are mixed only with "buffer-poor" neutral precipitation, it takes a very small amount of acid to lower the pH value to the 3.6 to 4.0 of the Danish raised bog. These acids further act as antibiotics and cause an acid tanning of the skin, as can be seen in the Grauballe man.

Today, very few untouched raised bogs are found in Western Europe, for the peat has been utilized as fuel since before the birth of Christ. Indeed, many bog bodies are placed in peat diggings of the Iron Age: For example, a wooden peat spade from the Iron Age was found just beside the Tollund man.

DANISH BOG BODIES

The distribution of bog bodies is extensive geographically as well as in time. If one fo-

cuses on Denmark, however, most of the bog bodies are undated, owing to the fact that they were found before such scientific methods as pollen analysis and carbon-14 dating were in use. It is quite characteristic also that the bog bodies are naked or accompanied only by simple, uncharacteristic articles of clothing difficult to date. Of the finds that can be dated, either scientifically or culturally, almost all are from the period around the birth of Christ, approximately 400 B.C. to A.D. 400, which is known in Danish archeological terminology as the pre-Roman or Roman Iron Age.

Fortunately, a number of the best preserved Danish bog bodies are among those that have been dated and carefully examined, all of them excavated within the first 10 years following World War II. This was a period during which peat was still being dug for fuel, but, unfortunately for bog body research, this practice has now ceased. Among the Danish bog bodies that were scientifically excavated and examined, we must make special mention of the three bodies from Borremose found in 1946, 1947, and 1948; the Tollund man of 1950; and the last one on the scene, the Grauballe man of 1952.

BODIES FROM BORREMOSE

The three bodies from Borremose were excavated in a stretch of boggy land that surrounds a unique fortified Iron Age village dating back approximately to the birth of Christ (Figure 10.1).

Borremose body 1946 (Figure 10.2) was found 2 m beneath the surface of the bog in an upright, strongly contracted position, which can best be explained by assuming that the body had been placed in the bog in a sitting position; the upper body had then, by its own weight, sunk down toward the thighs. A birch stick had been placed above the body: This is often seen with bog bodies and is undoubtedly intended to prevent the corpse from "going again" (i.e., returning to life). The find was excavated by S. Vestergaard Nielsen, Director of the Aars Museum, and Knud Thorvildsen of the National Museum (1947).

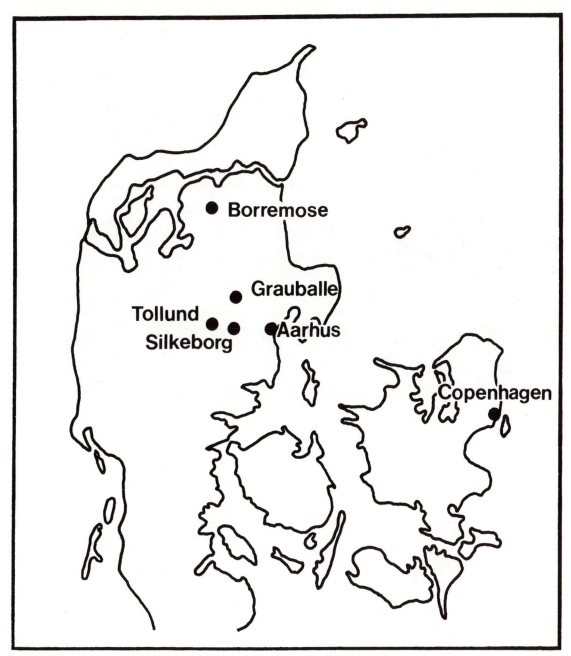

Figure 10.1.   *Locations of bog bodies found in Denmark. (Map by Timothy Motz, Detroit Institute of Arts)*

The body was that of an adult man who had been quite small, scarcely more than 155 cm tall. Because of the acidity of the bog, the bones were decalcified and soft, but covered with skin, sinews, and muscle tissue. The face, lower body, sex organs, hands, and feet were especially well preserved. The left eye was intact; at the beginning of the excavation it was closed, but by the end it had opened: the eyeball protruded, in color yellow white,

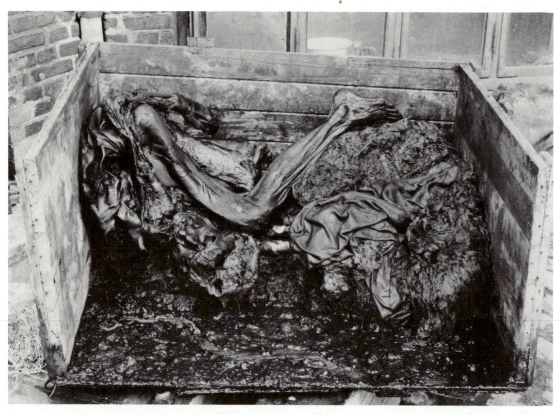

Figure 10.2.   Borremose man 1946 lying in the crate in which he was moved from the place where he was found. National Museum, Copenhagen.

with a dark iris. The nose and lower part of the face were undamaged. The tongue was well preserved. The teeth, of which only a few were left, were loose. Scattered beard stubble 6 mm in length was found on the upper lip, cheeks, and chin, corresponding to about 2 days' growth. The back of the head had been crushed, so that the cranium was open and the brain matter visible. The edge of the break was not new; that is to say, the head had been crushed before the body was deposited in the bog (Figure 10.3).

Of the inner organs, the intestine and its contents were partly intact. The large intestine contained his last meal (about 40 ml.), which consisted of about 65 percent spurry and 25 percent pale willowweed. Some animal tissue was found, which in all probability came from the intestine itself, and also a few short animal hairs, most probably hair from mice, which are always found in grains and seed (Brandt 1951).

The arm bones of the Borremose man were whole, but a break was found in the right thigh just above the knee. The shaft of the bone protruded through the skin on the underside of the thigh. The sharp edges of the fracture indicated that the break had occurred before the bones were decalcified by the acid water of the bog. The hands were well preserved, narrow, and finely formed, giving the impression that they had not been used for rough work. The fingernails had dissolved. The feet had high insteps, and the toes were in normal position. The toenails were loose; they were attractively formed, curved regularly, and had been cut or trimmed.

A rope 94 cm long and 1 cm thick was tied

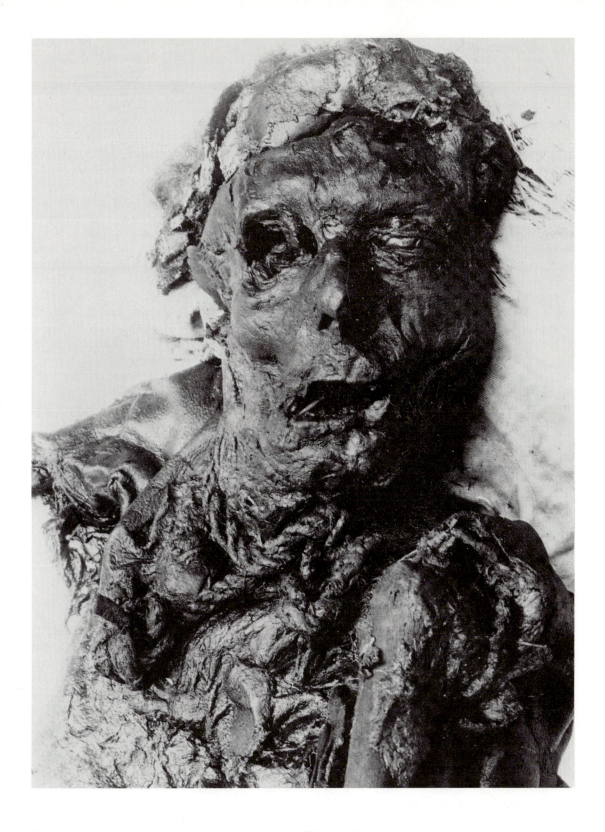

Figure 10.3.   Borremose man 1946, with the noose still around his neck. National Museum, Copenhagen.

around the neck and pulled so tightly that the neck measured only 37 cm in circumference. This rope was very likely the cut-off end of the cord with which the man was hanged. Whether the mutilations already mentioned – the broken skull and thigh – were inflicted before or after the hanging, or whether they had been a contributory cause of death, could not be ascertained. Apart from the rope, the body was naked, but two fur cloaks, almost alike, lay by the feet. These were, presumably, his only articles of clothing, corresponding to the Germanic style of dress mentioned by Caesar: "They wore only short fur cloaks but were otherwise naked."

The pollen test conducted at the National Museum indicated that the man was buried in the bog within the first 200 years after the birth of Christ. The Borremose body 1946 is dated by the carbon-14 method to 650 B.C. ± 80 years; that is, to the final period of the Bronze Age. None of the carbon-14 datings mentioned in this chapter have been calibrated.

Borremose body 1947, which was found about 1 km from the 1946 body, was too decomposed for the sex to be established. The body had been placed on its stomach in an Iron Age peat digging. Above the body in the peat digging lay sticks and heather twigs. The upper part of the body was naked; the hips and legs were covered with a woolen blanket, a shawl, and a ragged piece of cloth (Thorvildsen 1952). Some parts of the body were greatly decomposed. The stomach and part of the lower portions of the body were completely gone; part of the upper portion of the body had also disappeared; the head, the esophagus, and the left shoulder, complete with arm and hand, were preserved. The back of the head was pressed flat, and the skull was crushed so that the brain matter was visible. The hair, which had been darkened by the bog, was short – only 3 to 7 cm long. Around the neck was an ornament consisting of a leather string with an amber pearl and a pierced conical bronze disk. The right leg was

broken 10 cm below the knee joint; the break was not new, but must have occurred when the body was deposited. It cannot be determined with certainty if it was inflicted before or after death. The flattening of the skull was probably caused by pressure from the peat.

Near the upper part of the body, there were some small bones belonging to a baby, which may indicate that a mother and her new born infant had been deposited in the bog together. The cause of death could not be established. The date was established from the remains of a clay vessel of pre-Roman type that lay in immediate contact with the body. Pollen analysis of the body showed that it dates back to about the birth of Christ. The carbon-14 method placed the date at 430 B.C. ± 100 years.

In 1948, continued digging revealed still another bog body, 2 m under the surface in an Iron Age peat digging like the others. The dead person was a plump woman, lying on her stomach. Her right arm was bent at the elbow, and her right hand was resting on her chin. The left hand was propped against the left shin; the left leg was bent at the knee and pulled vigorously up toward the abdomen. The back of her head was intact, showing distinct signs of scalping. The face was crushed, and this must have been done before the body was deposited in the bog, for pieces of the skull were mixed with small pieces of brain matter. This could not have been caused by the pressure of the peat, as the back of the head would also have been crushed and this was not the case. Most of the scalp with hair on it had been loosened from the skull by the scalping and lay above it in the bog. The hair appeared to have been of medium length. The excavation was carried out by museum conservator B. Brorson Christensen.

The dead woman had been laid in a rectangular woolen blanket, 175 by 115 cm, but was otherwise naked. It is possible that the blanket had acted as a kind of skirt. The carbon-14 method dated the body to 530 B.C. ± 100 years, and a carbon-14 test used on the mate-

Figure 10.4.   Tollund man at the National Museum, Copenhagen. Lars Bay, Silkeborg Museum.

rial, where the humic acid had not been extracted, indicated 610 B.C. ± 100 years. The woman had therefore lived during the transition period between the Bronze Age and the Iron Age. Pollen analysis indicated that the body had been deposited about the time of the birth of Christ.

THE TOLLUND MAN
The Tollund man (Figure 10.4) is among the best preserved ancient bodies that are still extant, and his unbelievably well preserved head is without equal (Thorvildsen 1951).

He was found in central Jutland in May 1950 when two farmers, digging for peat, reached 2.5 m below the surface. A displacement in the peat layer showed that he lay in an Iron Age peat digging, which also contained a short wooden spade of the Iron Age type.

After calling the police, staff from the Silkeborg Museum, acting on the advice of Professor P. V. Glob, decided to send the body to the National Museum. It was still lying in the peat where it had been discovered, so the whole block was crated and shipped to Copenhagen. There the final excavation and examination took place under the direction of museum conservator Knud Thorvildsen.

The body was that of an adult male approximately 1.60 m tall; it lay in a natural sleeping position resting on its right side. The body was slightly contracted, the knees completely pulled up, and the arms bent so that the left hand lay under the chin and the right near the left knee – a position often encountered in bodies from ordinary Iron Age graves. One must assume that he had been placed in that position on purpose, which makes him different from other bog bodies, whose place-

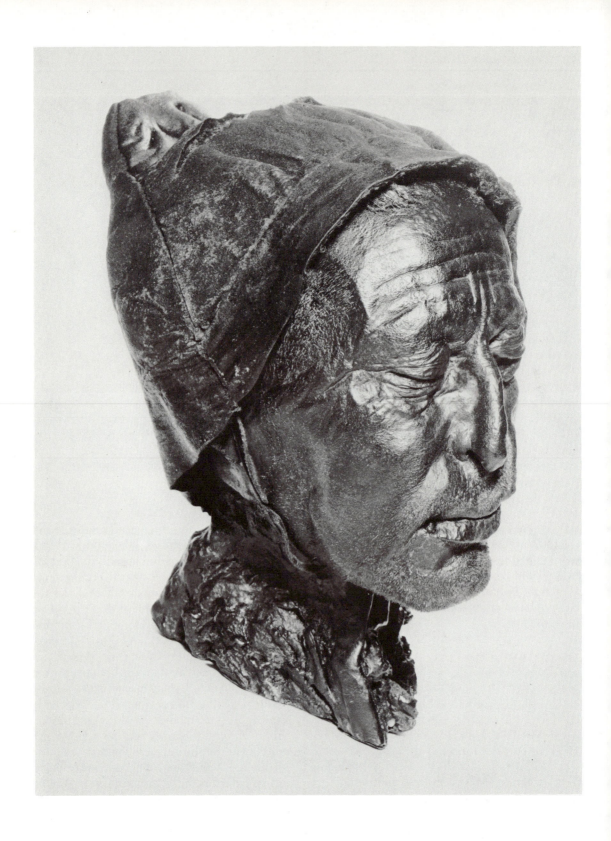

Figure 10.5. *Tollund man's head after conservation. Lars Bay, Silkeborg Museum.*

ment is more haphazard. He must have been placed in a sleeping position either within the first 8 to 12 hours after death (before rigor mortis had developed) or 1 to 3 days later (the time when rigor mortis would have worn off).

The skin and most of the soft parts were intact: Only the skin of the hands and their soft parts had disappeared; the arms and legs were partially dissolved. The skin of the up-turned side had begun to disappear, but the rest of the body was intact; the sex organs were well preserved. The best preserved part was the head (Figure 10.5), with its com-posed, sleeping expression. The wrinkled forehead and closed eyelids and lips were in such good condition that the man looked like a living person who had fallen asleep. The hair was completely preserved; it was cut short, but in no particular style. There was 1 to 2 mm of beard stubble on the upper lip, the chin, and the cheeks, which represents about 48 hours' growth, unless it is caused by post-mortem contractions of the skin. The eye-brows were also intact.

Dissection showed that the inner organs (heart, lungs, and liver) were very well pre-served, but unfortunately they were not ex-amined further. The alimentary canal, with stomach and small and large intestines, was intact. This was examined by Dr. Bjovulf Vimtrup and Dr. Kay Schaurup, anatomists, and Dr. Hans Helbaek, botanist, for evidence of the dead man's last meal. The contents of the stomach and small intestine were modest, only 0.5 and 10 ml; the large intestine con-tained 260 ml. This indicates that the meal was consumed 12 to 24 hours before death.

The body was naked, except for a narrow leather belt and a pointed hood made from calfskin, with the hair on the inside. The hood was kept on the head by a thin thong under the chin. Even while the corpse was lying in situ, it could be seen that a rope made from two braided thongs was pulled tightly around its neck. One end of the rope was tied to form an open loop through which the other end was pulled, so that it circled the neck. The free end of the rope measured 1.25 m and had

been sharply severed, so it had probably been longer. The rope was pulled so tightly around the neck that it had left a visible furrow in front and on the side of the throat, though there was no mark in the place where the loop was fastened. In order to find out whether the cause of death was ordinary hanging with dislocation of the axis or slower choking (for the rope was undoubtedly the cause of death), the neck and head of the corpse were exam-ined and X-rayed by Dr. Chr. I. Bastrup. His examination led him to believe that the cervi-cal vertebrae had not been dislocated and the axial process had not broken, as one would have expected if the man had been hanged by falling with the noose around his neck. Un-fortunately, most of the bones and teeth were so decalcified that they were difficult to evaluate. As far as could be observed, the wisdom teeth had erupted and the teeth were in good shape. The eruption of wisdom teeth indicates that the man was at least 22 years old. The X-ray pictures showed also that the brain had shrunk in a peculiar fashion (Figure 10.6). As a result of the decalcification, sev-eral bones were also bent and modeled in a peculiar way.

Analysis of the stomach contents showed that they consisted of a pure vegetarian por-ridge or gruel without any trace of animal content. According to the examining physi-cians, animal remains ought to have been present if they had been ingested just prior to death, considering the excellent state of pres-ervation of the body. The porridge was a combination of grain and weed seeds, to which had been added fat from linseed (*Linum usitatissimum* L.) and gold of plea-sure (*Camelina linicola* Sch. & Sp.). The grain varieties were naked and covered barley (*Hordeum tetrastichum* Kcke., var. *nudum*, and *H. tetrastichum* Kcke.), and the most im-portant of the weeds was knotweed (*Polygonum lapathifolium* agg. and *P. per-sicaria* L.). The examination showed that the water drunk with the meal must have been bog water as small leaves of sphagnum were found among the stomach contents. The Tollund man had also suffered from the intestinal parasite *Trichuris* in rather large numbers (over 100 in a 24- by 24-mm slide preparation). The composition of the meal helps to confirm the dating of the Tollund man as the relationship between naked and hulled barley corresponds to the time of the birth of Christ, and linseed and spelt, which were also found in the stomach, are first reported in the Danish flora about 400 B.C. (Helbaek 1951). By the carbon-14 method, the Tollund man is dated to 210 B.C. ± 40 years.

Unfortunately, after the detailed examination was concluded, preservation was attempted for the head only. Apart from the bog body from Rendswühren in North Germany, which was preserved in 1871 by smoking it at the local butcher's shop, no one at this time had any experience in preserving bog bodies. The method used consisted of first replacing the bog water contained in the cells with distilled water containing formalin and acetic acid. The liquid was then changed to 30 percent alcohol, and later to 99 percent with the addition of toluol. Finally, the head was placed in pure toluol, which was generally saturated with paraffin. The paraffin was afterward replaced by carnauba wax heated to different temperatures. This preservation process made it possible to retain all the correct proportions and the facial expression, but the head as a whole shrank about 12 percent; nevertheless, it is today the best preserved head of any person from ancient times. The rest of the body was dried up and thus partly destroyed.

Two feet were kept, however, one in water and one in formalin. In 1976, the foot that had been kept in water was dried and treated with wax: This caused it to shrink about 25 percent. The foot that had been kept in formalin was preserved by freeze-drying: This produced a fine result with practically no shrinking.

THE GRAUBALLE MAN

The last well preserved bog body is that of the Grauballe man, who was found in 1952 about 20 km east of the place where the Tollund

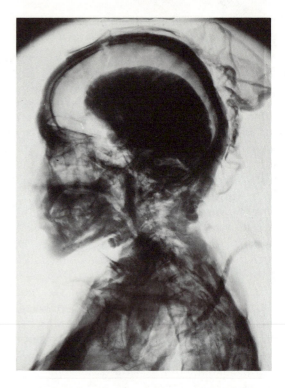

Figure 10.6.   X ray of the Tollund man's head. The brain has shrunk, but is still preserved.

man was found and 10 km north of the town of Silkeborg (Glob 1956). While digging for peat in a small bog, the cutters accidentally struck a body that was clearly placed in an Iron Age peat digging. The size of the digging could not be ascertained, as the greater part of the surrounding peat was gone when the people from the museum arrived. The corpse was placed in the digging slightly on a slant. It lay on its chest with the left leg almost stretched out and the right leg and arm bent. The pressure of the peat had deformed the head slightly (Figure 10.7).

Professor P. V. Glob requested that a crate be constructed around the corpse and the peat in which it lay, as had been done with the Tollund man. The crate with its contents was then taken to the Museum of Prehistory in Aarhus, where the examination could be continued and preservation procedures carried out.

A plaster cast impression was taken to re-

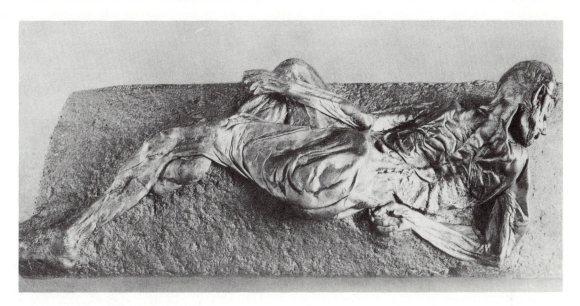

Figure 10.7.   Grauballe man at the Museum of Prehistory, Aarhus. Forhistorisk Museum, Aarhus Kommunehospital.

cord the body's position and size in case shrinkage occurred during the preservation process. A pathological, anatomical, and forensic examination of the body was performed by Professor Willy Munck (1956). Professor Carl Krebs and Dr. Erling Ratjen X-rayed the body (1956). External examination showed that the head was bent slightly backward and turned a little to the right. On the left side of the forehead there was a slightly curved depression 10 cm in diameter. The left earlobe was well preserved and, close to the opening to the ear, some irregular defects were seen, which probably occurred after death. The eyes were tightly shut and the eyeballs completely flattened and dried up. The color of the iris could not be determined, but the eyes probably had been quite dark. There were no eyebrows present. The mouth, which was slightly open, appeared to have been quite large. Teeth found in the upper jaw were 4+ and +3, 4, 5; in the lower jaw −1, 2, 3, 4, 5. The teeth were very black and worn on the masticating surface.

On the front of the neck was a large wound whose upper edge began 5 cm below and 3 cm behind the right ear. It ran upward and forward, a little above the lower jaw, and the edges were smooth, except for a notch in the middle of the lower side. The tongue was shriveled, but so well preserved that its shape could be recognized, including the tip. The epiglottis could be seen, but the gullet and the esophagus had been severed by the throat wound. The lungs seemed not to be fastened to the wall of the chest. A large, soft, red mass, approximately 15 by 10 cm and covered by a capsule was found at the site of the liver. The intestine with its contents was removed. In the scrotum a flat solid body was recognizable, presumably a testis. The stomach, spleen, pancreas, suprarenal gland, kidney, ureter, and bladder were not recognizable.

There was some reddish hair on the top of the head and a few strands of beard on the upper lip and chin, approximately 2 or 3 mm to 1 cm in length. A microscopic examination of the hair from the head indicated that it was of medium thickness and probably had been dark: The reddish color was attributable to the action of the bog water. The hair of the beard was somewhat thicker than that of the head.

The purpose of the X-ray examination was to look for signs of violence, to determine the age of the man, if possible, and to decide whether the bone system showed traces of disease. There were no signs of any serious illness marking the bone system. There was a skull fracture in the right temple region, and the left shin bone was fractured. It could be seen that the skull was partly flattened and depressed toward the middle, and at the back of the crown there was a 2- by 1-cm break in conjunction with a linear fracture. The other skull deformations were attributed to the pressure of the surrounding peat mass. The break on the tibia was oblique: The fracture line began 10.5 cm under the knee on the outside of the under part of the leg, traveling downward and inward to the inner side 14 cm from the knee. The fracture had been open. There was no sign of callus formation on the ends of the bones and no break in the fibula. Both the skull fracture and the leg fracture must have been inflicted immediately before or after death. The break in the tibia without an accompanying break in the fibula suggests a direct blow to the shin. A fall or similar accident would, as a rule, have caused a break in the fibula.

A second group of deformations and fractures must be attributed to postmortem displacement resulting from the pressure of the peat.

X-ray pictures of the thoracic portion of the spinal column indicated the beginning of rheumatoid arthritis, a disease that seldom occurs before the age of 30.

The cause of death was undoubtedly the long cut from ear to ear, which was so deep that it had severed the gullet. The wound must have been inflicted by another person: Its direction and appearance rule out the possibility of suicide or of an injury inflicted after death. Whether the man was knocked unconscious before his throat was cut could not be determined. The skull fracture seems to have been caused by a blunt instrument. It could not be determined whether the oblique fracture of the tibia had occurred before or after death.

The teeth were examined by two dentists, Friis and Warrer (Glob 1965). In the upper jaw there were 7 teeth in their proper positions, in the lower jaw only 5; but 14 sockets for other teeth were clearly visible, and 9 teeth were found in several different parts of the mouth. The teeth were very small. One tooth had been lost long before death, as the socket had healed. Some other teeth showed periodontitis and caries, which at times must have caused toothache. One bad tooth had caused malocclusion. The wisdom teeth had not erupted.

The preservation of the right hand and foot was so good (Figure 10.8) that the papillae lines could be clearly seen. To find out whether these lines corresponded with what is found in people living today, Inspector C. H. Vogelius Andersen of the Police Criminology Department in Aarhus examined both the fingerprints and the footprints (1956). The right thumbprint was the clearest and could immediately be classified as a whorl pattern, a so-called double-curve pattern; the right middle finger showed an ulnar loop pattern. The fingerprint expert came to the conclusion that if one had had a fingerprint card index from the time of the Grauballe man, it would have been easy to identify him! The two fingerprint patterns occur with a frequency of 11.2 and 68.3 percent, respectively, in the present-day Danish population. In other words, there was nothing irregular about this fingerprint, so far one of the oldest found anywhere in the world.

The alimentary canal contained food remains from the man's last meal. The content of the intestine was approximately 610 ml, more than double the amount of food found in the Tollund man (270.5 ml). How far these volumes correspond to the amount of food eaten cannot be estimated. Food remains of the same type were evenly distributed throughout the entire digestive canal, from stomach to intestinal outlet, indicating that the Grauballe man must have eaten just before he was killed. The examination was conducted by Dr. Hans Helbaek (1959), who also examined the Tollund man. In contrast to the Tollund man, the Grauballe man had eaten

Figure 10.8.   *Grauballe man's right hand. Forhistorisk Museum, Aarhus Kommunehospital.*

animal matter as well as vegetable matter, for 15 tiny fragments of greatly dissolved bones were found. A bone specialist, Conservator Ulrik Møhl, was of the opinion that the bones might have come from the ribs of a small pig. Thus it can be shown that the Grauballe man had eaten meat along with the vegetable soup or porridge. The latter consisted of cultivated seeds as well as weed seeds, just like the meals the Tollund man and the Borremose man had consumed before death. The soup of the Grauballe man had consisted of barley (*Hordeum tetrastichum* Kcke., var. *nudum* and *H. tetrastichum* Kcke.), seeds of knotweed (*Polygonum lapathifolium* agg. and *P. persicaria* L.) and soft bromegrass (*Bromus mollis* L.), and small quantities of wheat (*Triticum dicoccum* Schuble) and oats (*Avena sativa* L.). In addition, there were seeds of over 50 varieties of weeds, some of them certainly gathered on purpose, but the rest probably harvested by chance along with the cultivated varieties. Two of the plants are, furthermore, found near the coast (from Grauballe to the coast is approximately 50 km); the presence of seeds of these two plants must indicate that either a trade in foodstuffs operated or the Grauballe man had been near the coast immediately before his death. In addition, two small stones and a small piece of charcoal were found in the intestines, indicating that he did not chew his food very thoroughly. Like the Tollund man, he suffered from intestinal worms (*Trichuris*).

As with the Tollund man, there was no trace of fresh fruit, vegetables, herbs, or berries, which one would expect at a time of year when they are available. Death, therefore,

Table 10.1. *Dates of eight Danish bog bodies determined by carbon-14 method*

Body name	Specimen number[a]	Date	Source of information
Grauballe man			Tauber (1956)
Sample with humic acid	K-503A	A.D. 310 ± 100 yr	
Sample with humic acid extracted	K-503B	55 B.C.	
Borremose 1946	K-2813	650 B.C. ± 80 yr	Thorvildsen (pers. comm. 1977)
Borremose 1947	K-1395	430 B.C. ± 100 yr	Thorvildsen (pers. comm. 1977)
Borremose 1948			
Sample with humic acid	K-2108A	610 B.C. ± 100 yr	Thorvildsen (pers. comm. 1977)
Sample with humic acid extracted	K-2108B	530 B.C. ± 100 yr	Thorvildsen (pers. comm. 1977)
Huldremose	K-1395	A.D. 30 ± 100 yr	Munksgård (1973)
Krogens Møllemose	K-2132	A.D. 80 ± 100 yr	Munksgård (1973)
Haraldskjaermose	K-2818	450 B.C. ± 80 yr	author's data
Tollund man			
Sample A	K-2814A	250 B.C. ± 55 yr	author's data
Sample B	K-2814B	180 B.C. ± 50 yr	author's data
Average		210 B.C. ± 40 yr	author's data

[a] Identification number assigned by the National Museum of Denmark, Carbon-14 Dating Laboratory.

probably occurred during either the winter or early spring in the case of both the Grauballe and Tollund men.

After this thorough examination it was, fortunately, decided to attempt to preserve the whole body. Dissection had shown that the acid bog water had acted as a tanning agent on the skin, and it was decided to complete the tanning nature had begun. The process used is technically known as pit tanning; it lasted 18 months. The body was placed in an oak tub, and the tanning solution was continually concentrated through the gradual addition of oak bark (875 kg was used). Following this treatment, the body was soaked in a solution of Turkey red oil and then dried. This process prevented any change taking place in either the appearance or the size of the Grauballe man.

CARBON-14 DATING OF DANISH BOG BODIES

As mentioned before only about 10 percent of the Danish bog bodies have been dated, almost all to the period from 500 B.C. to A.D. 400. Eight were dated by the carbon-14 method at the National Museum. Data on these bodies are given in Table 10.1.

CULTURAL CONDITIONS IN DENMARK AND NORTHERN GERMANY DURING THE EARLY IRON AGE, 500 B.C.–A.D. 400

The period of these dated bog bodies, in Danish archeological terminology, is pre-Roman Iron Age (earlier called Celtic Iron Age) and Roman Iron Age. Both periods are prehistoric.

The pre-Roman Iron Age (500 B.C.) is the first Iron Age period in Scandinavia and northwestern Germany and is simultaneous with the end of the Hallstatt culture in central Europe and the La Tène culture (also called Celtic culture). Although central Europe is dominated by these widespread geographic cultures, the influence of the Germanic peoples who lived in northern Europe does not seem to have been very marked. During the pre-Roman period, Denmark was a peasant community, with people and animals living under the same roof, each at its own end, in rectangular houses measuring about 15 by 5 m. The houses were sometimes isolated, but are also found in small villages. Some houses were larger, indicating a social division within the community. Cremation was the usual funerary custom; the cleansed bones were placed in a clay urn, often in a graveyard. In bog burials, sacrificial objects were placed above the body – jewelry and clothing accessories, clay vessels with food, sometimes even, as at Dejbjerg and Rappendam, carts, and in one instance at Hjortespring, a war canoe, 13.5 m in length, filled with war gear.

Around the time of the birth of Christ, during the reign of Emperor Augustus, the Romans pushed the boundaries of the empire outward to the Danube and the Rhine, but the emperor's plan to extend the boundary farther north by subduing the Germanic tribes ended abruptly when the Roman commander Varus, in A.D. 9, was totally defeated by the Germanic chieftain, Arminius, only 300 km south of the Danish border. From then on the border remained along the Rhine and the Danube until A.D. 260, when the empire collapsed.

Extensive trade developed between the Roman Empire and the Germanic community, giving rise to the name Roman Iron Age (A.D. 0–400). This followed on the end of the pre-Roman Iron Age without any obvious cultural change. These trade connections were the source of many Roman accounts of the Germanic peoples, of which Tacitus' *Germania* (A.D. 98) was certainly the most significant, although he himself probably never visited Germany. These Roman sources are the subject of considerable dispute, for they usually seek not only to give a description of the Germans, but to picture the Romans and their deeds in a favorable light in contrast to the more primitive Teutons. Archeological material is much more reliable, consisting of grave finds, settlements, and sacrificial finds.

The reason people from the Iron Age were executed and then placed in a bog has been disputed at great length, and it is far from decided whether this was regular, routine punishment, perhaps followed by sacrifice to the gods in the bog, or a straightforward sacrifice. There is also the possibility that some of the bodies represent victims of murder or robbery.

The punishment theory has its origin in the work of Tacitus, for he says: "The coward, the unwarlike, the man stained with abominable vices, is plunged into the mire or the morass, with a hurdle put over him." The sacrifice theory also originates with Tacitus. In his description of rites connected with the worship of Ertha, or Mother Earth, he concludes with the words: "Afterwards the car, the vestments and the divinity herself are purified in a secret lake. Slaves perform the rite, who are instantly swallowed up by its waters."

These quotations do not explain why corpses were placed in bogs and lakes without the grave goods and food that other people had in normal graves, but they do raise the possibility that the reason may have been punishment or as a sacrifice to the gods. As the Danish and the northwestern German groups of bog bodies include men, women, and children, both whole bodies and parts, usually showing signs of violence (crushed limbs or skulls) over and above what would have been necessary for execution or sacrifice, it is difficult to imagine that these people were selected merely to be given to the gods. Perhaps they had, in one way or another, come into conflict with society and been executed.

More detailed examination of all the bog bodies found in Denmark and northern Germany should enable us to arrive at an explanation. The most important thing is exact dating. The carbon-14 technique can be used on even the most poorly preserved bodies, as long as it is chemically possible to remove humic acid and whatever has been used for preservation. The time of year the executions took place is also significant. The Tollund man, the Grauballe man, and possibly, the Borremose man 1946 were killed either during winter or in early spring; this implies a seasonal condition for the sacrifice. The papillae patterns on the feet of both the Tollund man and the Grauballe man and those on the hands of the Grauballe man indicate that these persons were not manual workers, but had a superior position in the community, perhaps chieftains or priests, possibly both.

However, lacking standards of comparison, it is impossible to reach a firm conclusion.

There is an interesting find from Rappendam on Sjaelland (Kunwald 1970). Carts or parts of them were offered as part of the sacrifice, along with a woman about 35 years old, though only her skeleton remains. The connection between carts and human sacrifice is mentioned in Tacitus' description of ceremonies for the fertility goddess Ertha, and Professor P. V. Glob believes that most of the Danish and northern German bog bodies are sacrifices to this goddess.

As well as giving a possible explanation of the legal and religious structure of society, the bog bodies offer an unusual chance of getting to know how people in the Iron Age lived. And the most fascinating aspect may be the discovery that an Iron Age person, if dressed in modern clothes, would look just like a person living today.

BOG BODIES ON EXHIBITION IN DENMARK AND NORTHWESTERN GERMANY

A list has been compiled by Dieck (1965). The largest collection is in the Landsmuseum, Schleswig, Germany, where the man from Rendswühren, who was found in 1871, is displayed. He was naked except for his left leg, which was covered by a piece of leather with the hair side in. His head was covered by a rectangular woolen blanket and a fur cap. The cause of death was a triangular hole in the forehead. He was preserved by smoking. At this museum also there are two bodies, a man and a woman, which were found in 1952 only 5 m apart. Both were dated to the period just after the birth of Christ, but it cannot be proved whether they were deposited at the same time. The woman, who died at about the age of 14, had been drowned. Her head and limbs are well preserved, but her chest is considerably dissolved. The hair had been light blonde; on one side of the head it was only 2 mm in length, but on the other side it was 4 to 5 cm. She was naked apart from a fur collar

and a cover over her eyes; this latter may possibly have been a cover for the mouth.

The man's skin and the hair on his head were preserved, but the bones were totally decalcified. The hair was presumed to be dark, going gray; its length was 2 to 2.5 cm. He is estimated to have been middle-aged. He was most probably choked by a hazel stick which lay around his neck. Both bodies were covered by thick branches and the girl with a rock as well.

The Gottorp Museum has the Damendorf man, but this body was washed out and only the skin and the hair remain. He was naked, covered by a cape and other apparel, including shoes. A 2-cm-wide split in the chest area tells us the cause of death. Also at this museum there is the Dätgen man and a single decapitated head; both have a characteristic hairstyle, with the long hair gathered in a knot. Tacitus mentions that the Germanic tribe, the Suevi, wore their hair this way.

The Tollund man is on exhibition at the Silkeborg Museum and the Grauballe man at the Museum of Prehistory in Aarhus; both museums are in Jylland. The National Museum in Copenhagen is planning an exhibition of the bodies from Borremose, but it is not yet known when the exhibition will be ready. There are other bodies in storage at the National Museum, but these were not preserved and as a result have shriveled up. They may, however, repay further study.

Since this chapter was written, another specimen has been recognized, after being in the National Museum since 1938. This is the Elling woman, found in the peat only 90 m from the Tollund man. She was about 30 years old and was dressed in a sheepskin cloak with the furry side next to the body. Without doubt, she had been hanged like the Tollund man. Carbon-14 dating placed her at 210 B.C. ± 70 years, which is almost the same as the Tollund man.

At an examination performed by Silkeborg Museum staff in 1976 it was found that the body had dried up into a mummy since its original discovery in 1938. No signs of dis-

ease were found, so the woman had apparently been quite healthy. Her hair was in good condition and was elaborately braided. Presumably she, like the Tollund man, had been sacrificed to the gods.

REFERENCES

Brandt, I. 1951. Planterester i et moselig fra Borremose. *Aarbøger for Nordisk Oldkyndighed og Historie* 1950:342–51. English summary.

Dieck, A. 1965. *Die europäischen Moorleichenfunde.* Neumünster: Karl Wachholtz Verlag.

Glob, P. V. 1956. Jernaldermanden fra Grauballe. *KUML* 1956:99–113. English summary.

– 1965. *Mosefolket.* Copenhagen: Gyldendal. Also published in English.

Helbaek, H. 1951. Tollundmandens sidste måltid. *Aarbøger for Nordisk Oldkyndighed og Historie* 1950:311–41. English summary.

– 1959. Grauballemandens sidste Måltid. *KUML* 1958:83–116. English summary.

Krebs, C., and Ratjen, E. 1956. Det radiologiske fund hos moseliget fra Grauballe. *KUML* 1956:138–50.

Kunwald, G. 1970. Der Moorfund in Rappendam auf Seeland. *Prähistorische Zeitschrift* 45: 42–88.

Lange-Kornbak, G. 1956. Konservering af en Oldtidsmand. *KUML* 1956:155–9. English summary.

Lund, A. A. 1976. Moselig. *Wormianium* 1976.

Munck, W. 1956. Patologisk-anatomisk og retsmedicinsk undersøgelse af Moseliget fra Grauballe. *KUML* 1956:131–7.

Munskgård, E. 1973. *Oldtidsdragter.* Copenhagen: Nationalmuseet. English summary.

Tacitus. *Germania.* In *Complete Works.* New York: Modern Library, 1942.

Tauber, H. 1956. Tidsfaestelse af Grauballemanden ved kulstof-14 maling. *KUML* 1956:160–3.

Thorvildsen, E. 1952. Menneskeofringer i Oldtiden. *KUML* 1952:32–48. English summary.

Thorvildsen, K. 1947. Moseliget fra Borremose i Himmerland. *Nationalmuseets Arbejdsmark* 1947:57–67.

– 1951. Moseliget fra Tollund. *Aarbøger for Nordisk Oldkyndighed og Historie.* 1950:302–9. English summary.

Vogelius Andersen, C. H. 1956. Forhistoriske Fingeraftryk. *KUML* 1956:151–4. English summary.

11

Mummification in Australia and Melanesia

GRAEME L. PRETTY
Senior Curator of Anthropology and Archaeology
South Australian Museum
Adelaide, Australia

ANGELA CALDER
Honorary Associate in Anthropology
South Australian Museum
Adelaide, Australia

Any description of mummification in Australia and Melanesia is made difficult by the irregularity of the evidence about funerary customs. There are two reasons for this. First, the accuracy of ethnographic reports has varied considerably, both spatially and temporally. Second, the variability and complexity of mortuary practices in these regions have continued to defy systematization. Mummification was considered to be only one component in a spectrum of cultural rituals associated with death and was practiced by relatively few tribal groups.

The most adequately documented area for this practice is the Torres Strait Islands. Ethnographic accounts for the entire region, however, have proved exceptionally valuable sources of information about the techniques involved and the diverse motives for the preservation of the dead. In Australia, study of the corpse was instrumental in determining the suspected agent of death; by contrast, Melanesian customs were concerned more with maintaining the physical integrity of the deceased. Similarly, preservation techniques ranged from simple procedures involving natural desiccation by solar processes to more complex methods of smoke drying corpses.

A further problem has been created by vagueness in the definition of *mummification* and the use of the word. Whereas accidental preservation of exposed bodies by desiccation occurred widely and randomly, purposeful preservation of bodies, or true mummification, was seldom recorded for Australia or Melanesia.

Despite these limitations, the evidence for mummification in this part of the world deserves serious attention. First, it refines our knowledge of mummification as a globally distributed custom. Second, this type of research also provides uncontaminated source material for biological assessments of indigenous populations in regions where hybridization has recently occurred.

DISTRIBUTION

In Aboriginal Australia a great range of mortuary rituals was employed in the disposal of the dead. The processes involved were either *simple* (primary disposal) or *compound* (secondary disposal) (Hiatt 1969:104). Simple disposal was characterized by the use of only one procedure, at a specific time, and was generally spread across the south of the continent. Compound disposal, of which mummification or desiccation was occasionally a part, was widespread in the northern part of Australia. Desiccated and partly decayed bodies have been randomly reported from widely scattered localities, as well as preserved parts of bodies such as hands and organs (Howitt 1904:459–460; Mathews 1905; Dawson 1928). Although smoking and drying techniques for preserving bodily parts were widespread, deliberate mummification was restricted to five main areas (Berndt and Berndt 1964:392–394; Figure 11.1). These were the lower Murray River and Adelaide Plains (Angas 1847a; Flower 1879; Taplin and Meyer, in Woods 1879:20–21; 198–200; Tolmer 1882:273; Stirling 1893; Basedow 1925; Elkin 1954:313); Gippsland

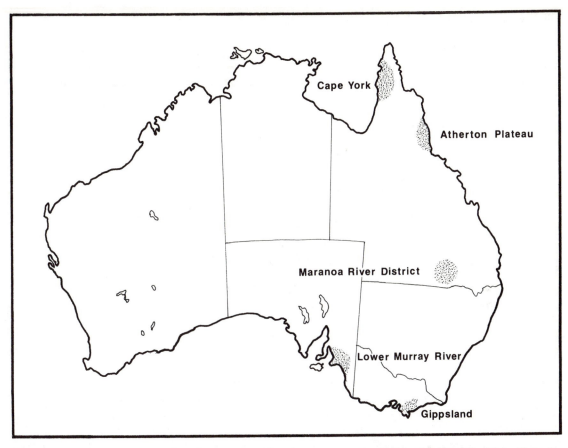

Figure 11.1.   *Areas in Australia where mummification was practiced. (Map by Timothy Motz, Detroit Institute of Arts)*

(Howitt 1904:459–460); the Maranoa district in southeastern Queensland (Howitt 1904:467–468; Hamlyn-Harris 1912b; Bull 1965); the Atherton Plateau near Cairns (Roth 1907:366–403; Hamlyn-Harris 1912b); and Cape York (McConnel 1937).

In Melanesia the preserving of fleshed and integumental parts and whole bodies appeared to be an extension of a widespread tradition of conserving relics of the dead as memorials. The best known example of this practice was the Melanesian penchant for preserving heads, usually as trophies. Deliberate mummification of whole bodies was, however, performed in several distinct localities (Pretty 1969; Figure 11.2). One area where the practice was common until very recent times was the Central Highlands in a

locality inhabited by the Kukukuku tribes (Simpson 1953:163–166; Bjerre, 1956:85–89; Pretty 1972:20–28). Numerous references exist to mummification in surrounding areas (Rhys 1947:148; Le Roux 1948:747–755) as far south as coastal Port Moresby, west as far as the Wahgi valley, and toward the north coast where the Buang tribes smoke dried bodies (Vial 1936:37; Girard 1957).

Another main center was in West New Guinea, where the custom extended along part of the southern shore of Geelvinck Bay and into the ranges east of Wissel Lakes (Held 1957:177–178; J. V. de Bruijn 1963; personal communication). Closer to Torres Strait, in an area enclosed by the tract of swampy, low-lying country that extends from the lower Fly River across into Irian Jaya, there were fre-

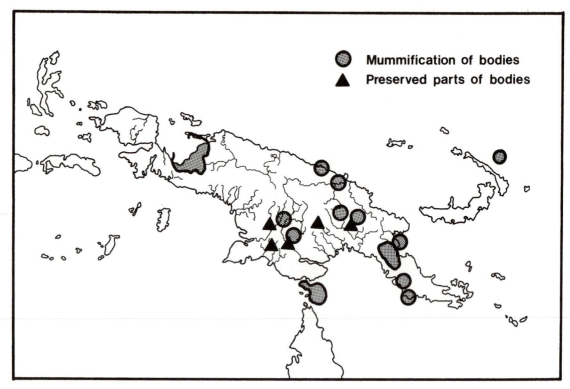

Figure 11.2.   Areas in New Guinea where mummification was practiced. (Based on Pretty 1969; map by Timothy Motz, Detroit Institute of Arts)

quent references to the preservation of sections of bodies and occasionally entire corpses (Haddon 1935:332–333).

A third important center for mummification was the Torres Strait (Pretty 1969; Figure 11.3). There the practice was confined to the eastern islands (Pretty 1969:35), which Haddon distinguished culturally from the western group (Haddon 1935:322). However, most reports have concerned Darnley Island (Flower 1879; d'Albertis 1880; Sengstake 1892) and the mummy collected by Macleay in particular (Hamlyn-Harris 1912a; Elliot Smith 1915; Dawson 1924; Fletcher 1929; Abbie 1959; Pretty 1969).

The distribution of mummification in Melanesia was not restricted exclusively to the aforementioned areas. As mummification was not an obligatory ritual for many tribes, its practice was sporadic. This behavioral flexibility was demonstrated at the 1963 Mount Hagen Agricultural Show, when a community from Laiagam, not known as practitioners of mummification, brought in attendance the preserved body of one of their fight leaders. While alive, this leader had expressed a desire to see the show, but died 2 years prematurely. His kinsmen had preserved his body and carried it to the show in accordance with his wishes (S. G. Moriarty, 1965; personal communication).

ORIGINS

Prehistorians consider that island Southeast Asia was the area from which Australia and

Figure 11.3.   Areas in the Torres Strait where mummification was practiced. (Based on Pretty 1969; map by Timothy Motz, Detroit Institute of Arts)

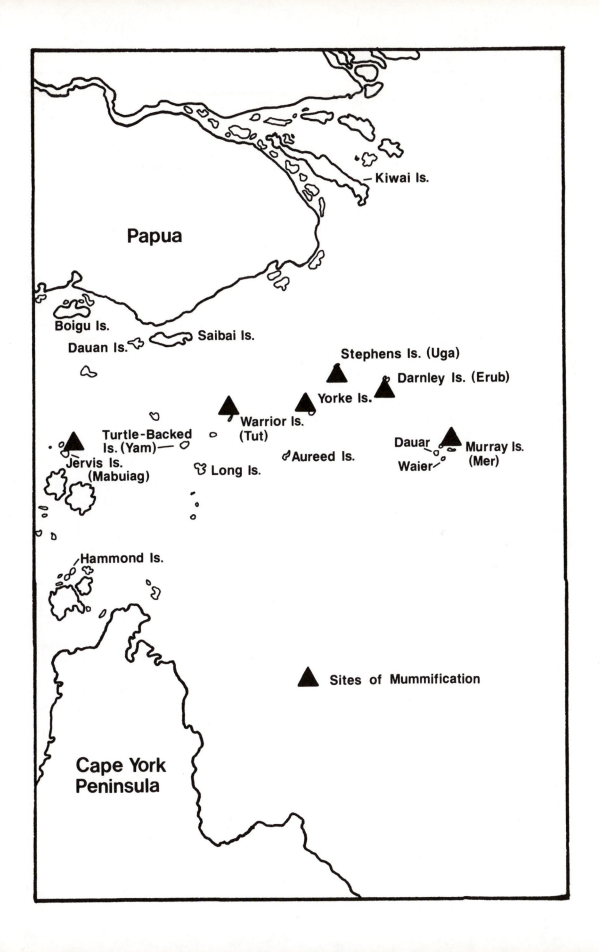

Kiwai Is.

Papua

Boigu Is.

Dauan Is.

Saibai Is.

Stephens Is. (Uga)

Darnley Is. (Erub)

Yorke Is.

Warrior Is.
(Tut)

Turtle-Backed
Is. (Yam)

Dauar

Murray Is.
(Mer)

Aureed Is.

Waier

Jervis Is.
(Mabuiag)

Long Is.

Hammond Is.

Sites of Mummification

Cape York
Peninsula

Melanesia were first settled (Mulvaney 1969). This event occurred some 40,000 years ago during the last glacial epoch and at a time when the lowered sea levels resulted in an extension of the main land masses and the linkage of Tasmania and New Guinea with the Australian continent. Archeological research has shown that since first settlement, Aboriginal societies have been adapting to changing local conditions and that much social and cultural diversity has ensued (Mulvaney and Golson 1971). Such variation has occurred within both Australia and New Guinea, the latter being subjected to a greater range of outside influences owing to its proximity to both Southeast Asia and the Pacific.

Unlike other regions, which also had extensive antiquities, Australia and Melanesia have no mummies of any great age. In this region, deliberate mummification was never intended to prolong the corpse's existence for more than a few years at most. Therefore, the identification of ancient mummies from prehistoric skeletal remains has proved extremely difficult.

One promising aspect, which may be linked with the origins of mummification but which has not yet been adequately examined, is the antiquity and distribution of compound funerary modes. All known specimens of historic mummies were from compound contexts. Compound burial practices in this region extended over a long period of time. However, to date there is no information to suggest that simple primary inhumations were as ancient as compound methods.

Prehistorians are presently unable to determine what funerary customs were practiced by the ancient people of Trinil, Modjokerto, and Ngandong in Java because the remains recovered have come from disturbed stratigraphical contexts. However, the finds from Niah (Howells 1973:177) and the interral of cremated ashes at Mungo (Bowler et al. 1970) were indicative of compound disposal modes. Careful excavations have also distinguished secondary from primary burial at Roonka in South Australia.

There, preliminary interpretations suggest that this practice may have been widespread throughout southern Australia during the period from 7000 to 4000 B.P. (Pretty 1977). The presence of compound disposal is indicative of a milieu in which mummification may have occurred, but extremely rigorous archeological observation is necessary before such conclusions can be definitively reached.

Information about burial customs became more detailed from the late sixteenth to midtwentieth centuries, during which period European explorers, traders, administrators, missionaries, and scholars made ethnographic comments about the region. None of these reports were sufficiently comprehensive to give insight into the origins of mummification, and few provided explanations for the distinctiveness of the practice in such widely scattered localities.

Taplin was one author who sought explanations for the origins of the practice by studying the Narrinyeri, a confederation of aboriginal tribes who lived at the mouth of the Murray River (Taplin, in Woods 1879). He explained the distinctiveness of mummification to this community by relating it to a unique mythic hero, Ngurundere, from whom the tribes claimed their descent. This custom and a sense of community cohesion were reinforced by tribal sanctions that held all other tribal groups as enemies. The Narrinyeri, then, represented a people who, in a region characterized by simple disposal methods, practiced a highly complex mode of funerary disposal that incorporated mummification (Angas 1847b). Other scholars of the Narrinyeri have used this evidence for mummification as a tool for interpreting the prehistoric settlement patterns of the lower Murray River (Stirling 1911; Pretty 1977).

SOCIAL AND RELIGIOUS BELIEFS

The stimulus for preserving whole bodies, parts of bodies, or human bones in Australia and Melanesia was generally attributable to one or more of the following sentiments:

1. A simple compensatory and restorative reaction to the loss of a relative or friend and the sense of grief this caused
2. The performance of a formally sanctioned duty to a certain class of person
3. The fulfillment of obligations to avert mischief by the spirits of the dead
4. The bearing of symbols of status; for example, the jawbone of her dead husband borne by a wife as a sign of widowhood

In the majority of instances where the motives for purposeful mummification were recorded, the custom accorded largely with the first of these sentiments – the playing out of a compensatory reaction to grief. Apparently, mummification in this region was neither a formal observance nor a mode of treatment conferred upon all members even of a certain class. The process and motives were limited by temporal considerations, for once the mourning period with its associated rites was over, the corpse was finally disposed of by procedures such as burial, cremation, or exposure to the elements.

This range of reasons for preserving the physical remains of the dead bore parallels to similar motives that governed several other aspects of mortuary practices, many of which were incorporated into mummification rites. Mourning observances often involved the demonstration of grief by self-inflicted injury or token cannibalism of the corpse. In some areas, inquests were held to divine the inflictor of death by a study of the deceased's entrails, resulting frequently in long-term vendettas.

This plethora of funerary behaviors was inevitable in small-scale societies whose religious systems provided no transcendental dimension to death. Death was a disaster that ranged in severity according to the social status of the deceased. Small children, women, and senile persons were generally of less importance than warriors or leaders. In such an emotional situation the feelings of grief and revenge felt by relatives often determined the funerary procedures. Mummification was an exceptional treatment conducted under special circumstances. It was an expensive process and placed considerable demands upon kinfolk.

The desperate and vindictive attitude to death of these societies and the consequent motives for mummification stood in marked contrast to other regions, such as ancient Egypt or Peru, where mummification was performed to celebrate beliefs about the afterlife. On the other hand, the actual mode of disposal corresponded to practices elsewhere, in that selection for mummification was based on the status of the deceased.

Although basic social and religious beliefs concerning the disposal of the dead were similar in Australia and Melanesia, there were distinguishing features in both regions. These differences were based more on a change of emphasis than on any single observable factor. In Australia the aim of mummification was to obtain an accommodation between the dead and the living; in Melanesia the aim was generally to prolong the physical presence of a dead relative in defiance of decomposition.

TECHNIQUES

In Australia the techniques used generally involved the exposure of the corpse in a tree or on a specially constructed platform (Figure 11.4). Initially the body was tied into a sitting position, often with limbs flexed against the chest or abdomen. The corpse was left in the open until the tissues were desiccated by the sun, and then deposited in the branches of a tree or on a wooden platform. In some localities, preservation was accelerated by sewing all the orifices closed and smoking the body while it was on the platform. Sometimes the body cavity was opened and the intestines removed in order to refine the drying process. Putrefying fluids were often collected and used in allied rites. When dry, the epidermis was peeled off and the pale corpse

Figure 11.4.   Mode of preparing the bodies of the warriors slain in battle among the tribes of Lake Alexandrina. After a fight is over, the corpses of the young men who have been killed are set up cross-legged on a platform, with the faces toward the rising sun. The arms are extended by means of sticks; the head is fastened back; and all the apertures of the body are sewed up. The hair is plucked off, and the fat of the body, which had previously been taken out, is mixed with red ocher and rubbed all over the corpse. Fires are then kindled underneath the platform, and the friends and mourners take up their position around it, where they remain about 10 days, during the whole of which time the mourners are not allowed to speak; a guard is placed on each side of the corpse, whose duty it is to keep off the flies with bunches of emu feathers or small branches of trees. The weapons of the deceased are laid across his lap, and his limbs are painted in stripes of red and white and yellow. After the body has remained several weeks on the platform, it is taken down and buried; the skull becomes the drinking cup of the nearest relation. Bodies thus preserved have the appearance of

mummies; *there is no sign of decay; and the wild dogs will not meddle with them, though they devour all manner of carrion.*

was smeared with red ocher and grease or decorated by painting totemic designs on its face and chest. Body hair was either cut off or pulled out and used for making waistbands and other personal ornaments (Berndt and Berndt 1964:392ff).

In Melanesia the methods employed varied slightly between the inland regions and the coastal and island areas. The most detailed accounts have come from Torres Strait (Haddon 1912; 1935; Hamlyn-Harris 1912a; MacFarlane, in Haddon 1935:325–326). In Torres Strait, the dead body was set apart for a few days. It was then taken out from shore in a canoe, where the swollen outermost epidermal layer was stripped away. Viscera were removed through an incision in the side between the ribs and the hips and then thrown into the sea. The abdominal cavity was filled with pieces of palm pith and the incision sewed up. The brain was removed after screwing an arrow through the back of the neck and into the foramen magnum. The body was then returned to the shore, lashed to a rectangular wooden framework, and hung up to dry behind a grass screen. Punctures were made at the knees and elbows and in the digital clefts on the hands and feet to drain off bodily fluids. The tongue, palmar tissue, and soles of the feet were stripped off and presented to the spouse.

Months later, when the drying process was complete, the mummy was decorated. Artificial eyes of shell with pupils of black beeswax were cemented into the orbits, the earlobes were decorated with tufts of grass and seeds, and the wrists and ankles were sheathed in bands of palm fronds. The whole body was then given a coating of red ocher. The loins were covered, in the case of a woman with a petticoat, and in the case of a man occasionally with a shell pubic ornament. The decorated mummy, on its frame, was then tied to the center post of the bereaved spouse's house and when, in the course of time, it fell to

pieces, the head only was retained.

On mainland New Guinea, the techniques of mummification differed in several details. For example, preservation of the body was obtained largely by smoking. In Torres Strait, drying in the open was the major agent. Although a fire was kept constantly burning near the mummifying corpse, this was considered to be more for the deceased's comfort than for preservation. Additional differences in technique were found in the Tauri–Lakekamu watershed area of central New Guinea. Evisceration was not practiced here, and the body and limbs were arranged in a squatting position, except during smoking, when the hands were tied to a house beam. The origins of the techniques of smoke drying are not definitely known, but the preservation of meat and game employing similar smoking processes was known by the Wahgi and Tauri (Kukukuku) tribes.

EXAMPLE OF A MELANESIAN MUMMY: TORRES STRAIT SPECIMEN IN THE MACLEAY MUSEUM, SYDNEY

The Macleay Museum in the University of Sydney contains the preserved body of a male Torres Strait islander (Figure 11.5). It was collected from Darnley Island in 1875 by the Australian zoologist Sir William Macleay. In 1914, during a session of the British Association for the Advancement of Science, it became a focus of attention when put forward by Professor Grafton Elliot Smith as a conclusive demonstration of ancient Egyptian influence on Oceanic culture. For various reasons, no comprehensive description of the mummy appeared until 1969, when Pretty published a detailed examination of the specimen and reviewed the controversy surrounding Elliot Smith's diffusionist hypothesis (Pretty 1969). The Macleay specimen is an excellent example of the Melanesian technique of mummification, and Pretty's report is the basis of the description presented below.

Figure 11.5.   Torres Strait mummy in the Macleay Museum, University of Sydney. (From Pretty 1969)

General description. The mummy is that of an adult male, 177 cm in length with a breadth at the shoulders of 35 cm. It was lashed to a wooden frame of two verticals and eight crosspieces at the head, under the armpits, and below the knees. The body must have been dried in a vertical position, as its weight, suspended from under the shoulders, caused sagging at the breast and the head to sink into a deep cleft formed by the clavicles, which raised the shoulders to a position level with the ears. Facial features were restored and the whole body coated with red ocher. The skin, where exposed, was parchment yellow except on the back of the left hand, where some of the original melanin, dark gray in color, was retained. The mummy's state of preservation was good, though there had been some postmortem insect attack around the jaw, mastoids, upper part of the breast, abdomen, and posterior surfaces of the legs. Loss of some of the distal phalanges of the left foot probably occurred during the mummification process, as the remaining bones were exposed and splashed with red ocher.

The head. The head (Figure 11.6) was shaved and the crown painted an even black from the forehead around and behind the ears and across the lambdoid region, where the cranium lay against the topmost crosspiece of the frame. No hair was found, the only potential sample from the left cheek being identified as a vegetable fiber. Like the rest of the body, the face was thickly coated with red ocher and the features considerably restored. The shrunken orbits were filled with a black mastic that had discolored the overlying red ocher to gray and had cracked the painted surface along its junction with the facial tissue. The artificial lentoid eyes were shell, and measured 4 by 1.5 cm. Emphasis was added to each eye by setting a spot of black resinous material in the center to imitate the pupil and by ringing the margins with flattened strips of the same substance to represent eyelids. The nasal septum had been pierced in life, but the hole plugged postmortem with a rod of coral-line material broken off flush with the nostrils. The mouth had opened and the lips had parted, exposing the teeth. Both upper central incisors were displaced after death but were located radiographically, one being lodged in the posterior pharynx and the other in the chest.

An interesting feature of the head was the double strand of rolled two-ply twine that ran across the center of the oral cavity. This was inserted to fix the jaw firmly to the head and made demands on the skill of the mummifiers as the twine was passed between lower lip and teeth, over the teeth and across the oral cavity, and joined with the other end of the string at the base of the jaw. This technique was well known and is beautifully illustrated by a decorated skull (Figure 11.7) from Hammond Island, Torres Strait, which is housed in the South Australian Museum (registration number A.17907). In this specimen and in some other mummies, notably the one described by Flower (1879:391), there was a supplementary lashing binding the ramus to the zygoma on each side. This was unnecessary in the Macleay specimen because the tissues surrounding the jaw were well preserved.

Only part of the ears were present, but sufficient remained to show that the lobes were intact at death. From them hung threaded strings of seeds broken in half and threaded through the ends. They were identified as Job's tears (*Coix lacrymi*). The brain had been removed, and examination from behind showed a vertical incision at the nape of the neck. Probing demonstrated that the cranial cavity was empty, and radiographs showed that the articulation of the foramen magnum and the first cervical vertebra had been disrupted.

The techniques for keeping the head upright were complex. A vertical stance during drying would incline the head to fall forward on the chest, but this was prevented by two devices. First, a double strand of flat three-ply plaited twine was passed across the forehead again and across the other side, being finally

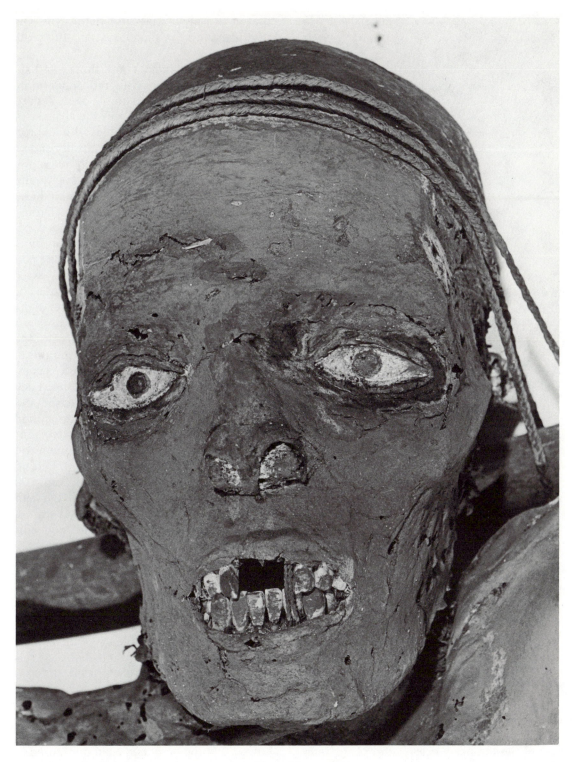

Figure 11.6.   *Head of the Macleay mummy. (From Pretty 1969)*

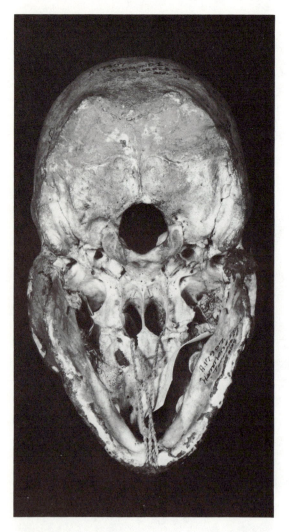

Figure 11.7.   Hammond Island cranium (A.17907) showing attachment of mandible to skull by lashing. (From Pretty 1969)

colored gray about the region of the eyes. The significance of the punctures remains problematical.

Thorax and abdomen.   Both thorax and abdomen were painted with red ocher more thickly on the front than on the back. A curious feature of this region was the absence of lateral shrinkage of the skin, leaving no protruding outlines of ribs either ventrally or dorsally. X rays confirmed that all ribs were present. The navel was discernible and penis and scrotum complete. There was no pubic hair.

The abdomen was clothed with a dress consisting of a fibrous material passed between the legs and kept in place by a waistband. The waistband had a zigzag pattern woven into it and was wound twice around the body and knotted at the front. The tie-ends were of blue calico, a reminder of the islanders' frequent contact with Europeans prior to Macleay's visit. Tucked into the waistband front and back were two lengths of teased-out or beaten fibers identified as coming from the bark of a species of fig. Each length had been doubled over, creased and drawn together to form a knob, then stuffed into a waistband behind, while the free ends had been carried out across the abdomen and tucked under the waistband in front. Behind and within the bark fiber was a length of twine, decorated at intervals of 6 to 8 cm with fronded insertions of plant material from a species of ginger. Darnley Island men normally went naked, but pubic coverings were known for other male mummies (Flower 1879; Hamlyn-Harris 1912a).

On the left flank was an incision 8.5 cm long, which had been sewed together with rolled two-ply twine by a running suture and finished by knotting at each end. Ethnographic accounts were explicit about an incision at this site for removal of the viscera and, for the Macleay specimen, this was confirmed by X rays that were consistent with complete removal.

The limbs.   Close examination of the limbs showed that the body had been punctured at the joints to allow putrefying fluids to escape,

knotted under the crosspiece. Second, the chin was probably supported by a small wooden prop, as the skin was pinched and depressed both beneath the chin and on the breast just above the sternum. This latter method was recorded by both Haddon (1912) and Hamlyn-Harris (1912a), but lashing the head to the top crosspiece was unusual.

Curious features were two punctures in the skin of the forehead at each end of the temples. The surrounding tissues had been dis-

thus confirming the observations of Haddon and Hamlyn-Harris. Also as a result of drainage and drying, shrinkage had occurred, which necessitated retying the lashings at fewer sites. Primary lashing sites, distinguished from the furrows and wrinkling they had left on the skin, were situated in positions suited to the binding of a body in a vertical position. The hands had originally been lashed to the frame across the wrists, so that they lay with the palms flat against the frame rather than facing the sides of the body. The feet were originally lashed to the double crosspiece at the base of the frame, which also served to support the feet. Shrinkage through drying had pulled both feet a few centimeters above the basal crosspiece, but their former contact with the base of the frame was shown by the presence of strips of skin which had remained across the soles of the feet. Other primary lashing sites were located underneath the knees and slightly above present lashing sites.

Drainage was effected by making holes in the skin at the joints, and mourners further helped to expel putrefying fluid by stroking and kneading the limbs. In the Macleay specimen, drainage punctures were identified at the knees and on the back of the left hand where the skin was drawn back. Elsewhere they proved difficult to identify because of fractures and deterioration of the tissues. There were breaks in the skin of the hand between the first and second fingers and on the right foot between the hallux and the second toe. Another hole was located on the inside of the right arm at the elbow. Longitudinal wrinkling and folding of the skin at the joints, in particular at the knees, was suggestive of manual drainage.

Both fingernails and toenails were absent, consistent with ethnographic records of the removal of nails and palmar skin, which were peeled off and presented to the spouse.

The limbs were decorated at the ankles and wrists with bands of palm leaf, 4 cm wide. Each band consisted of two partly overlapping strips of leaf secured by wrapping and a

small flat knot. These had been put on before the mummy was given its coating of red ocher, as the skin beneath was free of paint. *Radiographic and gastroscopic examinations.* An X-ray examination of the mummy unexpectedly showed a close scatter of granular opacities in the region of the lower abdomen. From a radiological viewpoint there was doubt about whether this represented the stuffing of the abdominal cavity substances or arose from radiopaque material in the coating of the red ocher itself. Weighed against this latter interpretation was the complete covering of the entire body with red ocher and the fact that the X-ray opacities were confined to the abdominal region. To resolve the problem, a series of tests was undertaken on samples of red ocher.

The first problem was to determine the composition of the paint that was smeared on the mummy. According to Hamlyn-Harris it was a mixture of coconut oil and ocher, but Haddon claimed the mixture to be of ocher and human grease. The first tests on the ocher were made from a mainland Australian sample and mixed with coconut oil and lard. This mixture was smeared onto tracing paper and X-rayed on a 10-cm thickness of Masonite board using an 80-milliamps-per-second ray with an intensity of 58 kilovolts from a distance of 80 cm. The plates were blank, showing the red ocher to be transradiant.

On specialist radiological advice the experiment was repeated, as the X-raying of a layer of red ocher on 10-cm Masonite slabs was held to be an unsatisfactory comparison with the ocher on the mummy. The contrasts achieved between a layer of ocher on 10-cm Masonite and 10 cm of Masonite alone were held to be so slight as to escape detection. A similar mass of balsa, being transradiant, was considered to be a truer comparison. In the repeat test, a sample of red ocher confirmably from Saibai Island in Torres Strait was used. Three mixtures were prepared, ranging from fine powdered to medium grained and coarse granules. The radiographs were at 63 kV, exposed at 2, 4, and 6 seconds from a distance of

127 cm. The plates showed the red ocher to be transradiant except where it was in compact grains or masses, thus supporting the hypothesis that radiopacity would depend on the size of particles and their specific gravity, but affirming the essential X-ray transparency of red ocher.

Reexamination of the coat of ocher covering the belly did not reveal any granular surface texture, but the paint had been thickly applied to this area, so the possibility that the ocher was affecting the radiographs still remained. To decide the issue and find out what the abdominal cavity contained, a gastroscope was inserted deep into the body from an insect hole near the right armpit. With it, a series of 5-mm color transparencies was made of the body cavity. Their interpretation was limited by uncertainties, first about the precise locus of the photos within the cavity, and second by the absence of a scale. However, the photos revealed that the abdominal cavity was empty of viscera and contained several lengths of a vinelike plant buried in a matrix of dusty grass and granular material. The lengths of vine stem appeared to be circular in section and occasionally had thorns or stems branching out from them. The matrix was mostly organic, but was assumed to be crystalline in places, as it reflected the light from the camera flash. Among the matrix were some curious smooth-textured ovoid balls of unknown material, some of which adhered to the body wall and some of which had broken away from it. Pock-marked depressions appeared in the interior body wall where these ovoid balls had broken away. The balls were not punctured and, as they were unlikely to have been insect cocoons, their composition remained doubtful. They may have resulted from the drying of fatty materials inside the body cavity in combination with the granular material with which the cavity had been stuffed. The gastroscopic examination demonstrated, without destroying any tissues, that the body had been emptied of viscera through an incision in the side and the cavity packed with lengths of a light vegetable stem and some earthy debris.

Paleopathology. The most striking radiographic finding was the irregular thickening of many of the long bones. Changes were observed in the left radius, left humerus, right clavicle, right ulna, both femora, both tibiae, and the right fibula. In general the changes consisted of an irregular thickening of the cortex involving the shafts of the long bones and containing irregular areas of erosion that were of both a sclerotic and a destructive type, as seen by the formation of cloacae. The ends of the long bones were normal in appearance, as were the joints. The changes in the right tibia and fibula were especially interesting in that the lesions, which extended over several centimeters, occurred at the same level in both bones. The left radius and tibia were severely affected, whereas the left ulna and fibula were spared. These osteological changes are consistent with the diagnosis of yaws, but no complementary skin lesions were detected on the mummy's external surface.

No evidence of any bony defects or fractures within the skull or facial bones was detected, nor was there any indication of degenerative arthritis in the skeleton as a whole.

EXAMPLES OF AUSTRALIAN MUMMIES
Although several Aboriginal mummies have been recorded, none has been described as thoroughly as the Macleay Museum specimen. Preserved bodies and organs of Australian Aborigines were collected from early Colonial times onward. That recovered from Adelaide by Sir George Grey and presented to the Royal College of Surgeons (London) in 1845 was one of the earliest known. Flower briefly described this specimen as an adult male bound in a sitting position (Flower 1879:393–394). The legs were flexed in line with the sides of the thorax and abdomen and the forearms were crossed, with each hand resting on the opposite foot. All orifices were

sewed with a running suture, but the viscera had not been removed. The body had been decorated with ocher and the mouth stuffed with emu feathers. Ironically, Flower directed the body to be unfleshed and the skeleton preserved so that the specimen would be more instructive! Unfortunately, even this has since been destroyed when the college was damaged during World War II.

A more detailed account of another South Australian mummy found at Rapid Bay near Cape Jervis was given by Tindale and Mountford (1936:487–502). The specimen was excavated from Kongarati Cave and was found in association with a wide range of molluscs, some wooden fire-making implements, a bone point, fragments of netting, and a kangaroo-skin cloak. The mummy was that of an elderly female, buried in a slate-lined cist grave in a flexed position. The right side had been oriented in a northerly direction. In view of the charred nature of the spine and hips and the presence of fatty matter on the right side, the authors concluded that the body had been smoke-dried. A proportionate amount of decomposition had ensued to parts of the right side, and the chest was distorted as if the lateral walls of the thorax had been crushed. This was explained by the local custom of forcing out the dying breaths of an individual by jumping on the thorax.

A third notable South Australian mummy was located in cliffs above the Murray River at Fromm's Landing (Sheard et al. 1927:173–176). The preserved corpse of an infant about 2 years of age was found lying on a net bag filled with long grasses. The body had been placed on its left side in a crouched position and was covered with a further layer of loose grasses and a wallaby hide. Hackett's examination of the body indicated that a depression on the right parietal was probably caused by a fracture, but this had not been sufficiently serious to cause death as there were osteological signs of healing. Both this specimen and that found in Kongarati Cave are housed in the South Australian Museum.

Figure 11.8. *Mummy of Ngatja, from the upper Russell River, North Queensland. (From Klaatsch 1907)*

Other equally interesting mummies have been found elsewhere in Australia. Klaatsch (1907) has described his ruthless acquisition of the body of Ngatja (Figure 11.8); its present whereabouts are uncertain. An Aboriginal mummy from Morphett Vale is stated to be in the ethnographic collection of the Berlin Museum (Tindale 1974:55), and several specimens are housed at the Queensland Museum in Brisbane. The latter were all found in Queensland and have never been adequately examined, although Hamlyn-Harris gave a cursory account of them in his 1912 paper (1912b).

CONCLUSION

The nature of mummification techniques in New Guinea, Torres Strait, and Australia was such that the duration of a preserved body was only temporary. Concern expressed for a dead relative would not continue much beyond one or two generations, which eliminated the necessity of seeking more durable preserving methods. Consequently, as the practice of mummification lapsed with intensified European contacts, and with the introduction of Christianity in particular, the number of mummified specimens available to science declined. For this reason, scholars have had to rely more upon ethnographic and historical sources for details about funerary modes in Australia and Melanesia. One important advantage in such reports is their status as first-hand accounts of the rationale for mummification. The motives recorded and techniques described were as varied as the cultures in which mummification was practiced, a fact that runs contrary to the original diffusionist hypothesis proposed by Elliot Smith (Pretty 1969).

Ethnographic and historical records, however, are rarely sufficiently complete to enable prehistorians to reconstruct ancient mummification practices in detail, and further investigations of the few surviving specimens using modern scientific and medical acumen are required. More research about the disposal of the dead is especially necessary for clarifying traditional Australian Aboriginal thought.

It is clear that a great deal of uncertainty still remains about mummification in this region. There exists, moreover, important undescribed material whose study is long overdue and whose description will help dispel some of these obscurities. Similarly, the contribution of information from such specimens is of immense value to human biological and paleopathological research. The contribution of mummified material to research about indigenous peoples prior to recent hybridization will be extremely important. The authors have attempted to present a comprehensive survey of Australian and Melanesian mummification with a view to indicating appropriate directions for future research.

REFERENCES

Abbie, A. A. 1959. Sir Grafton Elliot Smith. *Bulletin of the Postgraduate Committee on Medicine, University of Sydney* 15(3):101–50.

Albertis, L. M. 1880. *New Guinea: what I did and what I saw there.* London: Sampson Low, Marston, Searle and Rivington.

Angas, G. F. 1847a. *Savage life and scenes in Australia and New Zealand.* London: Smith, Elder.

– 1847b. *South Australia illustrated.* London: Thomas McLean.

Basedow, H. 1925. *The Australian aboriginal.* Adelaide: F. W. Preece.

Berndt, R. M., and Berndt, C. H. 1964. *The world of the first Australians.* Sydney: Ure Smith.

Bjerre, J. 1956. *The last cannibals.* London: Michael Joseph.

Bowler, J. M.; Jones, R.; Allen, M.; and Thorne, A. G. 1970. Pleistocene human remains from Australia, a living site and human cremation from Lake Mungo, Western New South Wales. *World Archaeology* 2(1):39–60.

Bull, J. 1965. The sleepers in the ranges. *People* 16(11):12–13.

Dawson, W. R. 1924. A mummy from Torres Straits. *Annals of Archaeology and Anthropology* 11:87–96.

– 1928. Mummification in Australia and America. *Journal of the Royal Anthropological Institute* 58:115–38.

Elkin, A. P. 1954. *The Australian aborigines: how to understand them.* Sydney: Angus & Robertson.

Elliot Smith, G. 1915. On the significance of the geographical distribution of the practice of mummification: a study of the migrations of peoples and the spread of certain customs and beliefs. *Memoirs and Proceedings of the Manchester Literary and Philosophical Society* 59:1–143.

Fletcher, J.J. 1929. The society's heritage from the

Macleays: part 2. *Proceedings of the Linnaean Society of New South Wales* 54(3):185–272.

Flower, W. H. 1879. Illustrations of the mode of preserving the dead in Darnley Island and in South Australia. *Journal of the Anthropological Institute* 8:389–95.

Girard, F. 1957. Les peintures rupestres Buang, district de Morobé, Nouvelle Guinée. *Journal de la société des océanistes* 13:4–49.

Haddon, A. C. 1908. Sociology, magic and religion of the eastern islanders. In *Reports of the Cambridge Anthropological Expedition to Torres Straits*, vol. 6. Cambridge: Cambridge University Press.

– 1912. Arts and crafts. In *Reports of the Cambridge Anthropological Expedition to Torres Straits*, vol. 4. Cambridge: Cambridge University Press.

– 1935. General ethnography. In *Reports of the Cambridge Anthropological Expedition to Torres Straits*, vol. 1. Cambridge: Cambridge University Press.

Hamlyn-Harris, R. 1912a. Papuan mummification, as practised in the Torres Straits islands, and exemplified by specimens in the Queensland Museum collections. *Memoirs of the Queensland Museum* 1:1–6.

– 1912b. Mummification. *Memoirs of the Queensland Museum* 1:7–22.

Held, G. J. 1957. *The Papuas of Waropen.* The Hague: Nijhoff.

Hiatt, B. 1969. Cremation in Aboriginal Australia. *Mankind* 7(2):104–14.

Howells, W. 1973. *The Pacific Islanders.* Wellington: Reed.

Howitt, A. W. 1904. *The native tribes of South-East Australia.* London: Macmillan.

Klaatsch, H. 1907. Some notes on scientific travel amongst the black population of tropical Australia in 1904, 1905, 1906. *Report of the Eleventh Meeting of the Australasian Association for the Advancement of Science, 1907*, pp. 577–92. Adelaide: The Association.

Le Roux, C. C. F. M. 1948. *De bergpapoea's van Nieuw-Guinea en hun woongebied.* Leiden: Brill.

Mathews, R. H. 1905. *Ethnological notes on the Aboriginal tribes of New South Wales and Victoria.* Sydney: White.

McConnel, U. H. 1937. Mourning ritual among tribes of Cape York Peninsula. *Oceania* 7(3):346–71.

Mulvaney, D. J. 1969. *The prehistory of Australia.* London: Thames & Hudson.

Mulvaney, D. J., and Golson, J. (eds.). 1971. *Aboriginal man and environment in Australia.* Canberra: Australian National University Press.

Pretty, G. L. 1969. The Macleay Museum mummy from Torres Straits: a postscript to Elliot Smith and the diffusion controversy. *Man* 4(1):24–43.

– 1972. Report of an inspection of certain archaeological sites and field monuments in the territory of Papua and New Guinea. Typescript. South Australian Museum.

– 1977. The chronology of the Roonka Flat: a preliminary consideration. In *Stone tools as cultural markers: change, evolution, and complexity*, R. V. S. Wright (ed.), pp. 288–331. Canberra: Australian Institute of Aboriginal Studies.

Rhys, L. 1947. *Jungle pimpernel: the story of a district officer in central Netherlands New Guinea.* London: Hodder & Stoughton.

Roth, W. E. 1907. Burial ceremonies and disposal of the dead, North Queensland. *Records of the Australian Museum* 6(5):365–403.

Sengstake, F. 1892. Die Leichenbestattung aus Darnley Island. *Globus* 61(16):248–9.

Sheard, H. L.; Mountford, C. P.; and Hackett, C. J. 1927. An unusual disposal of an aboriginal child's remains from the Lower Murray, South Australia. *Transactions and Proceedings of the Royal Society of South Australia* 5:173–6.

Simpson, C. 1953. *Adam with arrows: inside New Guinea.* Sydney: Angus & Robertson.

Stirling, E. C. 1893. Report on inspection of Aboriginal mummy chambers at two localities on the Coorong, South Australia, 1893. Field notes in Department of Anthropology research file, South Australian Museum.

– 1911. Preliminary report on the discovery of native remains at Swanport, River Murray, with an inquiry into the alleged occurrence of a pandemic among the Australian aboriginals. *Transactions of the Royal Society of South Australia* 35:4–46.

Tindale, N. B. 1974. *Aboriginal tribes of Australia, their terrain, environmental controls, distribution, limits and proper names.* Berkeley: University of California Press.

Tindale, N. B., and Mountford, C. P. 1936. Results

of the excavations of Kongarati Cave, near Second Valley, South Australia. *Records of the South Australian Museum* 5(4): 487–502.

Tolmer, A. 1882. *Reminiscences of an adventurous and chequered career at home and at the Antipodes*. London: Sampson Low, Marston, Searle & Rivington.

Vial, L. G. 1936. Disposal of the dead among the Buang. *Oceania* 7(1):63–8.

Woods, J. D. 1879. *The native tribes of South Australia*. Adelaide: Wigg.

12

Japanese mummies

KIYOHIKO SAKURAI
Department of Archaeology
Waseda University
Tokyo, Japan

TAMOTSU OGATA
Formerly of Department of Anatomy
Niigata University School of Medicine
Niigata, Japan

Translated by R. FREEMAN
Waseda University, Tokyo, Japan

A RESEARCH AND CULTURAL HISTORY
KIYOHIKO SAKURAI

In a country of high humidity, such as Japan, the belief that mummification could not, and did not, exist would not be altogether unfounded, but rather more a matter of common sense. However, through our investigations we have been able to establish that mummification was in fact a very old custom in our country and one that was practiced right up until the early part of the twentieth century.

It is recorded that the great priest Kūkai (Kōbō-daishi, A.D. 774–835), who is famous not only for the studies of esoteric Buddhism he made while in China, but also for founding the Shingon sect of Japanese Buddhism, became mummified upon his death at Mount Kōya (a sacred mountain of this sect). In addition, during the eleventh and twelfth centuries there were many priests who voluntarily attempted self-mummification.

In existence today are the twelfth-century mummies of the Fujiwara family, a powerful clan of northeastern Japan, and, dating from the seventeenth to the twentieth century, the mummies of numerous priests. Apart from those of the Fujiwara family, all Japanese mummies are those of priests who voluntarily sought self-mummification.

The Japanese idea of mummification, practiced in accordance with Buddhist principles, was subject to a strong Chinese influence. In China, Buddhists had long been practicing mummification of the dead; these mummies were known as *nikustin* ("of the body or flesh"). The act of self-immolation in order to become a mummy was termed *nyūjō* ("entering into Nirvāna"). Priests who became mummies were given the title *nikushin-butsu* ("a Buddha of the body") or *nyūjō-butsu* ("a Buddha of Nirvāna") and were worshipped and respected in the same way as the Buddhist statuary.

In this regard, there was a great difference between the principles of mummification in China and Japan and those practiced in Egypt and South America.

This section describes mummies unique to Japan under the following headings: (1) mummies as recorded in literature, (2) existing mummies, and (3) the principles of mummification.

MUMMIES AS RECORDED IN LITERATURE
The number of mummies mentioned in Japanese literature is quite large. I should like here to introduce only a few examples.

In the *Genkō-shakusho* (completed in 1322) – a history of Japanese Buddhism and collection of priests' biographies covering a period of more than 700 years up to 1273 – it is recorded that in A.D. 1003 the priest Zōga attained *nyūjō* at the age of 87. In compliance with his will his body was placed in a large barrel, buried for 3 years, and then exhumed. At that time he was found to be in a state of perfect preservation.

This procedure of placing the body in a large barrel or earthenware urn and burying it for 3 years followed by exhumation was a

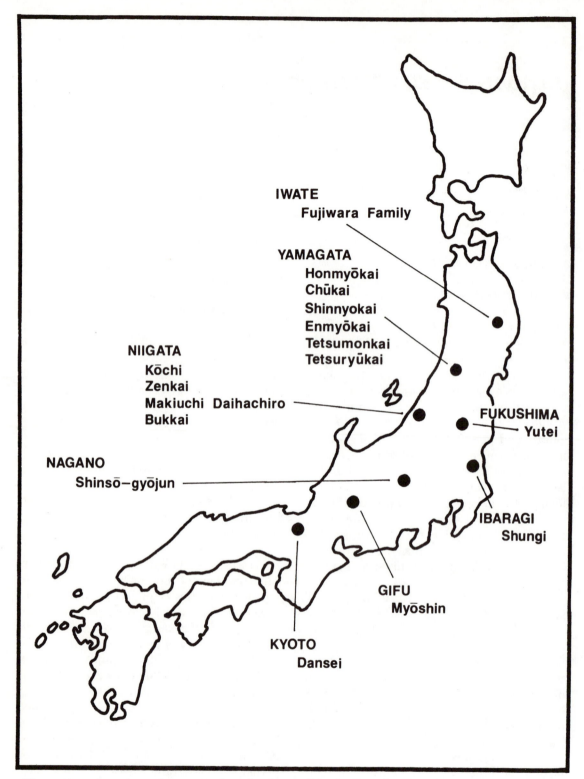

IWATE
Fujiwara Family

YAMAGATA
Honmyōkai
Chūkai
Shinnyokai
Enmyōkai
Tetsumonkai
Tetsuryūkai

NIIGATA
Kōchi
Zenkai
Makiuchi Daihachiro
Bukkai

FUKUSHIMA
Yutei

NAGANO
Shinsō–gyōjun

IBARAGI
Shungi

GIFU
Myōshin

KYOTO
Dansei

Figure 12.1.   Locations of mummies found in Japan. (Map by Timothy Motz, Detroit Institute of Arts)

Table 12.1. *Mummies of the Fujiwara family*

Relationship	Name	Date of mummification	Age at death (yr)
Grandfather	Fujiwara Kiyohira	1128	73
Father	Fujiwara Motohira	1157	Unknown
Son	Fujiwara Hidehira	1187	66
Grandson	Fujiwara Yasuhira	1189	23

method of mummification that had been practiced in China from the fifth to sixth centuries up until modern times. The *Genkō-shakusho* indicates that the practice was brought to Japan during the eleventh century.

However, whether or not the mummy of priest Zōga ever became the object of worship cannot be ascertained.

The *Genkō-shakusho* also contains an account of the priest Rinken who attained *nyūjō* in 1150. It is recorded that upon mummification he was duly enshrined at Mount Kōya. Thus it can be seen that by the middle of the twelfth century the practice of worshipping mummies of those who attained *nyūjō* had become established in Japan.

EXISTING MUMMIES

In Japan there are 19 mummies in existence. Figure 12.1 shows their geographical distribution. The following paragraphs describe several of the mummies in detail.

Mummies of the Fujiwara family (preserved at the Chūson-ji Temple, Hiraizumi City, Iwate prefecture). The 4 mummies enshrined in the Konjiki-dō (the Golden Hall) of Chūson-ji Temple are listed in Table 12.1. Whether these 4 examples became mummified through natural processes or by embalming is difficult to judge, for their internal organs have been devoured by rats. Different opinions are held by different scholars. However, there is general agreement that some form of embalming must have been carried out.

The Fujiwara family, a powerful clan of northeast Japan, created in this remote region a culture comparable to that of the capital of those days. It was undoubtedly to ensure the permanent preservation of the remains of the leaders of this powerful family that mummification was carried out.

Mummy of priest Kōchi (preserved at the Saishō-ji Temple, Teradomari City, Niigata prefecture). Born in Shimo-osa (the modern Chiba prefecture), Kōchi became a priest at Renge-ji Temple in the village of Ōura, which is in his native district. Later he departed on a pilgrimage to various provinces. His journeys took him to the northernmost parts of Honshū before he traveled to, and settled at, the temple of Saishō-ji in Echigo (the modern Niigata prefecture). There he attained *nyūjō* in A.D. 1363. His mummy soon became an object of faith and is displayed annually on 2 October, when it is worshipped by numerous believers.

The head of this mummy is yellowish brown in color. Its soft tissues have dried and adhered, although those of the face have almost completely fallen away, exposing the bone. The skin and tissues covering the area from the head down to the small of the back have been well preserved, but there are large cavities made by rats in the stomach and chest. In literature of the nineteenth century, this mummy is recorded as being in a state of perfect preservation. It is believed that deterioration advanced rapidly following the Meiji restoration and the subsequent neglect of their traditional practices by the Japanese.

Mummy of priest Tetsumonkai (preserved at the Chūren-ji Temple, Asahi Village, Yamagata prefecture). This is a compara-

Figure 12.2. Mummy of priest Tetsumonkai.

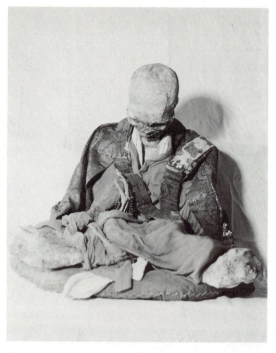

Figure 12.3. Mummy of priest Tetsuryūkai.

tively well preserved example (Figure 12.2). Tetsumonkai was an ordinary day laborer who, in his youth, killed a samurai in a fight over a woman and subsequently fled to the sanctuary of Chūren-ji Temple on the slopes of Mount Yudono, a sacred mountain of the Shingon sect. Upon becoming a priest, he built roads and constructed bridges for the benefit of the local inhabitants and visited various provinces in order actively to engage in the propagation of Buddhism. In his final years he settled at Chūren-ji Temple, where, for a period of 3 years he abstained from the five cereals (rice, barley, corn, millet, and beans). Upon his attainment of *nyūjō* in 1829, priests surrounded his body with numerous large candles, drying it out by means of the candles' heat.

Mummy of priest Tetsuryūkai (preserved at the Nangaku-ji Temple, Tsuruoka City, Yamagata prefecture). This person, a disciple of Tetsumonkai, attained *nyūjō* in 1868 (Figure 12.3). Although it was his wish to attain a state of mummification, he became sick and died during the course of his ascetics. Other priests buried him in an underground stone chamber (cist) beneath the temple, but

later exhumed and embalmed him so that, unlike other mummies, his internal organs have been removed. To do this an incision about 18 cm in length was made across his lower abdomen and then sewed up with linen thread. X-ray examination shows that the abdominal cavity had been packed with lime, indicating that this mummy owes its preservation entirely to embalming rather than to natural processes.

Mummy of priest Bukkai (preserved at the Kannon-ji Temple, Murakami City, Niigata prefecture). This, the most recent of Japanese mummies, is that of a priest who practiced asceticism at Mount Yudono before attaining *nyūjō* in 1903. In accordance with his will, priests constructed an underground chamber and enshrined his body. After 3 years they were supposed to exhume and mummify it. But in Japan at that time exhumation became forbidden by law; so that Bukkai remained buried just as he was.

In 1961 we excavated his tomb. At about 1 m beneath the stone slab covering the grave,

Figure 12.4.   Burial chamber of priest Bukkai. The ceiling stone and front wall have been removed.

there was a skillfully constructed chamber of hewn stone, measuring 1.25 m along the sides by 2 m in depth (Figure 12.4). Near the floor of this chamber was a shelf of iron bars upon which the strong wooden coffin had been placed. As the body had been in the earth for a long time, although parts of it had mummified, the remainder had become a skeleton.

PRINCIPLES OF MUMMIFICATION

With the exception of those of the Fujiwara family, all Japanese mummies are of priests who achieved mummification through their own volition, even though other priests had to assist the process of transformation. What was it that inspired them to undertake this? It was a principle that developed from the Maitreya faith – faith in Maitreya-bodhisattva, the Buddha of the future.

They believed that 5,670,000,000 years following Śākyamuni's (Buddha's) attainment

of Nirvāna, Maitreya will appear in this world for the salvation of all sentient beings. As priests, they wanted to assist Maitreya when the time arrived. They believed that in order to do this, they should await his coming in their earthly form – that is, as mummies. This was the principle, and although there arose many legends (starting with Kūkai) of famous priests who attained mummification, quite a large number did in fact achieve this condition. For both the mummies described in literature and those that are in existence today, the principle behind their mummification was tied to the Maitreya faith.

Following the seventeenth century, as the Maitreya faith became combined with the Shūgendō or mountain asceticism of Sangaku-sūhai (a primitive form of mountain worship), many priests of the lower orders, living in the strict feudal society of the Tokugawa era, turned to mummification as a form of self-assertion.

CONCLUSION

In this section I have endeavored to explain something about Japanese mummies. The method by which mummification was achieved is not yet clearly understood. However, from records and from tradition, the following process may be deduced:

1. By gradually reducing the body's intake of nutrition over a long period, the body's constitution was altered to one that was strongly resistant to decomposition. Abstaining from the five cereals was for this purpose.
2. After death the body was interred for 3 years in an underground stone chamber (cist); it was then exhumed and dried.

As explained previously, the mummies of the Fujiwara family appear to have undergone some form of embalming. Where did knowledge of this art of mummification come from?

In the book *Kitaezo-zusetsu (An Illustrated Book of North Ezo)*, compiled by the early nineteenth-century explorer, Māmiya Rinzō, there is an account of a custom among the Ainu of Sakhalin of mummifying their chieftains. Also, Aleut mummies have been discovered on Kagamil Island in the Aleutian chain. Although the practice of mummification cannot be found among the Ainu of Hokkaidō, the fact that many of the mummies that exist today come from the northern part of Japan suggests that mummification as it developed in these northern regions is an influence that must be taken into consideration.

RESEARCH BY NATURAL SCIENCE
TAMOTSU OGATA

Books and articles on Japanese mummies have been published in great numbers (Andō 1961). We, the members of the Group for Research on Japanese Mummies, have been doing extensive research, primarily on the mummies of people who devoted themselves to Buddhism. The following discussion is restricted to mummies whose general examination was completed between 1959 and 1969.

To the author, the most interesting question is whether these remains were artificially mummified. The investigating commission has carried out a great deal of research on the famous mummified remains of four generations of the Fujiwara clan. Their efforts to decide whether the mummification was artificial or natural produced two opposing points of view (Furuhata 1950; Hasebe 1950; Suzuki 1950). The mummies we examined are quite different from those of the Fujiwaras, many of which show obvious traces of treatment. An investigation of these mummies therefore will suggest the solutions regarding the question of artificial mummification in Japan.

RESEARCH MATERIALS AND METHODS OF INVESTIGATION
The nine mummies discussed here are all Japanese males who devoted themselves to Buddhism. The dates of their deaths range from the period of the Northern and Southern dynasties to the Meiji era – that is, from 1363 to 1903. Their deaths were caused by starva-

tion as a result of asceticism and by illness after asceticism. The remains show various stages of mummification, and one is almost a skeleton. Osteology, craniology, and somatology were applied according to the mummies' conditions. X-ray examination was also used on occasion. The reconstructed statures are calculated by Pearson's formulas. Fingerprint studies were done sometimes by using alginate impression material to make a plaster model and sometimes by the naked eye at autopsy. Blood groups were determined by an absorption test against anti-A, anti-B, and anti-O agglutinin serum, using skin and/or muscle tissue.

A lightweight, portable X-ray machine was used.

RESULTS
All mummies but one were considerably damaged by rats and insects.

Kōchi Hōin. Most of the remaining skin is well preserved, but almost no viscera remain, and there is no evidence that the brain and viscera had been removed. It is therefore impossible to decide whether artificial methods of mummification had been used. The mummy is in a sitting position. It weighs 4.7 kg and is 159.9 cm in height. Many of the teeth had fallen in his lifetime. It is reported that he died at the age of 82. X-ray examination shows the closure of the principal sutures of the skull is not complete. The bones of the lower limbs are more developed than those of the upper limbs. The vertebral column is highly kyphotic. Several sparrow-egg-sized shadows, the origins of which are unknown, are observed in the internal surface of the right parietal bone. Cervical spondylosis and osteophytes are seen on the anterior walls of the bodies of the fifth and sixth cervical vertebrae. Lumbar spondylosis with osteophytes is seen on the anterior walls of the bodies of the second and fifth lumbar vertebrae; the intervertebral disc spaces are narrow. The blood group is AB.

Shungi Shōnin. The skin is relatively well preserved and there are remains of hair. Although there are no viscera, there is no evidence that the brain or viscera were removed. The mummy weighs 4.1 kg and is 157.2 cm in height. It looks rather like a turtle, because it bent forward when put into the cavity of a seated stone image of *Amida-Nyorai* (Amitabha Buddha). Its hands are clasped in prayer. The cervical vertebrae show luxation. The alveolar part of the mandible and the alveolar process of the maxillary bone are highly atrophied. All the teeth were lost in his lifetime. It is impossible to measure the orbit because both upper and lower eyelids are mummified in a closed state. X-ray examination shows that the closure of the principal sutures of the skull is moderately complete. The vertebral column is highly kyphotic. It is reported that Shungi Shōnin died at the age of 78. The bones of the upper and lower limbs are particularly well developed. The right thumb shows a radial loop fingerprint; the blood group is O. The bodies of the sixth and seventh cervical vertebrae show spondylosis with osteophytes.

Zenkai Shōnin (Figure 12.5). Most of the skin is well preserved, and the hair, penis, and scrotum remain. Most of the surface is brittle, and the color of the body is yellowish brown. Although there is no evidence that the brain or viscera were extracted, only the penis and scrotum can be found. Zenkai wears the same clothes and a pair of tabi as at the time of his death. His hands are clasped, and the wrists are tied together with string. A straight, deep furrow is seen from the right to the left lumbar region through the umbilical region at a right angle to the axis of the body. It seems to be a ligature mark that was made when the body was tied with string to a prop on its back to make it assume the desired posture for mummification, thus maintaining an exceedingly good sitting position. The soft parts may have decomposed at one time, but are well preserved. The lower legs are relatively short. The body weighs 7.0 kg and is 160.3 cm in height. The blood group is O. The upper and lower eyelids of both eyes are closed. In spite of its good posture, the vertebral column is highly kyphotic. Most of the molars of the maxillary bone fell off in his

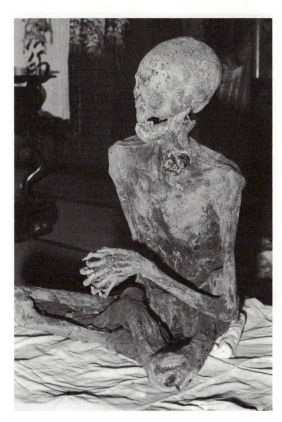

Figure 12.5.   Mummy of Zenkai Shōnin.

lifetime, and the bone has become highly atrophied. X-ray examination shows that the closure of the principal sutures of the skull is almost complete. It is reported that he died at the age of 85. X rays reveal many fairly large, oval shadows around the right internal surface of the occipital bone, the right orbit, both maxillary sinuses, and the vertebral column, but their origin is uncertain.

Chūkai Shōnin (Figure 12.6). The skin is well preserved, but the soft parts of the lower body have largely disintegrated. There is no evidence that the brain and viscera were extracted. The mummy is 159.1 cm in height, weighs 6.0 kg, and has blood group A. It is in a sitting position. Several ligature marks can be seen in the cervical region, on the right frontal chest wall, and from the right lumbar region to the left through the umbilical region at a right angle to the axis of the body. Old pieces of cloth are found attached to the im-

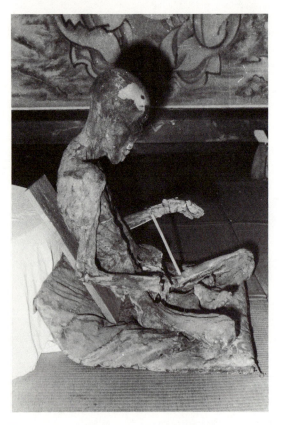

Figure 12.6.   Mummy of Chūkai Shōnin.

pressions caused by the rope. This suggests that Chūkai's clothed body had been tied with string to prevent it from falling forward in the mummification process. The upper and lower lids of both eyes are closed, and most of the soft parts under the headgear are decomposed. The facial part below the headgear is painted with something black (presumably Chinese ink), and most of the upper lip and some of the lower lip are shaped and mended with black substance. A board is tied to the back of the mummy to keep it in a good sitting position, and the left forearm is supported by a piece of wood to keep it forward and holding a bamboo stick. The mending of the face and the attempts to maintain the mummy's posture were performed after the second stage of treatment and will not, therefore, be discussed here. X rays show the closure of the principal sutures of the skull to be moderately

complete. Dental attrition is light, and the alveolar process of the maxillary bone and the alveolar part of the mandible are not much atrophied. According to the temple records, Chūkai died at the age of 58. The lower parts of the legs are relatively short, and the whole body is of slender frame. On X rays, spondylosis can be seen in the bodies of the fifth and sixth cervical vertebrae and the thoracic vertebrae. There are obvious osteophytes and osteosclerosis caused by osteoarthritis on the margin of the acetabulum. There is slight kyphosis of the vertebral column. The temple records say that Chūkai's corpse was smoke-dried, which probably explains its black brown color.

Shinnyokai Shōnin.   The skin is relatively well preserved but looks black brown, possibly because the body was smoke-dried during mummification. The skin surface is covered with innumerable white spots. The body weighs 6.0 kg and is 156.9 cm tall. The blood group is AB. The inferior aperture of the pelvis is wide open, and part of the diaphragm and urinary bladder remain, but there is no evidence that the brain and viscera were extracted. The mummy is in a crooked sitting posture, almost falling backward. The vertebral column is remarkably kyphotic, and a deep furrow is seen from the right lumbar region to the left through the umbilical region at a right angle to the axis of the body. A shallow furrow is also seen in the fifth intercostal space of the right side of the chest wall parallel to the ribs. These furrows may have been formed when the body was tied to a prop on its back at the time it was mummified. X rays show the closure of the principal sutures of the skull to be moderately complete. All the teeth had dropped out in his lifetime. The alveolar process of the maxillary bone and the alveolar part of the mandible are atrophied. Shinnyokai is reported to have died at the age of 96. The skeleton is delicate. The lower parts of the legs are relatively short. X rays show five oval shadows on the left scapula, but their origin is uncertain. Spondylosis can be seen in the lower thoracic vertebrae, and

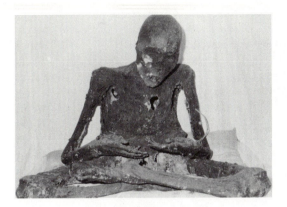

Figure 12.7.   Mummy of Enmyōkai Shōnin.

the body of the twelfth thoracic vertebra has
been deformed into a wedge shape. In front of
it, a new bone with a sharp margin is observed. It is not known whether the new bone
was formed as the result of a compression
fracture during his lifetime or because of
spondylosis. There is a postmortem fracture
in the second lumbar vertebra. The bodies of
the third, fourth, and especially the fifth lumbar vertebrae have been deformed into a
wedge shape. The acetabulum protrudes
slightly into the pelvis.
*Enmyōkai   Shōnin   (Figures   12.7   and
12.8)*.   The soft parts are brittle but thicker
than those of the other mummies. This body
has also kept its original shape better than the
others, though the lower part is not well preserved. The skin is atrophied, and there is no
sign that the brain and viscera were extracted.
The area from the right cheek to the upper and
lower lips has been mended, and the surface
is painted black brown, as is the rest of the
body. The upper and lower limbs were
painted black brown (presumably by per-
simmon tannin) after being tied with twine in
several places at a right angle to the axes. The
parts beneath the twine are not painted and
look light black brown. As the body had possibly been smoke-dried first, it was undoubtedly painted during the second treatment. X
rays show the closure of the principal sutures
of the skull to be almost complete. There is
slight dental attrition. Enmyōkai is said to

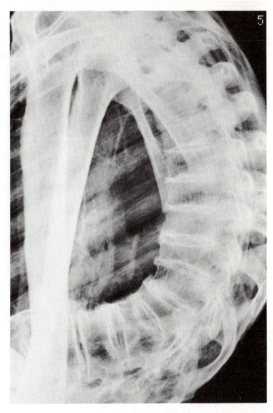

Figure 12.8.   Mummy of Enmyōkai Shōnin.

have died at the age of 55. The vertebral column is highly kyphotic and has the shape of a
bow. The body is 164.7 cm tall and weighs 6.8
kg. X-ray examination shows spondylosis in
the thoracic and lumbar vertebrae. Both the
twelfth thoracic vertebra and the first lumbar
vetebra, constituting the apex of kyphosis,
have deformed into a wedge shape. In the hip
joints, osteoarthritis is seen, but there is no
sign of osteoporosis. Because of its corpulence
it is believed that the body became mummified after it had decomposed.
Tetsumonkai Shōnin.   This mummy has
suffered serious damage. The remaining skin
is black brown, and hair also remains. There
is no evidence that the brain and viscera were
extracted. Part of the diaphragm and the left
lung remain. Temple records report that the
body was smoke-dried using big candles immediately after death. This suggests that the

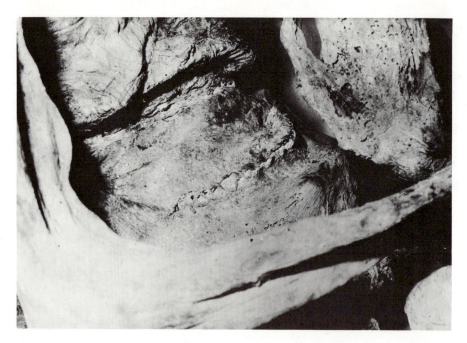

Figure 12.9.   Mummy of Tetsuryūkai Shōnin, showing the incision, extending from the right to the left iliac regions through the hypogastric region, with a continuous suture applied.

color of the skin may possibly be attributable to soot. A distinctive feature of this mummy is that the soft part of the face, from the frontal to the mandible part, has disintegrated and seems to have been mended with something black. It was painted over with yellow paint, then probably with black Japanese lacquer. Dental attrition is fairly advanced, and in X rays, the closure of the principal sutures of the skull is nearly complete. It is said that Tetsumonkai died at the age of 62. Long symmetrical ligature marks can be seen on both sides of the chest. They are like those of a cord used to tuck up kimono sleeves. They were probably left when the upper part of his body was tied to a prop on his back to make it assume a sitting position during the first stage of mummification. It is said that Tetsumonkai extracted his left eyeball and cut off his external genital organs himself. A soft part, which may have been his scrotum, was preserved separately. Tetsumonkai's blood group is B, and this was also the blood group of the scrotum. It may be assumed, therefore,

that this scrotum belonged to him. The mummy is 162.1 cm tall and weighs 5.0 kg. The bones of the lower limbs are well developed. The vertebral column, especially the lower lumbar vertebrae, is highly kyphotic. The left thumbprint, and possibly the right also, show an ulnar loop. In X rays, many oval shadows, origin unknown, are observed in the nasal cavity and in the right and left maxillary sinuses. Spondylosis can be seen from the eighth to the eleventh thoracic vertebrae. In the body of the twelfth thoracic vertebra, a compression fracture, possibly posthumous, can be clearly seen.

Tetsuryūkai Shōnin (Figure 12.9). This mummy is very well preserved because it was treated by a special method. The skin, especially of the face and head, is black because the body was dried over fire. A curved incision approximately 18.0 cm long runs from the right to the left iliac region through the hypogastric region. The thoracic, abdominal, and pelvic cavities are filled with lime powder and some has spilt from the inferior aperture of the pelvis. The incision is continuously sutured. The forearms are relatively long. The body, 159.2 cm tall, is in a sitting position. The vertebral column is highly kyphotic. Slight dental attrition can be seen in X rays; the closure of the principal sutures of the skull is almost complete. It is said that Tetsuryūkai died at the age of 62. The mummy weighs 15.0 kg, heavier than the other mummies, but this is because of the weight of the lime powder. The left thumbprint possibly shows an ulnar loop; the index finger a whorl; and the middle finger possibly a whorl. The right thumbprint possibly shows an arch and the middle finger possibly an ulnar loop. The blood group is A. Osteoporosis is observed in the vertebrae. Osteophytes are found on the upper margins of each acetabulum, and osteoarthritis is also seen. Periostitis can be seen on the medial side of the upper part of the left femur. There is slight osteoarthritis in the left patellofemoral joint. The cortexes of the medial sides of both tibial shafts have become rough. It is uncertain whether this is attributable to the posttraumatic periosteal reaction.

Bukkai Shōnin.   Immediately after his death in 1903, Bukkai was put in a wooden coffin and was placed in a stone room with special devices; we excavated his body in 1961. Many bones were separated at the joints. The soft parts had decomposed and were attached to the bones like dirt, but some skin of his back was mummified. There is no evidence that the brain and viscera were extracted. The body was probably in a sitting position when it was placed in the coffin, but it was not so at the time of our excavation. Four teeth were left on the mandible. The alveolar part of the mandible was atrophied, and the roots of the teeth were exposed. X rays show the closure of the principal sutures of the skull to be moderately complete. Bukkai's age at death is said to be 76. The body is 158.2 cm in height and weighs 7.2 kg. The lower leg bones are sturdy. Linea aspera of the femur is well developed; the tibia is nearly platycnemic; and the fibula is thick. These facts suggest that

Bukkai made ample use of his lower limbs. In X rays all the vertebrae, from the second cervical vertebra down to the fourth lumbar vertebrae, show various deformations attributable to ankylosing spondylitis, which results in a bamboo spine. An abnormal finding is that the right fifth rib and left fourth rib are bifurcated where they touch the cartilage. In addition, bulging or spinous cortical thickening is seen in the interosseous crest of the right radius and ulna and the head of the left fibula.

LIVING ORGANISMS FOUND INSIDE AND OUTSIDE THE BODIES

All mummies except Bukkai, who was buried in the ground, had been damaged by rats, although the extent of the damage varies. In particular, the viscera were eaten, and the destruction was accelerated by rat excreta. Flies generally got into the bodies during the period of decomposition with moisture. They laid eggs in the remains either at the time of death or during mummification. The season of death and the condition of the mummies when they were placed on the ground can be deduced from the pupal sloughs of the flies that remain in the bodies. It should be noted that the lunar calendar was used before the fifth year of the Meiji era (1872) and the solar calendar after that. Among those who were mummified on the ground and in the cold season, flies were observed in Zenkai and Kōchi, although the records say that the priests' deaths occurred in January and October, when such flies as *Lucilia*, *Sarcophaga*, and *Calliphora* were not likely to be active. It seems, therefore, that either the viscera were kept damp until spring or the dates of death were recorded incorrectly. It is recorded that Shungi died on 15 February, was placed in a hermetic place after 17 days, and then was taken out. However, the finding of pupal sloughs of *Sarcophaga* suggests that this body had been placed in a spot where there were many flies or that it was taken out of the hermetic place with wet viscera. It is recorded that Chūkai died on 21 May and was taken from the ground after having been buried. Pupal sloughs of *Lucilia* found in the remains indicate that the viscera were still moist either when he died or when he was taken out from the ground. Pupal sloughs of *Fannia canicularis* adhered to Shinnyokai (the date of his death is uncertain) and those of *Lucilia* to Enmyōkai, who died on 8 May. This implies that these priests' viscera were still damp when their bodies were placed on the ground. If the record of the temple of Enmyōkai is correct, the priest's viscera must have been in a condition that allowed flies to adhere to them immediately after the priest died. As these examples show, pupal sloughs of flies can be a valid and important clue in determining whether the dates of death shown in records correspond to dates suggested by the condition of the body, as well as in understanding the whole process of mummification.

DISCUSSION

The mummies discussed in this section were not natural mummies, nor were they found by accident. Their mummified condition can be seen with the naked eye. They were made and enshrined in temples by people who wanted to preserve them and who believed in the religious ideas of Buddhism. It can be said, therefore, that all were mummified intentionally. Unlike Egyptian mummies, the viscera do not seem to have been extracted, except for the mummy of Tetsuryūkai in 1879 or 1880 in the Meiji era. This was treated by making an incision, filling the cavity of the body with lime powder, and applying a continuous suture. Most of the viscera of the seven mummies other than those of Tetsuryūkai and Bukkai were eaten by rats, but some viscera obviously remain in two of them. There is no evidence that brains were extracted.

The most important stage of mummification is the first one, because it is then that the dead body is made into a mummy. In many cases, mummies were treated several times, but the later forms of treatment are not dis-

cussed here. According to the records, some bodies were smoke-dried in the first treatment, and indeed, black soot could be observed on their skins. The most notable feature of these mummies is their posture, which is related to the tenets of Buddhism. Many were mummified with the lower and upper eyelids closed. The position of the lower limb is different in each mummy. In some, the joints were broken and the bones separated, so that the original position remains uncertain, though it was probably a sitting position. In many mummies, the heads were bent forward and in some their palms were pressed together in prayer, as in the case of Zenkai, whose wrist joints were tied with string. However, the original forms were destroyed as time passed, and the upper limbs are now in various attitudes.

Unlike the Egyptian method, neither oil nor resin was applied during the first stage of mummification, although, in Tetsuryūkai's case, filling the body cavity with lime powder helped good preservation. Modern medical techniques had presumably been introduced by the time this work was performed. People capable of applying a continuous suture must have been exceedingly skillful.

Fingerprints could be investigated in only three cases. This had nothing to do with the period of the mummies, but was the result of damage by rats and insects and of corrosion. Blood groups were determined for all except Enmyōkai and Bukkai. Blood grouping was not possible in Enmyōkai's case because of decomposition and in Bukkai's case because of corrosion of almost all the soft parts.

The mummies are enshrined as objects of religious worship at their respective temples, which were far removed from cities. It was therefore necessary to take X rays with a lightweight, portable machine. In addition, in the case of the mummies with soft parts remaining on the bones, special devices were used to emphasize the bones. Senile spondylosis was found in almost all. Bukkai exhibited ankylosing spondylitis. Some remains had osteoarthritis in the hips and knees. Some had periostitis or periosteal thickness of the cortex. In some cases, fracture of the vertebral bodies was reported, but this may have been a posthumous modification. Many oval shadows were found in the skulls and on the scapulas and the vertebral column, but the origin of these is uncertain.

As is obvious from this discussion, these nine mummies were in the process of rapid deterioration. From the very beginning of the examination, the author, together with Sōjirō Maruyama, has aimed at achieving a better state of preservation for the mummies. Preventive measures against microorganisms, insects, and rats were taken, and decomposing parts were tied together with twine and fixed with glue.

CONCLUSION

This investigation of nine Japanese mummies dating from medieval times (1363) to the present (1903) has shown that many were mummified by artificial means.

ACKNOWLEDGMENTS

The cultural history presented in the second part of this chapter is derived from the following sources: *Mummies in Japan* (1961) by the late Professor Dr. Kōsei Andō, the previous head of our group, and "Research by Cultural History" by the late Professor Andō and Professor Kiyohiko Sakurai in *Research of Japanese Mummies*.

As reported in the second section of this chapter, its author took part in anatomical and anthropological studies of mummies. The following staff of Niigata University School of Medicine contributed information in their professional fields: the late Professor Emeritus Dr. Shungo Yamanouchi and Professor Dr. Rokurō Shigeno for medicolegal studies, Professor Emeritus Dr. Shūei Nozaki for review of X rays of mummies, and Professor Emeritus Dr. Sachū Kōno for observations

on alterations of bones seen in X rays. Together with Dr. Ryūhei Homma, the author dealt with living organisms found in and around mummies.

Thanks are due every professor and doctor for his help. The author wishes to thank Mr. Akira Matsumoto, lecturer of Nihon University, for his help during this investigation. The author would like to express his gratitude also to the following people for their help: the staff of Shōnai Hospital, Tsuruoka City, Yamagata prefecture, for radiographic studies; Professor Dr. Susumu Saitō, Mr. Yoshinobu Ikegami, and the late Dr. Hiromasa Muraki for identifying species of living organisms; and Mr. Sōjirō Maruyama for helping mend the mummies.

Gratitude must also be expressed for the encouragement and assistance of the priests of the respective temples.

REFERENCES

Andō, K. 1961. *Mummies in Japan*. Tokyo: Mainichi Newspapers. In Japanese.
–   1969. Preparation of Nyūjō mummies. In *Research of Japanese mummies*, Group for Research of Japanese Mummies (ed.), pp. 83–95. Tokyo: Heibonsha. In Japanese.
Andō, K., and Sakurai, K. 1969. Research by cultural history: Extant Japanese mummies. In *Research of Japanese mummies*, Group for Research of Japanese Mummies (ed.), pp. 21–82. Tokyo: Heibonsha. In Japanese.
Furuhata, T. 1950. Blood groups, fingerprints and teeth of four generations of the Fujiwara clan. In *The Chūsonji Temple and four generations of the Fujiwara clan*, pp. 45–66. Tokyo: Asahi Shimbun. In Japanese.
Hasebe, K. 1950. Various questions on the remains. In *The Chūsonji Temple and four generations of the Fujiwara clan*, pp. 7–22. Tokyo: Asahi Shimbun. In Japanese.
Suzuki, H. 1950. Anthropological observations on the remains. In *The Chūsonji Temple and four generations of the Fujiwara clan*, pp. 23–44. Tokyo: Asahi Shimbun. In Japanese.

13

Miscellaneous mummies

ANTONIO ASCENZI
Professor of Morbid Anatomy
University of Rome
Rome, Italy

AIDAN COCKBURN
President, Paleopathology Association
Detroit, Michigan, U.S.A.

EKKEHARD KLEISS
Professor Emeritus
Department of Embryology
Universidad de los Andes
Mérida, Venezuela

THE INFANT MUMMY OF UAN MUHUGGIAG

ANTONIO ASCENZI

The mountain range called Tadrart Acacus, situated in southern Libya (Fezzan), extends to the east of the Ghat oasis and covers a surface of about 6,000 km². A large area of it was explored by Mori during the winter of 1958–1959 on the occasion of his fourth paleoethnological expedition (Mori 1960). Almost at the end of the mission, in the Tagzelt Valley a deposit was discovered under a natural shelter called Uan Muhuggiag. Like the other shelters in the zone, the walls and ceiling are covered by more than 100 rock paintings, indicating that the site was actively used during the prehistoric era. The shelter faces south and is situated at the base of a tall rock wall that borders the southeastern end of the Teshuinat's wadi. At its entrance, the shelter is about 40 m long by 3.5 m high. Its depth does not exceed 4 m.

The height is not uniform, but progressively decreases to 90 cm at the level of the inner wall. In contrast with the other decorated shelters in the same zone, the floor here is a mixed deposit of sand and randomly distributed ashes. The surface of the floor is situated 1 m above the bed of the wadi and is separated from it by bulky rocks that have facilitated the settlement of the deposit (Figure 13.1).

In order to examine the structure of the deposit, an excavation was made measuring 160 by 80 cm and running east and west. In this way it was established that the deposit reached a depth of about 1 m and rested on sandstone flags. On the western side of the excavation were found fragments of long bones from animals and of bone tools. The eastern side of the excavation revealed a clear stratification caused by alternating layers of coals, ashes, and fibrous matter. Under the lowest layer of coals, the sandstone floor showed an intentional circular excavation 25 cm in diameter but only 3 cm deep. Here a spherical object was found, completely masked by a layer of randomly distributed vegetable fibers, measuring approximately 25 cm in diameter. When the vegetable fibers were removed, the mummy of a child appeared, almost completely wrapped in an envelope of animal skin and bearing a necklace of little rings made from the shells of ostrich eggs (Arkell et al. 1961).

Dating by the carbon-14 method was carried out by Professor E. Tongiorgi at the University of Pisa using two different types of samples: the lowest coal layer of the deposit and the envelope of animal skin. The first sample was 7,438 ± 220 years old; the second 5,405 ± 180 years old.

As far as the soft tissues are concerned, the child was in a good state of preservation, very much like that usually found in mummies obtained by drying. The body was in an unusual position, with an extreme flexion of the trunk and a forced rotation of the head to the right side. The upper right arm was extended and adduced somewhat posteriorly, that is, behind the trunk. The right forearm was flexed. The legs were in a squatting position near the head, but it was not possible to deduce their exact position because a partial dislocation had occurred (Figure 13.2).

Figure 13.1.   The shelter of Uan Muhuggiag. (Courtesy of F. Mori)

A careful examination of the abdominal walls revealed a long incision in the anterior wall, apparently for the purpose of removing the thoracic and abdominal viscera, of which no vestige could be seen. This agrees with the conclusion that the corpse's extremely flexed position could not have been assumed unless the trunk had previously been eviscerated. Between the edges of the abdominal incision lay a very irregular and bent cone 10 cm long. Its maximum circumference reached 6 cm. It was arranged in such a way that only its apex protruded from the incision. The structure consisted of a light and porous conglomerate of black mold mixed with granules, probably vegetable seeds.

The region around the external genital organs was badly preserved, so that the sex remained undetermined.

Anthropological research consisted of descriptive morphological, anthropometric, radiological, histological, and chemical examination. By these means it was possible to deduce that the child had negroid characteristics and that at the time of death it was about 30 months old. The skull showed the following main features: pentagonoid form with sharp occipital heel, protuberant forehead of infantile type, dolichocephaly near to mesocephaly, camecephaly, and tapeinocephaly. The face revealed an obvious prognathism, with a Camper's angle of 70°.

A careful examination of soft tissues and a radiological investigation of the skeleton failed to reveal any change that could be interpreted as responsible for death.

Samples of soft tissues prepared from the scalp and the trunk were hydrated, fixed in formol, embedded in paraffin, and sectioned for examination under the optical microscope. Hydration in saline solution showed that imbibition was similar to that occurring

Figure 13.2. The infant mummy of Uan Muhuggiag. (Courtesy of F. Mori)

when air-dried tissues receive this treatment. Microscopic examination revealed that tissue structure was not well preserved. The tissue was in no way different from that of a Peruvian mummy chosen as a control, in which mummification was carried out by drying process. There is evidence, therefore, to support the view that in the child of Uan Muhuggiag mummification was obtained by drying after removing thoracic and abdominal viscera.

This conclusion emphasizes that the spontaneous preservation of bodies in warm and dry environments probably played a major role in suggesting to ancient populations the

ways in which artificial mummification could be obtained. This was also the view of Pettigrew (1834), De Morgan (1896), and Elliot Smith and Dawson (1924) regarding the origin of mummification practices among the ancient Egyptians.

THE FROZEN SCYTHIANS OF SIBERIA
AIDAN COCKBURN

The Scythians were a nomadic pastoral people living in southern Russia north of the Black Sea. They formed part of a group of similar peoples inhabiting the vast, treeless

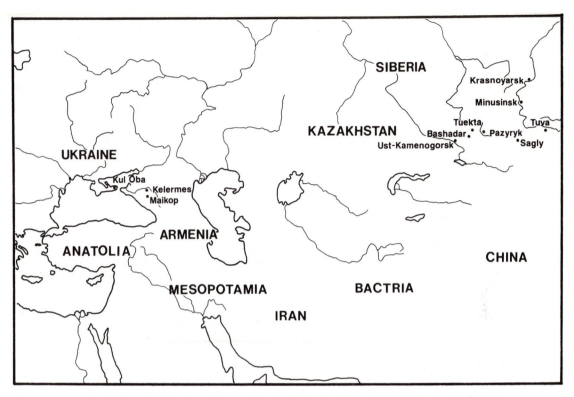

Figure 13.3. Burial sites of the Scythians. (Map by Timothy Motz, Detroit Institute of Arts)

territories that extend from Europe to China north of Greece, Persia, and India, and include Siberia (Figure 13.3). The term *Scythian* is used to cover the cultures of all these peoples. The key feature of all these cultures was the horse.

Herodotus visited Olbia in the course of his travels and wrote an account of the Scythians. His work is the basis of half the information in this section. The Scythian form of mummification is described by Herodotus, but few of these bodies have survived. The account is fairly explicit, assuming that the process used for preserving the king's body was also followed for the common people in preparation for the 40 days of exhibition.

The tombs of their kings are in the land of the Gerrhi, who dwell at the point where the Borysthenes is first navigable. Here, when the king dies, they dig a grave, which is square in shape, and of great size. When it is ready, they take the king's corpse, and having opened the belly, and cleaned out the inside, fill the cavity with a preparation of chopped cypress, frankincense, parsley-seed, and anise-seed, after which they sew up the opening, enclose the body in wax, and, placing it on a waggon, carry it about through all the different tribes. On this procession each tribe, when it receives the corpse, imitates the example which is first set by the Royal Scythians; every man chops off a piece of his ear, crops his hair close, makes a cut all round his arm, lacerates his forehead and his nose, and thrusts an arrow through his left hand. Then they who have the care of the corpse carry it with them to another of the tribes which are under the Scythian rule, followed by those whom they first visited. On completing the circuit of all the tribes under their sway, they find themselves in the country of the Gerrhi, who are the most remote of all, and so they come to the tombs of the kings. There the body of the dead king is laid in the grave prepared for it, stretched upon a mattress; spears are fixed in the ground on either side of the corpse, and beams stretched across above it to form a roof, which is covered with a thatching of twigs. In the open space around the body of the king they bury one of his concubines, first killing her by strangling, and also his cup-bearer, his cook, his groom, his lackey, his messenger, some of his horses, firstlings of all his other possessions, and some golden cups; for they use neither silver nor brass. After this they set to work, and raise a vast mound above the grave, all of them vying with each other and seeking to make it as tall as possible.

When a year is gone by, further ceremonies take place. Fifty of the best of the late king's attendants are taken, all native Scythians – for, as bought slaves are unknown in the country, the Scythian kings choose any of their subjects that they like, to wait on them – fifty of these are taken and strangled, with fifty of the most beautiful horses. When they are dead, their bowels are taken out, and the cavity cleaned, filled full of chaff, and straightway sewn up again. This done, a number of posts are driven into the ground, in sets of two pairs each, and on every pair half the felly of a wheel is placed archwise; then strong stakes are run lengthways through the bodies of the horses from tail to neck, and they are mounted upon the fellies, so that the felly in front supports the shoulders of the horse, while that behind sustains the belly and quarters, the legs dangling in midair; each horse is furnished with a bit and bridle, which latter is stretched out in front of the horse, and fastened to a peg. The fifty strangled youths are then mounted severally on the fifty horses. To effect this, a second stake is passed through their bodies along the course of the spine to the neck; the lower end of which projects from the body, and is fixed into a socket, made in the stake that runs lengthwise down the horse. The fifty riders are thus ranged in a circle round the tomb, and so left.

Such, then, is the mode in which the kings are buried: as for the people, when any one dies, his nearest of kin lay him upon a waggon and take him round to all his friends in succession: each receives them in turn and entertains them with a banquet, whereat the dead man is served with a portion of all that is set before the others; this is done for forty days, at the end of which time the burial takes place. [Herodotus, *Persian Wars*, Book IV:71–73]

In the 1860s, the archeologist V. V. Radlov excavated two large burial tombs in the Altai Mountains and found, among other specimens, some fur garments in excellent condition. In 1927 a Soviet archeologist started to investigate a stone mound near Shiba in the Altai Mountains. The finding of metal, wood, and bone stimulated further work on similar mounds in the region.

In 1929, S. I. Rudenko opened a mound in the Pazyryk Valley, and this was so rewarding that he continued with other mounds, for another four decades, except during World War II. The reason these graves were so important lies in the fact that they had partially filled with ice, which preserved soft materials like flesh, skins, and clothes.

A typical tomb has been described by Artamonov (1965). The builders first dug a rectangular pit about 5 m deep and 8 m wide. Inside this, they built a double-walled framework of wood, filling in the space between the walls with soil or rock. At one end, a space outside this framework was left open to receive the horses that were sacrificed in the funeral rites. The body of the king and his wife or concubine were placed in the inner chamber in a coffin made from a hollow tree trunk, together with a variety of household goods and treasures. The whole was then roofed in with beams and bark and covered with soil. The tomb was finished by laying a stone platform about 40 to 50 m in diameter. The completed tomb rose 4 to 5 m above ground level.

Water soaked through into the tomb, or possibly moisture condensed from the air, and in those cold conditions froze to form layers of ice over the contents. The tombs had been robbed, probably by the Turks who invaded the Altai Mountains after the third century B.C. The bodies inside had been mutilated in a search for ornaments; arms and legs had sometimes been amputated, and in one instance, the heads of both a man and a woman had been cut off. In spite of this, the bodies were in a good state of preservation, with skin and hair still intact (Figures 13.4 through 13.6). During the excavations, the ice was removed by pouring in hot water and then removing it with the thawed-out ice.

The bodies had been embalmed by a process not unlike that of the Egyptians, except

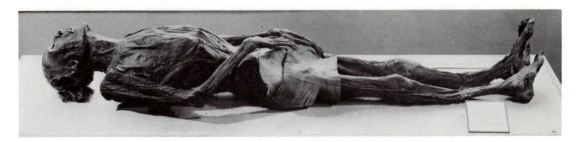

Figure 13.4. Mummy of a leader of the fifth Pazarokovsky cavalry, fifth to fourth century B.C. Excavated by S. I. Rudenko, 1949. (Courtesy of Imperial Ermitage of Lenin, Ministry of Culture, USSR)

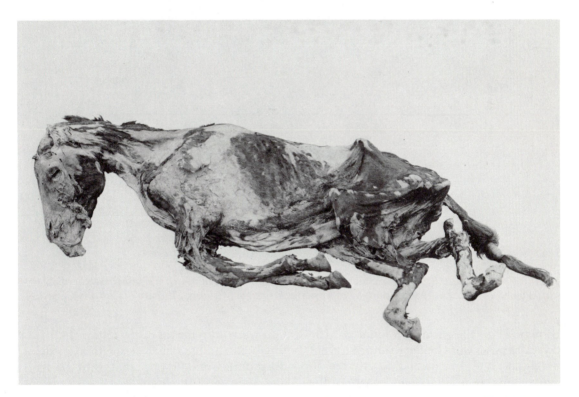

Figure 13.5. Mummified horse of the first Posiranov cavalry, fifth century B.C. Excavated by M. P. Groznov. (Courtesy of Imperial Ermitage of Lenin, Ministry of Culture, USSR)

that natron was not used. The brains, internal organs, and sections of muscle had been removed, and the cavities stuffed with grass or hair to maintain the shape of the body. The skin was then sewed up with thread made of hair or tendon. The heads were wholly or partially shaved, but before burial hair had been attached artificially to the women and beards to the men.

The horses buried with the king were not touched by the robbers and were recovered in excellent condition.

Most of our information comes from the work of Rudenko in five barrows of the Scyth-

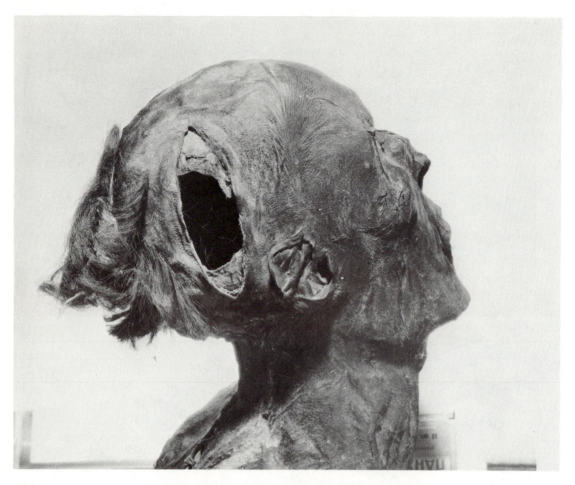

Figure 13.6. Mummified head of a leader of the fifth Posiransky cavalry, fifth to fourth century B.C. Excavated by S. I. Rudenko, 1949. (Courtesy of Imperial Ermitage of Lenin, Ministry of Culture, USSR)

ian period in the Altai Mountains. The Pazyryk barrows were looted in antiquity, but enough specimens remained to provide an adequate picture of the life and death of the chieftains buried there. The work has been published in English (1970) and is the source for the following account.

Burials took place in spring, in early summer, or later in autumn. This required the bodies to be preserved until burial could take place, but apparently only the chiefs and nobles were embalmed. Whether the common people were kept for burial at special times of the year is not known.

The three key features of full mummifica-tion were (1) removal of the entrails, (2) slitting of the limbs, sometimes with excision of the muscles, and (3) trephination of the skull and removal of the brain. To remove the entrails, an incision was made in the abdominal wall from the ribs down to the iliac bone. After the organs had been removed, the incision was sewed up with sinews, except that the woman in one barrow had been sewed with black horsehair cord. The treatment of the muscles varied from one body to another, but in general the slits in the skin of the limbs followed a common pattern. The cuts were made on the inner aspects of the arms and legs and ran deeply down the full extent of the limbs to the hands or feet. Presumably some preservative had been introduced, possibly salt, but this has not been identified. In other parts, such as the buttocks or shoulders, punctures with the point of a knife had been made, also probably for the introduction of a preservative. In some of the bodies, the muscles had been removed and replaced by padding, such as horsehair. This leads Rudenko to ask if these could have been examples of ritual eating of the body after death. Herodotus reports this custom as being quite common and says that it was habitual among certain tribes to kill off their old people and eat part of the flesh. These events were happy occasions with rejoicing; unfortunate persons who died of illness were buried without being eaten and were lamented by relatives and friends because they did not live long enough to be killed.

Removal of the brain was a common practice. In barrow 2 of the Pazyryk barrows, the skin over the parietal bone in the man had been cut away and pulled back, then crude tools such as chisel and mallet had been used to knock out an irregular disc of bone. The brain had then been removed and the cavity filled with soil, pine needles, and larch cones. The plate of bone that had been struck out had been replaced, and the skin sewed back with a cord of twisted horsehair.

The custom of burying a horse with its rider was very ancient and persisted into recent times in one form or another. The Turks maintained it into the first millennium A.D., and in the east Altai it persisted among the Telesi up to the end of the nineteenth century. The horses found in tombs in the Altai were presumably the favorite steeds of the buried princes and kings, although some kings had numerous horses buried with them.

GUANCHE MUMMIES FROM THE CANARY ISLANDS
AIDAN COCKBURN

The Canary Islands were invaded in 1402 and subsequently colonized by the Spaniards. They were occupied by an indigenous people called the Guanche, of unknown origin, who practiced mummification for their aristocracy. At the time of the occupation, there were probably thousands of mummies in ancestral caves, but nearly all have been lost and today only a few are left, scattered in museums around the world.

The Canary Islands are volcanic and rise from the ocean floor in very deep water. There is no possibility that they were at any time linked to West Africa, from which they are separated at the closest point by 107 km of ocean. This, of necessity, implies that the original immigrants had boats big enough to sail the open sea. The voyages of vessels like *Kon Tiki* have shown that such journeys can indeed be made. Irish monks with frail craft made of skin discovered Iceland and may even have reached America, so it does not seem unlikely that groups of peoples passed from Africa to these islands during an early period of man's history. At the time of discovery, the islanders did have boats, but these were rare and communications between the islands must have been infrequent. Tenerife itself, being 12,000 ft high, can be seen from a long distance.

Whatever method was used, the fact is that the crossing was made not only once but probably a number of times. It seems obvious that several races colonized the island, for the dominant groups were white with fair hair; others lower on the social scale were much darker, with black or brown hair. Their language was a mixture of Berber, Arabic, and other tongues. Who they were is a mystery. There have been numerous speculations, starting with Cro-Magnon man, but most are only guesses. While in West Africa, I heard legends of a king who heard of land to the west and sailed away with his tribe to look for it. This was told to me in connection with America, but the Canaries seem much more likely.

Hooton (1925) gave as his opinion that the first settlers probably came from Africa south of Morocco during the Neolithic period, bringing with them sheep and goats, but no knowledge of cultivated cereals. They survived in a relatively unmixed form on the island of Hierro. The invaders probably came from the Anti-Atlas and Atlas regions and penetrated only the southern islands. They were probably brunet whites, whose sole cultivated cereal was barley. About the same time another race of tall blond whites arrived. They were very warlike and probably came from the Atlas ranges of Morocco and Algeria. A fourth invasion affecting the eastern islands has been named "Mediterranean" and came when bronze was already in use in the eastern Mediterranean. These people probably spoke Berber.

Almost certainly, the islands were visited by the Phoenicians, for they established colonies along the West African coast; Hanno sailed that way in his famous voyage from Carthage, and others seem to have made the complete trip around Africa about 600 B.C. Other casual visitors in recent times would have been Arabs and Berbers.

BURIAL PRACTICES

The common people of the Canaries were buried either singly or in groups in simple trenches or holes, covered with dry stones. These tombs are indistinguishable from those of the Sahara.

The leaders and aristocrats were mummified and placed in mortuary caves. In 1526 Thomas Nichols was shown a cave in Guimar containing 300 to 400 mummies (quoted by Hooton 1925), and the Guanches said at that time that there were more than 20 such caves on Tenerife, but only 4 or 5 of these have been found. A famous cave between Arico and Guimar was explored in 1770 and contained 1,000 mummies.

These caves were plundered, partly to supply an important ingredient in medical preparations popular in Europe at that time, and partly by the modern natives, who destroyed them. Very few of these mummies survive today. There are no known complete ones in the islands themselves.

The embalming processes in Tenerife were recorded by two early visitors to the island, Espinosa and Abreu Galindo (see Hooton 1925). There was a professional class of morticians who were social outcasts, just as in Egypt. The bowels of the body were removed and the body washed twice a day. Espinosa says that the embalmers forced down the mouth a concoction made of mutton grease and powders of various sources, and Galindo records that the body was anointed with sheep butter, then sprinkled with a powder of dust of decayed pine trees and pumice stone. The incision in the abdomen was semilunar below the ribs, and sometimes all the viscera were taken out. The brain was removed from the head by means that are not clear, and the cavity was filled with a mixture of sand, ground pine bark, and juice of mocan.

There is a good deal of doubt on many points, especially the means of removing the brain, but it seems generally agreed that drying the body in the sun took 15 days. One observer says the body was smoked at night. After this time, the corpse was sewed up and wrapped in leather from sheep specially chosen for the purpose. Many other skins were piled on top, some being wrapped round the body.

Some of the mummies were enclosed in coffins made to fit them and constructed from tree trunks hollowed out for the purpose; others were arranged in rows simply in the skins in which they had been wrapped. The bodies were then placed in inaccessible mortuary caves. A few of the remaining Guanche mummies are in the Museum of Archaeology and Ethnology, Cambridge, England, and one was made available for examination to Brothwell et al. (1969). Their report is a detailed one and should be consulted for specific items. Briefly, it can be said that there was a remarkable similarity in the process of embalming to that practiced in Egypt. This has been known for a long time, but the present study confirms it. The position of the body, arms, and hands, and the presence of subcutaneous packing for the tissues are characteristic of mummies of the Twenty-first Dynasty of Egypt. However, the skull had been crushed, so that details regarding either the condition of the brain or its absence were not available, nor were any packages of organs discovered, either inside or outside the body.

The mummy had been radiographed by Scales in 1927, and he had reported evidence of rickets. In the later study doubt was cast on this diagnosis, and an alternative one of osteoarthritic disease of a degenerative type was substituted. The more recent films failed to demonstrate any opaque material in the skull apart from fragments of bone.

The tissues were not as well preserved as in Egyptian mummies, but were good enough to reveal certain features. Among these was anthracosis of the lungs, an indicator of exposure to smoky fires. Air pollution existed on the Canary Islands long before modern civilization arrived there.

THE MARQUISE OF TAI
AIDAN COCKBURN

Of all the mummies known to the authors, this seems to be by far the best preserved. We have not seen it in the flesh, but an hour-long 16-mm movie of the autopsy in color was lent to us by the Chinese government, and this left no doubt about the incredibly good condition of the tissues. The elasticity of the skin was such that when a finger was pressed against it, the skin rebounded to erase the depression formed, and the joints could be flexed without apparent damage. No other mummy described in the literature has similar capacities (China Reconstructs 1973; Group for Research on the Han Cadaver of Mawangtui 1976).

The lady is said to be the wife of Litsang, the marquis of Tai, who was chancellor of the principality of Changsha, Hunan, in the early Western Han dynasty, about 2,100 years ago. When she died, it is said that she was buried according to the Chinese Book of Rites.

There are many tombs in the Changsha area of Hunan, most of which were looted by robbers in the 1930s and 1940s. However, two huge mounds remained untouched until the present government began the task of excavation. It was a formidable undertaking, but after 4 months of digging the workers finally reached the tomb at the bottom. It was worth the effort, for there was a series of coffins, one inside the other, the whole covered with 5 tons of charcoal to soak up any water that might penetrate the thick layer of clay surrounding the coffins. The gorgeously decorated coffins lay inside each other, until finally, in the center, was the dead woman.

A description of all the art treasures found does not belong here. Some can be seen in the National Geographic Magazine of May 1974. It is the body that interests us. This had been immersed in a solution containing some mercury salts and then sealed hermetically, so that the fluid was still present 2,100 years later. The Chinese scientists who examined the body came to the conclusion that the exclusion of air had been primarily responsible for the preservation of the body. They claim that aerobic organisms would quickly exhaust all the oxygen present and produce an anaerobic environment in which decay could not take place. The mercury solution would play a minor disinfecting role. This may be correct, but no one has yet shown that the simple exclusion of oxygen will preserve a dead body as well as this. Perhaps the mercury compounds were more important than was thought by the investigators.

Apart from this, the autopsy revealed a great deal. The Lady Ch'eng was about 50 years old, somewhat obese, 154 cm tall, and weighed 34.3 kg. As mentioned earlier, the skin was elastic and in good condition, as was the brownish black hair. She had 16 teeth, with some crowns badly worn. One important point was a perforation of the right eardrum, this being the earliest recorded instance of such pathology, except for mummy PUM II, who was probably living a little earlier. The brain had shrunk to about one-third normal size, which is roughly the same as in Egyptian mummies where the brain is present. All the internal organs were intact and in situ, even the pulmonary plexus of the vagus nerve, the thoracic duct, and the artery to the appendix. In the stomach and intestines there were 138 muskmelon seeds which the lady must have eaten shortly before dying.

The causes of death were twofold. First, a gallstone about the size of a bean completely obstructed the lower end of the common bile duct, and this must have caused excruciating pain. Second, her arteries had many atheromatous plaques, as well as showing arteriosclerotic changes, and her coronary arteries were particularly affected. The walls of the left coronary artery were severely involved, about three-quarters of the lumen being blocked by disease. The diagnosis was that she suffered from severe biliary colic that resulted in coronary thrombosis and death. It is very rare for the cause of death to be diagnosed in an ancient body, apart from accident or violence.

Other pathologic conditions were identified. There was evidence of tuberculosis infection, indicated by calcified tuberculosis foci in the upper lobe of the left lung; blood fluke (*Schistosoma japonicum*) ova were found in the connective tissue of the liver and the walls of the rectum; ova of whipworms (*Trichuris trichiura*) and pinworms (*Enterobius vermicularis*) were present in the intestines; the fourth intervertebral space was narrowed and had a bony outgrowth that could have caused severe back and leg pains. Paintings of the lady show her walking with a stick, and this is the probable explanation. Her right forearm was deformed as the result of a fracture that had not been properly treated. Altogether, the autopsy shows a picture of an elderly lady suffering from the traumas and hazards of her age and time.

The tissues of the body, although shrunken, were in good condition. The brain had disintegrated into a crumbling mass, but the different layers of the abdominal wall were clearly discernible and the contours of the abdominal organs visible. Under the electron microscope, details of some structures could be distinguished. Her blood group was found to be A.

Some elaborate studies on the body tissue were conducted by anonymous Chinese scientists; the paper was published in 1976 and authorship listed as the Group for Research on the Han Cadaver of Mawangtui. Nothing of note was uncovered, apart from striations on muscles, collagen fibers, and amino acids. It is unfortunate that the body was preserved with formaldehyde after discovery. In view of the fact that it had survived for 2,000 years, was it really necessary to do this immediately? Could the body not have been kept as it was or at least placed in a refrigerator? We paleopathologists must have closer contacts with the archeologists who are the first to discover these bodies; unless we do, biochemical and immunologic studies will be hampered at the source.

Still, the Chinese did remarkably well with their marquise of Tai; perhaps someday scientists from the Western World will be able to see this most remarkable body from antiquity.

HEAD HUNTERS OF THE AMAZON
EKKEHARD KLEISS

Head hunting is undoubtedly one of the oldest forms of primitive warfare. To behead the defeated enemy was a custom common in ancient Assyria and could be observed still in the twentieth century among savage tribes in many parts of the world. Paleolithic heads discovered in Bavaria, carefully decapitated and buried separately from the bodies, suggest that head hunting already existed in prehistoric times.

In Europe, before World War I, Montenegrins used to cut off the head of a victim, which was then carried by a lock of hair as a trophy of victory. Later on, during the Balkan war of 1912–1913, this form of head hunting was replaced by cutting off the nose and the upper lip with the mustache. Both cases indicate the great importance attributed to hair, which plays a predominant role in the magic concepts behind these cruel customs.

Of the forms of head hunting that are so widespread all over the world, we can only quote some examples. Herodotus tells about head hunters in Asia who did their grisly work during or after the battles. In the first half of the twentieth century, many hill tribes in northeastern India, especially in Assam, as well as several tribal groups in Burma, in the Malay Archipelago (e.g., the Ibans and formerly also the Kadazans of Borneo) and in Indonesia in general, still devoted themselves to all kinds of human sacrifices, combined nearly always with decapitation and frequently with cannibalism. The Igorots and Tagalogs of Luzon, Philippines, abandoned such practices in the middle of the twentieth century. The Asmat and other southwestern Papuans reverted during World War II to tribal fighting and head hunting, which they had formerly given up, and the practice still persists locally in New Guinea as well as in other parts of Oceania, sporadically associated with cannibalism.

Several tribes in Nigeria and other African tribal groups frequently carry out human sacrifices similar to the head-hunting customs of Indonesia, along with cannibalistic rites. North American Indians, when fighting against the white settlers, took the scalp rather than the whole head; they considered the hairy part more important than the rest because the soul was located in the hair.

Finally, of the South American head hunters, who most likely came from the Caribbean area and extended their domains to pre-Andean and trans-Andean regions, Jibaros of the basin of the High Amazon River deserve our attention on account of their skill in preparing shrunken heads or *tsantsas* (Figure 13.7). These great warriors not only exerted a strong influence during the last cen-

turies on other tribes in Ecuador and Peru, but also resisted successfully all attempts to civilize them or to suppress head hunting. Although officially the preparation of tsantsas is strictly forbidden, nobody can really enforce the law in the jungle, and ancient customs persist even in modern times.

The Indonesians and other head hunters dried, smoked, or mummified the whole head of their foe, sometimes preserving tattoo marks and even the actual features of the victim. They also skinned the head and painted the skull with ash, chalk, and ocher, in this way preparing trophies of a macabre beauty. All these are more or less in the original size of the human head. The Jibaros, however, shrink the tsantsa to the size of a fist or of the head of a small monkey, maintaining during all this reduction the original features, like a portrait or a caricature.

The preparation of a tsantsa is a laborious process. First, the head has to be cut as near to the trunk as possible, preserving all the skin of the neck. If the victim was slain near the village of the head hunters, the preparation starts immediately, and this, according to the opinion of some experts, gives the best results. On the other hand, transportation of the head through the jungle during several days undoubtedly produces a certain degree of putrefaction, which facilitates the next step, the separation of the skin from the skull. After receiving authorization from the chief of the tribe to make the tsantsa (this is given in a solemn ceremony), the head hunter, sometimes assisted by more experienced fellow tribesmen, makes an incision in the midline of the scalp, from the crown to the occipital bone or even down the whole dorsal portion of the neck. Then he separates the scalp from the roof of the skull. This is quite simple, as the tissues can be separated easily with the bare hands. The halves of the scalp hang outward like two inverted sacks. The more complicated part of the dissection is to separate the skin from the bones of the face, a process for which the Indians use sharp bamboo

Figure 13.7.   Tsantsas. (Courtesy of Dr. Etta Becker-Donner, Völkerkundemuseum, Vienna)

knives, shells, or flint stones. Sometimes they break the bones to facilitate their extraction. Great care must be taken to preserve the eyelids, lips, nose, and ears. The preparation of the neck is similar.

The process of shrinking the head is another toilsome task. If the head was fresh, the natural retraction of the skin at once reduces the mask to half its original size or less. In any case, to avoid further decay, the head is put into a bowl for several days with a decoction of plants, probably rich in tannin and other coagulating agents that will preserve and shrink the tissues at the same time. Sometimes the prepared skin is boiled in these extracts of plants and barks. Then the openings of the mouth and eyes are sewed with plant fibers, often fixed to small painted wooden sticks; with religious rites this closure avoids the evil spirits, execrations, or other calamities that might come out of the orifices. The cut in the scalp and neck is also sewed, practically disappearing under the abundant hair. The head has now been transformed into a sort of sack, open only where the neck was severed from the trunk.

Into this sack, the Jibaro carefully pours hot sand that has been heated in the shard of a used pottery vessel (both details are important for the success of the preparation); some tribal groups also use three hot pebbles taken from the next river and rolled around in the inside of the sack. This ritual is to avoid any evil reaction from the spirit of the victim. At the same time, it burns away any excess of connective and other tissues, thus helping to shrink the skin in a proportioned way. On the outside, the skin of the face is frequently anointed with vegetable oils or fat, and the features are constantly modeled as their size is gradually reduced. Because of the smoke from special plants or woods, the plant extracts, and the powdered charcoal, this whole procedure produces the dark color typical of tsantsas, even if the victim had been a white man (this can be proved, at least in some cases, by the hair distribution – e.g., mustache – and by other details of the features).

During the whole time the head is being prepared, the head hunter must observe strict rules of fasting and other rituals, otherwise the spiritual success of the procedure would be in danger. When the work is finished, there is a big fiesta for the tribe, with special purification rites for the successful head hunter and introduction ceremonies for the tsantsa, which nearly always belongs to the whole clan as a sort of talisman.

This ideological framework demonstrates clearly that head hunting in general and the making of tsantsas in particular are not at all the result of bloodthirst or cruelty, but of spiritual concepts, as is typical of primitive religions.

Although we cannot discuss here all the details of the ideas or beliefs that induced primitive men to practice head hunting, basically there is a concept of the existence of a material soul. This soul matter has its seat in the head and can be stored and added to the existing stock of an individual or of the whole tribe. Its possession transfers to the owner of the head trophy certain qualities of the victim: strength, courage, sagacity, and so on. Similar ideas are associated with cannibalism, because the eaten parts of the foe's body transfer analogous qualities to the eater, an idea still believed by many primitive populations. Human sacrifices of any kind, including head hunting, are intimately related to fertility rites (the cycle of life), to the initiation of boys to manhood, to better status in the other world, where the head of the victim will assure his services to the owner, and to immanent or real power in the widest sense of the word – for example, related to the building of a new long house or the launching of a war canoe. The special importance of hair has been mentioned already and may be compared to the Biblical story of Samson and the use of amulets, arm rings, and necklets made from the hair of slain foes and therefore of magic virtue. In the British Museum in London, there is the tsantsa of a sloth, considered by the Jibaros and other South American tribes as the forefather of mankind, probably because of its hairy aspect. Because of the reduced size of the tsantsa itself, the hair of the head, which was practically never cut during the life span of the victim, seems extremely long and is frequently braided and/or adorned with feathers or beads.

Because of the commercial interest in tsantsas all over the world, fake ones made from the heads of monkeys or with the hairy skin of other animals abound on the market. In some cases, especially when they were made by the Indians themselves, their identification as fakes is rather difficult. However, even in such specimens, we must admire the masterly skill of primitive men.

REFERENCES

The infant mummy of Uan Muhuggiag
Arkell, A. J.; Cornwall, J. W.; and Mori, F. 1961.
    Analisi degli anelli componenti la collana della

mummia infantile di Uan Muhuggiag. *Rivista di Antropologia* 48:161.

De Morgan, J. 1896. *Recherches sur l'origine de l'Egypte.* Paris: Leroux.

Elliot Smith, G., and Dawson, W. 1924. *Egyptian mummies.* London: Allen & Unwin.

Mori, F. 1960. Quarta missione paletnologica nell'Acacus (Sahara Fezzanese). *Ricerca Scientifica* 30:61.

Mori, F., and Ascenzi, A. 1959. La mummia infantile di Uan Muhuggiag: osservazioni antropologiche. *Rivista di Antropologia* 46:125.

Pettigrew, T. 1834. *History of Egyptian mummies.* London: Longmans.

The frozen Scythians of Siberia

Artamonov, M. I. 1965. Frozen tombs of the Scythians. *Scientific American* 212:101–10.

Herodotus. *Persian Wars,* Book IV, pp. 71–3. Quoted in S. I. Rudenko. *Frozen tombs of Siberia: the Pazyryk burials of Iron Age horsemen.* Berkeley: University of California Press, 1970.

Rudenko, S. I. 1970. *Frozen tombs of Siberia: the Pazyryk burials of Iron Age horsemen.* Translated by M. W. Thompson. Berkeley: University of California Press.

Guanche mummies from the Canary Islands

Brothwell, D. R.; Sandison, A. T.; and Gray, P. H. K. 1969. Human biological observations on a Guanche mummy with anthracosis. *American Journal of Physical Anthropology* 30:333–48.

Hooton, E. A. 1925. The ancient inhabitants of the Canary Islands. *Harvard African Studies* 7:40–5.

The Marquise of Tai

Group for research on the Han Cadaver of Mawangtui, Shanghai Institute of Biochemistry, Academic Sinica, and Hunan Medical College. 1976. The state of preservation of the cadaver of the Marquise of Tai found in the Han tomb no. 1 in Mawangtui near Changsha as revealed by the fine structure of the muscle and other tissues. *Scientia Sinica* 19:557–72.

1973. Study of a body 2,000 years old. *China Reconstructs* 22(10):32–4.

Head hunters of the Amazon

Cranstone, B. A. L. 1961. *Melanesia: a short ethnography.* London: British Museum.

De Graff, F. W. K. 1923. The head-hunters of the Amazon. In *Encyclopaedia Britannica.*

Durham, E. 1923. Head-hunting in the Balkans. *Man* 18.

Heine-Geldern, R. v. 1924. *Kopfjagd und Menschenopfer in Assam und Birma.* Vienna: Anthropologischen Gesellschaft.

Hodson, T. C. 1912. Head-hunting among the hill tribes in Assam. *Folklore* 20.

Karsten, R. 1923. *Blood revenge, war and victory feasts among the Jibaro Indians of Eastern Ecuador.* Smithsonian Institution, bulletin 79. Washington, D.C.: Smithsonian Institution.

– 1935. The head-hunters of Western Amazonas: the life and culture of the Jibaro Indians of eastern Ecuador and Peru. Helsingfors: Akademische Buchhandlung.

Kleiss, E. 1966. Tsantsas: ein Mythus wird Maskottchen. *Wiener Tierärztliche Monatsschrift* 53:482.

– 1967. Zum Problem der natürlichen Mumifikation und Konservierung. *Zeitschrift für Morphologie und Anthropologie* 59:204.

Kleiss, E., and Simonsberger, P. 1964. *La parafinización como método morfológico.* Mérida: Universidad de los Andes.

Paredes Borja, V. 1963. *Historia de la medicina en el Ecuador.* Quito: Casa de la Cultura Ecuatoriana.

Sowada, A. (O.S.C.) 1968. New Guinea's fierce Asmat: a heritage of headhunting. In *Vanishing people of the earth.* Washington, D.C.: National Geographic Society.

Thomson, C. J. S. 1924. Shrunken human heads. *Discovery.*

Index

Aboriginal Australia, 194
abscess
    In Aleutian mummy, 131
    Psoas, in Egyptian mummy, 31
acromegaly, in Egypt, 40
adipocere, in Aleutian mummy, 131
age at death
    PUM II, 56
    PUM III, 92
    PUM IV, 99
Aleutian and Alaskan mummies, 118–34
alimentary diseaes, in Egypt, 39
Allison, Marvin, 157–9, 163, 165, 166
Altai mountains, 228
Amazon head hunters, 234–6
Anasazi (Navajo for ancient people), 103
Ancylostoma duedenale (Peru), 159
anthracosis
    in Aleutian mummy, 131
    in Guanche mummies, 233
    in Nakht, 79
    in PUM II, 65, 69
    in St. Lawrence Island Eskimo, 121
anus in PUM III, 89
apatite, in Aleutian mummy, 130
Arabs, 1
Arizona State Museum, 108–9
arterial disease
    in PUM II, 69
    in St. Lawrence Island Eskimo, 121
    in Tai, Marquise of, 234
arthritis
    in Aleutian mummy, 127
    in Egypt, 36
    in Japanese mummies, 213–9
Ascaris, 66, 80
asphalt, 1
asphyxiation, in Eskimo mummy, 123
Aswan dam, 2–4
Australia, 194–210
Austrian preservation of royalty, 7

bacteria
    in Aleutian tissues, 131
    search for, in PUM II, 56
    viable in soil, 4
balsam of Tolu

origin of, in South America, 169
use of, embalming, 151
Bangladesh, 7
Bartonella bacilliformis, 163
Basket Makers, 103–17
biochemistry
    of Nakht, 83
    of PUM II, 66, 69
blood cells
    in Eskimos, 123
    in PUM III, 89
blood groups
    Aleutian, 130
    Aleutian mummy, 132
    in Japan, 216–22
    in Nakht, 82
    in North America, 111
    in Paracas, absence of, 140
    in Peru, 166
    Tai, Marquise of, 234
bog
    biochemistry of, 178
    biology of, 178
    preservation in, 177
bone
    disease of, in Egypt, 34
    disease of, in PUM II, 69
    disease of leg, in PUM II, 66
    of PUM III, 92
Book of the Dead, 27
Borremose bodies, 178–83
    dating of, 182
    last meal of, 180
brain
    in Aleutian mummy, 128
    in Australia, 200, 202
    extraction of, in Peru, 139
    in Nakht, 76, 83
    not extracted, 140
    of PUM IV, 99
    removal of
        in Australia, 202
        in Canary Islands, 232
        in PUM II, 55
        in Scythians, 229, 231
    St. Lawrence Island Eskimo, 121
    Tai, Marquise of, 234

Buddhist monks, 7, 211–23
burial customs (Australian), 198
Burton, Sir Richard, 5–6

Cairo (Egypt), School of Medicine, 2
Canada, 4
Canary Islands, 231–3
cannibalism
    in the Amazon, 235
    ritual among the Scythians, 231
canopic jars, 18, 26–7
Canyon de Chelly, 103
Canyon del Muerto, 103, 108
caries (in Egypt), 46
Carrión's disease, 163
CAT scan (in Nakht), 83
Chile
    frozen Inca mummy, 1
    mummification in, 138
China, 233–4
    ancestor worship, 7
    use of jade, 7
circumcision
    PUM II, 55
    PUM IV, 98
coffins, 25
    Nakht, 72
    PUM II, 52–70
    Scythian king, 228
    Tai, Marquise of, 233
coprolites (Aleutian mummy), 128, 130
Corfu, 8
coronary disease
    Aleutian Eskimo, 124
    Marquise of Tai, 234
cotton
    Peruvian, 141, 143, 145, 147, 151, 157
    in PUM II, 54, 69
cranial deformation, 139
Cruikshank, George, 11
cryogenics, 8
Cryptocotyle lingua, 123, 127
cultural diffusion, 2
culture(s)
    Cuzco, 143
    Early Iron Age, 190
    Huari, 141
    Tiahuanaco, 141
Currelly, C. T., 71–2
Cuzco
    culture, 143
    funeral rites of Inca, 149

Dashur, 18
dating
    Danish bodies, 190
    Little Alice, 115
    PUM II, 67

PUM III, 88
ROM I, 72
St. Lawrence Island Eskimo, 118
Uan Muhuggiag, 224
Dawson, Warren R., 2, 11, 17, 30
death, 6–7
dentist, first in history, 50
dentition
    in Aleutian mummy, 130–2
    attrition, 45
    bridge in Egypt, 50
    caries in Egypt, 46
    in Danish bodies, 177–93
    in Egypt, 45–51
    occlusion in Egypt, 49
    periodontal disease, 45, 132
diffusion concept (Elliot Smith), 201, 298
Diodorus Siculus, 16, 21
disease
    in ancient Egypt, 29–44
    in Peru, 157–76

eardrum perforations, 69, 88, 233
Egypt, mummies of, 1–102
electron microscopy in Nakht, 87
Elland mummy, 192
Elliot Smith, G. 2, 11, 17, 30, 35, 201
environment (in Peru), 136–7
Etruscan text (in mummy wrappings), 5–6
eyes
    artificial (in Australia), 200
    histology (PUM II), 66
    Macleay mummy, 202
    of PUM II, 55, 66
    of PUM III, 88
    of PUM IV, 98

fingerprints
    of Grauballe man, 188
    of Japanese mummies, 216–21
fractures
    of Borremose man, 180
    Danish body, 182
    in Egypt, 36
    "fractures" in PUM II, 52
    radiology, 287
    St. Lawrence Island Eskimo, 123
Fujiwara family, 211, 213, 216

gallstones (in Egypt), 32
Genkō-shakusho, 211, 213
Giza
    Hetepheres, (Queen), 17
    homogeneity of nobles' appearance, 49
gout (in Egypt), 37
Grauballe man, 186–90
gynecological disorders (in Egypt), 42

Harris's lines
  in Egyptian mummies, 30
  in Nakht, 74,79
  in PUM III, 85
head
  of Macleay mummy, 202
  of PUM III, 89–92
heart (in Nakht), 76
hepatitis, 83
Herodotus, 71
  Egyptian mummies, 15–6
  head hunters of Asia, 235
  mummification, 3
  packing of cavities in Egyptian mummies, 21
  ritual eating after death, 231
  on Scythians, 227
Hetepheres (Queen)
  burial of, 23
  coffin, 25
  viscera, 17–8, 26
hieroglyphics
  of Nakht, 72
  of PUM III, 88
histology
  in Nakht, 77
  of PUM II, 65
  of PUM III, 92
histoplasmosis (in Eskimo), 123, 125
Hooton, E. A., 231
Horses, 229
Hrdlička, Aleš, 125, 127
Huari, 141

Ica (Peru), 139, 157
  thyroid disease in, 166
  tuberculosis in, 159
Inca
  display, 151
  funeral rites, 145
  mummification, 151–3
infectious diseases
  in Egypt, 30, 32
  histoplasmosis, 123
  in Peru, 163
inscriptions, (PUM III), 88
insects
  head lice, 111, 115, 141
  in Japanese mummies, 221–2
  PUM II, 64–5
  in PUM III, 93
  PUM IV, 96
  Sarcophaga, 221

Japan, 211

kidney disease (in Egypt), 38–9

lead (in PUM II), 66, 69
Lenin, V. I., 8

leprosy (in Egypt), 30–1
Libyan mummy, 224–6
lice (head), 111, 115, 141
Lima (Peru), Museum of Health Sciences, 157
linen
  in Egypt, 72–3
  from PUM II, 53
  from PUM III, 86
Little Alice, 114
Little Wren, 127
liver
  cirrhosis, in Nakht, 79
  in Nakht, 76
  in PUM III, 89
Lucas, Alfred, 11, 22–3
lungs
  in Aleutian mummy, 127
  in Nakht, 76, 79
  in PUM II, 58, 65

Macleay, Sir William, 201
Macleay mummy, 201
McCuen Cave, 109, 112
Maitreya faith, 215
malaria, 167
mammoth (frozen), 1, 4, 6
Mammoth Cave, 115
Marquise of Tai, 1, 233–4
Melanesia, 194–210
mercury (in Marquise of Tai), 1
Metropolitan Museum, 27
Michigan expeditions, 45
Middle Kingdom, 19
mummies
  of animals, 4
  definition of, 1
  exhibitions of, 192
  of great leaders, 7
  numbers of, 3
  used instead of coal, 4
mummification
  Aleutian, 126–7
  of animals, 4
  in Australia and Melanesia, 194, 199
  on Canary Islands, 232–3
  in Egypt, 19–20
  experimental, 3
  in Japan, 212–23
  in Peru, 135–6, 138, 145, 154
  of Scythians, 230
mummification (natural), 1
  in Egypt, 13
  in North America, 103
  in Peru, 135, 156–7
mummy (individual specimens)
  PUM II, 52–70
  PUM III, 85–93
  PUM IV, 93–100
  ROM I, 71–84

mummy bundles (Peru), 139
Murray River area, 198

Nakht, 71–84
National Museum of Natural History, 52
natron, 1, 301–11
    in experimental mummification, 3
    in Herodotus, 16
    lack of in ROM I, 83
    in mummification methods in Egypt, 22
    PUM II, 57
neutron activation analysis, 130
New Guinea, 194
New Kingdom, 22
New South Wales, 194
nutrition (in Peru), 167

ocher red
    in Australia, 200, 202, 204, 205–6, 207
    head hunters in Indonesia, 235
Old Kingdom, 13–4, 19

packages in PUM II, 62
Painted Cave, 103, 109, 111
Palermo, Sicily (Capuchin catacombs), 7
papyri (medical), 29
Paracas Necropolis, 137, 140
paraffin wax preservation, 8
parasites
    Ancylostoma duodenale, 159
    Ascaris, 66, 80
    Cryptocotyle lingua, 123, 127
    Enterobius vermicularis, 234
    in PUM II, 66
    in ROM I, 79
    Schistosoma haematobium, 79
    Schistosoma japonicum, 234
    Taenia, 77, 79, 81
    Trichinella spiralis, 80
    Trichuris trichiura, 171, 186, 234
pelvic organs (PUM III), 89
periodontal disease (in Egypt), 45
Perón, Eva, 8
Peru, 7
Peru (periods)
    Colonial, 145
    Early Horizon, 139
    Late Horizon, 143
    Late Intermediate, 141
    Middle Horizon, 141
    Preceramic, 138
Petrie, Flinders, 17, 18
Pettigrew, Thomas, 11
Philadelphia Art Museum, 52
pleuritis, 133
pneumoconiosis, 65, 69
pneumonia (Klebsiella pneumoniae), 133
pollen tests, 182, 183
pork, 84
porotic hyperostosis (in Peru), 166

predynastic period, 11–2
priests (mummified), 213–9
protrusio acetabuli (of Nakht), 74
Ptolemy, 1

Queensland, 207

radiology
    Aleutian mummy, 127
    first pharaoh, 2
    of Grauballe man, 187
    Japanese mummies, 217
    Macleay mummy, 204
    of mummies, 30
    of Nakht, 74
    of PUM II, 52
    tests for paint on Australian mummies, 205
    of Tollund Man, 185
renal disease, 205
resin
components of, in PUM II, 62
    in Egypt 22
    in PUM II, 54, 57, 70
    in PUM III, 89
respiratory disorders, 40
Roman period (in Egypt), 1, 96
Royal Ontario Museum, 71
Rudenko, S. I. 228–230
Ruffer, Sir Armand, 2–3, 30
Ruffer's fluid, 3

sacrifices
    in Asia, 231
    in Denmark, 177–93
    frozen, 153
    horse sacrifice, 228
    mummy bundles, 153
    in Peru, 149
    by Scythians, 228
St. Lawrence Island, 118
salt (for mummification), 22
sandals, 107–8
Saqqara, 17
scalping, 182
Schistosoma, 3, 79, 234
Schistosomiasis, 30, 71, 79
Scythians
    burial mound, 228
    Herodotus, 227
    mummification prctices, 227
    sacrifices, 228
    of Siberia, 226
sex of PUM III, 92
Shakespeare, 14
Short Cave, 116
skin
    change of color in PUM II, 56
    elasticity of in Marquise of Tai, 233
    of Nakht, 76
    of Scythians, 228

skull, reconstruction of, in Nakht, 76
smallpox (in Egypt), 32
South Australia, 198, 207
spinal cord (in PUM II), 55
spleen
    in Nakht, 76
    in PUM II, 65
Stalin, J., 8
stomach contents
    Grauballe Man, 189
    Tai, Marquise of, 234
    Tollund Man, 183
symposium, *Death and Disease in Ancient Egypt*, 52
syphilis, 31

Taenia, 77, 79, 81
Tai, Marquise of, 1, 233–4
tattooing
    in Alaska, 119
    in Peru, 140
Tello, Juan, 130–40
temporal bone
    disease in Aleutian mummy, 133
    disease in Egypt, 31
    eardrum, perforation of, 69, 233
    Nakht, 80
    in PUM II, 69
    Tai, Marquise of, 233
Tennessee, 116
Texas Cave, 109, 114
textiles
    in Egypt, 11–28, 52–100
    in Peru, 136, 139–140, 143, 145, 147, 151, 157
thalassemia, and porotic hyperostosis, 167
thyroid disease (in Peru), 166
Tiahuanaco
    hookworm in, 159
    verruga in mummy, 163
Tollund Man, 183–6
    dating, 186
    last meal of, 183
    preservation of head, 186
tomography in Nakht, 74
Toronto Academy of Medicine, 71
Torres Strait, 2
    centers for mummification, 196

trace elements
    bone in PUM II, 68
    PUM II, 57, 66, 69
    in resin in PUM II, 68
trepanation
    in Peru, 165
    by Scythians after death, 230
Trichinella, 80
Trichuris trichiura, 171, 186, 234
tsantas, 235-7
tuberculosis
    in Egypt, 31
    in Peru, 157–9
    Tai, Marquise of, 234
tumors
    in Egypt, 37
    fibroadenoma of breast in PUM III, 93

Uan Muhuggiag, 224
unfused epiphyses (of Nakht), 74

Vandal Cave, 103, 109–10
vascular disease
    in Egypt, 37
    Tai, Marquise of, 234
Ventana Cave, 106, 109, 113
Venzone, mummies of, 8

weaver (Nakht), 72–3
weight of PUM III, 92
West New Guinea, 195
wisdom teeth of Nakht, 74
Wood Jones, F., 35–6
wrappings
    Peru, 138–54
    of PUM II, 53
    of PUM III, 86
    of PUM IV, 94
    of ROM I, 73
    skins of Aleutian mummy, 126–7
    used to make paper, 4

xeroradiography (of Nakht), 74

yaws (Australia), 206

Zaki Iskander, 11
zinc in PUM II, 68–9